The World We Came to Find

The World We Came to Find

Woodstock (left), Wales (right) & Morris the Cat (center)

John R Morris

The World We Came To Find
© Copyright 2017 John R Morris All Rights Reserved.
While the accounts of this book are factual, many of the names have been changed as well as the designations of certain locations, roads, and properties traveled through. These changes have been made purposefully throughout this narrative in an attempt to maintain the privacy and anonymity of the people the author encountered as well as to disguise the places he may have unintentionally trespassed on during his journey.
All other names of those living or dead or places either real or fictionalized have been authorized and do not in any way cause purposeful or accidental disclosure of personal or harmful information in a way that would encroach upon an individual's private life.
The author does not condone or suggest the actions of the things he has done within the context of this book to be carried out by any other person.
That much should be obvious by the end of the book.

ISBN: 0997459212
ISBN 13: 9780997459210

In the Press

"The message in The World We Left Behind *is one that seems to resonate with a huge portion of the population, no matter their gender, their job, or their financial position, and Morris' struggle to achieve enlightenment while being challenged continually by forces over which he has no control, is a situation that speaks to the internal battle that rages in many of us."*

San Francisco Book Review

"There are some parallels between Morris' book, The World We Left Behind *and Cheryl Strayed's bestseller,* Wild. *Morris presents a realistic view of the people he encounters during this trip. His best work comes near the end of the book where he describes a one-day solo hike."*

Portland Book Review

*"*THE WORLD WE LEFT BEHIND *is part gripping travel diary and part emotional exploration, a young man finding himself amidst the natural beauties and dangers of the wilderness. The emotional force*

of the story is amplified by Morris's starkly honest and compellingly vivid writing style. Morris has a wry, humorous, engaging tone and an innate descriptive ability that makes his journey come to life." ★★★★½

IndieReader

"Such a good read! Insightful, funny, exciting and revealing. A realistic account of an Appalachian Trail thru hike complete with the quirky misadventures that such a quest brings to the unprepared. I can't wait for volume 2 and 3."

AT Library

"The World We Left Behind is instantly engaging. Morris displays a keen eye for detail in every descriptive passage and brings raw nature to life. Dialogue is sharp and involving, and the characters he meets leap off the page. The reader will feel drawn in to the whole experience due to the atmospheric and colorful picture Morris paints. It is a page-turner to the end of the volume." ★★★★½

Self-Publishing Review

"The World We Left Behind by John R. Morris is an excellent snapshot into one troubled man's journey to discover his life's meaning." ★★★★

David K. McDonnell for ReaderViews.com

Dedicated to all of you.

My readers, my fans and my trail followers. You were my light on and off the AT. Your unending support, and the confidence you instilled within me was the only reason I ever had the determination and courage to complete my journey.

Thank you all for helping me succeed, and live my dreams.

It's only because of you all, that I did.

Table of Contents

In the Press · v
Preface · xi
A Word from the Author · xiii

Chapter 1	Going On Alone ·	1
Chapter 2	New Beginnings ·	32
Chapter 3	Flipping North ·	92
Chapter 4	Katahdin & the 100 Mile Wilderness · · · · · · · · ·	126
Chapter 5	The Journey South ·	152
Chapter 6	A Friend, Says Goodbye · · · · · · · · · · · · · · · · ·	193
Chapter 7	The White Mountain Range · · · · · · · · · · · · · · ·	227
Chapter 8	And so, I Hike Alone… · · · · · · · · · · · · · · · · · · ·	319
Chapter 9	A Winter Daisy ·	426
Chapter 10	Delaware Water Gap ·	485
Chapter 11	The Way Home ·	580

Preface

<u>September 9th 2013 Rangeley, Maine – John Morris</u>

The long road, which awaits me.

The dusty abandoned highways that call out to me, and moan through the soft cries of insincere laughter...

....and the whispers of dissidents.

Their engines, their horns, their people smiling behind the steering wheels, long gone.

This dusty, dirt road...that leads to a cul-de-sac of dead trees, and dead ends.

The AT, my yellow brick road back to home.

Places in the sand to draw tired lines in the afternoon sunset. Dusk just a few minutes away. And night claws across the skies, scarring it with purple, pink, and blood stained gashes colored in brilliant hues.

The hush of the leaves blowing gently in the breeze. The harmonic chirp of the crickets at night; as they sing me to sleep.

The last remaining lightning bugs strain to light up the night fields I walk through, like a billion neon stars flashing and fading around me.

I want to leave.

My fear coursing through me so swiftly, I can feel it in my teeth. In my bones, whenever I think of tomorrow.

I want to watch the sun rise one more time, before I die. I want the fever eating away within me to subside long enough for my eyes to see one more smile.

I want to run my hands through the tops of the vast wheat fields, and hide behind the corn stalks.

I yearn to sip water unfiltered from the stream.

To meet the colors of dying leaves with wonderment and awe.

It is the big city that calls me, to leave my wilderness haven. To take me away from my passion, my life, my desire...and my will to live.

The cold society, the hardened metal of change, and the greedy concrete sidewalks that soak up all of humanity. The polluted air, the sail boats of trash, drifting down rain choked gutters.

Bleak reality, where opinions hurt you. Peace of mind doesn't exist...unless you can find it by some chance on the rooftops atop the rest of the world.

I hate to leave my home.....

....but life beckons me, to do something with myself.

I feel this place slipping through my hands, as I step onto this asphalt pathway.

As I walk the trails of my dreams, existing only in my mind now.

As my gait wavers painfully up stubborn mountain paths; in disintegrating boots.

As my strength weakens, and my joints grind together as if filled with splinters of glass.

Goodbye...my home.

Goodbye until the joyous day I come back.

Wait for me...

...Wait for me in all the bittersweet glory that is you.

For when I come home, I know I will no longer be as happy as I am in this moment...

.....of absolute freedom.

A Word from the Author

FROM READING MY FIRST TWO books in this three-part series, you've already come to find I didn't stick solely to the Appalachian Trail during my trek north, in 2013.

In fact, at the end of *The World We Left Behind: Book Two*, you the reader found Torry and I rafting in an inflatable rowboat made for a lake, down the Shenandoah River.

This was very purposeful at the time, because we had both wanted to break away from the "Purist" lifestyle we'd initially set out with, on March 17th, 2013. Our plans had morphed, and thus warped our vision of true "ultimate freedom" and what it encapsulated by being free of "rules" and time limits, and restrictions. During our time in the wilderness, Torry and I had come across many other hikers that took this purist title seriously enough, that they would even step to the exact spot on the AT that they had left off on maybe a day or two before, and then proceed walking North again.

Now this wasn't to say that I didn't respect these hikers who wanted to hit every last inch of the Appalachian Trail, because I did. However, I enjoyed the genuine spontaneity of walking wherever the hell I wanted to walk—too much to become chained to just this one path. My hike teeter-tottered on not only a search for freedom, but understanding in my life and desire to make a father proud back home, out of my own self-doubt.

Suddenly, this meant that I could wander, without fear of having to turn back and re-hike whatever I might have missed. It meant that I could potentially see, and experience many more different places than those hikers that stuck solely to that 2-foot wide narrow path from Georgia to Maine.

With our departure from the trail, Torry and I found our new approach to hiking north as adding a dash of chaotic adventure into the mix. Having lived almost religiously according to AWOL's 2012 Appalachian Trail Guide up to that point in time, it was refreshing to keep the book closed as we changed routes and read digital maps—choosing to meander through towns or places that "sounded cool" as opposed to not having been given a choice by staying locked to this one path in the woods.

It was easy to feel as if the book stripped away the *mystery* of simply coming upon a sight or a view all on your own, having discovered it by yourself instead of reading of its existence, days beforehand.

There was this overwhelming sense that I could find something out about myself in the woods and in the middle of nowhere within this maze of forests, streams, mountains, valleys, rivers (and later, towns). But not to sound negative by any means—I slowly became skeptical of that very fact with every step I took towards the finish line.

Walking a narrow trail doesn't always just reset everything wrong with your life, and I would come to learn that by the end.

I regularly needed daily reminders during the eight and a half months I spent out there. Reasons to make sense, of what I was doing and putting myself through. I sought out self-confidence and pride, as I tried to live my life for a father, who had spent so much of his own life, living and working for his family. It was both admirable but sad in a way because it meant that he hadn't had the time to complete such a hike or an adventure of his own. In a sense, I wanted him to feel what I felt out there each day and to live through my words and journal entries.

I had tasked myself with a mission to bring my mother and father a rock back, from the summit of Katahdin.

This solid, concentrated piece of earth that would tell the story of everything I had given up in 2013 resembling a normal life, and in turn; everything I had traded to gain, during my search for adventure.

This tiny stone existing as proof, that I had done it. I had conquered my fears, broken through a wall of self-doubt and returned home with different opinions of "success" than I had before originally setting out.

It was the only thing, worth living for.

A portion of the Level 3 rapids you encounter on the Shenandoah River.

CHAPTER 1

Going On Alone

I STARED AT THE LIFE jacket Torry had left behind, fiddling with the cinch straps upon it.

I then looked at the oars strewn carelessly into the boat by two tired hikers, now turned wandering nomads somewhere along the way. Nomads that over time, had grown apart and had become complete strangers to one another.

Above me, night had started to creep in and the sun had already begun setting rather rapidly; leaving only tendrils of light within the skies.

I glanced down at my phone and sighed, before typing onto my tiny four-inch screen: *You know, Melody was right about you. You really are a selfish individual after all.*

I then let loose all of my anger and pent up frustration over the last few days, into verbal bashings I would find I was never proud of later, after having read them over again. They were thoughts and hidden concerns or opinions that had built up over the course of our adventure together. Things I had seen Torry do, and the careless ease with which he could so callously do them.

His response was simple enough: *You are right. I am selfish. However, you are mistaken on a couple of points. I didn't ditch you over a pack of cigarettes. I left because there has been tension between us for days: bickering, anger, and swearing. The look of disgust you gave me when I asked if you'd pick me up a pack of cigarettes was the final straw for me. I'd have gone to get them myself if I hadn't been staying to watch our gear. I had enough on my credit card for one pack. Secondly, why is it so wrong that I walked off? What you mistakenly label cowardice is just simple preference. I prefer to get back to working. What's wrong with that? Anyway as I said before good luck, take it easy.*

I stared at that message for some time, not fully able to absorb the words sitting on the screen. Too frustrated and angry, to accept it.

Let it go I said to myself finally.

He doesn't owe you anything. Nobody does. This is where you pick yourself up, and finish this journey on your own.

After a while, I absorbed the rational voice speaking to me. I re-inflated my leaking water raft and gave a final glance back towards the road Torry had disappeared down.

Thank you I finally conceded, in my mind. The only reason I had made it that far, was because of him. And if nothing else, I at least owed him that much recognition.

In a sense, it was both exhilarating and scary, going off on my own. I hadn't been expecting the sudden turn of events, and as a result, I knew then and there that I would have to become stronger on my own since I no longer had somebody there to talk me through my lacking self-confidence issues any longer.

I was three days away from Front Royal, Virginia by river.

I didn't know the outcome of my future anymore and there were no longer any presumptions to be made. There was only going forward, without pause.

My journey through the night down that river alone was peaceful all the same. A massive thunderhead followed over me for quite some time down the river, lighting the skies with warnings and threats that would later prove to be empty.

The tired part of me began to hope it would let loose and rain, if for no other reason than because it would force me to seek cover and sleep. However, the stubborn part of me would insist I continue paddling occasionally and drift along in the current for the next 36 hours instead.

It was 1 A.M. when I stopped on a peninsula in the river to check my location over my smartphone. With Torry's body weight, and pack weight now absent, I found that I had been moving rather rapidly through the river. Three times as fast, to be exact. I had managed to make quite a bit of mileage in the short period since his departure.

As I climbed from the boat, I wriggled my toes into the soft sandbar and felt the deafening roar of cicadas calling out into the night around me. But upon closing my eyes to allow the sound to pull me into a mantric state, I heard the high-pitched whistling from an air leak on my boat.

"Awesome..." I muttered, as I opened my eyes and knelt down in the sand. I was quick to find that somewhere along my drifting down the river, a rusted fish hook had clung into the port side of my vessel. Between paddling and drifting, I had taken to re-inflating the sagging sides quite regularly while thinking to myself that there were probably dozens of obscure and impossible-to-find holes existing underneath. This sudden discovery however, helped diffuse that fear just a bit.

I removed a piece of duct tape from my backpack that would have to suffice for the time being as a temporary patch.

"Guess that solves it!" I tried to say enthusiastically.

I sat in my boat, in the dark and ate a raspberry cream cheese Danish, trying to temporarily put the whole thing out of my mind. I was out of drinking water, but I had a mouthful of warm, flat Pepsi which I complimented my Danish with.

The night was alive with strange sounds. Now and then, something would take off, crashing through the woods. Immediately, my headlamp would beam into the darkness, only casting enough light to make the creatures eyes glow as they stared back out at me. Certainly they were just as scared of me, as I was of them. Right?

I rowed back towards the middle of the river, nervously all the same in the rare case that they weren't animals, so much as they were monsters. "Much better," I assured myself, continuing to enjoy my raspberry cream Danish while drifting along.

Along the way, I would fall asleep several times as I lay tucked within the confines of my raft; for as much as an hour. Many times, I would only awaken when hearing the sounds of small approaching rapids or an animal call I'd never heard before—screeching out into the muggy summer night.

As 3 A.M. rolled around, I had become so exhausted that I had begun to see fantastically odd things. Logs in the middle of the river took the shape of people with dark, featureless faces; watching me. These creatures stood under the backdrop of the moon.

Maybe they were Angels? Maybe they were Demons?

Or maybe there were both.

Lightning bugs flying about these objects made the figures occasionally appear to be taking distant drags off of a neon cigarette, as they leisurely gazed at my drifting vessel.

At times when the wind blew, I would see pieces of trash become arms that bent or broke unnaturally back and forth, and in all the wrong directions. Howls of the wind were their cries, as they arced their broken limbs in my direction, reaching out towards me. And as my imagination grew, I also began to see empty black eyes with no souls, and mouths that ripped like rough charcoal lines from ear to ear.

I could take no more of these tired disillusions.

I needed sleep.

So I pulled my boat up against the bank of a pasture where sleeping cattle stood motionless no more than 10 to 15 feet away from me. Some looked at me nonchalantly, not nearly bothered by my presence.

Others, more perturbed with my being there waved their heads up and down quickly in challenge, and false charged two or three steps before stopping.

But I was too tired to run, and ultimately too tired to care. Somehow, I drug myself out from the boat and into the soft, dew covered grass blades.

I took my time deflating the damaged air chambers on the raft that I had recently discovered. I then repaired all but a few. This included a small seam rip in the front of the raft that I hadn't yet fixed from the day before.

When I was done, I slept on the floor of the re-inflated raft and wrapped myself in my tarp. It had taken seconds before I was lost in slumber.

I was met with a beautiful morning when I awoke, and fresh dew blanketing the tarp I had used for warmth during the night. The rain clouds from the evening prior had gone, and only the moisture of a few sprinkles during the early hours of daybreak remained. I must've been so tired, that I had slept right through the precipitation only because my hair was matted and drops of water fell from my beard to my chest, as I sat up.

It was odd, how much the landscape changed when it turned from night to day. The pasture was no longer just a black, featureless expanse. It had transformed under the sun, into a lush green field, rife with wildflowers of every color in the rainbow—amongst rolling hills. I stared in awe and removed my camera from my backpack to take pictures.

"Amazing..." I whispered, in wonderment. I raised the camera, and watched as the dead battery notification beeped, swallowed the entire screen and image, and then went black.

"Of course. Why would you have any power?" I asked sarcastically, tossing the damned thing back into the boat.

Breakfast that morning was simple. Starving, I chomped upon a 6-pack of crushed and partially-melted mini chocolate donuts which I chased with 5 ounces of filtered river water.

I looked at the maps and the river ahead for the days yet to come. This had been completed by utilizing what little remaining power my smartphone had left.

"Only 15% battery life remaining." I read the notification warning out loud. I was going to need to find a source of power soon if I had planned on effectively navigating to Harper's Ferry.

Minutes later, I shoved off from the shoreline with an audience of cattle watching me as if I was out of place for having ever stopped there. Simple expressions of concern or confusion as to who or what I was...and what it was that I had been doing there upon their territory to begin with.

I had reached Luray Avenue a few hours later and pulled up into the boat landing, decidedly stretching my legs.

Nearby, two men talked to each other from within their vehicles. They were parked side by side in the gravel lot of the boat ramp. From what I had overheard, they talked about politics and of how cruddy they found our government and current politicians to be. I unpacked my things from the boat and glanced up at them from time to time.

It was hard to disseminate what the black guy was saying between all of his jargon and his thick Jamaican accent thrown in, though.

As I looked down at my dying phone, I used the last couple of minutes of life it still had left on the battery to check my bank account and my dwindling funds. Having seen what little money I had left, the screen suddenly died.

So there I was in the middle of nowhere, with no clear direction of where to go to resupply or what to do next. I had thought I'd reached Front Royal finally, but I no longer even knew that for certain.

As I no longer had any food available, I didn't want to pass up the opportunity for a hitch into the nearby town.

So I took a deep breath and slowly approached the two individuals.

The words were there, but I had been too scared to ask. Instead, I had submitted to complicated directions towards the nearest motel.

"Well, you know where the main strip is from here, right?" the redneck with the thick southern accent asked me.

"I'm not actually from here," I replied, with a nervous smile. I wondered immediately if that had been a smart thing to have said, seeing as I was alone out here now. If the man had potentially wanted to take advantage of my ignorance, he might have been able to in that moment.

After the directions he had given me seemed too incomprehensible to understand, I thanked him all the same and figured I would be better off walking down the road until I found a house. Maybe then I could ask somebody *else* for the nearest town. Only because the mans directions had me going left, right, under places, through someone's backyard and behind a church to the left of a cemetery. By the end, I was supposed to have been petting a pit bull named "Butch" to ensure safe passage through an alley somewhere.

"Th…thanks." I stuttered, more confused than I had been before asking him anything.

So I went back to my boat and began deflating it. I rolled it up as tightly as possible and slipped it into a black garbage bag. I was now carrying a 47 lb. raft, a 50 lb. backpack and ten pounds of miscellaneous items such as life jackets, paddles, canned food trash, and a raft pump amongst other things.

While I had thought of stashing the boat in the woods nearby, I didn't want to risk somebody simply walking off with my stuff when I was no longer there to prevent it from being stolen. The Hot Springs incident back in North Carolina had destroyed my trust and belief in people, as well as the hope in the kindness of strangers.

I began to struggle with the load I was carrying, as I walked down Luray Avenue. I dropped the bag onto the scorched earth and sighed, wiping sweat from my eyes. When I started walking again, the plastic sack began to tear in half. As I leaned over to grip the deflated boat from the bottom, two empty water bottles from my backpack fell out onto the gravel lot in the process.

"Well isn't that JUST GREAT!" I shouted angrily, stomping the ground in a tantrum.

The sun was hot and relentless as I bent down to collect my things. When I stood, I felt just a little dizzy from the head rush.

As I started walking again, the Jamaican man who had overheard and seen my dilemma pulled up to my side in his purple Dodge Caravan.

"Cha mon! We a'go to da Pioneer. Would take ya'z to da Skyline but you don't seem 'twa be a battybwoy. Lots o' rudeboyz dere tho. Not'cha style." He said.

"I'm sorry?" I asked, as I dropped the ton of bricks in my arms to the earth and smeared more beads of sweat from my eyes.

"You's tol' mah friend back dere datcha needed tah find da nearest place tah stay didn't 'cha?"

I nodded my head, still trying to process what a "batty boy" was. Only half of everything the man said, was really discernible.

"My names John, what's yours?" I asked offering him my hand. He shook it gratefully.

"Dale Trejean Francisco. Ja one en' only. Come yah, see dis'. Twas a bad bwai me self back in dah day." He said, handing me a picture from his wallet. I rubbed more streams of perspiration from my eyes as I looked it over.

In the folded Polaroid picture, I could see the resemblance of a young teenage boy holding what looked to be a pistol of some sort as he crossed his arms over his chest. On either side were two other individuals in a typical gangster pose. The kid on his left in the picture had shades on, and an AK-47 propped across the back of his shoulders. The other kid on his right held two machetes in an X across his bare chest and had long dreads hanging down across his face.

I smiled as I handed the picture back.

"Should I be worried about riding with you?" I asked with a nervous laugh. And truthfully, I *was* just a bit nervous. I didn't think you offered somebody a ride and then showed them a picture of how dangerous you once were (or possibly still are) as a "welcoming" of sorts.

Dale reached over and opened the rear sliding door from the inside for me.

"Set'cha tings down mah friend." he offered. I immediately began to think that in doing so, he would speed off with my items and thousands of dollars in gear, cameras, flash drives and chargers. Reluctantly, though, I did as he said. I then handed him his picture back.

"Dat are Damselfly Dready on ja right, and Dungle dere on'cha left. Tink he wah from West Kingston. Dey wahz mah crew." He said in reflection.

I began to wonder how rude it would appear if I had suddenly taken my things back out of his vehicle and said I'd rather walk.

"Looks like a tight crew," I replied, unsure of what else to add.

"Coo yah. Yah'z best be believin', bruddah. Let's be ridin'." He said, stuffing the picture and wallet back into his pocket.

As he drove, he asked what I did for a living. It was a funny question, only because I knew the answers would always make me appear to have been rather reckless. How different I had become in those months out on the Appalachian Trail, as I had gone from a secured lifestyle, to never knowing what was going to happen next. To put it into perspective, I had drifted down a river asleep, only waking and navigating rapids when the roar of the river had awakened me. I slept on the shoreline in a rubber raft in a pasture overnight next to cattle, and now I had been picked up by a Jamaican man who was taking me into whatever the nearest town was.

You truly never knew what was going to happen next. And while that was a little scary when put into perspective against my previously scheduled, and productive life back in civilization— it was also rather exhilarating.

I explained to Dale that I had quit my former security job and sold everything I had owned to hike from Georgia to Maine. When I did, he burst out into laughter with awe, as he questioned every aspect of how I lived on a day to day basis.

After giving him my story, he told me he was in a gang growing up but that he had met a father figure in a "Big Brother" type program that had changed his life forever. After college, Dale came to America where he spent six years seeing and traveling the country by van.

"I worked sum time wit dah Babylon in Trinidad myself." He said. I wasn't sure what "Babylon" was supposed to have stood for, but I nodded my head in agreement. Upon further discussion, though, I was sure that it was some authority or law enforcement organization because Dale had explained to me that he had been helping in gathering information against known drug runners in the country at the time.

When he dropped me off in front of the Pioneer, and I thanked him; he slowly canted his head to the side.

"You gon' be oh-kay John. I can see it, yah. You's gonna make it fah." he said, shaking my hand. I shook back and smiled.

"I dunno Dale. Maine is a long ways away." I replied. Simply thinking about it was almost maddening. Mostly, because I wasn't even halfway there yet.

"Life is like a blink of da eye. People come and go each deh. Nevah knowin' when dey gon' draw dere last breaf. But you's got tah tink, dat when it comes your turn tah pass on tah dah otta side; you's got a story tah tell ol' Saint Pete at dah gates." he said with a warm smile crossing his face.

"Take care, Dale," I replied, feeling emboldened by his speech.

"You too, my brahtta," he replied. I watched him as he drove away and wondered why he had gone out of his way to help me.

The world was slowly opening up to me, and I was beginning to change with it, one encounter at a time. And with it, an immediate sense of guilt came over me, for my prior hesitance in jumping into his vehicle.

When I walked into the office of the Pioneer Motel, I was greeted by a tired, and rather angry looking Asian man.

"Yeah?" He had asked before I had even spoken one word. The air conditioning in the place had apparently been broken, and it was strikingly hot and humid inside the office. Sweat was pouring down in streams along the bridge of the manager's nose and the valleys of lines along his aged face.

"Need a room for one night. One person." I replied.

He sighed and shook his head slowly, almost as if bothered by the request. He glanced down at my backpack and the large trash bag I had in tow. There was an awkward pause before he stated: "Fifty dollar. Won't be ready till 1 o'clock."

"Thanks." I said, rolling my eyes.

I walked around to the side of the building where there was a balcony with outdoor patio furniture. There was a woman in her early 50's who was smoking outside, looking at me cautiously as I approached.

I was hot, soaked in sweat and just plain tired as I began to sit down. No sooner than my butt had glanced the surface of that wrought iron furniture, than the woman sharply spoke to me in surprise and anger in her tone.

"What the *hell* are you doing?" She asked, in a threatening pitch.

I was stunned. So much so, that I immediately shot up from the seat as if I'd just broken the law.

"I was just sitting down..." I began.

"Why?" She asked harshly.

"I....I don't know...I was tired?"

"So what?" she countered.

I gulped, slightly frightened at her sudden outburst.

"Am I not allowed to sit here?"

"No, you're not." She replied quickly.

"Okay then. Sorry." I said as I began to walk away.

"Where are you from?" She asked suddenly.

"Nowhere near here, thank God." I responded almost rather appreciatively. The response from both the motel manager and her had set me off.

"You homeless or something? 'Cause I don't have any money." She added rather immediately if for no other reason than to shut me down from asking long before the words had ever hypothetically left my mouth.

"Look, I don't want or *need* your money, lady. I'm hiking the Appalachian Trail. I have been aqua blazing since Port Republic, Virginia and I was just looking to rest for a moment." I returned, half expecting her to understand everything I'd just said to her.

Like most, she hadn't.

She didn't understand what 'Aqua-blazing' was or what the Appalachian Trail was either. So like I had for Dale, I gave her my story. She began to open up then, and relax if only a little bit once she had learned more about me. Possibly because she no longer thought of me as some beggar.

She told me a little bit of what to expect from the town of Front Royal, starting with the Skyline Motel and what a dangerous place she had thought it to be.

Apparently, she had used to be a pizza delivery driver in that town and had almost been sexually assaulted thereupon delivering an order. She also said that meth labs were being run out of the rented rooms there.

When I asked about a safe place to stay the night in town, she grimaced.

Supposedly a local power dam was in an outage and most of the contract workers that had come to town, had filled the cheapest of Front Royal's motels. She went on to explain that there wasn't going to be much for vacancies around town, if any.

I thanked her, and not soon after I was up and on my way. The heat and humidity had been getting to me, and I needed a place of reprieve to retreat to. Something with some sort of A/C. I found the Scottish Inn just about 200 feet down the road.

Surprisingly, it appeared empty. There wasn't one car in the entire lot.

Piles of old carpeting littered the corner of the properties parking area, next to the entrance. I'd actually thought for a moment that the building was potentially abandoned, based on just the outside look of the structure with sagging, dry-rotted wood paneling and grass turning the parking lot into a field. The sign on the door towards the motel's office read in highly expressive letters: *"Rooms at only $39 a night!"*

When I pulled upon the handle of the office lobby door, it was locked.

"Damn..." I muttered. I shuddered at the thought of having to return to the Pioneer and wait outside in the sun until I either dropped dead or accidentally sat on a hypodermic needle just laying around out there.

Just as I was starting to turn away, though, a woman came from the back of the office and unlocked the lobby entrance for me.

"Are you guys open?" I asked the woman who apparently had no verbal response for me, whatsoever.

In fact, she could barely look me in the eyes, as she gave me keys to a room and took my credit card from my hand.

"I guess that's a yes," I replied, for her.

When I opened the door to a disparaging room, with mildew on the walls and strange stains all over the floor; a feeling of disgust rolled over me immediately. The rented space had the odd scent of vomit, and there were house flies in swarms, as if a plague had been set loose inside the decaying space.

I had noticed more and more in these privately owned motels, that your physical appearance would often dictate the kind of rooms that the staff or owners stuffed you into. As a hiker, you didn't normally give a damn because at some point you had probably slept in worse conditions. In truth however, I had had enough of it.

I angrily walked back to the office and told the woman I wasn't going to stay in such a revolting room.

"No refunds. Read *there*!" The Indian woman hissed, pointing at the very sign I wish I had seen earlier. Then again I wondered how it would have affected my purchase having not been shown the state of the room pre-picked for me, beforehand anyways.

"Fine, no refunds. But you had better give me a cleaned room then." I replied just as angrily in tone as she had given me.

"The room is cleaned. We don't have any other rooms available!" She shouted back, apparently trying to sway me by raising her voice louder this time.

"There's no cars in your parking lot! NOBODY WANTS TO STAY HERE! IT'S FILTHY! Give me a new room or give me my MONEY BACK!" I yelled. A man came out then from the back of the office.

He began to talk to her in Hindi, and then he started raising his voice back at her before she threw her hands into the air and walked into the apartment behind the counter; slamming the door behind her. The man apologized and gave me a different room that had two beds in it.

But when I opened the door to what would be my 'humble abode'; I found it was also moldy, with thousands of stains all over the floor.

The beds appeared in shape, like a giant U and dead bugs of almost every variety in the world laid in permanent rest in their rust stained bathtub tomb.

"Only the best, for Morris the Cat," I muttered sarcastically, collapsing upon the dirty bed. Dust flew up in huge plumes that left me in a coughing fit over the next few hours.

I was tired, and I certainly wasn't going to argue for another room. Besides, the other spaces were probably all just as shitty as the next, if not worse.

It was June 25th, 2013.

I watched the weather channel and local news, learning that the next week had been calling for showers and thunderstorms. It had truly been my intention to leave Front Royal, Virginia that very day. Only that somber bit of news made me want to enjoy the very thing I'd be missing over the next week.

Being dry, that is.

I walked around town much like a tourist does and probably just as noticeable as one, and window shopped for things I wished that I could afford.

When I got back to my motel, I found that Dozer, Sadlack, Helmet Hair and his girlfriend, were staying at that same motel that I was. They sat on the second-floor balcony with their legs dangling over the edge and cigarettes perched between their lips.

"Well, well...look what the Cat drug in," Sadlack said with a sardonic grin.

I smiled up at them all with my hands in my pockets.

"Where's your boyfriend? I thought you guys were inseparable?" Helmet Hair asked me, as he took a deep drag on his cigarette and expelled bluish gray smoke from his nostrils in two thick streams.

"He decided to go back home." I replied.

"Well, it's good to know we're not the only ones giving up and going home." Dozer exclaimed as Helmet Hairs girlfriend immediately agreed with the statement.

"You're leaving the river? Or the trail entirely?" I asked them, taken back in surprise.

"I'd say both." Helmet Hair answered for the lot of them.

"So did your shitty little rubber boat finally crap out on you? Is that why you're leaving?" Sadlack asked in a rather cartoonish sympathetic tone.

"No. The raft is excellent." I replied, unbothered by his bullying.

"Then why are you getting off the trail?" Dozer asked me.

"*Torry* left the trail. The thing is," I said as I cupped my hand across my eyes to shield them from the sun.

"I'm still going on, alone." I finished.

Sadlack's face dropped rather suddenly into a scowl. Meanwhile, Dozer laughed and slapped his knee.

"That's awesome! I hope you make it man!" He exclaimed with genuine excitement.

Sadlack quickly gave a disparaging look towards Dozer as did Helmet Hair; almost as if they didn't approve of his enthusiasm for me.

Dozer noticed the expressions and immediately looked down towards the ground as if in shame, as Sadlack stood up slowly and came down the motel's side stairs.

As he approached quite aggressively and rather swiftly, I felt he was going to charge me at any moment out of anger. Maybe it enraged him to think that I was still going forward after he had given up? He had ragged on Torry and me early on the Shenandoah River.

Constantly expecting our boat to fail, and repeating it to us every time he saw us or we passed each other along the way.

"I'm almost certain I've met you before." Sadlack said, still approaching me rather quickly. I tensed my body.

Dozer and Helmet Hair had gotten up as well from their balcony seats and had muttered inaudible comments with concerned looks upon their faces as they followed down the stairs.

"It was a while back. Way at the beginning of the trail now that I think about it." Sadlack added as he stopped three feet away from me.

I watched his friends trailing up behind him.

"You asked us about the White Mountains...and we blew you off. It wasn't the NOC...was it?" He asked out of contemplation. Suddenly, I recognized him.

"It was Neels Gap." I answered. His facial hair and shoulder-length head of hair made him appear to be an entirely different person.

And it had taken me all of this time to realize it.

"That right! That was just before me and Shannon hooked up." He exclaimed as if I should have known exactly who he was speaking of. When he saw the confused expression upon my face, though, he clarified.

"That cute hiker that was with us at the picnic table. It doesn't matter. She was just a quick piece of ass." He stated rather crudely. I nodded, catching the disgusted look on Helmet Hairs girlfriends face once she'd heard the rude comment. Maybe insecurities in her mind were now starting to leak into her brain after having heard the comment.

"You were a jerk to me for no reason. All I had wanted to know was how hard the White Mountains were. I was new and naïve to the AT. But you laughed in my face and scoffed when all I wanted was information. Because you and your buddy there couldn't be bothered. Could you?" I asked as I walked by him towards my room.

"You know why we're getting off of the river? And well...the trail too?" He called out to me. I stopped and turned to face him with no response.

"Poor planning and too much partying. It cost us two hundred and eighty-five bucks a person to rent those canoes for a week. And now we have to return them today. We haven't even reached our original destination and to do so would cost more money that we don't have." He exclaimed.

"I don't see how that's my problem." I replied rather coldly and with no sympathy in my voice. And inside, I sort of smiled proudly to myself as I thought about my raft. Especially considering for eighty dollars I not only would complete the aqua blaze but could send the raft home and keep it if I'd wanted to once I was done with it.

"It's not *your problem*. You're exactly right. I'm just saying, I gave you a hard time in the beginning. And look at where you are now. And look at where I am." He explained out of reflection. I looked towards Helmet Hair who I had recognized now as the guy that had been with him at Neels Gap when they had both been too snooty and too bothered to answer any of my nubile questions. Instead, both choosing to ridicule my lack of knowledge and my overly hopeful initial determination.

I had come a long way since Neels Gap and only now, was I starting to feel like an entirely different person.

Sadlack offered his hand to me in those next few moments. I looked first into his eyes and then to his peace offering again.

"I won't lie. I didn't see you making it this far. But you surprised me." He exclaimed with maybe just a tad of jealousy in his tone.

I walked over and firmly shook his hand. There was regret in his eyes as he nodded his head.

I started to turn away until he added:

"The White Mountains that you were asking about back in the beginning?"

"Yeah?"

"They'll be hard. You haven't seen anything like them. But South Western Maine will be the most taxing part of the whole journey. Especially this summer with the black flies and the clouds of mosquitos you'll be contending with. Good luck, Morris the Cat." He said as he walked back upstairs towards his room. His friends either nodded or waved me goodbye as they followed their leader.

I thought over what he said, as I returned to my room.

There was something so ominous about that eighty-seven-mile mountain range. It struck mystery, fear and curiosity into my mind like a mythological beast I would someday have to battle.

If only because I wasn't sure what I was supposed to expect.

There was fear, but behind that excitement. And in a sense, I felt that made me courageous and determined to try.

The tremors had come back again during the night. I didn't understand them nor why they occurred. My jaw would involuntarily stiffen and then my hands would begin to shake wildly whenever I moved them a certain way. My muscles felt tightened and spasmed almost regularly now.

I simply hoped it was new stress or fatigue issues and not something underlying or worse. All the same, the restlessness had caused me to awaken quite early, and as a result I was already packed and ready to leave.

It was 7:45 A.M. and I was watching the Indian woman from the office lobby, pushing a cleaning cart from room to room as I stepped outside. I was confused, because no one else had stayed at the motel overnight that I was aware of, except for me. What she was exactly cleaning, I wasn't sure—if not the already filthy rooms she had been renting out to imaginary customers.

I took a deep breath of fresh air and immediately felt the mildew and black mold spores which had invaded my lungs during the night; expelling from my respiratory tract upon exhalation.

"Check out time at 11 A.M.!" The woman shouted rudely at me, apparently still angry from our confrontation the day before.

"What was that?" I asked, purposely pretending to have not heard her. I set my backpack and the garbage bag which housed my raft within it outside the door to my room.

"Check out in ten minutes, or we charge you another day!" She replied just as rudely as she had before, only now the check-out time had changed to 8 A.M.

"Sorry, didn't catch that. Say again?" I said, opening the door to my room.

"CHECK OUT NOW!" She screeched, slamming a handful of towels down upon the cart.

"Lady, you need to speak up. I can't seem to hear a word you're saying." I replied, slamming the door shut behind me.

I began packing away extra rolls of toilet paper. You always needed more toilet paper out on the trail and could never really have enough.

I took my daily ibuprofen and thyroid medication and proceeded to walk out the door to my room again. The woman was waiting outside by it.

"You leave now?" She asked impatiently.

"Come again?" I asked, tossing her the key to the room and cupping a hand over my ear to reflect that I was hard of hearing.

She dropped her broom and scrambled for the key a second in the air, before grasping it.

She began cursing at me in Hindi, then made a spitting sound in my direction as I walked off and slung my pack over my shoulders.

A taxi had pulled into the parking lot to drop off some potential customers staying at the motel. I asked the driver if she could give me a ride to the river via Luray Avenue and she agreed that she could. As I got into the cab, the Indian woman went up to the driver side window and exclaimed in a calmed and warning voice through her broken language that I was "bad" and that the driver shouldn't be giving me a ride because I may, in fact, be "dangerous". I looked at the Indian woman from the back seat and rolled down the window.

"Seriously? Are you *crazy* lady, or what?" I asked, laughing at the woman's questionable behavior. She began yelling at me in broken English and with her native language mixing in again.

"I'm ready to go, whenever you are." I told the taxi driver as I rolled up my window in the shouting woman's face. The driver nodded and slowly took off.

As our taxi drove away, I crossed my eyes rather childishly at the motel owner's wife and circled my finger against the side of my head mouthing: "Craaaazzzyyyyy...."

This made her even angrier, and she started shouting louder just as the taxi pulled a right onto Criser lane.

"Jesus! What was the deal between you two?" the driver asked, adjusting the rear view mirror to look back at me.

I just laughed as she drove me back towards the river.

Bright skies grayed, and then darkened with the promise of rain. As droplets sporadically began to fall, I sought shelter beneath a thick-leafed tree whose name I did not know.

The wind blew, and the river became a sea of brown leaves drifting slowly by. They danced, or glided across the glass surface with every slight gust.

Strangely enough, they reminded me of the brown eyes or hair of every woman I have ever loved in my past. And within their depths, just as quick with which for you to drown; clearly in love.

And as the wind shifted, the current pulled these leaves along, and the ripples in the surface of the water flowed parallel in the wrong direction.

Breaks in the sun came only for a moment, if only to exclaim quite proudly "I'm still here..." amongst the precipitations still coming down around me.

Untying from beneath the branch of the tree to which I had anchored, I let the wind push me.

The whisper of the trees was always so haunting when I found myself lost in thought. I heard laughs or voices from the past that I knew were not there. I saw smiles and faces in the clouds above me and felt the touch of summer caressing my cheeks as I squinted my eyes north.

I had found simplicity while sitting in the river, just drifting along on my raft. Frogs and crickets chirped away into the evening, and the air began to cool down quite significantly. There existed no skill in not caring. And sometimes I was appreciative of that.

I had finally made it to Warren Dam, just as the skies opened and a monsoon let loose upon me.

Here, you portaged to the left side of the Shenandoah River through an incredibly lush, dark and thick forest that opened to an expansive field on the other side. I quickly propped my raft upside down against the side of a large oak, deep inside the forest after scouting ahead, my path of travel.

I sat there beneath my rubber raft shelter, as the rain pounded down in droves for 45 minutes around me. While it rained, I dried off beneath my boat-made shelter and ate a late lunch which included:

1 Chocolate Chip granola bar
1 Cosmic Brownie
1 can of Tuna
1 Apple
And a 32oz bottle of purified river water.

As I was packing my trash away, I came across a nearly empty box of Torry's PallMall menthol 100's inside one of the garbage bags. Tucked within the half soaked pack, were two crushed and bent cigarettes and a third that had been broken into two pieces.

As I glanced back out at the torrential downpour, I perched a bent menthol cigarette between my dried out lips and muttered to myself: "Guess I ain't got nothin' but time." I lit the end of the tobacco stick and took a slow drag. I watched as rain drops tore the smoke clouds apart before my very eyes as I exhaled.

Afterward, I quickly scrambled back into the river after the rain had momentarily let up. I had seen yet another dark collection of clouds headed in my direction and wanted to get a head start on their arrival.

They were never able to catch up to me though, as the recent down pouring had hastened the river's current quite a bit.

Instead, the sun came out and left me with a rather beautiful atmosphere rich in the smells of an after shower scent, nature and wildflower fields steaming beneath summer skies.

Damselflies (which look a lot like dragonflies only not as big) came out in swarms. Like protective little fairies, they landed on or around and all over my boat or on my knees or hands. Almost hundreds of them I would say, that accompanied me in a rainbow of colors.

But they were not pests. They didn't bite you or suck your blood or sting you in any way.

Instead, they were catching and eating all of the nuisance flies out there, such as mosquitoes. It was like I had acquired a flying-insect-protective-escort down the river. Sometimes, one or two would land on me while chomping a horsefly they had caught or a mosquito they had managed to snatch out the air. Others were lightly snacking on gnats or bugs with names I was not entirely familiar with.

I was their perch and they, in turn, had become my source of entertainment.

Much as they'd perch on each of my extended fingers like gaudy jewelry pieces.

As the night came on, they slowly took their leave a few at a time until I had one more left. Resting upon the back of my hand, this particular damsel fly had a distinctive red tint to its rainbow of possible colors.

I held the creature up to my face and watched as it canted it's curious head from side to side, looking at me.

There was something so intelligent in its nonverbal expression that made think that this tiny little creature had become curious in trying to decipher what I was.

And then in the blink of an eye, the little creature flew away.

That evening, the river had finally started moving a lot faster. It's funny to think of 2 MILES PER HOUR as swift, but you have to look at it like this. Say from 7 P.M. until 7 A.M. I stay in my boat, sleeping, drifting, eating, and generally being worthless and lazy by not paddling one bit.

In a 12 hour period just floating alone, I just knocked out twenty-four miles of river overnight, doing NOTHING.

Not a bad deal. Come morning after sleeping all night while doing this exact thing; I'd come to find that my body was rather refreshed.

The sunlight filtered in slowly enough to wake me rather calmly, and quietly.

I opened my eyes to find a pasture drifting by in my field of vision with curious horses watching me from behind the fence.

I sat up slowly and massaged the crick in my neck out as I tried to take in my surroundings. It was 8 A.M., and while I was rather hungry, I didn't have the energy to pull anything out from my pack or look for food nearby.

Instead, I read over a few text messages I had received from Woodstock.

He had explained in his letter, that he and his car crew were still four days away before they reached Front Royal which was only a memory in the past to me now.

And while they had officially invited me to join their group once learning of Torry's departure, I had contemplated hiking ahead of them on my own once I'd reached Harper's Ferry. It was my belief that they would eventually catch up to me while walking their average sixteen to twenty mile days.

Maybe it would give me time to adjust to their pace? Seeing as how Torry and I never seemed to average more than thirteen miles a day if we were lucky.

That wasn't to mention I was damn near close to experiencing atrophy in my legs due to non-use over the past week while aqua blazing, so I would need a readjustment period to be sure.

When I arrived at Watermelon Park, as I had assumed they did, I was offered the option to camp.

The property housed a small general store, fire pits, coin showers and plenty of space to call home for a night. The only problem was, I couldn't justify paying fifteen dollars to camp there when instead I could find a patch of land somewhere down the river for free. So instead of purchasing a campsite, I bought some drinks, paid $.50 cents for a four minute shower and charged my phone and backup battery on an outlet outside of the shower building.

The skies looked miserable, and I was beginning to wonder how I was going to cook the hot dogs I'd bought two days before in Front Royal when it appeared you weren't allowed to make a fire on the property unless you were paying to stay overnight.

It was of no consequence, only because I left just as the owner started getting impatient with me. She had caught me charging my phone and kept asking how long I was planning to stay in the area.

So I departed the park, thinking about the rain. I then looked at the design of my boat and had an idea. I tied a tarp down in front of me to the bow up front and then to the starboard and port sides. I brought it all the way up to my waist like a blanket. It did a better job at keeping me dry within the raft, and as it started to rain, I threw it completely over my head and continued drifting down the river.

After a couple of miles, I fell asleep for thirty minutes only to awake to somebody shouting: "No one's in the raft!"

"Someone needs to stop that thing!"

Those were followed by: "I see a foot hanging out! Whoever it is might be hurt!"

"I think the guys dead!"

"Hey! Are you okay?"

I peeked my head out from beneath the tarp, and suddenly I found around ten to fifteen people on either shoreline and two people looking down from atop the Harry Byrd Highway Bridge upon me.

"Is everything okay?" I asked, just a tad confused over all of the hubbub.

"We thought you were dead!" Somebody shouted from the shoreline. I glanced up at the structure above me just in time to see an eight-year-old boy spitting over the bridge railing and then an adult I presumed to be his father smacking him in the back of the head.

"I'm fine! Thanks!" I replied. Their faces all appeared to drop; maybe more irritated at me for not needing help, than relaxed in knowing that I was okay.

As I continued down the river, the rain got worse.

The woman at Watermelon Park had told me I wouldn't be able to find a place to sleep—until I had reached Harper's Ferry.

But she was wrong.

There were several islands in the river along the way, and they didn't belong to anybody but the state of Virginia.

I chose one such place that at first I thought would be overgrown with vegetation. It turned out however, there was a well-established path from the sandy port side inlet to the middle of the island. There, within a massive clearing I came upon a rock fire ring and a rusty foldable metal chair to sit on!

I went to work quickly gathering wood and then proceeded to make a quick fire. I cooked and ate six plain hot dogs charred over the flames, with no buns or condiments, for dinner. They hadn't spoiled after two days in a hot backpack and tasted so darned good; I didn't feel they needed mustard or ketchup or buns to taste any better than they already did.

After eating, I took a bar of Ivory soap and went to work bathing myself in the river as well as scrubbing down my nine-day dirty, mildewy and sweat soaked rags I had the gall to call "clothes".

I was tired of smelling so badly and I had begun to break out rather severely from laying up to 12 hours sometimes in my raft filled with muddy river water. I had patches of rash all over my body as if a collection of river bacteria had started to work its way inside my flesh.

After bathing myself thoroughly and lathering the areas with soap, the skin irritations subsided completely, over the course of two hours. I went back into the river water to take another swim but couldn't stand the many minnows which were giving me exploratory nips. They were like biting piranha! All were attacking my thighs, calves or the sides of my stomach!

I got out and threw my clothes on so that they would dry quicker. I packed all of my things so that if the rain got bad and the island started to flood, I could make a hasty escape.

The scary thing I had noticed after hanging my hammock tent was that the islands highest point was actually about twenty feet above the river. There was backwash and deadfall as high as an additional 10 - 15 feet in the branches of the trees above my head, where the river had flooded over the island completely at some point in the past.

It was 7 A.M., and I hit the river like an Olympic champion for all of three strokes until five seconds later I was snoring with my head dangling out the back of the boat and with a leg thrown over one side.

I drifted a bit, listening to music over my phone and scoping out Harper's Ferry on Google maps via my smartphone. It appeared that there were plenty of islands in the area to choose from, for camping to save money. I also needed to find a taxi to drive me to the post office so that I could ship my boat home, though.

As always however, I responded as I did with most problems: "Eh, I'll worry about that later."

'Later' was seriously, like THE NEXT DAY.

Oh well. 'Winging it' hadn't failed me thus far, so I guessed I would, in fact, worry about it later.

I crossed into West Virginia at 8:56 A.M. and later down the river after the sun had turned my flesh into a darker tan of leather; I was paddling past a recreation area for RV camping.

As I rowed ever so delicately, trying not to stretch the raw flesh on my arms and neck, a cop pulled up on the side of the road and asked to see my life jacket.

"Who needs that, when I've got *these* babies," I called out to him in jest, while flexing my imaginary biceps for him.

There was an awkward silence, and I frowned when I saw that the officer wasn't laughing.

So I took out my life jacket and showed it to him.

"Have a nice day." Was his reply, as he got back into his truck. I guess he hadn't found me very amusing.

I pushed on over a set of class 2 rapids that finally did in the bottom of my raft.

As I drifted slowly away I felt the middle of my vessel sinking into the water enough to make it impossible to drift anymore.

When I reached Interstate 9, I found out why the water had been moving so slowly.

There was another dam crossing to make. The Millville Hydroelectric Dam to be precise.

With the help and direction of town locals, I walked half a mile with my heavy backpack to scout out portage safely on the other side. I then had to walk back to retrieve my boat and repeat the process. Finally, I had to go back a third time for the oars, air pump, trash bags and other miscellaneous items before I continued down the river just as it was beginning to turn dark. The weather was calling for rain through the night, and it had just started to sprinkle. I saw the last rapids just before Harper's Ferry. Unfortunately, it was 9 P.M. and after understanding the scope and magnitude of these perilous waters, I found that I was in no rush nor did I have any intention to pass over them in the dark.

I scouted the woods around the area and found a section of thick vegetation that I had to bushwhack through, literally fifty feet from the start of those rapids.

I then hung up the hammock between two trees hanging over the water.

I was on the river as soon as 7:30 A.M came upon me the following day. I hit the first set of rapids and plowed through. Then I saw the second set and made a dead stop. I pulled up on shore when I saw the sudden drop in the level of that river. Surely I wasn't meant to make it over these in my chintzy rubber raft?

When I looked up information over my smartphone, regarding those particular rapids I found that they had been called "The Staircase" and that with over a mile and a half in length—they dropped some fourteen feet in elevation. Unprepared and improperly trained people had died on these rapids as well. And even if you happened to get past them in your boat, you were not allowed to pull up onto Harper's Ferry, WV. The U.S. Forest service forbade it for some reason.

I wasn't looking to chance losing everything I owned by sinking my craft or possibly drowning when I was only two miles away from Harper's Ferry.

The CSX Railroad ran along the left side of the Shenandoah River around twenty feet up along a boulder-ridden bank. So I deflated my raft and sadly began to tie it onto my backpack.

I was going to have to walk the rest of the way via the railroad; hefting this 47-pound beast in the process.

I felt that I was probably better off just pitching the whole thing into the first dumpster I came across in town, to be done with it.

So while walking down the railroad tracks with a 100 pounds of gear on my back, I came across two guys who worked for River & Trail adventures. They were making their way to the start of "The Staircase" rapids via the railroad tracks, wearing life jackets.

"Hey there. How're you do…?" The man began before I cut him off.

"FREE RAFT!" I shouted, tired, falling to my hands and knees dramatically in the baking sun.

They exchanged confused glances towards each other as I threw my backpack off and looked up at them with sweat pouring down my face.

"Um…you for real?" The taller of the two asked.

I told them my story and how I'd only paid $80 for the Seahawk 4 online at Amazon, and that it had gotten me from Port Republic, Virginia all the way there to Harpers Ferry (176 miles) in ten days. I also told them that it would cost almost just as much just to ship the thing back home.

I no longer had a need for it, and I didn't want to tote it around in my pack either or go through the hassle of trying to sell it. Besides, who would buy it? It'd been patched up three times already!

So they took it, graciously!

I felt free and amazing after unstrapping it from my back and handing them the oars, the pump and the Styrofoam noodle floaters and life jackets with it.

As they hefted the craft in their arms, they looked a little reluctant after taking it off of my hands.

"Jesus, you weren't kidding. This thing weighs like a ton of bricks!" The shorter guy complained as I was walking away.

I smiled, mostly because it was no longer *my* problem.

And though I didn't yet know it, I was about to have a new adventure starting out ahead of me.

Crossing the Winchester & Potomac Railroad Bridge over the Potomac River in Harpers Ferry, West Virginia via the Appalachian Trail

CHAPTER 2

New Beginnings

As I walked along the tracks, I came to realize doing so in crocs was almost entirely too painful to continue.

I zipped off the bottom leggings of my pants, threw some clean hiking socks on and put my boots back on as well. It was time I started donning my hiker clothes again now that my days as a *river vagabond* were over.

The railroad tracks were narrow and hugged a gigantic granite rock wall for a short time. The stone pass was evenly parallel to the river crashing and rushing by thirty feet below on my right. Pine trees and cedars lined the tracks intermingled with oaks, sycamores and maples and the heat of the sun and mist from the river complimented the views with bright splashes of rainbows.

I passed over a small railroad bridge that had signs stating "No Trespassing" and kept walking until the tracks intersected with Highway 340, Shoreline Drive, the Appalachian Trail and a greenway that ran through Virginius Island.

Virginius Island had been a thriving community in the 1800's. It had been separated from Harper's Ferry by a human-made canal. The canals and locks served to power cotton, flour, iron, lumber and grain mills on the island. It also acted as a home for many residents.

All that remained were ruins of that prior history.

A flood in 1870 had wiped out 12 buildings and destroyed almost everything else. The river that had been the very lifeblood of the town had also become its destruction.

I explored these canals, and waterways while reading over the fascinating history of the area on weather worn information boards scattered throughout the park.

When I had finally reached the town, I was very self-conscious of my smelly clothes, soaked with days of sweat and mildew having stayed consistently wet while on the river. I received estranged looks from tourists and passerby's and did my best to avoid everybody as I looked down in passing.

I ate lunch at Cannonballs Deli, which existed as a restaurant beneath the street, and appeared to be about the size of a basement.

I didn't care how it looked because I was starving. I had a meatball sandwich with a side salad having craved something fresh and healthy after preservative filled carbohydrates and wood pulp infused pop-tarts for over a week.

Afterward, I was still hungry, so I added a bag of chips and six glasses of ice cold root beer to my tab.

As I waddled up the restaurant's stairs having gorged myself, I looked about my surroundings and momentarily felt lost.

I had made it here.

I had finished the river and had reached the unofficial halfway mark of the Appalachian Trail. But what happened now?

Looking around Harper's Ferry, I felt it was too densely populated and filled with wandering tourists to find a place to stealth camp overnight. After talking to a few town locals and shop owners as well as the famed AT Thru-hiker—Baltimore Jack, I was made aware of a nearby hostel right there in town.

Well, unfortunately for me, it was full.

As the sun started to set, I began to feel a lot like a lost puppy now that I no longer had Torry to give me guidance or direction. I sat upon a grassy knoll directly adjacent to a train station and thought about the things Melody had warned me would happen out here. The most pressing being her prophetic message that Torry would eventually leave my side.

And while there was initial anger towards him as he posted Facebook status updates and pictures of him partying back at home, I knew I truly had no right to be angry.

In the pictures he took, he held a beautiful woman (Pam) in one arm and a beer in his other hand. He was happy, and he was satisfied if only by the expression painted upon his face.

And the more I thought about it, the more I realized that I *wasn't*. Not satisfied just yet, at least.

I yearned for more adventure.

"Hold up. I'll be there in a moment," I heard someone say behind me.

A dirty hand, coated in five or six shades of dirt plopped down upon my shoulder suddenly.

I followed the wrist to the arm and then the arm to the person.

"Rambles..." I muttered both in surprise and regret.

"Isn't the best thing about this journey, how you can randomly stumble across old acquaintances out of nowhere?" He asked with a smile that showed his yellowish teeth and dying gum lines.

I nodded, leaning back away from his face and his soured breath.

"Can I get a cigarette from you?" He asked sitting down on the grass beside me. It was the only time I'd wished Torry was still here to engage the guy in a conversation about weed, all while I walked away.

"You really are a mooch, aren't you?" I asked, fishing around in my backpack for Torry's last and almost emptied pack of PallMall menthol 100's. I hadn't felt much like smoking since he had gone so there were two left. Inside the crumpled pack was a bent and contorted cigarette and one that had been broken in half.

I took the broken one and gave Rambler the pack.

He then quickly removed the one remaining cigarette and tossed the empty box into the grass behind him.

"Jesus dude. What's wrong with you?" I asked in disbelief as I grabbed his trash and stuffed it into my own pocket.

"I was gonna get it later. Maybe..." he said with a shrug, before laughing. It only took seconds within his company to realize why I didn't like the guy.

"Where's Stupid?" He asked, lighting the end of his cigarette.

"He got off the trail," I replied solemnly.

"Are you kidding me? No way!"

"Yeah. He was ready to go back home." I replied as Rambles nodded his head and took a deep drag from his crooked tobacco stick.

"Maybe he was tired of your nagging." He offered, as I glared over at him in response.

"I mean no offense. I thought for sure you woulda quit before he did."

"You know I've heard that a lot lately," I responded, rather annoyed with his presence.

"Well, I was gonna invite both you guys to Washington with us. A group of us thru-hikers are going for July 4th to see the fireworks. But since Stupid isn't coming..." he trailed off.

He didn't have to finish his sentence.

Rambler was a pothead, and he knew that I wasn't. He was looking for fellow smokers to split a room in D.C. and was well aware that wherever Torry went I usually followed. Only now, I was on my own.

So there was no reason to invite a buzz kill, blowhard like myself.

And that was just fine with me.

"Where are your friends? Sumpeach and Hammy?" I asked. He only shrugged in response to my question before getting up and chasing down a fellow thru-hiker without so much as a "thank you" for the cigarette or a "goodbye."

I began texting Woodstock shortly after Rambles departure, to follow up on our original plans we had made way back in Troutville, Virginia.

It seemed like such a long time ago now.

We had talked about my joining his group of thru-hikers who were using his car to hike the whole AT.

If you were curious, this was achieved by exchanging keys along the trail as two people completed a section north and two individuals walked that same section of the AT going south. Whoever was walking towards the parked vehicle then drove and picked the others up. This meant day hikes and slackpacking were possible as well as not having to be tied solely to expensive food or shelter options along the trail. This was good because sometimes when the nearest store was five miles away, you gave in to highway robbery priced food items at road crossings, marked up as much as 300%.

Woodstock exclaimed in response to me by text message that he would be reaching Harper's Ferry within four or five days, so I could either wait on him or hike ahead, and he would pick me up at whatever road crossing I came across.

When fact-checking the AT thru-hikers guidebook, I found that I wasn't all that far away from Pine Grove Furnace. The *official* halfway point of the Appalachian Trail.

But as I glanced down at the large patches of rashes on my legs and stomach, I thought I might just be better off taking a day to rest because Lord knew that after ten days on a river, I needed it.

I crossed the bridge on foot into Maryland at 11:02 A.M. and followed the Potomac River a ways, headed north. This part of the trail had many bicyclists flying by quite regularly. After a while, I got a little annoyed with them shouting out:

"Passing on your left!"

Or...

"Coming up on your right!"

Eventually, I crammed in my earphones and chose to drown them out altogether; choosing instead to take my chances at getting run over by some guy in sweaty spandex.

The trail went directly beneath Highway 340 before curving uphill quite a ways along Weaverton Cliffs.

When I got to the top of the ridge, I found it was 1:30 P.M. and I'd already knocked out 5 miles.

I ate a quick lunch...mainly to get weight out of my pack but also because breakfast that morning at the Northgate Inn had only been a small bowl of cereal and a cup of coffee.

When I made it to the civil war correspondent's memorial, I took pictures and then kept pushing on. I was drenched and had been without reprieve all day, whether from sweat or rain. The last five hours of the day had been accompanied by beautiful rays of sunlight tearing through leaf cover, but it did nothing to pull my thoughts away from the chafing that was taking place between my thighs and along my waistband.

After an 11 mile day, my feet were screaming with pain. I found the first clearing I came across and leaned against a tall oak.

My back had become so stiff from the weight it had stopped getting used to carrying. I felt like an old man as I threw my pack on the ground.

"You know what? I'm gonna give you a name." I said, looking down at my backpack. I'd thought of a few possible monikers, such as:

- PITA (Pain in the Ass)
- Two Tons of Fun
- Jerkface, Please Die

The last one might have been a little complicated. So instead, I went with the models name: Gregory.

Having satisfied my delusions, I hobbled down the hill a quarter of a mile towards Crampton Shelter. I needed water, having drained out all of my bottles due to the heat and humidity during the day.

There was a spring flowing straight out of the ground just before the shelter, so I knelt down, drinking from it thirsty and exhausted without filtering. I cupped my shaking, calloused hands into the cold liquid and took in mouthful after mouthful of water.

It was amazing, how incredible it tasted to a man on the brink of dehydration. Having drunk my fill, I started the long walk back up the hill.

I cooked hot dogs and shared them with a fellow thru-hiker who had set up nearby while I had been re-hydrating myself.

I'd done this more out companionship, as I hadn't talked to anybody that day and had felt rather lonely for it. He thanked me, offering some chicken and rice in return, but nothing for conversation.

He explained this, by telling me that he needed his rest.

So I let him be.

As I laid back in my hammock, I looked over status updates on Facebook. Not only Torry's but people I had once called "friends" that had chosen Melody in our breakup over me. Some had deleted me from their friend's list altogether as I searched for their names and never found them. Others had just forgotten I existed.

All the same, I sent out "Hello's" via the messaging system Facebook provided its members with. Only when I went to do this, I saw that I had already sent these same people "Hello's" maybe three or four times in the past with no response.

Bitter by this information, I bit my bottom lip and felt loneliness creeping its way back in.

I shut my phone off and laid my head back against the hammock feeling exactly as I had earlier that morning.

About a million miles apart from them all.

"Why must you attack my eyes? Seriously?" I asked the tiny creature, pinched between my thumb and forefinger.

Of course, I received no reply.

"I mean I understand you have to be quite brave to go for the eyes of a beast, thousands of times your size. But do you realize how annoying you are?"

I asked as the gnat struggled to free itself from my grasp.

I smashed the tiny thing between both fingers and smeared its guts upon my pants leg without remorse, as I continued hiking on.

As I walked, I was bombarded by hundreds of the creature's friends.

They were like little kamikaze pilots making last ditch efforts to crash into my eyeballs, crawl up my nose or dive into my ears having exhausted all other options.

I began smacking my hands together in a clapping motion for minutes at a time as I walked; accomplishing smashing three or four of these suckers in the process at a time. It was good at clearing my vision from the cloud of pests hovering about my face, if for only a few minutes of reprieve.

This action too had started to become a hassle, though, as sweat beading across my forehead had begun to drip down into my eyes.

I made my way along the trail and passed large collections of morning glories, thistle's, bluebonnets and Queen Ann Laces. These of course were accompanied by never ending fields of poison ivy glistening with their allergenic urushiol oils.

And while the flowers were beautiful, the Ivy reminded me that out here in nature there was always a 'Give & Take' of some kind.

As I rounded a corner, I saw Bitter Goat; a fellow thru-hiker whom I had first met back at Dick's Creek, in North Carolina. I could tell he recognized me, but not my name.

"*Fat Norris* or something. Right?" He asked, tapping his chin thoughtfully as he looked over at me.

"That was your first guess. Huh?" I asked with a sarcastic tone.

"The guy that was hiking with you. I think he went by, uh. Was it, *Dumbass*? Was that his name?"

"Close. His name was Stupid. He got off the trail, though." I clarified.

"Oh yeah! And you're *Morris the Fat*! Now I remember!" He said excitedly.

"Cat." I corrected him with a sigh, shaking my head from side to side.

"Morris the Cat! That's right!" He restated.

"How've you been?" I asked, leaning against a kudzu-covered oak tree.

"Well, I'm in the process of completing the Four State Challenge. It involves clearing forty-three miles within 24 hours." He exclaimed.

This was achievable because the Maryland section of the Appalachian Trail was so short, at only 40.9 miles along the entire 2,188-mile path.

So you started two miles South of Harper's Ferry on the Virginia/West Virginia border. You crossed the footbridge over the Potomac into Maryland for the next 40.9 miles until you stepped into Pennsylvania at Pen Mar Park, thus completing the four state challenge.

As I watched Bitter Goat changing out his bloodied socks and popping some ibuprofen, I didn't think I would have been very interested in doing that sort of challenge myself. When he explained that he had 25 miles left to hike until completing it, I definitely knew then that he had a hell of a lot of strength and determination. Far more than I did.

"I'm planning on resting up a short while at the Washington Monument. Maybe I'll see you there." he offered. I bid him farewell as he continued hiking on with a wave goodbye.

Once I had made my way to Washington State Park, I saw Bitter Goat again. There was a picnic building with a sign calling it the "Mt. Vernon Shelter" and that its use was by permit only. So I went to the visitor center and asked the employee behind the counter, if I could stay there overnight and if I was supposed to sign a permit.

The park employee exclaimed that because I was a thru-hiker I didn't need to sign anything and that it was perfectly okay to sleep there for the night. I passed on the information to Bitter Goat, and we both set up our hammocks there underneath the picnic shelter as if it was a genuine AT structure. It had a chimney and a fireplace as well as a fresh water faucet and outlets to charge our electronics. If anything, this was the ULTIMATE Appalachian Trail shelter just because of those things.

Furthermore, it was only three-tenths of a mile away from the Washington Monument summit.

But as we gathered wood, enjoyed a ten-minute sunset that broke through the clouds and ate dinner together; I began to wonder how Bitter Goat had intended on completing his four state challenge if he was setting up to sleep for the night.

I had been questioned one too many times during my journey of the way "I" had chosen to hike the Appalachian Trail myself. Criticized quite often for the way I did it as well. The HYOH (Hike Your Own Hike) philosophy had been abandoned by hardcore trail purists, and as a result you found yourself judged quite often by the hiking community based upon the way you chose to take on the trail. So I felt I had no place to challenge him or ask and instead, simply enjoyed his company without bringing the subject up.

Moments later as the park was closing, the volunteer caretaker of the property arrived.

He explained to us that the employee within the visitor's center had been wrong and that people weren't allowed to camp in ANY parks throughout Maryland, let alone the Mount Vernon picnic shelter.

I found that odd and asked him rather glumly if we needed to move on. The caretaker glanced over at Bitter Goat who wasn't any more enthusiastic about the news than I was, if by expression alone.

"Just tell me if I need to put *these* back on." Bitter Goat said, resting his pair of bloodied socks upon the picnic table for effect.

The act had worked perfectly in our favor, by the expression on the caretakers face as his eyes widened at the sight.

"Jesus…" he muttered under his breath.

He quickly straightened, and cleared his throat.

"Well, we ARE supposed to have some inclement weather later tonight," he exaggerated just a little bit. The area was expected to have light showers, but nothing more than that.

The caretaker went on to explain that he'd allow us to stay for that night only, but that we needed to be gone before 7 A.M. the following morning when the ranger came and opened the park.

"That's not a problem, we'll be gone before 6 A.M. if that's okay," I replied, answering for both Bitter Goat and me.

"That should be fine." The caretaker replied with a smile.

When he left, Bitter Goat and I laughed excitedly.

"That was good. The whole 'look at these bloody socks' thing you pulled right there." I remarked, as he just grinned and passed a toothy smile.

I awoke around 5:30 A.M. to Bitter Goat packing. When he saw me stirring about, he glanced in my direction before going back to packing his things.

"What time did you say the sunrise was gonna be, last night?" He asked me.

I groggily rubbed my sleep filled eyes.

"...Five....uh...five-fifty..." I muttered as I swung my feet to the cold, hard stone surface of the picnic shelters floor. I immediately shuffled my feet back and forth blindly trying to find my crocs, and slipping one on at a time.

With gray skies and thick fog that morning, there was no real sunrise. There was, however, a sickening, struggling light, that you could have kind of called a "Sunrise"; but it was one hell of a stretch.

I packed my things as Bitter Goat ate a quick breakfast and walked up to the Washington Monument. I wished him well and started my 2.9-mile hike to the US-40/I-70 highway. The morning was filled with random bouts of sprinkles and light misting that kept everything at an uncomfortably wet level. The terrain was so incredibly flat, it took no more than an hour to make the journey, and I had actually been taking my time.

It was strange to follow the path as it led directly between residential houses. I felt as if I was trespassing on people's property because the trail literally passed along the property line between homes on either side. The AT had become rather interesting in this section of the Eastern seaboard as we've moved out of Virginian farmland and into quiet suburbs and consistent state road crossings. After hiking between the houses, the trail then went down a set of stairs where it met with an arched fenced in footbridge that crossed I-70.

After crossing, the trail split to go 2.2 miles towards Annapolis Rocks. As the rain started to come down once again, I pushed on about a tenth of a mile through a small forest where the trail came across an abandoned section of roadway overgrown with weeds.

This area was once going to become the US-40 Bridge, but was canceled for lack of funding and had been blocked off instead with guard rails, empty beer cans and busted broken bottle barricades.

I hid beneath a patch of trees until the rain stopped and when it finally had, I moved to a set of steps leading into the parking lot. A troop of girl scouts passed me by, asking about my adventure after seeing the huge backpack I had on. It's amazing how transparent a thru-hiker can become, based on his or her appearance alone.

So I passed along some stories from my journey as they sat around and asked questions about what I carried, how I funded my trip, how often I stayed in a motel or hostel or what hostels we're even like. It was crazy how inquisitive they all were and how generally interested in hiking they seemed to of been. Especially because they knew all of the trail jargon I was using. They were asking about specific places, if I had been scared aqua blazing and if I had somebody waiting for me back at home.

"Family..." I replied with a smile as I thought about my sisters and my parents.

Each one of the scouts then went on to tell me how they couldn't wait to try a thru-hike someday themselves.

It was so refreshing to see youth with such a love for nature in this day and age when the internet, Facebook, video games and smartphones had begun to dominate our culture. The scout leader asked if I needed a ride somewhere, but I thanked her and explained I had one on the way that very moment.

"Stay dry."

"Be safe."

"Don't give up."

"You can do it."

"You're strong, just believe in yourself."

Each scout that passed me by had something encouraging and kind to say. As I sat there, I almost began to tear up. I sometimes wondered when I felt alone like I did and without direction, how it was that simple words of kindness could pull me out of such a depressing rut?

It had to account as one of the best moments I had out there yet.

After a text message explaining where I was, Woodstock and Wales arrived to pick me up, having effectively reached Harpers Ferry. After trading hugs, we laughed in excitement to see each other once again and started passing our wild stories back and forth to each other. It was good to see them both again, and some part of me felt as if I'd known them both far longer than the few months we'd all been out on the trail together. They were interested in hearing about the 10-day Aqua Blaze I took through the Shenandoah's and I in turn got to hear about the bears they'd seen by way of the trail.

"Gotta admit dude..." I began, as Woodstock looked up into the rearview mirror at me from the driver's seat.

"It's really good to see you both again," I said, wholeheartedly. Wales glanced back at me and smiled as he nodded his head slowly.

"It's good to see you too. But I've gotta ask..." Woodstock said, looking up at me in the rearview mirror again.

"Why did Stupid leave the trail?" he finished.

"He was ready to be done I guess. I'm not sure if our arguing had something to do with it, but I think it had a hand. I dunno..." I said looking out the window. I hadn't spoken to Torry since our last exchange of text messages, weeks prior.

I still had too much pride to admit that I was wrong for the way I felt. And as Woodstock glanced away and looked back towards the road, I wondered if he was in short—trying to discover if I was going to be a "problem child" in this new group. And it was the last thing I wanted him to believe I was.

We drove to the ATC Headquarters back in Harper's Ferry, where we all got the iconic picture of ourselves taken for the books out front by the sign on the porch, and as it had turned out, Stephanie had left me a box of extra food there. I was hiker number 881.

Inside the box, was an airplane bottle sized shot of apple pie liquor, some MRE's and a pair of red panties for some reason.

"What...the hell....is this?" I muttered, picking the panties up with the tip of a pencil.

"Oh my God," Woodstock said, snatching the panties immediately from me and stretching them out into the air before him.

"Gross, what if they're used?!" I shouted. He quickly tossed the panties towards Wales, who deflected them in disgust back at me.

"NO!" I said, smacking them down quickly into the box and closing the lid shut as if they were radioactive waste.

"Do we even KNOW if they've been worn?" Woodstock asked.

I shrugged and looked at Wales who only shrugged back at me.

"Are you willing to take a *smell test*?" Wales asked.

I shook my head in disgust. "Please God, don't," I said feeling sick just thinking about it.

"Do you guys dare me to?" Woodstock asked with a mischievous grin.

"I don't," I muttered. But Wales was smiling wide.

"I do." He said with a high pitched laugh, as he covered his mouth and shook his head from side to side. It was quite comical to watch Wales chuckle.

So that was how Woodstock took a picture next to the ATC sign, with the panties on top of his head. It was hilarious.

As I was window shopping for things I couldn't afford, we came across a topographical map of the AT. As the three of us looked at the length and studied the craggy ridges and mountains up north, we nodded in unison as we all agreed we hadn't seen anything tough yet, in the south.

"It's crazy, isn't it?" I asked with a slight bit of awe.

"It's rather exciting and scary at the same time," Wales added in wonderment.

"Sometimes I wonder how built up the Northern section of the trail really is." Woodstock added, just a bit cynically.

"What do you mean?" I asked, looking over at him.

"Well, technically it's the end of the trail. It's supposed to be daunting in a way, isn't it? Metaphorically speaking I mean. The *climactic ending*, to one hell of a journey." he exclaimed as I glanced back over the map.

"Yeah. I guess you're..." I began, until a young woman suddenly cut into the middle of our conversation.

"Excuse me? I'm sorry but, are you *Morris the Cat*?" the woman asked.

I turned slowly and looked upon somebody I had never met before with questions in my eyes.

"I am if I haven't done anything wrong." I said, with a nervous chuckle. She only smiled immediately as she looked towards her husband.

"This is the hiker I've been telling you about!" she said excitedly. I was still confused though as to if that was a right or wrong thing.

"How are you doing?" he asked, offering his hand. I shook it, glancing back and forth between them.

"I'm sorry, do I know you guys?" I asked as Wales and Woodstock had joined my side.

"I apologize. I just didn't ever expect to see you in person. My name is Dana, and I've been reading your journal entries for quite some time." she exclaimed. Suddenly I remembered the woman's name in my guestbook and her posts of encouragement she had been giving me. I still found it hard to believe that she had recognized me, though.

I felt that if anything, I looked a world apart from how I had upon first starting out.

"We're visiting from Pennsylvania. We've never thru-hiked ourselves before but we've always wanted to. By the way..." she said with a smirk on her face.

"Don't bullshit me now. Did you seriously take a raft down the Shenandoah River?" she asked. It felt so weird to be re-living these events in my mind, or through my stories mostly because I was now re-telling my first-hand accounts to people that had read my journey as if it was some mythological legend of sorts.

"Yes, I did. By the way, since you've read my journals you already know about Woodstock and Wales." I said, introducing them both to her as well.

"This is such a mind trip!" she said with a laugh. It honestly WAS a small world after all, when you thought about it.

So I retold my stories and adventures to her thus far, as she listened and laughed or commiserated with the things I had written in my journals. She went on to explain that she felt I was very depressed and that being alone on the trail now that Torry was gone was only going to make things harder.

But she went on to explain that she believed in me and insisted that I continue and finish the trail.

"Hear that guys? You gotta keep me going." I said to Woodstock and Wales both.

"We'll lose him at the first McDonalds we come across." Woodstock said sarcastically.

All the same, I told Dana that was definitely my intention. To finish the trail completely.

Just before leaving, she offered me a twenty dollar bill. I thanked her graciously but felt too guilty to accept her money. I wasn't a beggar by any means, let alone a mooch.

"Please? I really want to be able to say I helped you on your journey." she exclaimed, holding out the cash. I glanced back with uncertainty at Woodstock who only shrugged.

"It's not MY place to tell you whether or not to take her money. I don't have millions of fans throwing money at ME." he exclaimed cynically. I only rolled my eyes.

"I'm not leaving until you take it," Dana stated rather proudly.

Twenty bucks richer, I gave Dana a hug goodbye and thanked her from the bottom of my heart for the cash.

After we had left, I used the money towards lunch for Wales, Woodstock and me—choosing to feed the three of us via Dairy Queen.

"What are you writing about?" Woodstock asked me as he glanced up from the gleaming tool and ratchet set he had just purchased from Wal-Mart.

"Just the things that we're doing. What we've been up to, so on and so forth." I said shielding my face away from the sun. I looked back down at my phone and continued typing up conversations we had shared and the activities we had done together just days before.

"You're not putting *this* in your journals, are you?" he asked, removing the last bolt from the tire.

I slipped my phone into my pocket and knelt down upon the hot blacktop beside him, to assist.

"Ready?" I asked as he gripped the other side.

"One, two...THREE!" he replied as we both lifted the wheel off and sat it on the ground.

"Well?" he asked.

"Well, what?"

"Are you writing about what we're doing right now? I don't want to appear to be a bunch of con artists." He said, smearing sweat from his eyes.

"Con artists? How are we con artists? We bought some tools from Wal-Mart so that we could save money and change our own brakes. Then we'll return the tools just as good and new as they were before." I said.

"Sounds like a scum bag thing to do." he replied with a frown, while shaking his head from side to side.

"It's not like anybody gets hurt or ripped off. Wal-Mart gets their tools back, and they get paid for the groceries we purchased from them for lunch. And now we have a car with decent brakes to safely finish our hike."

"I guess..." he replied, disconcertedly. He still didn't seem all that comfortable with the idea.

I ran my hand along the smooth metal disk and shook my head slowly.

"It's a good thing we decided to change the rotors too." Woodstock stated proudly while watching me. I nodded agreeably before standing up.

"So do you want me to get that money back for you?" I asked.

"If you really think you can get a refund..." Woodstock said, handing me his credit card.

Ten minutes later I walked out of Wal-Mart: "Looks like you're eighty-one dollars richer." I exclaimed, clapping him on the back as I handed him his credit card back.

"You didn't even have my driver's license, though! They didn't ask for it?" He inquired as I sat in the passenger side front seat and he climbed into the driver's side.

"Nope. Guess I know how to charm the ladies," I said with a purposefully egotistical tone and a smirk.

"Yeah right. Or you were just lucky." he said flatly, as he started his car.

After returning the tools to Wal-Mart only two hours after having purchased them, Woodstock had been reimbursed for the cost of the tools and ended up saving over $300 dollars by fixing his brakes himself. Being frugal out here, when you no longer had a job or money coming in was sort of paramount to making for a successful journey at times. Trying to find 'life hacks' per se, as a way to get by.

We stopped at REI on our way back to the Fairfield Inn nearby in D.C. so that I could change out my broken water filter. The handle had snapped off while pumping water out of the Shenandoah River weeks before when Torry and I had been aqua blazing together. Meanwhile, Woodstock needed to buy a new platypus for himself.

As I handed the well-worn product over to the customer service representative, she scrunched her face up at the condition of the item.

"How many times would you say you've used this?" she asked.

I felt a bit thrown off by the question, only because I wondered if she was going to try to work with me or ditch the effort altogether and exclaim that there was nothing she could do for me.

"Does it matter? With me being an REI member and all..." I asked as if I held supreme powers because of the membership card in my wallet.

"Actually, it does." She said turning the broken water pump over in her hands as she inspected it.

"Like once, or twice..." I lied. It wasn't even a GOOD lie because the purifier was so worn there were holes in the fabric of the carrying case. Her facial expression immediately fell.

"Really? Just once...or twice...huh?" She asked clearly not believing me. She held up my water purifier in the air before me, showing the worn away painted company label.

"You know it's so weird. That thing got wet like one time, and suddenly all the paint on it just came off..." I trailed along.

"Worst lie, ever." she said, sighing and shaking her head.

"If I bat my eyelashes, in a flirting gesture...like this..." I said, batting my eyelashes just like I had said I would.

"Would it help me at all?" I finished as she chuckled lightly.

"How could I EVER resist THAT?" She asked sarcastically as she typed away at the computer. She went into the back storeroom and grabbed the exact model I had owned, only the new one was black.

"Thank you," I whispered.

"For what?" She whispered back staring at the screen as she typed away.

"You know, bending the rules." I replied.

"I'm not bending any rules." She replied just as quietly. She scanned the barcode on the water pump.

"Oh, okay..." I replied just barely audible.

"Why are we whispering?" She asked as she took my credit card and slid it into the reader.

"I...uh...I don't know...actually..." I replied, blushing immediately. I felt like an idiot.

"So you had a $3.30 credit. These have reduced in price." She said, handing my card back to me.

"Sweet! Thanks!" I said as she nodded with a smile.

"And try not to break this one. Okay?" she asked as I grinned.

"Have a nice day." She said as I wished her the same and we left.

"Ask for her phone number!" I insisted as Wales swiftly shook his head 'no'.

"She's not going to be interested in me guys, I know it." He replied with an embarrassed smile.

"Oh quit being a wimp. Just say you like her beautiful brown eyes." Woodstock offered as if he knew exactly what to say to attract a woman. Which was funny, considering he had actually confided in both Wales and I that he was gay.

"Look Wales. You're talking to a guy that knows how to talk to women." I began, with skepticism in my tone.

"Oh, here we go." Woodstock started, while rolling his eyes.

"Don't listen to him. Look, it's just a simple yes or no response. She either gives you her phone number or she doesn't. It's not a huge deal. Besides, if she rejects you—you'll never see her again anyways." I exclaimed as he nodded his head and glanced over at our waitress who was currently serving another table. She had a young, tanned, skinny build, and almost seamless asymmetrical facial features. She also had an accent, I wasn't sure I could readily discern of its origin.

Wales, being 20 years old was still quite an introvert. Woodstock and I found this odd, as he not only had a strong athletic build, but he was extremely tall and rather attractive as well.

Going out in public, he regularly had women staring at him or giving flirtatious looks that he never seemed to pick up on. Oh, how a thousand other guys would've loved to have been in his hiking boots.

"Wales, just tell her you have a raging erection. That's all you've gotta do. The end." Woodstock said, before bursting into laughter. I looked over at Woodstock with a tri-mixed expression of confusion, disgust, and laughter all at once.

"What the hells wrong with you?" I asked.

"Oh, you guys have it so easy, every day. *I'm* the one really suffering here, every day while hiking the AT." Woodstock explained.

"Wales, you've got these women eating out of your hand practically every day on AND off the trail. But you're too shy to do anything about it..." Woodstock ranted on.

"Meanwhile, I'm suffering out there in the woods, staring at delicious eye candy all day while hiking the trail, since it's clearly a sausage fest. And do you know how many gay guys are walking the AT? NONE! No one except me." he finished just a little more irate. But as he started to smile, I got to get a glimpse into Woodstock's personality and his exaggeration was also his form of humor.

"Can I get you guys anything?" Our waitress asked, suddenly taking the three of us by surprise.

"I uh..." Wales began, as Woodstock began to speak up.

"Go on Wales, just ask her!" he said suddenly.

Wales glared at Woodstock, turning several shades of red. Meanwhile, I burst out into laughter.

"Sheila, have a seat next to our friend Wales here. He's got something important to ask you." I said, pulling out the fourth seat at our table.

"No...I really don't..." Wales muttered, shaking his head from side to side.

"Wales, tell her what you said about having children and getting married someday," Woodstock added. I felt tears of laughter coming to my eyes as Woodstock joined in. I felt like the heat from the sun all day had somehow made us all delirious. And to a degree, I felt just a little inebriated because of this. It physically hurt to laugh with sunburnt skin, and a heat exhaustion headache pounding in the background. But it also seemed okay, because I was amongst friends and laughter seemed to drown both of those things out in retrospect.

Sheila sat down in the seat next to Wales and lightly touched his hand. It was almost as if she had already picked up on his interest in her. Then again, Wales wasn't exactly good at hiding it either.

Woodstock and I traded a surprised expression as Wales turned almost maroon at this point.

"What's wrong?" she asked, looking between Woodstock and I and then to Wales.

"I...well....you know, there's....really nothing...wrong..." he mumbled quietly.

"Wales, stop screaming at the poor woman! All she did was ask you a question!" I said suddenly, as Woodstock erupted into another round of laughter.

"I'm...not screaming...what are you two talking about?" He asked confused as if he literally believed the irrational statement.

"Wales here wants to know if you'd like to maybe go out on a date sometime," I said finally.

"I...didn't....ever say that..." Wales stuttered. Sheila's face went from surprised to disappointed once she had heard Wales' response.

"Oh...." she said looking down.

"I mean, I wouldn't be put off by it. I'm just stating that I didn't come into this restaurant with preconceived notions to ask a waitress out." Wales added quite curt.

The waitress reached into her apron and removed our dinner receipt to sign.

"Well I guess that's *your* loss." she exclaimed with no self-conscious feelings whatsoever as she set it down on the table and then stood, walking away.

"I swear Wales," Woodstock said in awe as he shook his head from side to side.

"You guys are being arseholes." Wales replied.

"I'm sorry? What was that?" I asked, feigning naïveté.

"Arseholes," Wales repeated.

"Ohhhh...well s'cuse me your majesty. Forgot we lived in London, we do we do. Gotcha, we're a buncha 'arseholes'. Hey, and I'd wager this whole idea was 'bullocks' too? Ro'ight-O." I replied in my best cockney accent.

"Here, I wrote this on the receipt. I'm gonna give this to her." Woodstock said.

The note was simple.

It stated: *I'd like to take you out to dinner sometime. My phone number is...* and then Woodstock, of course, added Wales' cellphone number.

Immediately Wales snatched the receipt away.

"No!" he said suddenly, but I had already grabbed the receipt away from Wales again.

"Well, well, Wales. Look at you, taking the time to write this beautiful note to our fantastic waitress Sheila." I said, waving the receipt back and forth in front of him as he glared and shook his head from side to side.

"You know what? It doesn't even matter because like you said. I'm never going to hear from her again." Wales spoke plainly.

"So...do you find *us* attractive? Wales and I, I mean." I asked with a slight bit of curiosity as Woodstock drove us towards the US-40

Bridge the next morning where I had left off along the Appalachian Trail almost a week before. Woodstock gave me a disgusted look, as Wales leaned forward from the backseat to listen in on his answer.

As he did this, Woodstock adjusted the rearview mirror to look back at Wales so that he felt a part of the conversation.

"Why is *that* always the first thing a straight guy asks a gay guy?" Woodstock inquired.

"I mean you're into guys. That's cool. But I would like to think I'm like, an 8 or a 9 in hotness," I offered as Woodstock laughed heartily at my response.

"I'm sorry, but did you say *8 or 9*? I'd say you're lucky if you managed to waddle your fat ass past a 3." he replied. My face soured immediately.

"Well, what about me? What number would you possibly quote me at being?" Wales asked with an excited expression.

Woodstock thought about it momentarily, as he adjusted the rearview mirror again.

"Well to answer that, you'd have to drop your pants."

"And now, I suddenly no longer want to be a part of this conversation. So anyways, about that local football team or something..." I cut in rather immediately as Wales threw up his hands in confusion.

"Why in the world would I need to do that?" he asked, as Woodstock merely grinned.

"Because, he wants to see what you're packing. Down *there*." I clarified for Wales, as I gestured towards his crotch.

"I like to think, I'm of a hearty length." Wales muttered, blushing quite profoundly.

I immediately burst into laughter, as did Woodstock.

"He's of hearty length, m'lord!" I mocked Wales in my best, horrible British accent.

"Wales, I'd say you're like a decent 7 or maybe an 8 on a good day. And no, I'm not attracted to either of you like that so you can both stop asking those stupid kinds of questions." Woodstock added, concentrating on the road again.

"Now that I think about it, and all the rooms the three of us have shared or the times we've all slept in the same bed; who's to say you're not getting off to seeing us naked?" I asked in contemplation.

"Please, stop flattering yourself. Wales is not my type. You're DEFINITELY not my type. You're more of a 'bear' anyways."

"A bear?" Both Wales and I asked in unison.

"Yeah, you're a *bear*. A bear is usually hairy. Never grooms their self very often. Never uses deodorant or cologne that much and is typical of a bigger, heftier build. You guys like to look and come off as a lumberjack tough guy, but you're usually sweethearts." Woodstock said to me, with a purposeful smirk; knowing he had gotten under my skin.

"How many different classifications of homosexuals are there?" Wales asked.

"No! Now wait a minute! I bathe regularly whenever I can, and I *always* use deodorant. And yeah I'm hairy, but I'll punch somebody in the face in NO TIME! No sweetheart here," I tried to reassure Woodstock. He only ignored me as he went on to answer Wales.

"Well, you have Otters, Twinks, Twunks, Yestergays, and Cub's—which Morris here can relate to at an earlier age." Woodstock said, nodding his head towards me.

I rolled my eyes.

"Then you have Chasers, and you have Lipsticks, Sandwiches or Jock's which is kinda self-explanatory." Woodstock rambled on.

"A *sandwich*? Really? Did you just make that one up?" I asked, still slightly angry over the fact that I was considered a three and apparently as a bear I was regarded as an unhygienic slob of some sort.

"Calm down, Morris. It's all in retrospect and singular to each and every guy. Some might say you're an 8 or a 9. But to me you're just not my type. I'm more into Twinks myself, which is kinda what I would consider our friend Wales here." Woodstock said, as Wales only gulped and then leaned further into the backseat.

"Hear that Wales? If your date doesn't go anywhere with Sheila these next few days; you have a fat gay guy here interested in you." I said, gesturing towards Woodstock.

But Woodstock's expression was less than friendly as he replied: "Now, now. No need to be angry or jealous. Besides, I don't think Wales has the guts to kiss the waitress anyways." he exclaimed, shifting the attention off of him and back onto Wales.

"If we kiss, we kiss. If not, I do not care." Wales replied rather snobbishly.

"Aren't you glad now that we left your phone number on the receipt? Now you guys are texting each other like crazy back and forth." I exclaimed. And just as I had, Wales, in fact, received yet another text message and we all laughed over that.

"I'm appreciative, but at the same time, I'm not. I live in North Carolina, and Sheila lives up here in Maryland. It's not as if things are exactly going to work out in the long run. So I'm not going to over think it. She's an attractive, Dominican woman with whom I am going to show all aspects of respect to," Wales said quite confidently.

"Well then," I said sarcastically as I tugged at my imaginary shirt collar and adjusted my imaginary tie.

"So Wales, how is this next section going to work? You see, we're dropping Morris back off at US-40 so that he can continue hiking North where he left off when we picked him up. And meanwhile, I'm going to walk south from the same spot he's starting so that I can connect the portion of the trail down to Harper's Ferry. But if you're taking an extra day or two off just to go on a date with this Sheila girl—how are you ever going to catch up to us?" Woodstock asked.

"I hike twice, maybe even three times faster than you guys." He said matter-of-factly.

"It's true. I've hiked with Wales on and off along this damned Appalachian Trail, and the one thing I've come to notice is that he usually is always struggling to hold back when it comes to hiking along side me." I said.

"That's fine and good and all. But I still don't know how this is going to work. It'll take two days for me to reach Harper's Ferry if I go at my own pace." Woodstock explained.

"Morris hikes four days north, and stops at a road crossing somewhere and waits for us. Meanwhile, I'll hike what's going to take Woodstock four days, in just two days. Because I'm faster than both of you." Wales clarified. And they would in turn trade keys along the trail.

"All this confusion, because of a woman…" Woodstock muttered, looking up in the mirror at Wales and then chuckling.

Rain pitter-pattered around the three of us, as we talked about various scenarios running through each of our minds. We had roughly ninety-five days to make it to Katahdin before Baxter State Park closed down for the season, on October 15th. That meant shelling out 11.57 miles every single day, without any more zeroes until we had reached the end of the trail.

"Or we could just flip-flop and hike south from Katahdin once we start seriously running out of time…" Wales interjected.

"True, but it may not even be an issue at all, with this terrain. We may be hiking as much as 15 to 20 miles a day from here on out till we reach the White Mountains." Woodstock added.

"But that's a bold assumption. When Torry and I originally planned for this trip, our itinerary had us doing 18 mile days all the way to Maine. We never factored in weather, or getting sick or spraining an ankle. We never thought about simply needing a day off to recharge." I said as Woodstock nodded his head in understanding.

"Still, we just got done taking almost an entire week off in D.C. In Damascus during Trail days, we took a week off there as well. We need to begin prioritizing our hikes." Wales insisted.

"Yeah. You know, now that I think about it. We should probably discuss all of this over breakfast too." Woodstock replied.

"Wait, what?" I laughed unbelievably.

"No guys. No more zero days. I just got done explaining that we've already taken nearly a week off." Wales said, shaking his head from side to side.

"I'm just saying, we have some important topics we need to go over. Maybe with a plate of bacon involved." Woodstock offered, with a shrug and a purposeful smirk. Ever the deceiver, and the enabler that he was.

"Well, that was all you had to say for me to give up hiking the AT." I said, throwing my backpack on the ground and heading back towards the car.

"Now wait a minute gentlemen. We can knock out this mileage right now and talk about taking a zero in four more days. Right now you guys need to hike." Wales exclaimed, trying to be the voice of reason amongst us.

"Oh yeah, says the guy taking a day off to meet up with some chick he met at a Golden Corral." Woodstock retorted just a tad sarcastically.

"On a date that *you both* set me up on." Wales countered.

"Now that I think about it. I wonder Woodstock, did *we* set him up on a date solely so that we could take another day off WITH Wales?" I asked, thinking back on the whole situation.

"Jesus Christ, we're never going to finish this trail." Wales muttered miserably, while collapsing his face into either of his hands.

"Okay, okay. I'm going. Let's hike. Morris, you go *that way*. I'm going south." Woodstock exclaimed finally.

I picked up my backpack begrudgingly and muttered "pink blazer" as I walked by Wales.

"Wasn't it *you* Morris that said it was about the Smiles, not the Miles?" He asked me. I just laughed as I spun around back towards him.

I gave him a majestic bow.

"Yes it was my friend, yes it was. It's good to see some of my wisdom is finally rubbing off on you." I replied. Wales was proper, initially quiet and very shy. Often I wondered if these traits had been ingrained in him while he had attended private schooling in the UK growing up, or if he had always been so introverted. Regardless, at times it was funny to see him snap or talk back to somebody which was so out of character for him to do with his quiet persona.

"Sure wish Wales would get us one more night at a motel, though in all honesty." I said as Woodstock added: "I know. It's only fair after we got him a girlfriend and we've been doing everything HE'S wanted to do on this trip so far."

I grinned at Wales as he sighed, with a guilty look.

"God, my legs ache." I grumbled as I fake-limped along the trail.

"If only Wales would get us a ROOM!" Woodstock moaned.

"Guys, you aren't fair..." He said sympathetically to us both.

"Oh no, don't you worry. You enjoy relaxing the next few days while we suffer like vagabonds in the middle of nowhere..." Woodstock replied, with a sad smile.

"I just wonder how cold someone can truly be when he sees his friends suffering and does nothing...let alone shell out a few bucks for a place to stay." I added.

"We could be watching MTV's Catfish in an air conditioned room with beds while sharing pizzas," Woodstock exclaimed, betting wildly on sympathy.

"Well...I..guess..I...could...look for something cheap..." Wales stammered, taking out his smartphone before Woodstock, and I both burst into laughter.

"You're so easy Wales. If I wanted to I could have you doing anything I wanted." Woodstock exclaimed confidently.

"We need to hike anyways." He added as I agreed.

Wales looked at either of us rather sadly, with guilt still in his eyes.

"We're just kidding dude, I promise," I said laughing as I walked over and patted him on the back.

We arrived at the intersection where the trail split North and South heading either across the footbridge or towards Annapolis rocks.

I wished Woodstock well and headed in the opposite direction.

Wales followed me for a while, talking about his excitement to meet Sheila, for their date later that evening. After half a mile of hiking, he received a phone call from her. And from what I overheard it was quite a frank conversation they had going on. I bid him farewell as he headed back towards the car excitedly, with a skip in his step.

And now, I was alone again.

The skies were gray, and a heavy drizzle came down rather consistently throughout the day.

The trail was rather nice for the most part, by which I meant the forest was removed of shrubs and bushes so that you could see a decent ways in.

The first two miles were a breeze despite the initial climb uphill. I passed a group of children who were being herded by two exasperated adults. They all looked at my backpack, and one kid even asked me how much it weighed.

So I took it off and let him attempt to pick it up. He couldn't.

Suddenly my backpack became 'The Sword in The Stone' as the other children tried to see if they could heft it one at a time as well.

When they asked why I was carrying so many things, I told them I was headed to Maine.

I got a few "Ohhh's and Ahhh's." Some of the children seemed blissful in the ignorance and naiveté of where Maine geographically sat on the world map. As if it was only a thirty-minute stroll further North through the woods.

I continued on.

My ascent was met with slippery rocks, boulders and generally what I had liked to all around entitle: "ankle breakers"

These rocks were usually anywhere from five to eight inches in diameter to a maximum of one or two feet. They had been placed as if a dump truck had driven down the trail with bedrocks bouncing out of the back. Usually, slick with algae or fungus of some sort, their un-sturdy existence posed painful to most long distance hikers. It was typical to roll your ankles on this kind of terrain quite quickly up to five or six times a day if you weren't careful.

I stopped at the intersection to Annapolis Rocks.

AWOL'S Guide labeled the view "Outstanding" so I walked a quarter mile there and back to see what was so amazing about it.

And while the view was okay at best, it was also quite dismal by the gray skies and thick clouds clogging the view. The wind had also started blowing, causing cold fat rain drops to sting as they hit my face or eyes.

It was 2:36 P.M. when I found that according to my guide, I had knocked out 8 miles despite the horrid terrain.

As I walked the ridges of Maryland, the trail simply became miles of boulder fields. With no trekking poles, I was slipping and falling left and right. My boots wouldn't grip a single stone let alone a sloped rock, and as a result, I'd sometimes slide, stumble and proceed to slam down clumsily upon my butt rather unexpectedly at times. There were several instances that I was either crawling on all fours or sliding down the stones rather rough and weathered surface just to get over the obstacle.

I passed a southbound hiker who asked me how far the next shelter was, so I informed her it was about six miles south. She, in turn, told me she had seen a bear and it's cub about a mile up North in the direction I was heading. I began to get excited. I left my ear buds out and turned off my music.

Only three miles later, no bear and no cub either made its presence known.

I was convinced that I had been cursed, to never witness one single bear the entire time.

The AT curved through Maryland farmlands and open pastures. The sun had come out at around 5 P.M. to bake away the moisture dripping off of everything. I say that because it got HOT towards the end of the day.

As a result, though, the world was illuminated with amber light. The fields smelled like warm honey dripping from blooming wildflowers of every type. Fog drifts and low banks of gray clouds floated in limbo. Caught between bright blue skies mixed with afternoon daylight and a lush green earth. Chest high grass glistened, with beads of diamonds clinging to the blades of leaves with which they hung. In the distance, farmers shoveled hay from the backs of their trucks to feed the cattle on rolling green hillsides. Chickens scratched and pecked at the ground, ignorant to the world around them.

And I walked north.

It was peaceful.

I took my morning pee the next day only to notice how incredibly dark brown my urine was. I had literally sweat without reprieve throughout the night, even after stripping down to my boxers.

I felt dizzy as I stood, and immediately began seeing sparks in front of my eyes. I quickly downed what little water I had left over from the night before, and then made my way towards the closest water source I could find. I didn't care that I was only in my boxers. I was too hot to care about anything anymore. Modesty had left me in those moments to follow.

I was only eight miles from the Pennsylvania border.

I knew I was getting close to civilization when I started seeing graffiti on the natural landscape. The trail went by Highrock which was littered in spray painted names, curse words or crude phrases as well as your typical teenage marijuana leaves and anarchy symbols for rebellion.

Too bad they couldn't have found more urban areas with which to take out their teenage angst instead of ruining the natural viewing area.

The rocky descent was by far the worst I had experienced thus far. Rock boulder mazes where the white blazes seemed impossible to find or even follow sometimes made for a harrowing drop in elevation. Slippery gravel at one point, caused me to lose balance, fall, and proceed to hit the back of my head rather hard, as it bounced off of the back of a jagged boulder.

Well, of course, it wasn't long before a beautiful goose egg-sized knot was throbbing at the back of my skull; as a result.

When I had finally reached Pen Mar Park, I was convinced that I was still dehydrated if only because my vision continued to blur and I regularly stumbled, tripped and started to fall more frequently.

I had been here several times before in my life. The dizzy feeling that felt as if all circulation had been cut off above my neck.

The fast heart racing.

A headache I'd tried to ignore for so long.

I could imagine myself in 3rd person view. But it seemed to happen so quickly I couldn't sit down before it started.

The last thing I remember saying out loud in a queasy voice, was: "Not again..."

I blacked out.

I woke up twenty-three minutes later with the taste of blood in my mouth. I was also shaking rather studiously and felt the heated sticky skin of my own cheek and the dirt clinging to it. I felt as if I was a fish out of the water, and left to dry in the sun.

There were bits of sand and debris upon my tongue.

I began coughing immediately, having inhaled dirt, small bits of leaves and who knew what else while my face had been plastered to the earth in my unconscious state.

I paced myself as I sat up, and color slowly seeped back into my vision as if dripping from a paint can onto a television screen. My hands wouldn't stop jittering. There was a sharp ache in my brain, and it was hard to focus my eyes. They felt dried out and coarse. Each blink felt like sandpaper being dragged across my ocular orbs.

I tongued the gash inside my mouth, resting against the inner cheek wall. I had bitten into it, upon my fall towards the earth. It stung on touch, but it wasn't too bad. What WAS bad, was that I felt a piece of one of my porcelain tooth fillings rolling around in my mouth. I spit it out into my hand within a mixture of blood and saliva, and then I began looking for the tooth it had come out of with my tongue.

I took a drink of water, and that's when I felt the exposed nerve ending in my left rear molar scream out in pain.

As I slowly got back to my feet, I used a nearby pine tree to help stabilize myself.

And while not exactly odd, that I would remember it at that particular place in time; a memory of my father came to mind.

He had once told me about Native Americans and how they used to use the sap from pine trees for not only cuts but as an antiseptic. He explained that they would pack it into tooth cavities as well.

When I thought of doing that myself, however, I realized I didn't need to take such a dramatic course of action.

Instead, I took an extended break, drinking the remainder of my water. My legs felt like rubber as soon as I had started walking again.

Once I made it into the parking lot area of the park, I refilled my water at a bathroom sink and attempted to find an outlet to charge my phone and camera battery.

No such luck.

So I sat at a picnic table, drinking more water instead and feeling as if my skull was about to explode.

My head was still swimming and as I slapped at a horsefly on the back of my head. In doing so, I was painfully reminded of the goose egg there from earlier.

Up to that point, I had either walked or rowed into every state thus far along the trail, and Pennsylvania would be no different.

So having fully rested, I followed the AT and took the path downhill and across some railroad tracks where there was a border sign that read like this: MD - PA.

I took a selfie in front of it for memory and continued on into Pennsylvania.

Having effectively crossed the state line, I began to break away from the AT yet again as the thought of a greasy hotdog with all of the fixings, filled my mind and pushed the fear of my chipped filling out completely.

I began walking an incredibly dangerous and narrow state road that hugged corners of mountains or hills and offered NO shoulders or ditches, let alone anything with which to safely travel on foot.

When I passed by a Sheetz gas station in route back towards the AT further north, I stopped in for a quick bite. Well that bite, turned into dinner, as I ordered four fully loaded hot dogs, a large root beer and a cup of fries for eight bucks! You couldn't beat the price, however my newly exposed tooth pain gave occasional reminders to slow down and eat slowly.

The entire meal had vanished inside of my mouth within the course of fifteen minutes.

As I sat outside at a picnic table with a view of the parking lot, I watched people eyeing me with caution as I only smiled with a mouth stuffed full of food, and waved kindly back at them. And though I was only acknowledged by four or five of the roughly thirty people or so that had passed by during my time out there; I was approached by one.

A man who introduced himself to me as "Don,"

He asked if I was hiking the Appalachian Trail with a pack as big as mine on. It was said more out of laughter than actual belief. He sat at my table, across from me. I exclaimed that indeed I was and had no shame to ask if he could give me a ride back to where I had left off from the trail at Pen Mar.

He then exclaimed that it wouldn't be a problem and offered for me to hop into his truck.

As he drove, he talked about how he had thru-hiked himself in 1971 with his ex-wife and an Alaskan malamute. Then in 1992 he had hiked it again, only this time by himself. When I asked what he did for a living, he replied that he worked at a local lumber mill, sharpening saw blades. I thought that it was very coincidental, only because that had been Torry's job a long time ago, and something he had been looking at getting back into again now that he was no longer on the AT.

Don must have suffered from a little bit of confusion in where I had explained I had intended to be dropped back off at. I say this because he drove me to a park a few miles up the trail and deposited me at Antietam shelter. I wasn't aware of this until both he and I walked to the shelter staged there in the park and I had a chance to look over my guide book.

"Uh, not to sound rude or ungrateful but you actually took me eight miles too far up the Appalachian Trail." I pointed out to him.

"Doesn't matter. You didn't miss much. Just lots of shrubs and poison ivy." He said with a non-caring shrug to accompany it. I thought about how devastating this might have been, had I been a purist thru-hiker looking to cover every inch of the AT. The thought that I would have to hike eight miles south and then eight miles back just to connect those two points would have led to an entirely wasted day unless I was somehow lucky enough to emerge from the woods and either pay for a ride *back* to the park or hope that I got a hitch.

These conditions were mostly why I didn't enjoy trying to be a thru-hiking purist. When situations like this occurred. Instead, while it wasn't entirely my preference towards hiking, it had offered me the freedom of choice. So instead of walking backwards, I decided to stay.

Don wished me well and left me to my own devices, as I walked around and explored the campsite. Suddenly, I came to find that I wasn't alone.

I heard a slew of heavy cursing, upon my arrival to the shelter. I turned the corner to see an older gentleman rolling out a sleeping bag. He continued cursing before looking up at me with one dead eye.

"So how the *fuck* did YOU get here?" he asked with quite a bit of hostility in his tone.

I was taken aback by the comment momentarily before answering, mostly because of the angry inflection in his voice.

"Th...there... was a guy that was kind enough to give me a ride here," I replied anxiously, setting my pack down. The older gentleman eyed me over, quite cautiously before nodding.

"Well, I'm not sure if you're hiking North or South, but I wouldn't plan on going up any fuckin' further tonight if I were you. You've got a bunch of stupid ass Boy Scouts up there hogging every damned piece of floor space. Two shelters and these damn idiots take every last spot." He went on, while I listened.

"They're lucky I don't call the police on their candy asses. The sign says *Groups of Ten or more must Tent*. But these fucking morons apparently can't read. By the way, what was your name?" He asked.

"Morris the Cat," I replied sheepishly. He nodded his head before going on.

"I'm Crazy Horse, and you apparently didn't catch me in the best of moods." He said in a grumpy tone.

"It's okay, we all have our bad days," I said as I took out my water bottle and sat by the fire ring across from him.

Crazy Horse was 65 years old and had been hiking the trail for 20 years. He explained to me that he had lost his right eye in the gulf war and had been in the Airforce all the way back to Vietnam.

He had hitchhiked across the country, and he had explained the bitterness that people in that lifestyle can grow into, seeped out of him in every negative curse word he spoke.

"People are maniacs. You have to watch everyone," he said, with just a hint of paranoia in his voice.

He gave me some stories about the people on the trail that we might've mutually met at some point. Then he went on to say: "The thru-hiker class of 2013 are some badass mothers. You told me you started March 17th? You guys got MY respect." He said, building my ego quite a bit in doing so.

As we traded stories on the hardships we'd both faced on the Appalachian Trail, I found that mine couldn't even scratch the surface to what he'd been through, himself. Anything from having a mentally ill hiker with PTSD pull a gun out on him, to riding in the biker gang called 'The Outlaws.'

We went back to talking about people we'd mutually met while on the trail after conversations of our pasts started to taper off. It was here, I had learned just a little bit more about 'The Legends' of the Appalachian Trail. People that either lived on the trail permanently or had hiked its full length more than a few times and had become celebrities of sorts.

He explained the history of a woman who called herself 'Jiffy.' She was a 6'9 blonde woman I'd seen in passing at a few shelters here and there along my journey thus far.

However, Crazy Horse explained that he was convinced this woman was transgendered. When I told him, I didn't know anything about that, and that she had seemed very kind to me, he gave me an awful gaze.

"That's because she was waiting for you to turn your head so that she could clock you with a branch and then have her way with you." He said smugly.

This 65-year-old man was the crassest person I had ever met in my life.

"She was kicked out of a diner because she was wearing a mini hiking skirt. She proceeded to make the joke that she had no panties on to the guy working behind the counter. Well, the bartender doesn't believe her, and comes around and sees a set of balls dangling over the stool and kicks her out." Crazy Horse went on to tell me assuredly as if he had seen this incident take place first hand.

I was convinced this guy, was in part either making these things up or was trying to be crude in an attempt to impress me.

And in a sense, as I talked more and more to him I wondered if there was any correlation between his trail name and actual mental state.

He told me things about Baltimore Jack and spoke of the kindness of Miss Janet. He then said some truths to the legends that accompanied these people as if he knew them personally. It wasn't my place to judge or make assumptions as my interactions with these two individuals had been nothing more than brief moments in time where I was either getting a ride by them or some sort of information, regarding food or local hostels.

"The local losers, punks, and thugs like to come up here and try to start shit or steal your things. I'm glad you're here. I'll freakin' cut anybody open that attempts to fuck with me." Crazy Horse said as he glanced over at his Rambo-sized knife.

I laughed nervously, unsure as to if I had just been involuntarily volunteered into his partnership.

"I've got your back," I replied, all the same. I'd have to sleep next to the guy and didn't want to appear to be at odds with anyone that had *his* angry mental state.

As we sat in silence momentarily, my eyes caught a flyer on the wall of the shelter next to Crazy Horse's set up.

All I could make out was 'trail magic' from where I was sitting.

"Hey, what's that flyer talking about? Trail magic?" I asked.

He promptly proceeded to reach up to the wall and rip the paper off of it in one quick swipe.

"Don't bother, it's bullshit." he said, balling it up and tossing it into the fire ring.

"Bullshit? What do you mean it's just bullshit?" I asked in surprise, as I started reaching for the paper beginning to burn inside the fire ring. I quickly thought better of it, though, just as it exploded into flames rather instantly amongst the coals.

"I just hiked from there today. There's no trail magic. Just a bunch of liberal yuppies sittin' around and bitching about gun control, and pro-abortion. Buncha fuckin' crybabies if you ask Me." he trailed off.

I sighed.

When morning came, I was out by 9:30 A.M.

I had 11 miles to get to Caledonian Park, where I planned to rest for a night before moving on to Quarry Gap shelter.

And boy did I ever blaze through those miles.

I took off with a strange amount of energy. The initial climb, while long—went by in a breeze as I ran up the mountain ridges and stopped at each flat spot or switchback end I came across.

And per usual, the views were nonexistent. It was rather disheartening at times to realize that despite whether or not the tall mountains the AT made you climb, had a view waiting for you or not; that they were going to have you chugging on up that mountain regardless.

The Boy Scouts were still milling around as Crazy Horse had claimed they were going to be the night before. And though Tumbling Run Shelter appeared to be a beautiful piece of land and a nice area for a quick break, I had no time to stop and enjoy its beauty. I needed to hike.

Besides, I hadn't been interested in conversing with Scout leaders asking about my backpack and the sheer enormity of it so I pushed on uphill before I could get dragged into more conversations about my adventure up to that point. I stopped on a couple of occasions to eat fresh ripe raspberries dangling idly along the sides of the trail.

That morning, I came to realize quite quickly that the day, was going to stand out solely as a day of finding dead animals along the trail.

While hiking, I came across a deceased bat on the side of the path as well as a baby cottonmouth somebody had stomped to death.

At the next water source, I came across a partially chewed chipmunk on the shore of the third stream crossing I had passed that day.

I took two sticks and picked it up out of the water supply, wondering how many hikers' bottles its rotting corpse had polluted.

After passing Snowy Mountain Road, I stepped off of the Appalachian Trail to use the restroom. I hadn't been paying attention to where I had been stepping as I clomped through the heavy leaf fall. Suddenly my left foot punched through something hollow, accompanied by a sickening 'crunch' sound. I immediately felt hundreds of little 'things' moving up my ankle and tangling their selves within the hairs on my leg.

As I glanced down, my face turned into one of terror. I found that my foot had accidentally punched through the rotting chest cavity of a partially buried and decaying dead deer. Maggots were swarming over my boot and crawling up my leg. While in mid-urination, I jerked my body about wildly, in disgust and surprise; spraying urine sporadically everywhere as I freaked out at the horror taking place on the forest floor.

The throat of the deer pulsed, filled with fly larvae as if some strange and erratic heartbeat had been pumping away inside the dead creature. Flies and millipedes crawled along a sky blue, glassy dead eye staring straight up at me; the intruder with its boot inside of its chest cavity.

I stumbled back, whimpering and shaking my foot maniacally as I finished peeing in mid walk. I began dry heaving, as black blood and rotted hunks of meat clung to the outsides of my sock and caked to my boots laces.

When I zipped up, I quickly went about shaking the remaining maggots off of my ankle and foot.

While I would have rather utilized the last of my wet wipes to bathe myself later that evening, instead I had chosen to use them to remove the brownish black guts of the deer from off of my ankles and socks.

"This is somehow your fault, Gregory," I said to my aptly named backpack.

Gregory's response was typical of an inanimate object, as it hung limply upon my back.

That's right, silent, inward laughing and amusement at my expense.

Truthfully, I just needed someone to blame.

The final descent followed roads on either side of the trail. It was strange to be walking the AT which mainly went through people's backyards at this point, and it had reminded me a lot of Maryland. Once I had reached Caledonia Park it was just a little after 2 P.M. in the afternoon.

I looked around for a place to charge my phone and then found a working outlet on the side of a swimming pool building, crowded with locals sunning themselves or teaching their children how to swim.

I sat at a picnic table tired, and irritable. It was always something to marvel, as I watched families playing together, and couples laughing and kissing each other. Only because each and every scene existed only as a somber reminder of what I didn't currently have.

"Just you and me, Gregory," I said, patting my backpack.

I ran a tired hand across my face and closed my eyes if only to imagine in those moments to come, that the heat was gone and in its place air conditioning was blasting away as I laid somewhere on a beach with a margarita in hand.

It was a dream that came and died, as the warm summer heat rolled in and pulled me from the ignorance of my dreams.

Amidst the smells of suntan lotion and cocoa butter, I began to daydream when suddenly I heard voices approaching my direction.

"I bet he won't remember us..." I heard distantly. I didn't initially believe the person or persons, to be talking about me.

"He will remember us. Just ask him because he probably knows where it's taking place." a woman's voice explained.

I lifted my head slowly and brushed sweat and anguish out of my eyes. The heat was definitely not helping the smell of the deer guts caked and dried on my left sock and boot. Nor was the occasional whiff of sunbathers coating themselves in oil.

I needed to find a bathroom with soap in it so that I could get to work cleaning my boots and leg off. As I started to stand, I was suddenly approached by two hikers whom I hadn't seen since Hampton, TN.

"Chuck...Norris....? The cat?" the guy asked me, quickly displaying he had no idea what my name was.

"I'm sorry?" I asked, cocking my head to the side in confusion.

"Norris the Cat?" he asked again.

I shook my head 'no', as I began to heft my backpack slowly.

I started to walk away until the girl spoke. "It's *Morris the Cat*, right?" she asked.

I acknowledged, with a tired sigh and turned to face them slowly. I was exhausted and rather saddened by the fact that there seemed to exist no signs of trail magic in the area. Staring at the many other families and couples who were grilling hamburgers and hot dogs had started to wreak havoc on my patience, and now I had become a bit hungry.

All I wanted to do was wash my foot off and hike away from the pleasantries of the park that I didn't get to be a part of.

"That's correct," I stated, robotically.

"You were just going to walk away, despite the fact I almost had your name right?" the guy who had gone by 'Frodo' asked me with distinct awe and slight anger in his voice.

"I'm sorry, I just want to hike away from all of this happiness, and the incredible smells of cooked meat wafting over here every five seconds," I explained.

"That doesn't give you the right to be a..." He began before his girlfriend, Winterbourne cut him off.

"Stop it!" She said sharply to her boyfriend.

"Look, we're just trying to find the trail magic that was supposed to be taking place here." the woman went on to exclaim to me with exasperation.

"Look around you," I said, waving my arms about.

"Where do you see any trail magic?" I finished, with a bit of annoyance.

"We were hoping you might know." she replied, as I only shook my head in response.

"I was told by a hiker that went by the name Crazy Horse that this trail magic event had already passed us. You see he's hiking south right now and so he's already been through here." I offered, as her boyfriend began to walk away.

"No. That's not true, and we heard different. Come on babe, let's go." Frodo replied angrily, as he began walking off.

It was clear to see we were all a little bit upset at what we had thought we would find here. Just another reason never to get your hopes up too soon, and to always expect the worst.

"Well, thanks anyways," Winterbourne said with a shrug as she started to chase after her boyfriend. I watched them for a bit before I felt my stomach growling quite anxiously at the thought of somebody such as a family or a group possibly offering me some grilled food if I walked by and looked hungry enough a few times.

And strangely enough, I had no shame at that moment to do such a thing.

But as I watched the young couple, and overheard their bickering and arguing I sort of found myself more engrossed in their drama than the hunger resting upon my stomach.

So I followed them, secretly hoping that they might find food their selves.

And sure enough, I would come to find that I had been wrong about the trail magic. And so had Crazy Horse.

"Morris the Cat!" Greenlight and First Gear both said at once as I approached them. There were quite a few other familiar faces amongst the thru-hiker community that were here as well.

"What's going on? Where's Woodstock? I heard you joined him and Wales and now you all have started driving up and down the AT!" Greenlight exclaimed.

"Well, something like that. I mean we're still hiking the trail and all, but we're using a vehicle mostly to get ourselves cheaper rooms, and food *away* from the AT. This way, these thieves can't exploit us and charge fifteen bucks for a bag of chips." I explained.

"You an Appalachian Trail thru-hiker?" A man suddenly called out to me.

He approached me with his hand out, and I shook it firmly and appreciatively.

"The names, Cook Doctor. My wife over there goes by Drumstix," he said.

"Morris the Cat. And yes, I am hiking on and off the AT this year, sometimes finding my own ways instead of sticking solely to the trail to do it." I replied.

"Well Morris the Cat, you will find showers over *there*. And when you get back we'll have some ice cold lemonade waiting for you. We're cooking smoked pork, grilled corn on the cobb and grilled baked potatoes with all the fixin's." he exclaimed.

I glanced over at Winterbourne and Frodo, and we laughed in awe. Forget the hamburgers and hot dogs we'd wanted; instead we'd just found heaven.

"Thank you so much." I said, with glassy eyes as I shook this man's hand again.

As more hikers settled in for the evening, we were all told we that we would have hash browns with gravy, French toast and ham, bacon and maybe even sausage for breakfast the following morning.

I stood in the shower for a good hour, lathering myself up from head to toe. After rinsing off, I then repeated the process four more times, while enjoying every second of the warm water.

After dinner, and once everyone's stomachs had settled; the trail angels broke out the Hershey bars, Graham crackers, and marshmallows for S'mores.

I helped myself to two, though I had been offered three more by the gracious hosts.

With a full belly and an evening spent talking to fellow thru-hikers as well as new people I'd never come across yet before that evening—I slunk back into the lair that was my hammock tent, to eat the second s'more alone. I watched the merriment on all of the hikers faces as they glowed bright orange in the firelight. And while I was sure that I would have been invited into their conversations on trail life, quite simply I felt a thousand miles away from them all. As if I didn't belong on their level. Because I hadn't experienced the same things, they had in their hiking bubble. I had been in one all my own, and that bubble no longer surrounded me.

I used my headlamp to illuminate the pages of my trail guide as I lay there.

Forty-Nine miles in three days wasn't too bad. I was actually rather proud of myself.

And while I always wondered how much harder things would get up North, I still held on to hope that I was ready for the challenge with open arms.

I received a text from Woodstock explaining that he was at mile 998 (still hiking south) and had around 13.3 miles left to go that day before reaching the car. He would then plan on driving and meeting me later that very night, where we would both stay at either Caledonia Park with the trail angels or somewhere else in the area that was free.

Well, I definitely didn't believe that I was going to make it to Pine Grove Furnace, the official halfway point of the AT (18 miles North) that day. However, I felt that I could at least hike up to the Shippensburg Road crossing which was eight miles south of that park.

This meant that my only goal was to make it as far as I could north before Woodstock picked me up.

The trail angels prepared us a breakfast of hash browns, sausage gravy on biscuits, and eggs mixed with mushrooms and cheese.

I bid everybody 'farewell' and headed on out towards Highway 233.

Along the way, I stopped to refill my water at a nearby hose outside of the pool area and unexpectedly came across an event taking place in what had been an empty field the day prior.

"What's going on?" I asked a ranger directing car traffic in the area.

"Arts and Crafts Festival. You should check it out. They've got some great food." He replied.

I supposed I looked hungry to him, despite the food already sitting within in my stomach.

Out of curiosity, I walked around a bit, admiring some of the hiking stick vendors that had made beautiful carved works of art that would've ultimately proved impractical for such long distances, due to their weight. There was chainsaw art and handmade necklaces with bead kits to create your own. Some former thru-hikers stood at vendor stands, trying to sell the books of their experiences to other hikers not willing to take on the extra weight of the item.

The food was cheap, but to a man with no cash, it was far too expensive.

So I walked down 233 past a beautiful waterfall on my right that tumbled down worn river rocks and boulders.

The road went by a peaceful pond with a gentle stream that poured from the overflow. A fern and stone wall bordered brook ran beneath the road and continued South without noticeable navigation other than the cut it had made into the land over time.

About a mile into the walk, there was a water purifying plant off to the left side of the road, which was fed by two or three natural streams.

The highway passed lush evergreen forests with bright green pristine grassy floors. Small babbling brooks intertwined between moss beds with as much direction as a pair of shoelaces tossed upon the floor.

Once I had reached the Michaux Long Pine Reservoir, I was dismayed by the strict rules associated with the lake. It stated no wading, swimming, camping, picnicking or ice skating.

It was solely for boating and fishing.

Through a series of forest roads and deer trails, I made it to the Michaux ATV parking lot .5 miles down the road from where the AT crossed Shippensburg Road.

I was out of power in both of my phone batteries and my external battery charger. I needed to find an outlet if I was ever going to make contact with Woodstock and tell him where I was at to pick me up later that day. However, power would have also proved to have been useless, as I also had no phone signal regardless. I started heading down the road.

I made the brash decision to move on another 8.8 miles to Pine Grove Furnace State Park, mostly because I had made such good time and I didn't want to sit around for five or six hours waiting on Woodstock. But more than anything, my deciding factor had been to charge my electronics at the park, and hopefully find a phone signal as well.

The sun ate way at my resolve however, feeding eccentricities and illusions such as water puddle mirages in the road.

I was thirsty again, and in my attempt to make mileage I had ignored taking 10 minutes to purify some water back at the reserve I had passed a few hours earlier.

As I swallowed and felt my dry throat click, I realized the error of my way had potentially put me at risk for another blackout.

Once I had reached the bottom of the hill, I found a stream to get fresh water out of, beneath a bridge crossing. Only the water was truly anything but fresh. Old cups and bottles filled with urine, old mattresses and chunks of shredded tires lay within the polluted water having been dumped over the edge or washed downstream by the careless.

The surface of the water had a fine sheen of oil residue across the top as well.

And while I was confident I could have filtered the water and been just fine, I didn't want to chance it either.

I came to a crossroads then that led back to Caledonia State Park towards the South, the town of Shippensburg to the West, and another small town called Arendtsville towards the East. Finally, to the north, Pine Grove Furnace State Park sat just waiting for my arrival.

I took Pine Grove Road towards the AT Museum while cars flew by, and my boots lazily slapped upon the asphalt surface of the road. There was always a love-hate relationship with walking streets. The surface was hard on your feet and joints, causing your knees to hurt with the extra weight burdening your back. Especially considering that there was no give in the surface beneath your feet.

But the terrain always seemed to make up for that with me, as I was no longer stumbling across rocks or boulders just to get there. I wasn't twisting my ankles on rolling stones, and stumbling into partially hidden dead carcasses either when I went to pee.

Upon reaching the park, I walked past the General Store towards the Appalachian Trail Museum. Only as I showed up, the building had already been closed at 4 P.M. and I was only just late.

"Damn…" I muttered as I glanced down at my phone and then looked about briefly for a place to charge it.

The General Store I had passed by, looked promising as a place to power my things and get food or water. Only I didn't want to lose the chance to snag a ride back South towards Arendtsville where I could possibly have a better chance at finding a fast food restaurant and resting while I awaited Woodstock and Wales' arrival once they came to pick me up.

A young woman with blonde hair and a universe of freckles across her face was in the process of placing her newborn child into its baby seat, as I slowly approached. This was dangerous, mostly because she was a woman by herself and I was a strange man approaching her and her child in an empty parking lot. I didn't want to scare her off or give her a bad impression of me.

And so it started with me walking back and forth as the woman removed things from her stroller and put them into the trunk of her Subaru Forester. Once I felt her look up at me, I immediately glanced down at my phone to make it appear I had no intention of bothering her for anything.

I coughed, and the woman looked up at me as I smiled at her. She immediately gave me the most unconvincing return of my facial expression I had ever seen before in my life.

Apparently, all it took was standing near her, to make her feel creeped out by my presence. As she finished putting everything away, she finally shut the door and began to walk around towards the front of the vehicle. This was it.

She was about to leave, and I needed to make my move.

I hadn't bothered to attempt the ice cream challenge (if it had been available) nor did I visit the AT Museum because it had been closed. I needed to get to Arendstville, and my phone was at 10% power, and I had no way of recharging it.

With a dying signal that made attempting to contact Woodstock damned near impossible, I approached the woman feeling all but hopeless and scared at the thought that I would be left behind from the car crew.

"I'm so sorry to bother you, but I was wondering something." I began, as I approached the woman. Her calm demeanor dissolved, and the immediate expression on her face made me feel as though I was completely wasting her time just by approaching her with an apology.

"I don't have any money." She said quickly as she sat down in the driver's seat of her car.

"No, no, I don't need any money ma'am. You see my cell phone is dying and I need to get to Arendtsville to find some place to recharge it." I explained as she started her car and closed the driver's side door. I was losing this battle, and the only window of opportunity I had left was the fact that she'd left her car door window down.

"I don't see how that's *my* problem." she explained, dismissively.

"It's not. You're right. I'm sorry for bothering you." I said, with a tone of voice that had changed so dramatically and had sounded so defeated that I had actually surprised myself.

The woman glanced up at me then.

"I'm thousands of miles away from my home. I haven't seen my family in months, and I don't know where I am." I explained as my voice cracked on cue, and I felt my determinations all but die. I turned, without so much as another word and began walking back the way I had come, when I suddenly heard the woman call out: "Wait a minute."

I turned slowly with Oscar Award winning, humbled eyes as she was typing up an address on her GPS system.

"I'm headed to Gettysburg, not Arendtsville. But I suppose I can drop you off along the way, as long as you're not a rapist or murderer of some sort," she said cautiously.

I felt that it was an odd thing to say, seeing as how I highly doubted had I been either one of those types of people that I would have so candidly told her so.

"I'm just a hiker, trying to make my way to Maine," I said plainly.

She eyed me a final time and then told me to hurry and get in because she had to go.

So I jumped into the rear seat next to her infant child and held my backpack in my lap as the woman drove back 8.8 miles down the road I had just walked in the direction from Caledonia. It wasn't until she started off that I realized I should have sat in the front seat.

As she drove, she adjusted the rear view mirror not so much to see traffic as much as to view me. And there was a nominal amount of distrust in her eyes as she did this.

"It was a beautiful day out today, wasn't it? Kinda hot, though." I said, trying to cut through the tension and awkward silence in the air. I was most clearly aware of the hideous smell emitting off of my sweat covered clothes. And from the expression on the woman's face, I was sure she was too.

If only I had changed clothes before even bothering to approach the woman—maybe I wouldn't even have reached her in time to snag a ride?

"It was all right." the woman replied coldly. I felt she was no longer watching the road and instead quietly eyeing me alone within her rearview mirror.

The baby beside me had started to cry a little, and so I smiled down at him and made funny faces.

"He doesn't like that. Please stop scaring him." She said curtly after my third face. I gulped and apologized immediately.

"I'm sorry. I was just trying to make him laugh..."

"When was the last time you washed your hands? Please don't touch my child with your filthy hands." the woman asked with a hint of annoyance and sudden irritability in her voice.

"Ma'am, I'm not touching your kid at all. I was just making faces, trying to make him laugh." I explained as the infant started to cry a little more consistently now.

"He's crying because you're scaring him. When was the last time you've been to church?" she asked rather spontaneously.

"I...uh..." I began, unsure of how to answer such a random question.

"It's probably been well over a decade," I replied.

As we reached the intersection of Pine Grove and Shippensburg Road; I was suddenly well aware of where I was. I had WALKED here from Caledonia Park hours before, and now here I was again at the four-way crossroads that led not only towards Shippensburg to the west but Arendstville to the east.

The woman crossed the intersection and immediately proceeded to pull into a gravel lot on the adjacent side of the road. There, she stated quite clearly and concisely: "You need to just get out *here*. I'm sorry."

Truthfully, I hadn't said much to her as she had driven. What little I had said, seemed to only have irritated her more. Simply being in the car had caused her to snap at me like I had been the biggest thorn in her side.

"Did I do something wrong?" I asked. Maybe I smelled even worse than I initially thought?

I couldn't have done or said anything wrong because the closest thing I had potentially gotten out of line over, was trying to make her infant son laugh by making funny faces when he was crying. I didn't know what else it could have been?

"You really just need to get out right here, now please." She repeated a little more frantically.

What had changed? I thought to myself miserably.

I opened the door and grabbed my pack.

"I'm sorry if I did something wrong." I offered as she nodded her head, avoiding eye contact.

It was all so very bizarre.

"Can you tell me which direction Arendtsville is? Do you know if it's straight *that way*, or what roads I'm..." I began as she immediately cut me off.

"I don't know where your town is. Please leave," she said, with a small break in her voice as if she was on the verge of tears.

"Have a nice day," I muttered closing the door gently.

As she drove away, in the opposite direction from what I presumed had been towards Arendtsville; here I was in the middle of NOWHERE.

No phone signal, and only at 7% remaining charge on it.

"Great," I muttered, as I smeared my hands across my face, and took a deep breath.

I cupped my hand over my eyes as I looked up and counted the hours of daylight left in the sky. I did this by placing my flat outstretched hand beneath the sun and counted my fingers down towards the horizon. Theoretically, each finger accounted for about fifteen minutes. It appeared from my estimate that I would be losing light

The World We Came to Find

in roughly two hours since it was already 6:48 P.M. and the sun was starting to set.

I watched the flow of traffic for a bit to see the direction the majority of commuters were headed and then started walking if for no other reason than because I was hoping it was the direction of a town.

I walked through wheat and corn fields, as well as apple orchards as the light began to die. I cut across these farmlands and fields upon properties of people I would never know, as if some sense of entitlement had given me permission to trespass. My phone finally died on me thirty minutes later. However, I had made use of the time it had afforded me by drawing out a map in ink upon a waterproof pad of paper my sister Mary had given me as a birthday gift, before I'd set out onto the AT back in March.

I had come from remote mountain tops down into grand valleys with lush fields and rich harvests. Field workers pruned trees and gave me odd looks as I passed by.

I felt as if I was in an entirely different country as the atmosphere had changed and I no longer felt fear or nervousness often attributed to the claustrophobic feeling of closed-in forests.

When I was 3 miles from Arendtsville, I turned on my phone and knew I had maybe two or three minutes of power left before it died again. I made a last ditch call and was finally able to reach Woodstock.

"Finally! I've been trying to call you. Don't you answer your text messages or phone?" Woodstock asked in a rather annoyed tone.

"I'm sorry. This things about to die. I don't have much time left." I replied quickly.

"You're about to die and don't have time left?" he asked. I heard Wales laugh in the background, and suddenly I was angry if for no other reason than because my phone had seconds of life left, and these guys were making jokes.

"Meet me in Arendtsville at the A-Ville Inn. I'll be there." I replied.

"Where the hell is Arendtsville? I thought you were headed to the Shippensburg Road crossing?" He asked.

"I was, but then I decided to shoot for the AT Museum...and then some lady dropped me off in the middle of nowhere...and..."

The phone had suddenly died while I was in mid-sentence.

"ARGH!" I shouted, as I writhed the thing within my grip and had the sudden urge to slam it down on the ground; shattering it into a million pieces.

All I could do was make it to that Inn and hope that I could charge my phone.

It was dark once I had made it into town. I was able to turn my phone on again if only to see that Woodstock and Wales had both sent me five more text messages wondering where I was at.

Inside the A-Ville Inn, the room was packed with about thirty people too many. You couldn't find an outlet in there if your life depended on it, let alone walk into the room without accidently having violated somebody because it was so tightly packed with people.

I sat outside on the bench and continued to attempt to get any battery life out of the phone that I could. It would be an hour later when they arrived to pick me up.

"Well, that was a stupid idea. Why didn't you just wait for us in the park at the museum or the General Store?" Woodstock asked as he drove the same roads I had just walked to take to Arendtsville.

"Because I didn't have a signal there. My carrier sucks, and I felt if I had made it to a town I could have just sat inside a fast food restaurant, charged my things and waited on you guys with a phone signal. But I guess my plan fell through." I replied.

"Where are we heading again?" Wales asked as he peered out of the rear window from the backseat into the darkness.

"When I came out of the ATV Park to Shippensburg Road, there was a picnic shelter there in the parking lot. I figure it doesn't have any walls or anything, but it'll be free to camp underneath it tonight, and besides, it's not that hot or cold outside." I said.

They both seemed agreeable to the idea, and so our plans were tri-mutually met with interest.

But after setting out sleeping bags and pads upon hard picnic tables or benches not nearly long enough for our entire bodies, it was quickly seen how foolhardy and not thought out my idea had been.

"Wish Morris would've just gotten us a room somewhere..." Woodstock muttered.

"Here we go..." I said, shaking my head from side to side.

"We could be watching Catfish, or Bizarre Foods, or Wife Swap. Instead, we're getting eaten alive by mosquitoes out here it would seem." Wales joined in.

"Too bad. Get over it." I countered, rolling onto my side and placing my back towards them both.

"To think, we saved this guys life from heat exhaustion and being in the middle of nowhere. Now look how he repays us. Makes us sleep out here under a picnic shelter like dogs." Woodstock moaned, as the three of us burst into laughter.

I sat up.

"I'll buy us all breakfast tomorrow, asshole. Will that make you feel better?" I asked in a cartoonishly placating voice. There was an accepting silence that I followed up by breaking.

"Good. It's settled. Goodnight." I said as I laid back down upon the splintery and uncomfortable surface of that old and weathered picnic table.

"Sure could use some bacon *right now*. Not tomorrow morning..." Woodstock muttered, and we all burst into laughter again.

We awoke at 5 A.M. to wet clothes, dew covered sleeping bags and tired, sandpapery eyes.

The parking lot was a white wall of fog that had simultaneously soaked and enveloped everything we owned within it. We had gathered nearly four hours of sleep if we were lucky. Most importantly we hadn't been served a ticket or a fine for illegally sleeping beneath a picnic pavilion in a parking lot that we weren't entirely sure we were allowed to sleep in.

After a week of deliberations, we had finally talked about our best course of travel now that we had connected all of our pieces of trail on the Southern sections of the AT, and had more or less made it halfway along the Appalachian Trail.

We had decided the best plan was for us to flip-flop to Maine, then hike south and connect these points. The reason for this was due to the October 15th closing date of the park; in which hiking up Mt Katahdin was only achievable by proper gear and special permit.

My final connecting point and finish line would be Pine Grove Furnace State Park, and Woodstock's would be further South at Annapolis Rocks/US-70 Section along with Wales.

We talked about where we were each, monetarily. This was done so that we could be a bit more responsible with the rest of our funds as we pooled our resources together to make sure our three man crew finished the Appalachian Trail together. And ultimately I believed there existed a sense of camaraderie in that.

Iconic picture spot along the AT, showcasing Katahdin for those so close to the end.

CHAPTER 3

Flipping North

RAIN.

The scourge of the trail for the Class of 2013 Appalachian Trail Thru-Hikers.

Wales, Woodstock and I had wanted our ascent up Katahdin to be bright and sunny with great views and great pictures. Ideally, it would also be a lot safer if we weren't traversing five thousand feet inside a thunderstorm cloud as well.

Unfortunately for us, Mother Nature wasn't at our beck and call.

Due to the weather, park rangers weren't allowing hikers to summit and instead we were told we would have to hold up for the next two days unless the weather cleared sooner.

After driving several hours, we reached the small town of Millinocket, Maine and came upon this sobering news.

Out here it felt as if literally nothing existed so close to the Canadian Border other than lakes, ponds, and trees for sources of entertainment.

We found a rest stop just outside of town with a bathroom and picnic tables. We walked into the wood line where we set up camp for the night, just a hundred yards away from a destitute strip club that didn't appear to have much business.

Two bored strippers sat in the empty parking lot upon the wooden stairs leading inside the crumbling structure. Both were smoking cigarettes and had their heads held, looking down at their phones.

"What do we do if a cop comes and writes us a ticket?" I asked Woodstock.

He gave a disparaging look that spoke droves of his exhaustion from having driven most of the day.

"I don't know about you guys. But I don't see any signs saying we can't camp here. Do you?" He asked.

So we took advantage of our ignorance, staking a claim of "stupidity" should an authority figure come along to kick us off of the property.

I fell asleep in my hammock to the sound of a distant loon. It was both sad and beautiful amongst the evergreens we were camped in. The fog came in from the nearby lake and crept over our tents during the night, chilling us beneath a bright and silvery moon.

The occasional car had driven by, always making the three of us wonder what types of individuals were driving these abandoned and lonely roads at night. And wondering where they were going.

Throughout the night, constant the whine of mosquitoes hovering around the outside of my bug net left me staring wide-eyed up at my rain tarp.

They were so persistent that they had taken to digging their needle-shaped proboscis into the walls of the hammock, looking for the blood they had smelled in me.

"Morris, you awake?" Woodstock asked suddenly, the next morning.

I put my phone into my pocket and glanced out of the bug net surrounding me. I'd gotten barely anything reminiscent of sleep.

"Yeah, why?" I called back.

"The amount of mosquitoes outside of my tent are *insane*. We need to make a sprint to the car!" he said, as I rolled over onto my side and glanced towards his tent.

"How the hell are we going to take our tents down?" I asked, eyeing the black cloud of flying pests swarming around our camp like the plague. I wondered how in the hell anybody could live up here with swarms of these bloodsuckers, this thick. I could see myself as nothing but a sack of skin and bones after the thousands of these things buzzing about outside, had their way with me.

"Wales, are you up yet?" Woodstock asked.

There was a small groan, and then Wales finally answered in a weak voice: "Yeah..."

"We need to get out of here together. I don't want these things in my car." Woodstock said, as if Wales had been a part to the conversation we'd had only moments before.

"What *things*, are you talking about?" Wales asked.

"Look out your bug flap," I called over to him.

"Can't you just tell me?" He whined.

"Would you just look out of your damn tent window already?" Woodstock replied angrily.

Wales didn't know we hadn't meant for him to zip open his tent door and look outside with no bug net barrier in between. As soon as his tent flap opened, there was the sound of a scuffle, and then Wales was running out of his tent and waving his hands wildly about without a shirt on.

"Make a run for it!" I shouted in the heat of the moment as I launched out of my hammock and began disassembling my tent without direction or care. I wasn't trying to fold anything or make it pretty or convenient. I just wanted to get the hell out of there.

The cloud of mosquitos that had been waiting outside of my tent all night swarmed straight towards me but seemed to change direction rather instantaneously as Wales ran barreling through the brush by me.

Two landed on my face and immediately fell victim to my palm.

I waved my hands wildly, smacking maybe three dozen in the path of my defense with a single blow. All as the air I'd just cleared only clogged up again with more mosquitos in seconds.

Four more dive bombed my bare legs, as three more scattered about my left forearm preparing their stance to puncture my skin.

One sunk it's proboscis beneath my flesh, and I felt the tiny sting already beginning to itch on point. I crushed it with a quick swat. The result left the other two flying off cautiously, yet still hovering in close enough to show they weren't going anywhere.

Five or six more began to take my attention off of the swarm around my legs as they dive bombed my eyes, ears, and face.

I took off running around the rest stop, waving my hands wildly... and smashing clumps of them left and right with every swing.

Woodstock and Wales weren't doing any better. To picture Wales, just imagine a tall, lanky, 6'5 giant hopping over fallen logs and swinging his arms clumsily about in a forest as he crashed into tree branches, and stumbled wildly over logs. In between doing this, he would occasionally dash back towards his tent, to try and pick it apart before taking off from the mosquitoes gaining on him again.

We drove off, peeling our tires out of the gravel lot of the rest stop with anywhere between two or three dozen bites already raising into small little bumps upon various places on our skin.

"Wow. Worst place to camp. Ever." I muttered as I glanced back at Wales who was wiping a slick sheen of sweat from his forehead.

"I can't stop itching," Woodstock said, exasperating the point by scratching various places on his upper torso as he drove.

I leaned back in my seat and sighed.

We called the Baxter State Park Ranger office, only to receive some rather troubling news.

For starters, it would cost thirty bucks a night to rent a campsite at the base of Katahdin. While the price felt a bit hefty, we accepted that. Then we learned that for us to drive into the park itself to reach our campsite, it carried a fourteen dollar car entry fee. Okay, that was all right as well. We were done with the fees now, right?

Nope.

Almost as if some moron had decided it made that much more sense to do it, there was then a five dollar fee on top of that, just to park our car there overnight, after having driven it in to reach our campsite and destination.

We were bitter about the experience as a result.

Moreover, we had been unable to secure a campsite for the next two weeks because of the heavy traffic the park was receiving from out-of-towners. There would be no way to drive into the park, justify the price and hike up the final northernmost summit before closing time. We would need to have secured a place to sleep beforehand. Because of this, we had chosen to hike through the Hundred Mile Wilderness that preceded Mt. Katahdin while we waited for our spot within the park to open.

When we arrived at Abol Bridge, 15 miles south; it was bright and sunny, and 70 degrees outside.

Woodstock and I took off along the AT as Wales wished us well and drove the car 40 miles further south to where the hundred mile wilderness crossed an old logging road called 'Jo Mary.' There, he would begin his hike north to Abol Bridge. Along the way, we'd switch keys with one another.

I walked at a leisurely pace and enjoyed the comfortable surroundings and natural terrain. The forests were alive and vibrant. Green moss grew over everything, carpeting rocks, boulders and the forest floor like a giant green blanket.

Streams of sunlight poured down in bright rays, and the beams cut through the shadows like a flood light in the darkness.

We saw a few Northbounders who weren't very far from their goal. When we attempted conversations, or to congratulate them, they were short with us, and understandably so. Two days hike from finishing a 2,188-mile trail was a big deal. I didn't fault them for wanting to hurry and get it over with.

As Woodstock and I climbed Rainbow Ledges, we were given a fantastic view of Katahdin from a distance. We took pictures and sat on the rocky ridge line to admire the view.

As I leaned back and smiled up at the sun, I felt my hand squish into something resting on the granite rock beneath me.

I lifted my hand in disgust until I saw that what I had smashed had once only been a blueberry.

And there were THOUSANDS of these bushes surrounding me.

Even better, they were all ripe!

We spent half an hour picking wild blueberries and eating them until our stomachs were satiated with the sweet juices.

"This is incredible," I said to Woodstock who smiled back at me.

"Listen for a second." He said, as I stopped moving and did exactly that.

"What am I trying to hear?" I asked.

"Nothing. Isn't it great?" he asked.

Birds, weren't even chirping. There was an occasional breeze that ruffled leaves, but otherwise, it was the most silent moment I'd ever experienced before in my life. No airplanes, no distant trucks or train horns. There was nothing, but an occasional gasp of wind and even that flew in like a whisper.

The air was crisp as we walked along exposed rock trails that had been wearing away within the sun and rain over the course of millions of years.

We traversed across logs that had been nailed down into the mud and over the decades of use, had started to crumble. It made walking across them sketchy as they tilted left and right or sometimes just snapped in half under our weight.

It was a good idea having them installed at some point, until the upkeep had become rather infrequent. The boards had become so severely degraded that they were of no use to anybody anymore.

Strange fungal growths grew into the sides of the birch trees we passed, which looked like gray, upside down bells.

The smell of cedar and evergreen trees made the atmosphere feel almost like Christmas.

Along the path, we did our best to avoid moose droppings and eyed the monstrous tracks they had left behind with fear, curiosity, and anticipation of seeing one. Tree trunks within our vicinity had huge pieces of bark torn out of them, which the Bulls had raked their antlers across.

After hiking 8.1 miles, we came upon a stream that trickled down into Little Beaver Lake. We found a flat camp spot along the shoreline, looking down into the water.

This lake was crystal clear and the water, pristine and pure. You could swim out towards the middle of the body of water and still see the rocky bottom, 16 - 25 feet beneath you.

We undressed, and bathed—washing ourselves off and the salt crystals that had gathered on our bodies from the hours of hiking throughout the day.

Afterward, Woodstock and I made dinner and watched the sun die in hues of pink, purple and burnt orange along the shoreline. Far away loons sang eerily to us from unobservable distances.

And I was truly at peace.

I smacked at a yellow fly that was biting the back of my head. It would be the first of over a hundred more that I would count that day. One Hundred and Eighteen would become the ultimate total, and leave me feeling more bruised than anyone would have liked to be.

My neck and cheeks had become coated in broken legs, wings and a paste of smashed mosquito, horsefly, and yellow fly guts.

As the rain came down in droves around us, my soaking pants had started to chafe the insides of my thighs. The waist band on my pants had also begun to rub my flesh raw, leaving bright red scabs and spots of blood beneath my stomach.

Woodstock wasn't doing any better. The rain had turned cold, and fog from the many lakes or ponds that had surrounded us had begun creeping in during mid-day.

Woodstock explained that he had a friend at home who had hiked the AT in the past. He exclaimed that she had gotten bored once she had reached Virginia, and flip-flopped North to Maine to re-energize her enthusiasm to complete the trail. He also exclaimed she had only been doing five miles a day once arriving, because of how consistently wet it was.

She would later quit.

That day, I felt a breath behind her, as well.

I began wondering when the M.A.T.C. was last out and about on the trail as well. There were so many fallen trees across the path that people had started making NEW trails just to try and avoid them. Then I was surprised at whoever's bright idea it was to bring the trail, five feet away from the lake shore so that every time water levels were high due to rain (LIKE THAT VERY DAY) the trail flooded and left you walking through 3 feet of lake water or mud.

The path to Rainbow Brook lean-to crossed over a roaring stream.

After reaching the shelter, I saw that I was alone. I stripped off my clothes and wrung as much rain water from them as I could. I was cold, but not enough to be in any danger. I then removed my boots which were soaked. I wrung out my socks as well and sat my boots upside down to drain.

I threw my wet clothes back on as Woodstock arrived. Steam started to come off of my outfit. I knew my body heat was doing it's best to dry them but that would take quite some time, and the rain wasn't letting up anytime soon.

The trail went across a logging bridge then back into the conifer tree forest. We hiked up an arduous 800-foot mountain, climbing hand over hand up boulders or root walls. You see, in Maine, they didn't believe in switch backs. So when the trail went over a mountain it literally went straight up and down the other side.

For the next couple of days, we went from mossy cliff side paths to beaches, to traversing small islands via natural tree root bridges. Further, into the forests, the path trail crossed fallen logs over stony streams.

The scenery was magical. I've dreamt of fairy tale worlds like Maine or seen them in fantasy movies—but never thought for a moment I'd stumble upon them with my own eyes.

Woodstock and I had reached the campsite within an hour and a half, mostly because of our determination to eat town food instead of from our packs.

Woodstock pulled ahead, as I had decided to stop at the privy there. As I opened the door though, I realized rather immediately that this was going to be a first for me.

In fact, it was the first time I had ever seen anything like this at all.

The privy accommodated *two people*. By that, I meant the toilet had two side-by-side seats in it resting on a little shelf that housed the excrement below. It was almost as if you grabbed your loved one's hands at that moment you needed to use the restroom, and you both scrambled into the outhouse to take a romantic dump together.

But that wasn't all. There were about a thousand different species of spiders inside, most of which were as long and wide as a pack of playing cards.

I sat down warily, and looked at the register to my left as I brushed away huge walls of webs. I found it odd to have come across a "Poop-log-book" inside the privy. In fact, I had to admit, it was definitely spot on with a *two-seater outhouse* in "weirdness".

People had written things in the book like: "You're most likely pooping as you read this."

Or: "I'm watching you from the hole in the door."

And though *that* entry had been written from around a month before I had even gotten there, I looked at the hole beside the entrance door, all the same, searching for a voyeuristic eyeball and a hillbilly pervert.

Using the restroom in such a spider-ridden environment, especially while you're in such a vulnerable position can become nerve racking rather quickly.

I began to feel a little freaked out as I looked at some of the sizes of these arachnids, which were inhabiting this same space with me at that moment.

I spit a wad of saliva at one that was moving curiously back and forth in the corner, chasing imaginary prey every time the wind blew.

Funny enough, I nailed it! I was surprised at the luck of my aim. Well, spitting at the thing had proved to be stupid on MY part as well, because the creature took off in fright. Only it didn't run and hide in some dark corner far away from me. Instead, the thing ran *towards me* and up my boot. Goosebumps shot up the back of my neck, and I kicked my legs wildly, trying to knock the huge spider off.

It is important to remember that this isn't an easy thing to do with your pants around your ankles, mind you.

The pest held on while I bucked back and forth, trying to get it away from me anyway that I could—aside from touching it. As the arachnid reached my right calve, I swatted the beast with the privies 'shit register', but the spider was undeterred and maybe even emboldened by the act. It sprinted forward up my thigh, where I had managed to scoop the thing up as a last resort with the log book and flung it full force into the wall. There, the spider crumpled as it fell to the floor in a pile of upturned legs.

I was a bit shaken, and because of that, my next response was rather erratic. I felt something crawling on my back and immediately began swatting at my shoulder. Smacking at something that probably wasn't even there. That's when I put my hand down and what looked like either a brown recluse or wolf spider ran across it and beneath my butt.

It was too much to take at that point. I had lost my nerve, and these spiders were clearly in the process of trying to take back their territory from the giant, stomping around in their home.

I flew up in a panic and shoved full force into the privies door, only to be knocked back a couple of feet. I fumbled with the hook lock latch, opened it and finally shoulder rammed the door open, jumping out into the dirt.

I fell to my knees immediately because my pants were still down, and then I began rolling around—smacking myself wildly without direction with my privates exposed to the world. I felt sorry for any unfortunate hiker who had happened to be passing by at that moment in time.

Luckily, nobody had appeared to bear witness to my stupidity.

Lost.

Like three blind mice, stumbling around in the woods; crashing from tree trunk to tree trunk and Woodstock was behind the wheel.

"Shh, be quiet! This is probably somebodies property!" I whispered in a hushed tone from the front passengers' side seat, as we crept along in our vehicle through the dark. We were driving down what appeared to be a privately owned dirt road.

Wales had his head lamp on, occasionally looking out of the rear drivers' side, or passenger side windows for a clearing to set up a tent for the night.

"I don't think this is the right way," Woodstock said dully, glancing towards me for only a moment from the overgrown dirt road stretching out into the darkness before us. We were crashing through plants as high as the roof of the car.

"Well Google maps says we've already *passed* the Appalachian Trail. Oops, now I just lost my data." Wales exclaimed with confusion from the back seat. It had been *his* job to navigate since he had Verizon as a service provider and was the only one between the three of us with a signal to look up directions.

"We're gonna get shot to death. I know it." I said miserably, as I smashed my face against my hand.

"Maybe we should just go back," Woodstock offered.

"Oh wait...here we go. Okay, keep right at the fork here." Wales said, with a pleasant tone that only further instigated my anger. He pointed directly in front of us, from the back seat to where no fork in the road existed in front of our vehicle.

"Fork you say? What fork?! The HELL are you TALKING ABOUT?! I see a one-eyed cat sitting on a dumpster over there! *Nothing else is out here!*" I growled in frustration.

"Agh, never mind. Now Google Navigation says we're just floating in the woods, completely off of the road." Wales added, with a slight chuckle.

"Give me that DAMNED PHONE!" I shouted angrily, ripping my seat belt off as I made for him. I wanted to throw the thing in front of the car and run it over a thousand times.

"What? No!" Wales replied, backing up further into the rear seat while gripping the phone protectively against his chest.

Woodstock gave me a calming pat on my shoulder.

"We have to be near the trail head. The sign back there said 'Appalachian Trail This Way -->' so I'm pretty sure we're close." Woodstock added, peering left to right in the darkness.

"Oh, you mean that sign that looked as if it was scrawled out in BLOOD back there? Yeah, why don't we go THAT way?" I replied sarcastically.

Woodstock only rolled his eyes.

"If we keep going straight, we should supposedly find a parking lot according to AWOL's guide," Wales said, looking back and forth between his phone and the trail guide a little more frantically now.

So we kept forward, passing obscure or sometimes hidden roads with no trespassing signs on them.

"Let's check this small alcove," Woodstock said, pulling into a narrow drive, adjacent to a privately owned "Dead End".

Woodstock acted as the scout and walked with Wales' headlamp into the woods while Wales and I stayed behind in the car.

We were both unmotivated and too tired to do anything about it.

It wasn't long though, when Woodstock began heading back in our direction.

"Well, I guess he found us a spot. He's rubbing his hands together excitedly like he does when he's happy about something." I said to Wales who was busy, absorbed by his phone.

It was 10:30 P.M. when we reached our campsite on what looked to be a privately owned ATV trail.

"Nice place. What do you call this area, Woodstock? *Rapeville, USA?*" I asked, looking at the collection of old, weather-melted or soggy mattresses somebody had dumped into the woods along with old bags of trash and washing machines.

"It's not *that* bad," he replied.

"I just hope nobody runs us over or shoots our nuts off with a shotgun in the middle of the night!" I muttered, just as the rain started to come down around us.

"Morris, you realize that your negativity only stands to distance us further as a group, don't you?" Wales asked me as we trudged through the night with our packs bouncing up and down on our backs.

"Wales, haven't you realized? That's just who he is. A regular *Debbie Downer*." Woodstock added.

"Talk all you guys want. When Billy-Bob Dumbshit comes along claiming you've got a purty mouth, don't come looking to me for help." I exclaimed as we disappeared into the uncertain darkness.

I had asked Woodstock a semi-morbid question.

If he could choose his own death, *how* would he want to die and what did he want to do with his remains?

"I'd want to die by a heart attack, and then probably be cremated."

"Wouldn't a heart attack be painful?" I asked.

He shrugged.

"I dunno. I don't think so. What about you?"

"I think I'd want to go in my sleep. I like to believe I'd be having an amazing and beautiful dream that I never had to wake up from." I said.

He liked my answer, thinking it thoughtful.

But I wondered if my response had given him the impression that I had obsessively figured it out a long time ago. I suppose in a sense; it was true that I have always thought about death. Not for any particular reason either. Just because it was something that had always frightened me. Scared me into believing that I hadn't truly *lived*, before my opportunity to do so had been pissed away.

"What about your body?" He asked me next.

"Well, I'd like to be cremated as well and have my ashes dumped along Hammocks Beach, North Carolina out on a little barrier isle called Bear Island. It's a small strip of sand off of our coast." I said.

I had thought that one out too.

It was one of the best places my father had ever taken me camping as a child, and over my adult years, I had almost annually gone there as soon as I had learned how to drive.

From that conversation about our deaths, a dream had blossomed from a seed inside my mind, about that very subject later that evening.

I imagined that a faceless mortician had taken my ashes and dumped them into a trashcan along the side of a road like I was trash. And then some fat guy had waddled down the sidewalk, and thrown a half filled aluminum tin dish of uneaten spaghetti on top of my remains.

When I woke up, it was 1 A.M., and I noticed immediately that I had fallen asleep while in the middle of writing notes for my blog.

The writing application on my smartphones screen read: "kjjjjG fall sinto sunroof ggg zZZZZZZCC dammit stink"

I wasn't remotely certain what I had been thinking about when that garble of nonsense had spilled from my in and out, conscious state. However, the following morning I believed that there was fear of worthlessness, in my death. No greater glory other than just having existed, and then died with no real impact on those around me.

I looked over at Woodstock who was stirring the remains of a fire with a stick and walked over.

He craned his neck up towards me.

"Wanna make me some of that cocoa?" I asked. His face soured, mostly because his water was only now starting to boil, and he would have to wait all over again to heat up some more.

"Do you even have a cup?" Woodstock asked.

I shook my head.

"But I'll take that one right there," I said, pointing to his.

"Oh yeah? *This* one right here?" he asked, licking the edge of his cup.

"Never mind," I muttered.

We would head out around 10:30 A.M.; Wales and I going south while Woodstock drove even further south to hike north alone.

Just before our 1,400-foot ascent up Moxie Bald Mountain, Wales and I stripped our clothes off and went swimming for an hour in a stream.

The water was cold, dark and amber colored from the pine needles carpeting the forest floor around us as well as the bottom of the creek.

After getting in, we had minnows and small bream picking at our legs, thighs and feet.

"Christ, what the hell was that!" I shouted.

There was another quick nip behind my knee and I swirled around in the water violently.

"We gotta get outta here! Something is eating us!" I said, as I started to climb back out.

"Calm down, they're just little fish." Wales replied in a calm voice.

"Well, you enjoy yourself in there. I'm not getting eaten alive."

"You know they have spas, where fish eat the dead skin cells off of your feet." he explained.

I quickly reminded him however that we were in the wild and that these fish didn't know what "dead skin cells" or "spas" or even really what "we" were.

"They probably assume that we are dead animals and are trying to pick the flesh from our bones," I explained to Wales.

"That's a bit morbid." he retorted.

As soon as we got out of the water, many leeches began to swarm around the shoreline and then beach themselves upon the hot rocks cooking in the sun. Some shriveled up on the sizzling surface while others were able to escape back into the stream with only minor burns.

I was grossly fascinated by the creatures and shivered, wondering how lucky we had been to have not had one attach to us during our swim.

"Can you imagine if you had come out to find those things all over you, from head to toe?" I asked Wales, who chuckled and backed up out of the creek in disgust.

"I wonder if they smelled us in the water, and came to feast on us just now," Wales thought in recollection.

"Probably. Come on, let's go." I said, slipping my shirt back on and grabbing my backpack.

Scrambling up Moxie Bald going south felt a lot like climbing a 1,400-foot ladder, straight up into the sky. I sometimes had to pivot off of adjacent boulders to scramble across flat wall faces that were five or even six feet tall.

As I approached the false summit and second base of the last 300 feet to the top, I sighed out of relief.

The hardest part was done, and I'd only had .2 miles remaining.

On top of the bald, there were several hundred dead trees that had started to crumble under the weight of many years. Hikers had set up cairns which led from bare rock slab to rock slab; adrift in a sea of neck-high grass or overgrown weeds. It was reminiscent of a swamp at the summit; only there were no stagnant water sources or mosquitos. Only damp mud pits surrounded by bird feces.

I reached Wales who had been waiting atop the highest peak of Moxie Bald, where a sign stating "2,630 feet" had been propped up between piles of boulders. There were remnants of where an old fire tower once stood and the eyehooks that had been drilled down into the granite stone to help support it.

After eating and re-hydrating, Woodstock climbed the summit going north and joined us.

"How long you guys been here?" He asked.

"Ten or fifteen minutes. Don't worry; you're not that far behind." I said, as Wales nodded and palmed a handful of blueberries he had stashed away earlier into his mouth.

The three of us took a 20-minute nap under the sun, side by side before moving on.

During my continued descent South, I fell even more in love with the mountain.

We walked an exposed, flat rock ridge that edged downwards over the length of two football fields. Our only way of knowing we were headed in the right direction was the cairns people had left up. We were given a clear 360-degree view of the lakes and rivers at the base of the mountain. The cool wind danced behind us, to hurry us along beneath a bright, but soft sun.

We crossed beneath rock overhangs, one of which had a plaque installed in Memorial for an older gentleman who had died. It stated something along the lines of: "In honor of a man who loved to hike and climb. We will miss you Dad, Grandpa, Tony."

I wondered if this spot beneath the overhang had been chosen as a favorite place of his for a reason. I wondered if there had been, amazing memories shared there and if that was why the plaque had been set in that particular spot.

I blazed down past Moxie Bald Brook Lean-to, not bothering to stop and check in before reaching a river of boulders—three miles down.

When Wales appeared thirty minutes later, we took Woodstock's waiting vehicle and drove into town where we grabbed some gas for our 2-hour drive back up towards Millinocket the following day.

At times, Wales could come off as a very shy, and easily timid individual. Often, he appeared to have a hard time talking to strangers. In such scenarios, Woodstock and I capitalized on the moment, ribbing him on his inert demeanor. It wasn't done in a bullying gesture, so much as playful, friendly jest.

Woodstock and I had a mutual love at ruffling his feathers and so it happened that after our hike up Moxie Bald, I was driving us two hours back north towards the town of Millinocket in preparation of summiting Katahdin. Woodstock was sitting in the front passenger side seat, reading out different coupons he'd received in his email folder, from over his phone.

The most promising option he'd read for us had been a Pizza-Hut special claiming only $6.55 for a large, one-topping pizza.

So when we'd asked Wales to call and order three of them for us; he had become quickly absorbed by his own, ruinous progression of nervousness.

"This is Pizza Hut, how may I help you?" a bored, hurried teenager's voice spoke across the other end of the phone.

"Wales, I want some pizza! Come on!" Woodstock shouted suddenly in the background.

"Yes. I was...well I was just wondering if you happened to sell pizzas there," Wales asked, nervously.

"Wales! It's a *Pizza Hut* for God's sake!" I said, throwing my hands up into the air.

He gulped and looked away from us both, as the employee replied in an annoyed tone.

"Yes, this is a Pizza restaurant, so we probably sell pizza's here."

Wales cupped his hand over the receiver and looked back at us.

"What were you fellows ordering?" he asked in a hushed tone.

"Why are you whispering, Wales? You asking me out on a date?!" I purposefully shouted as he withdrew with a painstakingly angry face, back into the rear seat.

"Hello? Anybody there?" the employee asked in an annoyed tone over the line.

"Y...yes. We wanted..." Wales began, before pausing again because we hadn't yet told him what we'd wanted.

"Sir, you know you could always call back when you have your orders ready," the teen explained over the phone.

"Ask if they have ribs, Wales," Woodstock said, scrolling through his phone.

"They...they don't have ribs." he replied to Woodstock, not even bothering to pose the question.

"Sir, we don't have ribs," the kid over the phone confirmed.

"I know that. I was just answering for my friend," Wales assured him.

"Wales, do they have Sesame Seed Chicken or Moo Gu Gai Pan?" I asked him.

"Morris, this isn't a Chinese restaurant." he replied to me, with an angry tone.

"Oh okay. Then ask if they have General Tso's or Sesame Seed Chicken Pizza." I said, passing a grin towards Woodstock who was holding back his laughter.

After we had retrieved our dinners, we ate and drove back to our stealth campsite on the outskirts of Millinocket. It was 9 P.M., and rain had started coming down in droves. Bright flashes of lightning accompanied the storm, sending rumbles across the earth.

"We're almost there!" I shouted at Wales.

"I can't see you!" He shouted back, through the downpour. His voice was little more than a muffle as the precipitation didn't just fall in heavy drops; it came down in buckets.

I smeared the streams of rainwater from my eyes and looked down at the pond I was standing in. Sticks, leaves, and trash people had dumped alongside the trail all floated halfway up to my knees. The path had flooded from the storm, and water ran along the AT like a rushing stream; almost carrying us along with the current.

"Bring your headlamp over!" I shouted through the roaring rain.

Woodstock had quickly caught up with us and hovered behind me.

"We gotta get outta this storm. Where's the campsite?" he asked.

"We drew a map to it, but the inks run off," I said handing him the worthless piece of paper it had once been scribbled upon.

"You know, I have leftover pizza waiting for me in the car. Maybe I should just go back there," he replied, stuffing the soggy paper map back into the palm of my hand.

I saw the exhaustion and exasperation on Wales' face. He exactly how I felt.

"The guide..." Wales said.

"Let me see it," he asked, holding out his hand.

I ripped out the pages of the Appalachian Trail guide for the very section we were on, and gave them to Wales who was now reading the terrain we had ahead of us.

"It makes no sense. The guide says that *this* is supposed to be all flat. Right, *here* where this line is. But we have had to climb at least five or six hundred feet in the last hour." Wales said, handing me the papers back.

I stuffed them into my soaked pants pockets.

"I think we should go back." Woodstock offered.

"The three of us cramped into that tiny ass car of yours? No thanks." I said, shaking my head from side to side.

"You guys could stay out here in this shit then, and I'll just pick you both up tomorrow. Meanwhile, I'm going to a motel," he said, as he started to turn and walk away.

Lightning lit up the sky and then struck somewhere nearby. The ground shuddered, and I'd almost felt as if I'd been partly shocked by a traveling bolt. I immediately leapt into the air.

"Christ, we have gotta get outta here!" Woodstock shouted.

"I uh..." Wales began.

"Rethinking that plan, huh?" I asked, cutting him off. Wales was always quick to shy away from using funds to take shelter in a motel. Especially when we couldn't get the full benefit of the evening, due to how late it already was. In truth, he was right to feel this way.

"I don't have the money, Woodstock." I said, quickly deflecting my anger away from Wales.

"I'll pay for the room tonight. Come on." He offered.

The three of us rushed for the car. Occasionally unseen stones beneath the water's surface caused us to trip or fall hands and knees into the mud.

The wind picked up into heavy gusts, and branches began to fall in the forests surrounding us.

"Do you have a motel in mind?" I called out to Woodstock. His headlamp flashed backwards to me, blinding me as I held up my hands to shield my eyes.

"Nah, we'll have to search for something once we reach the car."

"I...I'm cold..." Wales stuttered, shivering as water cascaded from him like a waterfall.

"Come on buddy, we're almost back." I said, patting his shoulder and leading him ahead.

At stream crossings, huge logs or branches passed by in thick currents leading away into the darkness as we balanced our way over slippery rocks and stones to the adjacent side.

We slipped and fell across mossy rocks turned slick as ice by the rain and winced every time lightning crackled across the sky.

Upon reaching Woodstock's car, we piled in soaking and cold. The heat went on immediately, causing the windows to fog with the humidity inside. As we drove ME-11 back north towards Millinocket, we realized that we'd only be wasting our money for a place to sleep when it was already midnight. So instead, we pulled over for the night at a roadside rest area along the side of the road. There weren't any "No Camping" signs anywhere, so we set up for the evening beneath picnic shelters. Our plan had been much as it had always been before in the event someone came along to run us off of their property. To claim ignorance in not knowing any better.

And sure enough, that's when the local cops pulled up.

"Well, it doesn't say 'No Camping,' officer," I explained to the older one of the two men jamming bright flashlights in our faces.

"Let's see some I.D.'s." He replied.

"You guys thru-hikers or something?" the younger officer asked, handing me my driver's license back.

"Yeah, we are," I replied for us all.

After the officers had found that none of us had any warrants for our arrest, they told us that they would allow us to sleep there until morning despite the area being considered "Town property" that "Closed at 8 P.M.".

We thanked them and went to sleep.

I woke everybody up at 5:30 A.M. so that we could hurry and get on the road.

We spent the first 30 minutes of that morning arguing back and forth mostly because we were all so tired and grumpy from having to get up so early with barely any rest.

We argued about trivial things.

Anything from the differences between the two words "hypocrisy" and "contradiction" to: "Who closed their door the wrong way?" or "What if this random hypothetical situation happened?"

These became actual HEATED arguments!

Finally, to break up the anger and calm everybody down—I played a favorite soft song of ours called "Real Hero" by Electric Youth.

A round of "Aw's" went around the car, and everybody settled down as we enjoyed the soft voice of the woman singing over the car speakers.

That was until I asked a question.

"Why do you rub your hands together all excitedly when you hear good news, Woodstock?" I hadn't meant it as an insult, but I believed he took it that way. Before he could answer, I stated that I also noticed Wales covered his mouth like an Asian School Girl whenever he laughed excitedly.

"I don't know Morris, why do you bloat you gut out like a fat whale?" Woodstock asked in a dull tone.

I stared at him momentarily, and incredulously as silence met his question.

Then we all exploded in anger at once, throwing insults left and right.

Morris The Cat: *"Oh I don't know Woodstock. Why don't you wreck your car again and then find somebody ELSE to blame and pay for it, right Wales? You know, how Woodstock said it was OUR FAULT his car exhaust was cracked?"*

Wales: *"I don't cover my mouth when I laugh. What the hell are you talking about?"*

Woodstock: *"No Wales, you just flap your girly arms like a butterfly. On top of that, you slammed my rear door hard enough to shatter the windows."*

Wales: *"I didn't slam the fucking door! THIS is slamming the door!"* Wales shouted, opening and closing the door hard enough to rock the entire car.

Woodstock: *"Morris, you instigated yet ANOTHER FIGHT. Congratulations*

Morris The Cat: *"Sorry, what was that? I couldn't hear you over your INCREDIBLE SNORING THAT KEEPS EVERYBODY AWAKE AT NIGHT!"*

Woodstock: *"THAT'S WHY I ALWAYS HAVE EARPLUGS IF YOU NEED THEM, ASSHOLE! Oh, and by the way Wales, you were the one whining about the door being closed when me and Morris saw it was open."*

Wales: *"The fucking door was closed! You're both idiots!"*

Morris The Cat: *"Don't rope me into your drama, Tons o' Fun."*

After we had finished arguing, we sat in silence for a few moments, slowly drifting back into conversation as if everything was normal. We actually even laughed at the things we'd said to each other.

It was as if the arguments had never existed.

It was strange how that worked with the three of us.

How we could be at each other's throats one minute and then completely okay the next.

Thunder rocked us, and rain poured from above all day long as we sat out the storms, seeking shelter wherever we could find it within our tents.

The plan the following day was to be hiking the ten miles out of Baxter State Park after meeting our reservations there.

But as the night trickled on I was feeling worse and worse.

And my right ear was in a constant state of pain.

"Shhh..." She cooed softly against my neck.

Her hand rested peacefully upon my chest as she laid there beside me; watching me with her dark brown eyes.

Not just wanting, but needing my company just as dearly as I had needed hers.

Her delicate features matched her breathy whispers of love. I could sense she was fragile, though only a silhouette of her frame was all that bore her existence there beside me.

The morning sun seeped through drawn shades, illuminating pieces and fractions of her body in the light.

The brown of her eyes were all I saw in those moments; as the confetti of light that stole visibility through the darkness, ran from left to right and the sun rose and set by days.

It was odd how these seconds transpired in hours.

Only showing how endless 'time' was within her presence of a dream.

The heat from her hand was life, and I was the sole recipient of that very gift of touch. It gave me strength that withdrew every time she turned away.

And while rationale began to set in, irrational bliss was the only world I had wanted to live in.

Outside, my fever was sweltering, and sweat gleamed from my brow.

My eardrum throbbed in pain as I swung my head from left to right within this reverie.

This mysterious woman.

She haunted my dreams, regularly.

And her name was *Melody*.

In the fading tendrils of this bitter-sweet reality, I called out to her.

"Don't leave me..." I begged. My fingertips touched her lips as she faded without as much as a word of protest, having only responded with a smile.

Everything faded, and in her place was only the darkness of reality to greet me.

I awoke that morning, uncaring as I stared out into the black forest, devoid of any light.

I was detached upon awakening, as the hiking; and as every reason, I came to believe in for being out here seemed to be gone. Words and sentences were muffled from my comrades. The cold of the early morning couldn't find its way inside to chill me nor to make me feel empty.

Because I was already so numb and hollow.

That day we were out there to hike again, only I would drift down those same miles, almost never feeling the earth beneath my feet.

And when the rain would come, I wouldn't feel it streaming down my fevered brow.

Any views of nature's beauty would blur by.

Songs of cheerful birds would go unnoticed, unheard; and in the few moments that true sunlight touched my face, I would feel no warmth from it.

I was thousands of miles away in my mind, within a reality that didn't exist. My thoughts were broken as they played on 'repeat'; over and over...showing the same clip in time again and again.

Where was I amongst these stormy fields, and foggy overpasses? These dark forests, and empty wood lines.

How blindly I sought out answers and feeling.

I was sick, and drifting into these obscure dimensions from time to time while those that would care for me, looked on with worried expressions.

They reached out to me, telling me to "go on."

"You can do it."

"Don't give up."

And I wanted to please them. To tell them it was "All okay."

But I didn't always believe in that.

And while some found that self-doubt could be destructive; I tended to think it made me more real.

Colors vibrated in my eyes. Even streaking at times, as my head pounded with an incredible ache.

My forehead was hot, and my ear was throbbing uncontrollably again.

I made no illusion to my hiking partners that I was ill. I listened listlessly, comforting the decisions they made by agreeing to anything they said regarding the logistics of our trip. Undeniable, and undeterred by miles I once feared I couldn't walk.

I was in too much pain to care.

I wanted to feel the sharp pangs in my feet and ankles if only to draw away from the incessant and constant bleating of my eardrum.

Sounds reverberated between metallic walls, whenever anybody spoke. The feedback from those sounds occasionally led to an overwhelming squelch and ringing sound that was deafening.

And nausea became my closest friend; as well as my un-welcomed hiking partner.

Sure enough, it gladly grasped my hand with unyielding strength and stated in its dead voice: *Walk...*

And I obeyed.

"Are you okay?" Woodstock asked, as I slowly turned to face him. It seemed as if he had just asked the question despite my knowing my response had been delayed by several seconds.

"Something...doesn't feel right..." I replied.

He would ask other questions. Even well aware of the abnormal twitching I had made talk of in my right ear in the days past. He would go on to inquire if I needed to go to a doctor or stay behind and skip the 10-mile pre-planned hike.

But I stupidly told him I would be okay.

I was willing to push myself, if for no other reason than to say I tried.

I would fail from fatigue, fall from consciousness or die before I gave up without trying.

There was no way; I wasn't scaling Katahdin in the next few days.

My world was muted, and hazy.

Amber light poured into foggy afternoon skies where dragonflies danced back and forth between ethereal bands of sunshine. The broken surface of the streams we crossed scattered light like shattered glass; creating a rainbow of bright colors shimmering through the wild scents of nature.

I went to sleep, listening to these sounds as nausea overtook me, and left me emptying the contents of my stomach within the woods.

I parked the car and started slow, hiking North from Abol Bridge in the direction of Katahdin Stream Campgrounds. Meanwhile, Wales and Woodstock had left out that morning from camp inside the park and were connecting that same strip of trail headed south.

With the ground still slick from rainfall the days before, precarious steps were all I took as I swayed between trees and fought back the urge to vomit.

The right side of my head felt hot, and my ear was cloudy and clogged as if my ear canal had been packed with Vaseline.

I passed day hikers with no real excitement or interest in a conversation.

Their faces were just as enthusiastic as mine, on this cold, wet morning.

I smiled weakly at the handful of thru-hikers whose paths I happened to cross, as they passed me and their journey came to an end.

Before heading out that morning, I had met a guy at Abol Bridge who had hiked the Appalachian Trail in 1983. He called himself "Magic Mike" because he had regularly performed magic tricks while on the trail to help fund his adventure back in the day for spare cash or a place to stay overnight. I found his stories of getting hitches into towns or staying in someone's garage for free rather awesome after having shown the target a magic trick of some kind.

He explained that he and his family were staying the night in Katahdin Stream Campground and that he would give me a ride so that Woodstock and Wales wouldn't have to pay an additional fourteen dollar fee just to drive in and pick me back up at the end of the day.

And though I had offered him gas money, he wouldn't accept it.

I took off across the road towards the AT with a steady drizzle falling upon me...hoping that once I had reached the campgrounds, he wouldn't stand me up.

It was 3:45 P.M. when I reached Katahdin Stream Campground after starting at 10 A.M. that morning. Sure enough, when I walked to Magic Mikes campsite, he introduced me to his wife and son. His nephew was with them as well; 13 years old, uninterested in anything—with his hoodie covering his face and a Nintendo 3DS in his hand.

He looked bored and certainly not interested in the concept of camping or hiking.

But Magic Mike exclaimed his 8-year-old son Dylan wanted to thru-hike someday himself and had even already chosen a trail name for himself.

"I want them to call me *Boogers*." He said enthusiastically.

I raised an eyebrow and looked at his parents who smiled. I guess they didn't find the name strange.

"Why, Boogers?" I asked. He only shrugged before letting out an intolerable shriek and running off...laughing.

I covered my throbbing ear.

I wasn't sure how I was supposed to react to any of that, and luckily Magic Mike was ready to go.

So I said my goodbyes as Dylan waved from behind a boulder at me.

Meanwhile, Mike's nephew never even bothered to look up from his video game.

As we drove away, Magic Mike explained he was going to town to grab some soda and chips for their family's dinner, but that he could drop me off first unless I needed to pick something up there.

I thought it would be fun to surprise Wales and Woodstock with some foot long veggie subs from Subway...so I took the free ride into town with him.

He asked about my experiences while I had been out on the trail and I told him about my mistakes, my failures, and my learning lessons. He claimed he had been reading a guy's journal online with stories that were quite similar to mine. That's when I realized that I hadn't even given this guy my trail name yet, or even a name at all.

I apologized for being so rude, before telling him I went by the name "Morris the Cat".

"YOU'RE Morris the Cat?! I thought you looked a little familiar! So when are you planning to finish the trail already? At the rate you're going, you won't be done until December!" He laughed.

I chuckled lightly, and then shrugged as I stared out the window.

"Maybe I won't finish," I replied watching trees pass by along the side of the road while he drove.

"Hey...I wasn't trying to be a jerk or anything..." He quickly tried to clarify, but I held my hand up and smiled.

"It's not you. I just question how much more I'm willing to put up with sometimes. That's all. After six months in the woods day in and day out, you just about start to feel isolated." I tried to explain.

"But you aren't in the woods every day. I mean you disappeared into Manhattan for a week or two. Back in Damascus, you took a week off. You wrote that in your journal entries at least."

"This hike is what you make of it, right? We carve our paths out here. We hike our hikes the way WE want to walk them. Just like we are told to do from the beginning. If I stay out on the trail too long, I feel lonely, and miserable due to the constant rain, lack of social interaction, the bug bites and poison ivy, oak or sumac, cuts, and infections. Just the hardships of everyday life out here. What I'm saying I guess, is that I miss my home. I left North Carolina and a simple life behind, and there are days that I regret that decision. I honestly miss drinking beer, eating pizza on my comfortable couch and making a decent living—so that money isn't an issue. And as sad as it is, I actually miss my pretend ex-girlfriend as well, with our fake mutual friends that have all but dumped me." I explained as he listened.

"Now I'm two grand in debt to a credit card I can't afford to pay off. I owe three thousand to an apartment complex I left and abandoned early. And the only money I have left to carry me the rest of the way home is two grand. A thousand of which is nothing more than credit. I'm contemplating taking this money, and trying to get my life back in order." I ended.

Magic Mike smiled.

"Are you gonna make it?" he asked.

"I kinda feel burnt out at times."

Magic Mike went on to tell me about some of the hardships he had faced when he'd given the trail a go, back in '83. He even stated that there were places he wasn't even sure he knew where the trail picked up and that he was sure it was better marked now than it was back then.

"You guys these days have ultra-light gear, you have guidebooks with detailed maps and water sources listed in it. You have GPS satellites and prepackaged dehydrated food like Mountain House. It's easy compared to what we old timers went through." He said, almost with a bit of bragging in his voice. And he was right. I thought he had every reason to boast.

Mike pulled into an IGA, and meanwhile I went and grabbed food at the Subway across the street for me, Woodstock and Wales.

While standing there waiting for my food to finish being made, I received a text message from my phone carrier which stated: "As a reminder, your service will be discontinued as of Sept. 4th."

Well, this was NEWS TO ME?!

I received my subs, thanked the cashier and stood outside as I called my service carrier, Sprint.

"So there's nothing you can do? You do realize it's not my fault you guys don't have towers up ANYWHERE...right? What the hell am I supposed to do now?" I yelled into the phone.

"Sir, that's not up to me. We attempted to contact you several months ago with this same warning and we never received a reply."

"I'm hiking the Appalachian Trail. I'm not exactly in town to receive your messages every single day." I bitterly spat back.

"Okay sir, I don't even know what an *Appalachian Trail* is. But you need to understand that it's not cost effective for Sprint to keep you as a customer when it costs us just as much to pay service providers from the other towers you utilize when you're roaming." The client service representative replied.

"I have been with you guys for over nine years. When I first signed up, I was paying for unlimited talk, data, and text and roaming. I'd like to know when the hell Sprint decided to take away my unlimited roaming and then give me some arbitrary capacity limit they then NEVER TOLD ME ABOUT!" I shouted back.

I took a breath as the man talked, gave excuses and told me there was nothing he could do and that the decision was final.

"Hey, you know what? Don't bother. I'm sorry for yelling at you. It's not your fault at all. Have a beautiful day." I said briefly, just before simply hanging up.

It was time I started looking into purchasing a second phone.

Magic Mike dropped me off at Abol Bridge, saying just before I left: "A guy I knew once had a great saying. He wrote: *I don't want to die wondering what if, I could've done that. I want to die being able to say I remember when I did.* You know that quote?" He asked me, smiling.

I was amazed.

I did know the quote.

I had made it, during one of my self-empowering rants I had blathered on about in an attempt to inspire hope not only in myself, but in others before starting out on the Appalachian Trail.

I was impressed that this complete stranger had remembered it through all of my ramblings, and that this had been the second time in my journey somebody had quoted my own words to me.

"Don't give up Morris..." He said through his rolled down window.

I had heard those words before too. Many people had said them to me.

"I can't promise that I'll finish," I said. His face immediately began to drop.

"But I can promise that I'll *try*," I said as I held out my hand to him.

He shook it through the open window, smiling again and wishing me well as he drove off.

First day in the 100 mile wilderness while south bound, Woodstock and I stumble upon this incredible sunset on a crystal clear pond.

CHAPTER 4

Katahdin & the 100 Mile Wilderness

We were hiking at 7 A.M., and Wales had taken off ahead of us, jumping excitedly and clapping his hands together in anticipation.

A blink later, and he had completely danced out of our sights.

The first mile up Katahdin was flat. Here, we competed with other day hikers for a place on the trail ahead. While there were many instances of playing leapfrog with these other people, most times we found ourselves waiting in a queue. So we trudged along behind them in line or waited for them to climb that next boulder and heft their weight over the next ridge.

Sometimes we'd even assist them over rocks.

The first mile was very much a "warm up" stage whereas in the second mile—rocks and roots started to crowd and barge their way towards the center of the trail. At this point, we were trying to avoid small baseball sized stones that rolled around beneath our feet or the slippery root stairs coated with morning dew that offered absolutely no traction of any sort.

Upon reaching the Katahdin Stream Bridge crossing, this made for the perfect opportunity to not only fill up our water bottles but to use "The Last Privy" on the trail.

"Do you even have to go?" Woodstock asked as I stood before the door to the outhouse.

"By God, I'll squeeze a couple drops out of myself if I have to, just to say I've used the last toilet on the AT," I replied.

"What an accomplishment," Woodstock replied, rolling his eyes.

The trail started to gain a constant intensity by the third mile. Our warm up was thoroughly over. Now we had begun climbing hand over hand as we charged up rocky streams or utilized tree trunks, branches, and just a little upper body strength to pull ourselves up and over the boulder ledges.

"Whoa, watch out!" I heard suddenly and felt someone's hand tug the back of my shirt rather hard.

I looked back and saw Woodstock.

"What the hell are you doing?" I asked.

"There's *shit* on the trail. Look!" Woodstock said, pointing to the dark brown blob covered with toilet paper, directly in front of me.

I immediately felt sick, as other hikers behind us pushed past in disgust. They appeared almost accusatory in their expressions, as if I should have had the answers for why it was there.

"No consideration at all. You have to be a real scum bag to do this." I said, shaking my head from side to side as I stepped around the human turd.

As we continued to climb, we found even more defecation.

Now I want to make sure it's understood, that before you break the tree line—there was plenty of room to go off into the woods for just a little bit more modesty and cleanliness if you absolutely had to. However, some lazy hiker hadn't felt like doing that at all. Which also made me wonder how he or she got away with it, due to the gross amount of traffic on the trail that morning.

And it made me think how animalistic we as humans, still were. To give no regard to the hundreds or thousands of people behind them that could have accidentally fallen or stepped into this person's defecation.

I watched a kid stop, bend over, and pick up a feces covered piece of toilet paper on the side of the trail that had been covering yet another human poop.

"Mom, what's this?" he asked with blind naiveté.

"Don't touch that!" she screamed at him, before smacking his hand. The kids face immediately bound up in anger with tears on the edges.

Luckily I had a bit of Purell sanitizer on hand, and I squirted a blob onto his palms as I passed by.

Early that morning, a ranger had told us that there would be a total of five false summits before we reached the infamous Baxter Peak sign.

I had reached my first one, as I crawled out of the wood line at about 2.4 miles in. This was where the rock climbing began.

It was almost a lot like an adult's jungle gym. I had to put my back against stone walls, and shimmy up or pivot to an adjacent ledge by lightly jogging and then jumping from boulder to boulder.

In the last mile after finally topping the ridge line, hikers found themselves upon a rather flat landscape, devoid of anything other than small plants and shin-high bushes. We crossed Thoreau's stream where there was a plaque dedicated to him and the first book ever written about Maine's wilderness.

The last mile had us passing the pond on the mountain top and scaling Katahdin itself.

And the looks were deceiving.

"We're never gonna reach it..." I muttered breathlessly to Woodstock who wiped away beads of sweat from the corners of his eyes.

"You're right. We should probably turn around and go back home." He said, with a smirk.

I chuckled and thought it would've been the most angering and anti-climactic thing I could have ever done in my life—if just a few hundred feet away from the top I had said: "The hell with that. I'm going home" and turned to walk back down the mountain.

When we reached Baxter's peak, there was a crowd of 30 or 40 people in and around the sign and taking pictures. I snuck in snapshots of "The Cathedral" and the "Knifes Edge."

After eating a light lunch, we made the insane trek back down the mountain. By the halfway point my knees felt as if the cartilage between the joints had been reduced to grains of sand.

The bones screamed in agony during the decent. However, I was too filled with pride and ecstasy to care. I had conquered the Northern end of the AT, and I had been witness to some of the most impressive and incredible scenery my eyes had ever seen.

"What do you think?" Wales asked me, holding up a slice of his cheese pizza.

"It's alright, I guess," I said with a shrug.

Meanwhile, Woodstock had nearly wolfed down his entire pie.

We were celebrating the completion of Katahdin with Angelo's Pizza for dinner. We sat out front of The Pamola Motor Lodge with exhausted, but distant expressions as we re-lived the views from the day in our awe-struck minds.

"I still think you fellows should have attempted the Knife's Edge. It was remarkable." Wales exclaimed.

"Did you get any pictures of it?" I asked.

He handed me his phone. The picture he had taken was only semi-remarkable. Something you couldn't honestly feel or experience without being there in person.

"Well Wales, you forget we're not all built like an athlete such as yourself," Woodstock said, polishing the last bit of pizza sauce and grease from his fingertips.

"It's a bit sad, now that I've done it," I said out loud.

There was silence, as they both looked over to me.

"These last few days I was seeing the expressions of other passing hikers now getting to the end of their journey. Meanwhile, we're still so far from finishing ourselves. It almost all seems like a dream." I said more to myself than to either of them.

"You were all for flipping," Woodstock clarified.

"Yeah, I know. But think about it. We're never going to see a sight for the rest of our journey that's even remotely as remarkable as that ending we just completed today." I said.

"I'll be ending in Harpers Ferry," Wales said suddenly, as his face seemed devoid of all excitement.

"I think I end in a parking lot near Annapolis Rocks." Woodstock chimed in.

"And I end in a parking lot as well. But also a General Store and the Appalachian Trail Museum, in Pine Grove Furnace, Pennsylvania." I said with just a bit of a somber tone.

Before jumping back into the 100 Mile Wilderness, we were going to enjoy a day off.

We had utilized Priceline to secure a cheap room at The Pamola Motor Lodge there in Millinocket. The building had seen better days. The flooring appeared warped, and there was black mold in sections up on the ceilings. The cigarette burns in the mattresses, the pubic hairs left on the sheets and the television from 1975, had left our interest rather reserved.

"Christ, you call this a *celebration room*? I'm likely to catch crabs from the sheets here, instead of a decent night's sleep." I grumbled as I followed Woodstock upstairs.

Initially, Wales was still sitting in the car out front, playing on his phone. He had made plans to sleep outside rather than in the room with us.

However with five hours until dark, we had invited him to come up and use the shower before he took off with the car and left Woodstock and me to our humble abode.

As he showered, Woodstock watched television while I planned our course for the next few days hike. Suddenly, the phone to our room rang.

"Hello?" I answered.

"Hey, I'm going to need to see you and the fella stayin' in the room with you real quick downstairs."

I explained this to Woodstock, and we shrugged unsure of what to expect as we walked downstairs to the counter.

"Get out, no refunds!" the owner shouted at us.

"Or I can just call the police!" the owner added with contempt.

I laughed in awe, as did Woodstock at the gall of this guy.

"What would you be calling the police for?" Woodstock asked, with an incredulous and airy tone about him.

"You tried to sneak in a third person. It'll cost ten dollars extra for him."

"The website Priceline gives us a set price. I don't ever even have to pay YOU a dime, to begin with. You collect your money from Priceline. I've already paid sixty dollars and stated the amount of people that would be staying in the room. You can't just up and charge me ten extra dollars just because you want to." Woodstock replied matter-of-factly.

"Those are MY rules. You hikers come in here all the time and sneak your fuckin' friends in here. Not anymore. It's ten dollars an extra person." he said.

"You can't just make up the rules whenever you like..." I began.

"I can make up any rules I fuckin' want. I OWN THIS MOTOR LODGE." he snapped back at me.

"This *dump* you mean? You can have it, and we'll stay somewhere else. Just reimburse me." Woodstock said, leaning on the counter.

"I can't believe you, morons. You *criminals* come in here and try to steal money out of my families and my pockets." the guy's wife, who had also appeared to work the check-in counter whined.

"Lady, nobody's talking to you. Just shut up." I said annoyed, with a dismissive tone. Well her husband didn't like that very much.

"Don't talk to my wife like that. No refunds and you can get off of my property," he said, crossing his arms over his chest.

It was clear as day that Woodstock wanted to punch the guy in the face because lord knows I wanted to myself.

"Come on Woodstock, let us call Priceline and see if we can get our money back," I said.

"No. I'm not going anywhere, till this piece of shit gives me my money back. He can't just up and decide when and where he can add charges on for no reason at all." Woodstock said, looking at me flush faced.

That was all the owner needed to hear.

He walked into the back room and made a quiet phone call.

The man's wife then laughed and shook her head from side to side.

"You shoulda just left. Now my brother is on his way." The woman said with a confident smile.

"Oh No! Not your inbred brother. What's he gonna do? Give your husband a kiss?" Woodstock asked, instigating the situation even more.

"I'm about to kick this guys ass if you don't hurry and get here." The owner said louder, over the phone from the back room.

I already knew that this wasn't boding well for us and that if nothing else, we would, in fact, be ejected from the property. As a result, I asked Woodstock not to lose his cool while I went back upstairs to retrieve our things as well as Wales.

"Why are they calling the police," was the first thing Wales asked. His gaze lazily rolled over from watching Monty Python playing on television, to me.

"The owner and Woodstock got into it because he's trying to charge us an extra ten dollars for a third person to stay in here," I said with a sigh as I sat down on the corner of the bed.

"I'm not staying, though. I'm sleeping outside tonight." Wales replied, looking back towards the television.

"Yeah, but the owner doesn't believe us. Says hikers sneak in people here all the time."

"So let's just give the guy ten bucks," Wales replied distantly, apparently absorbed with the happenings on the TV more so than the coming of police officers.

I grabbed the remote for the television and turned it off.

"Hey!" He protested.

"I think the situations got too far past that option. Come on. Let's go." I said.

The police officer that appeared was clearly off duty. As we explained our side of the story to him; much as predicted, it was utterly pointless.

"Dude, let's go. This cop doesn't give a shit because he's related to the woman in there," I said.

The officer looked apologetic almost in his demeanor but held firm to the fact that we needed to leave or else we would be arrested.

"I want a supervisor out here," Woodstock demanded, as I sighed and shook my head. I glanced over at Wales who was watching the whole show from the comfort of the passenger's side front seat.

He looked more upset over the fact that he wasn't going to finish his Monty Python episode than he was that we were getting evicted from a room we had just paid for.

When a second police officer (Sergeant) arrived on the scene, he got us to move our vehicle to the opposite side of the road, and then he proceeded to explain that we would be arrested if we stepped back onto the property. It was two in the afternoon when this whole situation had kicked off, and now it was nearly four.

Finally, after joint reasoning between Wales and I, we got Woodstock to back off by practically pulling him to his car while he shouted angrily at the officer and the officer's supervisor.

The good news was, that after we had contacted Priceline, we were reimbursed, so the owner of Pamola Motor Lodge never got paid.

I had 900 miles remaining, and sixty of those existed within the Hundred Mile Wilderness. Over the course of the next few days, the three of us would get hit by an onslaught of storms and precipitation that would make hiking through those backwoods and swamps so much more unbearable than the mosquitoes had already made it.

I looked outside at the downpour from the safety of my hammock as Woodstock packed away his tent.

"We gotta get going. We're running out of time," he called out to me. I had felt the urge to pretend that I hadn't heard him when in fact I had.

The reason we were so behind was the day before we had only completed seven miles which had taken us to Little Wilson Falls, where we camped out for the evening under clouds of mosquitoes and blankets of ticks.

"My ear is still killing me. I think I have tinnitus or something. My eardrum won't stop twitching like crazy." I said, as I unzipped my bug net and swung my legs out. Immediately, I was greeted by the bloodsuckers impatiently awaiting me.

"You need to find a minute clinic or go to the hospital?" He asked, as he stopped packing his things and looked back at me. His face was sympathetic, and I was appreciative of that. He had been sincere, and it was one of the only times he hadn't been sarcastic in his response.

"We'll see," I said, with a forced smile.

A few days later, I had broken off of the Appalachian Trail altogether and had started stumbling down old logging roads that had made for easier paths.

I texted Woodstock and told him where I thought I was at.

"why the hell did you get off the trail?" he texted me.

"dunno. guess I thought I could cut some mileage by taking flat roads instead of those boulder fields they called the AT" I had replied.

I figured I was somewhere along Ki Road and I was passed by two trucks as I huffed along through the rain. I had planned on taking Ki to Katahdin Iron Works Road where I would hop back onto the AT and eventually meet up with Woodstock again. But for the time being that would have to wait because it was nearly dark and I needed to end my day.

I had found an overgrown road that looked as if it hadn't been driven on in almost a decade. I walked the shrub packed path as it curved through the forest and out of line-of-site from the road.

I then threw my tarp up and above the space between two trees that would house my hammock that evening. This would also aid in keeping out the heavy downpour of rain throughout the night.

Loons sang their eerie, sad song in the distance while rain pitter-pattered atop my tarp.

Despite the gross amount of body glide slathered on, my chafe still burned like molten metal had been poured on the flesh of my inner thighs, left to solidify, and then ripped off. It then felt as if somebody had then packed the fresh wounds with salt and lime juice.

I whimpered, waddling down the logging road like some morbidly obese penguin. My hair was wild, face unshaven and I had 'crazy eyes' darting around, back and forth. To take my mind off of the pain, I decided to play a rather amusing game.

I called this specific form of entertainment: Count to 30, 30 times. I'd done this plenty of times during my journey when I had gotten tired of 12 hours of walking and thinking. Once the fun of that game had burned itself out, I tried playing trivia with myself. However, that only ended up sucking, because I knew all of the answers to the questions I was asking.

At one point I had also started swinging my walking cane around like a sword, forgetting that it separated into sectional links for easy folding convenience. Well, it turned from a longsword into nun chucks, which with my horseplay, ended up smashing me in the back of the head.

Finally, I started kicking a rock. I had managed to kick it maybe two miles down the forest trail before I accidentally kicked it into a ditch filled with gray-green water.

I watched the rock which had sort of by that time, seemed to have become a friend; disappear beneath the surface with a couple of good-bye air bubbles floating up behind it.

I saw a section of woods standing between me and an adjacent roadway and burst into the tree line, hoping to cut off some mileage.

Unfortunately after struggling through thick shrubbery and small, tightly compacted fir trees I came to a stagnate pond that doubled as a deep mud swamp. I took off my boots and socks which I had no intention of getting any more wet than they already had from the rain the day before.

The water looked too deep to walk through with my backpack on, without getting it soaked so I needed to improvise.

I glanced down at my phone and saw that according to my map and GPS, I was exactly in the middle of NOWHERE. No forest path, no trail.

Nothing.

The road I had been walking upon had dead-ended two miles back and if I tried to go *around* the swamp, it was sure to add several miles.

I sat down and removed some Paracord from my pack that Torry had given me back in Waynesboro, Virginia.

It took maybe 45 minutes to an hour to find the pieces of wood I needed to build it, but I had strung together a makeshift raft. It dangerously dipped beneath the water once I placed the craft into the swamp. It hadn't been my intention to swim through the middle of a swamp, mostly because I wasn't aware of the wildlife in the area. I was used to growing up in the south, where cottonmouths swam the waterways, ready to bite you with their venomous fangs. I wasn't sure if I could expect the same thing up here in the North. In fact, I wasn't aware of any poisonous snakes in Maine at all and immediately realized how ill-equipped I was even when it came to basic knowledge.

As I looked down into that primordial soup, with potentially thousands of years of rotting vegetation and animal matter decaying on the swamp floor; I began to wonder if I would emerge from that bog with parasites and leeches coating every inch of my body.

When I put my backpack on the raft, it sunk precariously deeper than I had intended it to. The weight and balance seemed to have been off because my pack nearly rolled into the swamp to be lost forever.

So with me not knowing really how to build a watercraft, and with a way around the marsh looking as if it would have added a mile or two, I put the second level of wood on top and a thicker base piece to add to the buoyancy on one side.

Once I sat my pack on top this time around, it started to sink deeper than I had wanted it to once more. I was a breath away from saying the hell with it and finding another way, but took a moment to calm down.

It was at this time; most men usually trashed whatever they had been working on in anger, frustration, and hopelessness. But I knew, I didn't want to go back even more than I wanted to destroy my makeshift raft at that moment.

I tied a leash to the raggedy craft and took off everything but my boxers and threw my clothes on top of my backpack.

As I waded through a black and amber color toned swamp, I repeatedly had to remind myself that this wasn't North Carolina and I didn't have to worry about some poisonous snake or animal roaming around in the depths below. Hopefully. But then again, I wasn't so sure about that either every time I felt something brush against my thighs or feet.

"Stay calm. It's all okay..." I whispered out loud, as I swam.

I reached a rotted tree in the middle of the swamp, whose decaying roots dove straight into the gunk ten feet beneath my feet. As I clung to one of the roots, it suddenly snapped, and one of the largest spiders I had ever seen in my life had become startled and crawled out from a crevice down along my arm.

"AIIIIIIEEEEEE!" I screeched at the highest pitch humanly possible as I shook and flailed my arms about wildly. I dived beneath the surface of the muddy marsh water.

When I came back up, I looked around and no longer saw the spider. However, I felt something crawling on the top of my head and down along the side of my right temple. This resulted in eliciting another scream in horror, as I knew for certain that spider had clung to my scalp as soon as I resurfaced.

I dove beneath the surface of the water again and started to pull my raft through the water for at least twenty feet until I crashed into another old swamp stump. I resurfaced and tied the cord around my waist. After occasionally bashing the backs of my heels against my raft while swimming, I switched to simply tugging it by hand behind me.

Whenever I tired, I lightly gripped the edge of the raft and let my arms rest momentarily. As I did this, I saw a road crossing directly ahead of me at around seventy feet and began to pick up pace as I made my way towards it.

I had also started to tug too hard in my excitement because some of the branches had begun to separate. The Paracord began to slip off from around the edge of the branches I had tied it to as my raft started to disintegrate before my eyes.

I made a quick remedy in the marsh and then carried on in my rush to the shoreline.

Once I had reached the road, I had to wade through decades of trash bobbing along the shore. Bottles and cans or old pizza boxes half submerged and decaying beneath the water's surface. I pulled myself up and over a rusted drainage pipe, surprised at the intensity of the sun and how its heat had caused the drainage pipe to scald and literally sear my flesh. Once I got my pack up to the road, I was rather dismayed to see how wet it had gotten.

"Forgive me, Gregory; I've never built a raft before," I said to my backpack, apologetically.

Gregory didn't appear very forgiving and if anything—his silence spoke droves about what he really thought of me in that moment.

The path went downhill past a ton of raspberries on my left and right.

Coupled with these were blackberry bushes that had already begun ripening in the sun. I grabbed a handful of both kinds and scarfed them down greedily.

They were fat, juicy and sugary, with just a hint of sour tanginess to them. After eating my fill, I continued along until I came to yet another dead end.

"Christ, it's like a maze out here," I said irritably, as I threw my hands up into the air with frustration. Once again, I had no idea where I was, and my phone didn't have a signal which meant that trying to bring up a map was impossible.

When I turned to my right, a bright blue Chevy truck caught my attention. I hadn't even noticed that it had been there before, as it sat tucked away within a little cul-de-sac in the field.

There was an older fellow in the truck who was in his 70's. Once we had noticed each other, I immediately became aware of the scent of marijuana in the air. The old man quickly flicked the joint into the woods in front of him and tried to stash a little baggie with more in it.

I pretended I didn't notice as I walked up to his truck.

"H...hey there. You're sure in the middle of nowhere, aren't ya? You lost?" He asked me suddenly, clearing his throat with a half cough.

"Yeah, suppose I am. I was hiking through the Hundred Mile Wilderness and got bored. Guess I decided to get lost for a while," I explained.

I offered my hand as I approached his driver's side door.

"I'm Morris the Cat." I said being jovial. I felt bad he had flicked his joint away, thinking I was possibly a narc. However, I found it even odder when I looked down inside his vehicle that he wasn't wearing any boots or shoes. Not even socks or flip-flops.

Just a pair of pale, bony, bare feet resting upon his floorboard.

"Terry, nice to meet'cha. So you going to Katahdin?" He asked.

I thought my whole story would take forever to explain, regarding my flip-flop, so I just said: "Yeah, that's the plan."

"Well, you're almost there." He said taking out a cigarette from his shirt pocket.

"Could I get one of those...?" I asked.

"You smoke?" He asked, eyeing me cautiously.

"Occasionally, when I can afford it. Which isn't much these days." I replied truthfully.

"I mean, do you SMOKE." He corrected himself, emphasizing the word 'smoke.'

I knew what he had meant immediately.

Especially from being out here on the trail.

"Weed? Nah. But I saw you flicked your joint away. Didn't have to stop on *my* account." I said, lighting the Pall Mall Light 100 he had given me.

"Well, you coulda been a game warden sniffing around out here." He said laughing as he took a drag from his cigarette.

I smiled.

"I grew up, running around in these woods so I know this area well. Probably when I was in my early twenties, those trees weren't there," he said, pointing to the expansive tree line directly in front of us.

"Lots o' logging goes on out heer'yah". It was disheartening to hear that and the fact that the trail was always coming and going due to logging.

"But Gorman Campground Road is still there. Only now they have it barred off." He exclaimed.

I hadn't any idea what the hell he was talking about, as he re-lived his memories out loud.

"Well, how do I get back to the AT?" I asked.

"Theoretically if you go straight, you'll eventually run into it again down a series of old gravel roads." he replied.

Well that wasn't vague at all, was it?

I wished the man well, though he had been kind enough to offer me a ride.

I had gotten lost on my own, and I was determined to find my way back on my own.

The trees were thick and looked rather spindly and nubile for having been there for so many years. But the terrain was flooded. You could barely make out the ruts of old tire track trails littered with the fully grown trees, stumps or rocky mud pits sitting about like landmines.

I saw old, dry rotted and faded ribbons; pink and blue tied to random trees.

Maybe they are there to mark a border of some kind? I thought to myself.

I came across three blue blazes and began to follow them, thinking it was a trail of some sort until they stopped appearing. It was possible that they had been marked for cutting at some point in the past. It was also entirely possible they had only been there to mark yet another border.

I just didn't know.

As I stumbled through grass and shrubs as high as my neck; I tripped over a root, and tried to catch my balance. However, all I succeeded in doing was stepping into a pit and sinking up to my knees in black gunk.

I realized now why this road had no longer existed on any maps, despite the obvious in that it was overgrown.

It appeared that over the decades, it had nearly washed away.

There were old logging cuts that had been carved into the earth years ago. It was almost as if the vehicle that had created those divots in the land had driven right through the trees themselves.

I struggled to pull my legs out, losing both boots in the process as they were sucked from my feet. I reached down into the mud holes and pulled them back out.

As I sat in mud putting them back on, I was harassed by mosquitos and yellow flies biting me everywhere they could find open flesh.

I just needed to get out of there, so I followed a set of moose tracks, realizing that they were headed in the direction of Indian Pond.

If I had made it there...I could monitor the shoreline in the general direction of Katahdin Iron Works Road which the AT crossed.

The moose trail led to a waist high grass road that hadn't been driven on in seemingly forever. I could see why too. Every quarter mile there were deep, and steep stream crossings that looked impossible for anything other than an ATV to cross it with.

Eventually, I made it to a locked forest gate. This might have been the very one; Terry had mentioned.

It had an old faded sign that stated: "Do not block Emergency Access."

I wondered why somebody had locked the gate shut to begin with.

I had made it that far simply by guessing my way through the wilderness, and I didn't feel the specific need to add any more unnecessary mileage in search for the Appalachian Trail. So I followed the gravel road, instead.

Upon reaching the AT after a last five-mile sprint, I went half a mile down to where hikers were meant to ford the West Branch Pleasant River.

Just as I was about to cross, I found out from a ridge runner on the opposite side that I wasn't allowed to camp anywhere for the next 5 miles.

"Might want to stay on *that* side of the river!" he called over to me.

So I trudged sadly back across the river and set my tent up there. It was 4 P.M., and I was bushed. I was also many miles ahead of Woodstock.

After eating dinner, I crawled into my hammock and not ten minutes later I heard: "Morris?"

I guess it was a good thing I didn't have my earphones in at the time because I'd have never heard Wales call my name.

"What's goin' on dude?" I asked as Wales suppressed his excitement from seeing a familiar face after the days he had spent alone, and in the rain, we had been subjected to.

And it immediately felt good to complain about the weather. It was comfortable to trade stories about terrain and the way I had done the last sections of the trail.

"Of course you went off the trail. You HAVE to make your journal entries interesting *somehow*." He said laughing as I joined in.

While it had been a difficult experience, it had been a damn fun one now that it was over. It was also the first time I had ever built a raft as well. And while my pack had still gotten wet, who cared? I had made it!

Before dark completely settled in, Wales and I would check a couple of campsites closer to the road the way I had come to see if Woodstock had made it in that evening. However, we wouldn't see him that night at all.

In the morning we would continue on in opposite directions.

There was something to be said about these privies at times. The Carl Newhall Shelter definitely had something that needed to be said about them. Things that had been noted in the logbooks there as well.

This was, that the privy was *disgusting*.

I looked at the mounds of fecal matter nearly bulging out of the toilet seat itself within the outhouse and immediately felt as if I was about to wretch the scant remnants of my breakfast all over the earth. Instead I slammed the door shut and stepped back with disgust.

People had stopped using the privy due to its current state and had instead—started to defecate in the woods surrounding the dilapidated structure. Piles of used toilet paper surrounded the building and run off from past rainstorms had left a trail of flies and maggots in a turd filled, slow-moving yellowish stream behind the outhouse.

Inside the shelter, somebody had even smeared fecal matter along the walls.

As I looked at the destruction of the forest surrounding me, I felt sudden disgust towards fellow hikers due to the state of the forest in the immediate area. To simply toss used toilet paper on the ground without even attempting to bury it, was pathetic, to say the least.

Rather animalistic and lazy to be exact.

Over the next few miles, I cleared 900 feet and still had around 1,600 to go before I would summit White Cap Mountain.

I hit the first 600 feet straight up like a champ, though admittedly I did have to stop several times from lack of oxygen flowing to my brain.

I reached the Gulf Hagas summit at 2,680 feet or something, only to find I didn't care.

That was because there had been no views available, *to care about*.

I refilled my three water bottles at a nearby stream and began my next uphill portion. This was a 700-foot section that I knocked out in less than 30 minutes, but man was it exhausting. At this summit (West Peak) I threw my pack onto the ground and collapsed.

Had I really considered going as far as fifteen miles that day?

It was 3:36 P.M. and I was losing daylight.

Though I didn't trust AWOL's guide because of how often it had been wrong or grossly under exaggerated, a huge part of me had wanted to believe that I had no more climbs for the rest of the day. As I looked at his terrain map, though, I knew I was going to be disappointed.

I always was.

The trail went back down 150+ feet before the death march up White Cap finally began. My legs felt like jelly, and I was wondering how I had planned on handling The Green Mountains of Vermont or the White Mountain range through New Hampshire when these easier hills were giving me such a hard time.

As I summited and watched the sunset, I looked at my guidebook and found that I'd only hiked 11.5 miles that day.

I took out my phone and checked to see if I finally was able to receive a signal, so high up in the mountains. I wasn't that surprised to find that I had been roaming when I received a text from Wales.

The text message read: "Woodstock has been trying to reach you. he says he wont make it to the car til tuesday"

If that were the case, I wouldn't NEED to push out another five miles that day past Logan Brook shelter. Instead, I could take my time.

When I arrived at camp, there were two SOBO's (Southbounders) in the lean-to that called out a "Hello!" and a "How are you?"

I was slightly dismissive as I said "Hello" back and vanished quite quickly and purposefully from their sights. I was tired, hungry and in pain. Furthermore, I was convinced I'd never see them again anyways—as if that crass and selfish excuse was justification in and of itself to be anti-social.

After finishing my evening chores, I began to feel guilty for how I had ignored them. So I limped back up towards the shelter, apologizing if I'd been rude.

The older gentleman went by the name "Re-pack" while the other younger hiker went by "Patches."

There were a lot of "Patches" on the trail that year, and I found I couldn't keep up with them all.

Re-Pack had thru-section hiked sections of the AT in the past and was finishing up the trail this year. He was headed to New Hampshire where he would complete it within the next three weeks.

Patches, on the other hand, was in it for the long haul as a thru-hiker walking all the way to Springer Mountain, Georgia.

The infancy of my knowledge, as I listened to those that had done all of this before me, was eye opening.

I was by no means an expert, but they were both asking *me* questions about the trail further south, and it felt strange that I actually had the knowledge to share with them.

At the beginning of my journey, I had been in their shoes, asking and learning everything that I could. I had been laughed off and ignored by arrogant former thru-hikers that had long since failed themselves while I'd kept on. And it made me feel good to know that my responses never had to be anything like theirs had been to me.

Now, I could share what I had experienced firsthand.

The following day I came to a road crossing with a sign nailed into a tree reading: Jo Mary Rd - 13.8 M.

This meant that AWOL's 2012 Guidebook had been off by more than five miles.

Upon reaching Jo Mary Road, I waited for two hours before Woodstock walked in,

I waved my arms enthusiastically in the air.

"It's time for McDonald's, my friend!" I shouted happily to him.

"Oh man, I'm gonna order a ton of McDoubles," he replied.

After driving a few miles down the road to go and pick up Wales, we came upon a cable fence that had orange ribbons tied to it for visibility.

We were maybe fifty feet from Highway 11.

"What is that?" I asked, pointing towards the cable blocking our way.

Woodstock peered through his dirty windshield and then fished through papers and registrations stashed on his dashboard.

"You have to turn in the receipt Wales left us, for the entry fee," he explained. I took the receipt and started to drive on before Woodstock told me to hold for a moment.

"What's wrong?" I asked.

"The receipt is to drive ONE guy out. Not *two*. I don't want them to charge me for leaving." he explained.

"Do you have any cash on you?" I asked. He shook his head no, and I quickly explained to him that I didn't have any on me either.

"Where's your pack cover?" Woodstock asked as he hopped into the backseat.

"It's in the front pocket on my backpack. Why do you need it?" I inquired.

"I'm going to hide beneath it," he replied as he removed it and pulled it up and over his body.

"This is ridiculous," I began.

"Just drive!" He said in a hushed tone.

I parked at the cable fence, and got out; slowly climbing the wooden steps up the front porch and into the main office of what looked to be somebodies home. I stopped momentarily and glanced back at Woodstock who was childishly peeking out from beneath my pack cover.

I shook my head and walked in.

I handed the receipt to an old man, who squinted his eyes up at me from behind his desk and then glanced out of the window towards the vehicle.

"So why's yer buddy hidin' 'neath a tarp in the back seat of your car?" the man asked me. I felt like a complete idiot. Of course, I had to be the one going through this moment of embarrassment and not Woodstock, the guy causing it.

"I don't think he was trying to hide actually. I believe he said he was sleepy, so he may just be trying to shield out the sun." I lied.

The old man grunted as if that was the worst excuse he had ever heard.

Only he didn't know that when I lied, I tended to run at the mouth a bit more than usual as if I had to make up some grand story to explain unusual circumstances that would ONLY happen to me.

"I mean...I don't even know who he is. He just asked if I could give him a ride into town." I explained. The old man read over my receipt slowly.

"So your taller buddy the other day, said that only *one* of you were coming out. And that's what this paperwork here says too." He explained, as he sat back in his chair and set the receipt down on the desk in front of him.

"Well yeah, but that guy in the car is just hitching a ride with me from the trail crossing. I'm taking him to Millinocket for the night." I replied.

"Doesn't matter. It'll be twelve dollars." He said coldly.

"Hold on a second. You're charging for a guy LEAVING the trail?!" I asked.

"Well, your friend had to cross through the landowner's property to get here. So regardless of if he came in through the trail or not...he's currently sitting on our right of ownership now." The man finished.

I had the sudden urge to kick the old man's desk against the wall, pinning him behind it and shouting out the window to Woodstock to "Gun it!"

I would then kick open the door and hop into the backseat as Woodstock peeled off, leaving a cloud of dust in his wake.

In reality, I only shook my head in disbelief, thinking of the many fees associated with the AT through Maine. It made me never want to return to the state because of it—in all honesty.

"Well, I'll go see if he has any money," I said with a defeated tone as I walked out of the building to the car.

As soon as I had opened the door, Woodstock whispered: "Are we good to go?"

"Here's the deal. He saw you and said it'll be twelve dollars. They don't take cards, only cash. I told him you're just a hitchhiker I picked up on the trail while headed out."

"But I don't even have twelve bucks in cash on me and neither do you," Woodstock replied as he removed the pack cover from his head. He had been sweating profusely beneath it in the heat while hiding.

"Well, this was YOUR idea to hide beneath a pack cover when we were right in front of the shack, to begin with. As if he wouldn't see us." I complained angrily.

"Oh, because your *hitchhiker story* clearly went over so well with him." Woodstock shot back sarcastically. I only rolled my eyes as he got out and we both climbed the steps towards the gate house.

When we walked in, the old man looked back from the small television he had behind him, playing a Judge Judy rerun; and smiled up at us both.

"Twelve dollars please." the man said, holding his hand out.

"Listen. That's fine that there's a fee and all to leave, but I don't have any cash." Woodstock explained. The man smiled as if he'd heard the story a million times before.

"Well, that's unfortunate. I don't know how you're going to get past that gate unless you have some bolt cutters on you," he explained, as he swiveled in his seat and looked back towards the television behind him.

"You can't keep us, hostage, here," I said flatly.

"No, but I can call the police for trespassing." he replied with a light chortle.

We stood there in silence for a couple of minutes trying to figure out what to do, until the man finally spoke again

"So you're going to Millinocket tonight and coming back tomorrow to finish the northern portion of the wilderness?" The gatekeeper asked Woodstock.

"We're done with the Hundred Mile..." I began, as Woodstock elbowed me in the ribs and cut in.

"Yes, sir. After this kind man drops me off there in Millinocket, I'll be getting some cash out and coming back here to finish up North." Woodstock lied while nodding his head towards me.

I nodded along and agreed quite quickly, though I was almost certain the old man had seen right through our ruse.

"If I see you here tomorrow, the fees twenty-four dollars just for YOU." He said, pointing to Woodstock who nodded his head agreeably.

"Yes, sir. That is no problem." We both said almost simultaneously. Minutes later we were laughing as we drove off down Highway 11.

"Yeah, we'll be here bright and early tomorrow with your twenty-four bucks." I said sarcastically to Woodstock as he made a crude gesture with his hand and we both burst into laughter.

We had just finished the 100 Mile Wilderness completely having connected the Southern portions to the Northern section of the AT.

We wouldn't ever NEED to come back again.

Woodstock standing at the summit of Katahdin, overlooking the Cathedral.

CHAPTER 5

The Journey South

THE NEXT FEW DAYS ROLLED out beneath cold, but clear blue skies and with them, Avery Peak along with the Bigelows came and went. We made our lives easier in between each task of hills or mountain ranges along the AT that we were tackling—by essentially guilt tripping Wales into taking days off with us in between each summit. This was accomplished by going into town and watching movies or wasting money on alcohol and town food.

Our nights would then be made up of scouring the landscape, forest roads, logging roads and quite often private property just to find a place to sleep for the evening before driving along on our next big four or five-day excursion.

"Only 880 miles left to go," I said to myself out loud, as I stared down at my guide book. Suddenly, I felt the eyes of another person looking towards me.

It was 9:30 A.M. and I was sitting upon my backpack near the shoreline of the Kennebec River. It was here, I had read that according to the guide—an individual or volunteer from the MATC was present to Ferry you across by canoe.

I had wondered what would have happened if I had decided to swim across instead and how quickly I would've sunk beneath the water with my backpack on.

"You tryin' to cross?" the man in the canoe called out to me.

"Yeah, how much is it?" I asked. I thought it was only fair to assume there was some sort of monetary transaction that was supposed to have taken place.

"I won't charge ya, come on." he replied, pulling up to the shore.

The man running the canoe was kind and full of information as he handed me a waiver on a clipboard to sign, as well as a life vest to put on. This was releasing him from any liability in the event I accidentally drown while passing to the other side.

"So I'm just curious. What's the most asked question you get out here?" I wondered out loud. The man thought about it momentarily before responding.

"You get a lot of people asking about when the water levels rise out here. But there are so many hydroelectric dams that run off of this river it's not exactly an accurate or designated time."

"What do the dams have to do with anything?" I asked, just a tad naively.

"Imagine you're crossing a river that's waist deep here in the middle. Suddenly, in three to four minutes it's above your head as some hydro-electric dam releases water miles away upstream, unbeknownst to you," he explained to me. It was quite an image when you thought about it. Especially when imagining yourself in the middle of the river when it all happened.

Struggling for air with a sixty-pound pack clinging to your back and pulling you beneath the surface of the cloudy brown water did not sound like the way I wanted to go.

I found I lived for the moment in these days, only because one day the adventure would ultimately end. The money eventually runs out, and the trail stopped. It's only then our re-emergence into society begins, again. But we look at it with young eyes at times. It's like when you're a kid, and you say to yourself or to your parents: "I'm never gonna get old!"

Then one day you wake up, and you're 30, wondering where the time went.

I watched the silhouette of a man stumble back and forth at the Rangeley parking lot trail head.

He was screaming obscenities, in-between broken words of confusion and crying.

"Why...why, WHY?!" He shouted into the early morning with no one to answer but a far off bird calling into the dawn of morning.

He was picking up branches and smashing them, enraged, against trees and flipping off or shouting curse words at passing cars along the highway.

I watched quietly from within my hammock tent—hidden, unnoticed. I didn't want to be seen or confronted by the angry man.

He was just another trail stranger to me, only he appeared to be homeless and mentally unstable, and I didn't want to become a victim of his misguided rage.

He picked up his small backpack and threw it against a tree just before he began a vicious tirade of violently stomping and kicking the thing.

He collapsed moments later crying out loud: "It wasn't my fault. Everything was BECAUSE OF *BRUCE*!"

He cried into his pack for 20 minutes before standing and somberly putting it back upon his shoulders. His dark black hair was long and clung to his weathered, sweat covered face as he stole a glance into the woods. Even once in my direction.

I remained motionless, as he wiped his eyes and headed off west towards Rangeley with only the thoughts of whatever demons were torturing his mind as he walked along that busy highway.

I boiled a pan of water and tossed in two instant coffee packets, staring at my hands. They shook lightly for a moment without my own doing, before I closed them slowly and dug my fingernails into my palms. Bloodshot eyes looked out into the fog covered woods surrounding me as I removed the pan from the blue flames and turned the gas off on my cook kit.

I sipped the boiling, black substance resting in the pan—clenched between my quivering palms. I was watching squirrels fuss and false charge each other's territory in the branches of the cedar trees above me. They argued and made threatening noises at each other.

I packed my things and went into town.

The locals here could pick out a hiker rather quickly I believed. I didn't pretend to stand out from the crowd any more than anyone else. Though quite often I felt my Frankenstein-like pants made me appear a little more monetarily destitute than most others. My haggard appearance didn't help much either. I had sewn the crotch of my synthetic pants, and then a rip from the belt to the zipper. I had fixed a burn hole that had left a knife-like opening on both pants legs, and then a HUGE cut along the seat of my butt as well. Let me tell you something, in all honesty. By no means have I developed the art of stitching. Oh, I can stitch an opening closed mind you, but I can promise you it won't look stunning.

As the locals eyed me over, they attempted to engage me in conversation and their personal opinions.

They asked me if I'd heard of the missing hiker, Inch Worm. I had heard the name, but I had never met her in person. You could read all sorts of things about her on the flyers posted at trail crossings or in news reports about her disappearance on television.

"They should make it illegal for women to hike the trail." One of the elderly women sitting at the coffee bar insisted.

"I agree. Women aren't built to hike long distances." Another older man that could've been her husband threw in.

I couldn't believe that I was hearing a woman fight for a more sexist and misogynistic society.

"What do you think happened to her?" One of the elderly men asked me.

I had been pretending I hadn't heard them when somebody suddenly spoke up for me.

"She probably got lost and headed out West."

Somebody else said: "The husband probably got rid of her."

They then all started laughing.

I was angry, only because as a hiker myself, I felt a connection with other long distant hikers out there on the trail. I feared for the woman Geraldine Largay, also known as Inch Worm. It had been so long since she had last been seen. Because of that, you had to realize that there may have been a good possibility she had already passed away. Such a rude comment followed by laughter from the group of old folks there made me want to tell them all to *Shut Up* and to *Have Some Respect*. Instead, I kept my mouth closed.

I paid for my drink and left; for the "Town Jackals" to make their judgmental assumptions, spit their opinions and gossip about things they knew nothing about.

It had been quite refreshing to hear from my parents…much as it always was. I whined and complained about the trail, and they were kind enough to lend their ears and listen. My father told me of the people back at work, and my old job at the Plant that asked about me and how I had been doing on a regular basis. Some of these people he had mentioned, had still been following my adventures through my online journal entries. It was crazy to think I had gained such a huge following, doing nothing really but writing about my day to day hikes.

But it felt good to know that people cared about me.

I looked down at the stone sitting in the palm of my hand.

"I still have that rock, I got from the summit of Katahdin," I said, rolling it around and watching the sun glint off of precious minerals ingrained within it.

"So what!" I heard my mother say in the background. I knew now that my father had me on speaker phone because I had suddenly started hearing my mom sobbing.

"Anna, stop it." My dad tried to whisper away from the receiver.

"I don't care about *some rock*, I want my son back!" she shouted, as her voice quivered in-between the tears I knew were falling down her cheeks.

"Dad, tell Mom I'm going to be just fine," I said, shaking my head from side to side.

"She knows, she's just worried about you."

"We read that your cell phone lost service. How are you going to talk to us anymore?" my mother asked, as I heard her clearly taking the phone away from my father.

"Mom, I bought a new phone from Walmart, and it has the same phone number I had before."

"Well good for you. Why don't you just stay out in the woods and kill yourself then like we all know you want to do!" She spat sarcastically, before letting off another string of sobs.

My mother hadn't really meant that, naturally. But it had become clear to me that she thought that the sole reason I had left home in the first place to hike the trail—was because I had wanted to commit suicide. Her thought process (which was ironic when you really thought about it) was that I was on a drug-fueled binge, ready to go any day now. And as bad as I felt with her crying, I also found the whole situation too humorous to believe.

"Mom, you know that I love you guys. I'm not out here to kill myself." I said, half laughing over it all.

"I just want you to come home, Richard." She plead into the receiver.

"I will Mom. But you've gotta believe in me. You guys are the only reason I'm still out here anymore."

I had purchased myself a cheap hamburger and fries as I sat alone inside the building, playing around on my phone and surfing the internet.

I had been looking to purchase a new pair of Keens hiking boots, utilizing the promo code I'd gotten for returning my old ones that had fallen apart back in Bly Gap, North Carolina.

Only my card wouldn't complete the purchase online for some odd reason.

While I ate my dinner, I figured I'd worry about it later and blamed the spotty Wi-Fi signal for the issue. After I had cleaned the plate, I handed the same card to the waitress who would return only moments later to explain that it had been declined.

"You're kidding, right?" I asked in genuine disbelief. There was absolutely no way that there was no more money in my account, unless my bank hadn't been updating my transactions at all.

I asked her to try another credit card reader as I looked about, suddenly noticing I had garnered a few looks from the local populace of Rangeley—judging me and whispering under their breaths.

When the waitress returned, she exclaimed that it had still been declined, even after entering the numbers manually on both machines.

I felt a huge pit hit my stomach.

What was I going to do?

"I uh...I can go try an ATM machine if you'd let me leave and come right back." I offered. The waitress looked me over for a moment before speaking.

"You're a hiker, aren't you? Let me talk to the manager. I'll be right back." She exclaimed as she took up my empty dishes.

Talk to your manager? Oh yeah? Why? So he can call the cops on me? I thought to myself.

I began to look for the closest exit.

My mind was working fast.

I could head north towards Stratton, where I would meet up with Woodstock and Wales, having finished this section of the AT already. Bypassing anybody possibly waiting for me at the trailhead in Rangeley. Hell, I could orienteer off the AT altogether.

I nervously downed the rest of my water and found within my gall that I was only seconds away from standing when I heard a group of teenagers by the door, pointing and laughing at me.

"That has gotta be embarrassing..." One of the guys giggled. I had the sudden urge to beam him square in the face with anything I could potentially grab at that moment. Instead, I merely glared before looking away.

Then, the waitress came back.

"So since your meal was so cheap, the manager said that dinners on the house." She said, handing me proof of the receipt exclaiming my card had been declined.

I took the slip and ran my thumb across the words, smearing the barely dried ink which had been printed only moments before.

"I....I can't accept that. Is there anything I can do? Dishes or something?" I asked in all seriousness. I wasn't even sure if that was how things worked these days in this situation. I had only seen this representation in cartoons or movies growing up, and for some reason, I had believed that was how the world actually worked. As if I could get off of paying for dinner by doing a little work around the restaurant in exchange.

The adults at the table behind me laughed once they had heard me offer help in return for my dinner. I felt my face explode into dark shades of red from both embarrassment and shame.

I'd never been on such public display with something as humiliating as this before. The eyes of the entire restaurant were now looking at me and burning right through.

"No, it's probably just something wrong with the card. The bank declines these things whenever they are worried that it's been stolen all the time." She explained, trying to comfort me. I knew exactly what she had been trying to do. She had been trying to save me from the grief she saw the rest of the restaurant giving me with the expressions on their faces. I knew then, that I appreciated her for that.

"I've got five dollars in cash in my backpack. Let me at least get you a tip." I asked as I stood.

"No, no, that's fine. You probably need it for emergencies or something." She said with a slightly awkward expression.

"I'll be right back. Just wait here." I said standing.

I jogged past the table of laughing teens.

"Run Forrest, run!" One of them called out to me...as I headed towards my pack outside. I returned with a five dollar bill; all the cash I had on hand, from a waterproof wallet holder my father had purchased as a gift for me before I'd left for the trail.

I thanked the waitress wholeheartedly for the assistance, as I handed her the crumpled bill. I asked her to apologize and to thank the manager for me as well, which she smiled complacently and agreed to do.

As I walked towards the exit door, I felt the amused faces of everybody who had found my ordeal hilariously entertaining and had made comments under their breaths or out loud during the entire incident.

"All set then?" One of the teens muttered in ridicule, while the rest of his friends chuckled along.

I stopped, feeling my anger rise rapidly. I clenched my fists and collected my thoughts. I then took a deep breath and slowly opened my fingers as I turned to look down at him. It was sudden that I realized he was such a coward, he didn't dare to look me in the eyes when he made the comments.

"God forbid, you should ever find yourselves in this situation someday. Broke, and surviving off of the kindness of strangers. I hope the people around you that day, treat you with the utmost respect. The very kind you couldn't find in your own hearts to show me." I said as I walked out.

They could've started laughing again for all I cared once the door had closed behind me, but at that time the entire restaurant was silent after hearing what I'd said to them. I liked to think that it was a moment of reflection, as if they had somehow learned from what I'd just said.

Upon calling my bank, I found that I only had $375 dollars left in my savings account. According to my bank, I had over drafted around thirteen dollars thus far from my checking account. Still, most of that $375 had been set aside for my portion of the gas money for the vehicle Woodstock, Wales and I had been sharing.

So the new shoes I had tried to order inside the restaurant would have to wait...which was going to prove to be torture to my ankles and feet over the next few hundred miles.

In particular through Mahoosuc Notch and the North Western part of the White Mountains.

It was September 15th, and Stephanie would be summiting Katahdin that day. As I stood there in the parking lot looking up at the mountain standing before us, I felt just a tad lonely knowing that she was soon on her way back home to friends, family and loved ones.

Meanwhile, Woodstock, Wales and I were still struggling with the weather conditions and the northern most section of the Whites, and we had nearly 800 more miles to go to complete it.

Woodstock and I had decided we would be starting at the Rattle River parking lot where the Appalachian Trail crossed Highway 2. Now while he had to remain enslaved to the Appalachian Trail to hit every last White Blaze; I planned on enjoying my freedom to find my own way by taking a different path up to the trail.

I had done some research on the always unfaithful Google Maps application over my smartphone and had found Millbrook Road which led to an "Austin Brook Trail."

Reading up on the trail, I found it was an attractive path for snowshoeing during the winter months. It led to Gentian Pond shelter along the AT over the course of 3.5 miles, effectively cutting off 10 miles of the Appalachian Trail.

Once again I had found an easier, more direct and sensible path for a trail that offered no mercy for a full backpack.

After Wales had dropped me off on Millbrook Road, I made my way past a boulder vehicle barricade to a stream with an obliterated bridge. I looked momentarily from side to side to find the best possible way across the bulging waterway.

It didn't look as if there would be an easy way to cross, so as Wales drove away, I began to remove my socks and shoes slowly.

The water was liquid nitrogen, and when I reached the opposing bank, I expected my feet to start crumbling and shattering apart beneath my weight having been frozen through.

I could have sworn that it was maybe half a degree away from being completely frozen over completely.

The rocks, though rounded by the rushing water for who knows how many decades were still sharp with the weight of the pack upon my back assisting in bearing down upon them. The water got as high as my mid-calve in the center of the stream before slowly reducing in depth with each step towards the adjacent shore.

I reflected in amazement at how much we relied on boots and socks these days. I could never imagine traversing these mountain ranges barefoot or even in simple moccasins like Native Americans had. The sheer splintering of stones seemed to wreak havoc upon the squishy, tender soles of human flesh.

Gray skies were all I had to greet me, and the temperature wasn't very accommodating either. It was in the low 60's which wasn't too terribly oppressive. I lifted my face towards the clouds and felt a cold wind say "hello" with a decent cutting snap into my sides.

This trail appeared to be an old logging road by the age of the trees as well as the aggravated earth, and the ruts left behind. There were streams, and nubile meadows filled with decaying tree stumps tilted left or right like tombstones of the past.

Side roads crossed this way and that way through overgrown shrubbery and cut off vehicle access by huge boulders or manmade ditches too steep or high for even ATV clearance.

As I walked, I eyed the rocky, craggy looking mountain ridge I'd be summiting within a few hours.

There were sections of slippery rock slides to traverse and impossibly high boulders to contend with along the way. Due to the torrential rains, we'd suffered over the past five days; streams were everywhere...even going down washouts which looked as if they hadn't seen water in years. The trail literally became a river sometimes, and I was a leaf trying to fight the impossible current straight up.

When I finally reached Gentian Pond Shelter, it was 2 P.M., and it had taken me 2 hours to clear the 3.5 miles.

It appeared to be a fantastic place to stay. It had a huge mountain reservoir a mere 20 yards south from the shelter and an open faced, wonderful view of the valley I had just climbed up from. I rehydrated and marveled at the landscape painted before me.

I believed Woodstock would be reaching the site that night. However, I had planned on going on alone.

When I reached the AT, I was reintroduced to the purposefully unnecessarily difficult terrain that I had become accustomed to.

If you had ever walked a cattle path before in your life, then you knew the muddy conditions of the trail and what to expect. But that wasn't my biggest issue. That was nobody's fault because a lot of people simply have to hike the trail through snow, thunder and rain. And it clearly erodes the path over time into these deep mud pits, stomped with boot prints up as high as a person's knees at times.

No, my issue was not only with AWOL's guide but with the dangerous boulder scrambles I came across. To make hikers take this trail up flat, slippery rock paths, where the stones slid out from beneath your feet like ice, seemed a tad ridiculous. At almost a 90 degree angle, there were no handholds or rebar ladders like we'd seen further up north.

Here, a hiker had to kiss a rosary and hope for the best. AWOL's guide wasn't making things any better, either. As always, it seemed he was wrong about the heights of the terrain in the book. I literally laughed out loud, thinking he potentially got bored and just guessed what the terrain was like while scribbling jagged lines maniacally up and down without any rhyme or reason.

"Calm down…" I said finally and stopped to take a deep breath. False summit after false summit later, I began to laugh while 2/3's the way up Mount Success.

"Calm down John, just calm down. This is Gregory's fault for being so fat! Let's blame *him* for a while." I said in a soothing voice. I mean what else could I honestly do, punch my frustrations out on the trail?

At the top of the summit, I never actually found a sign of any sort saying I had reached the top. Instead, I wandered blindly around in the mist as fat, cold drops of rain sporadically landed atop me. I walked across rotted planks, where occasionally I'd set my full weight on only to find my foot sink halfway up to my knees.

"Just, smile," I said, shaking my head with rage building behind that falsified, happy expression.

"Oh little Johnny, just smile so that you don't get angry…and start STOMPING THE SHIT OUT OF THESE ROTTEN BOARDS!" I shouted out in rage. The plank was splintered and broken anyways and didn't support anything. I purposefully stepped off into the mud, allowing my feet to become completely submerged by the black goop.

"I hate you!" I shouted as I struggled to pull one foot out at a time. I stomped on the board, lost balance and fell back into the mud even angrier than I was before. This time I was completely on fire.

"AGHHHHHH!!!!!" I screamed as I stood up immediately, covered in gunk. I ripped my backpack from my shoulders and launched far enough to almost clear the other side of the mountain. I then went to raise my foot again, if only to stomp the hell out of the rotted plank. Instead, my boot came off, and my barefoot smashed down on the board painfully enough to show me it wasn't completely rotten.

Now I was howling in pain as I gripped my aching heel and then fell over into the mud again.

I sat there miserably, and then looked at myself in the reflection of the water slowly gathering on the surface of the muck I was unintentionally bathing myself in.

"Feel better?" I asked my reflection after my little temper tantrum had subsided.

Strangely enough, I did.

Invictus had been at the next shelter. I hadn't seen her in quite some time. Actually, I hadn't seen her since back in Virginia when she, Roadkill, Torry and I had hitched a ride from the Captains into Troutville. After that, she and Roadkill had come strolling in at nearly midnight during a thunderstorm after having completed a 22-mile day through Tinker Cliffs and McAfee's Knob.

From where we met that day, she still had over 500 miles to go to my 788. We spent the evening catching up on old times.

"I haven't seen you in so long. Where are all of your friends? Rainapple, Bear-cloud…Roadkill?"

"Some of them flipped north. A few others got off of the trail altogether." She said, smearing the rain away from her face.

She opened her arms suddenly.

"I haven't hugged anyone in a long time." She offered, with a slight shrug. She was smiling, though there appeared to be a bit of loneliness residing behind her eyes.

I gave her a warm hug and looked up at the skies above us both.

"Think this will stop anytime soon?"

She let go and looked up as well.

"Think happy thoughts, and it will."

Well, I tried her plan of action. My happy thoughts were of eating pizza and taking an airplane back home.

The rain never let up, however, and continued on throughout the night.

The following morning, I wasn't looking forward to hiking. It was bitterly cold, and both my socks, and my boots were still soaked. The clothes I had wrung out and hung in the shelter were just as wet as they had been the day before. As if they had magically reabsorbed the water I thought I had rid from them.

I scaled wet algae or moss covered rock slabs that sometimes went from a 45-degree incline to a 90 degree one. I traversed up and down rebar ladders that had strangely been placed in easier spots to traverse than in the places they were needed and non-existent in the miles before.

While I could say that I sometimes hated this trail, I couldn't lie either. It was also incredibly beautiful. I took rebar ladders or hand holds in straight up rock climbs to the Goose Mountain intersection, and for some reason felt emboldened by what I had just done. As if I had just completed an American Gladiators course of some sort, just before Nitro or Thunder shot me on the side of the head with a nerf ball.

According to the sign at the top; to enjoy the view, I'd have to walk .1 mile straight up another boulder scramble behind me.

And strangely enough, .1 miles looked a lot like .3 from where I was standing. I wasn't going half a mile out of the way and back just to see a little more clearly what I was al-ready seeing at the base of the tip.

So instead, I continued down a narrow ridge that showcased the next 1.5 – 2 miles or more along a distant, open exposed bald ridgeline. I would traverse downhill about 500 to 600 feet immediately, then climb straight up the mountain top directly in front of me that was shaped like an enormous granite ball.

I'd then go down THAT distant mountain (whose shape now re-minded me of a #2 pencil eraser); about four-tenths of a mile before walking what looked to be a narrow bog along the ridgeline.

In the distance, I could see three people already walking across the ridge. I also watched somebody carefully climbing the hand over hand boulders in front of me.

I slowly made my way towards victory.

As I reached the summit of the adjacent peak opposite Goose Mountain, I enjoyed the view for a total of 8 seconds before saying: "The hell with this cold! I'm outta here!"

It seemed as if the heat of the sun baking the granite rock was causing the cold air up top clashing with it, to whip violently about the mountain which wasn't helpful when my clothes were still soaked from the rain the day before.

I walked towards the north (or should I say I was shoved north), where it looked as if the trail ended on a cliff overlooking a long narrow ridge 500 feet below me.

No, it didn't end. It just dropped off and expected you to climb straight down with your big ol' backpack on. That, or you could just fall to your death. Whichever was more convenient for you at the time.

I let loose a sigh, as I navigated the slippery slides called a trail.

The path weaved in and out of a rather impressive plank, and bog system further down.

For the most part, I found myself going down the mountain on boards in a switchback like motion with slip resisters nailed into them. That or more straight down rebar ladders drilled into the rock.

Some of the placement of these ladders were confusing in that they were placed in manageable sections like before, where they seemed completely unnecessary.

As I reached the bottom, I met up with Invictus who was cursing the trail just as much as I had been.

"Okay. Tell me the logic in rebar stabbing into the wall *there*," she said, pointing behind us.

"But right *here* I've got to literally jump down ten feet and hope I don't break my ankle." Invictus finished, as she stared down the edge in front of us.

"Well, I'm not entirely sure it could break your ankle..." I tried to comfort her until I thought about my recent ankle injury and the amount of pain and damage I had done just by rolling it along. Add the force of over three hundred pounds with only granite rock to cushion the sprain, and you could see what she meant.

"I'm wrong. It could totally break your ankle." I clarified much to her dissatisfaction. I looked around at the bushes beneath us and then glanced up at a group of hikers far ahead of us.

"How the hell did *they* get down this?" I asked her.

"Well, they're young you see. Athletic, and built with perfect genes. They could have probably done a backflip, or used a ray of sunshine as a fire man's pole and swung down in their perfect little worlds." She said sarcastically. She was also pointing out the obvious without actually saying it. She and I were both out of shape.

We walked and talked as we slipped and sunk upon half or wholly submerged planks over mountaintop bogs after having navigated the cliff side by my helping lower her down and then handing her backpack to her. Meanwhile, for me, it was every man for their self.

As we walked, I realized it was literally a swamp up here on this ridgeline. It began to get rather ridiculous as well because some of the planks weren't even supported. You'd just step on them and sink up to your crotch in ice cold, sewage smelling, black gunk.

One such time, Invictus took a dangerous step on a worthless crumbling board and fell on her ass into the muck; sinking thigh high.

I offered her my hand while we laughed, pulling her out of the gunk pit.

"Great, now I smell like shit." She sighed, bitterly. "It's okay, I smelled like shit long before I ever stepped into one of these bogs," I said, reassuringly.

We re-accessed which way we were going.

"Well, sorry about this 'super fragile alpine vegetation' but there's simply no other way to go," I stated as I took the point and guided the both of us around the sinkhole.

"Fragile Alpine vegetation my ass. This shit survives on top of Mt Washington in hurricane force winds and below freezing weather. You think my walking over it is going to destroy it?" Invictus added as I laughed.

There was really no other way to go, and I was NOT going to wade through the waist-deep mud in my only pair of clothes, in this freezing weather any more than I already had.

I began to pull ahead of Invictus, and soon she was completely out of sight. I had really wanted to hike with her, if for no other reason than to have conversation with somebody I knew. But I was also really anxious to get to the next shelter before nightfall mostly because of the events that afternoon. After sinking in mud holes throughout the hike, and the fact that the Appalachian Trail had indeed become the *Appalachian Stream* ALL DAY LONG. Muddy water had literally been absorbed as deep as my bones. My feet were swollen and soaked, and the flesh had rubbed off raw.

Later in the evening after having reached the shelter, I set up my tent and began boiling water not only for my dinner but for some tea as well. The wind had become disastrous and after washing off most of my clothes I strutted around camp in my long johns, crocs, and dri-down jacket after having rinsed the majority of mud from my body.

By the fire somebody had started, I dried my boots and socks as best as possible as well as my clothes before settling in for the night. Invictus had reached camp an hour after I had arrived and had contemplated going on before fearing the Mahoosuc Notch we were only a mile away from.

The Mahoosuc Notch was considered to be the hardest 1.1 miles on the entire Appalachian Trail and would definitely take some time to tackle. Trying it in the dark seemed a little too hazardous for our liking.

Wales would come in later that evening as well, with 22 miles remaining as he headed south. He explained that the two and a half hours it had taken him to tackle the Mahoosuc Notch had been exhausting.

As I listened to his stories, I had a pit in the bottom of my stomach only because I would be tackling it in the morning, myself.

I've come to realize there's a bit of irrationality in me when I awake first thing in the morning.

You see, I remembered I had left my shoe insoles outside of the shelter in the open to dry by the fire. When I awoke, I had HEARD the rain coming down. But it was so cold and miserable outside of my sleeping bag that I tried to rationalize with myself while half in and out of consciousness by saying to myself:

Eh, the rain will stop, and they'll dry out by morning.
WELL I'M AN IDIOT.

There you go. Happy now, folks? You finally got the truth out of me if you hadn't figured it out already on your own after all of this time.

I resided in pitiful reluctance as I watched the water droplets fall, each landing on the insoles and soaking into the already drenched spongey material.

The day, while it had originally called for sunny skies, was cold, gray and horrible of course. I mean sure, why not? It was not only the scariest part of the trail I was about to hike but the hardest too. Of COURSE, it had to start raining. I mean it only made sense, right?

I didn't want to walk through, but I didn't have much of a choice either. And as I sat there I started thinking of excuses, such as waiting on Woodstock to come along so that we could complete Mahoosuc Notch together. But then again, it sort of felt like a rite of passage that I do this on my own. I risked death, to face the most intense part of the AT on my own, as a man.

Minutes later: *"I don't really think I'm a man at all actually. Hahaha (insert nervous, and shameful cough right here). Wanna hike with me? Please?"* I begged Invictus as she shook her head from side to side.

"No way dude! Not in that shit out *there*. Whatta'ya crazy?" she asked. I sighed, poking my bottom lip out childishly as I looked out from beneath the awning of the shelter. I then glanced over at Wales who was packing and getting ready to head on down the trail in the downpour himself, as he continued south.

Why can't I have his enthusiasm? I thought pathetically to myself.

As I made my way over, my first step from out of the shelter had my crocs sinking four inches deep into a mud puddle outside the shelter—if only to get me realizing just how miserable my day was going to be.

I asked Wales if he thought I could honestly do 9.7 miles that day, what with the Mahoosuc Notch and the rain and everything jumbled together.

He looked doubtful, though, stating he had broken up the last 10 miles going southbound because of the terrain and how tough it had been on his knees.

While disheartening to hear; the urge to stay there at camp was strong, but the urge to go on and get the section over with forever was stronger.

I started off into the cold, wet rain after bidding him adieu, no longer looking for excuses to clasp to.

"I just can't hike in this damn weather, did you know that?" I said suddenly to my backpack. Why I was talking to my backpack, I wasn't even sure. But I felt like, after everything we had gone through together, it sort of made sense to speak to the thing.

"Greg, if I'm not soaking myself from sweat, I'm getting wet by the rain on a daily basis. I don't think I've ever had one day of dry hiking this entire journey."

Greg didn't have much to say on the subject, and sort of just hung there—bouncing along and weighing me down painfully on bruised shoulders.

"Can I ask you something?" I said out loud once I was earshot away from the shelter and looking like a complete psycho as I talked to my own backpack.

Greg gave no answer, so I figured he was all right with it. Yes, that's right—I had even decided to give him a gender and treat *him* as a sentient being of some sort.

"Okay, so your right shoulder strap seams have ripped away from the rest of the backpack. I have soaked you in bleach and water in a bathtub for 4 hours, and your shoulder straps still smell like spoiled bologna, rotten ground beef, and parmesan cheese mixed with onions and garlic. Oh, and when a mouse chewed open your front pocket back in the Smoky Mountains, it also destroyed the zipper which means I can no longer use that pocket anymore. Now when I fell down that hill back at Pine Swamp Branch, just before The Captains, you did save my life. Well, at the cost of snapping your plastic strap buckle in half that is after it got caught in the Y of those two trees. I mean do you ever get tired of suffering along with me?" I asked.

Now while Greg obviously didn't answer me, I imagined he did. In fact, I only say that because when I adjusted my slipping straps and tightened the buckles I could swear I almost heard a mumble much like that of a child.

"I dunno" it had said.

Well, that was it. I was CERTAIN my backpack had answered me. I also knew that had another human been there they'd have said it was nothing more than the sound of the buckle scraping along a worn nylon strap.

"Well, that's fine with me Greg. I agree. Nothin' is gonna keep us down today. Not even ol' battle scars buddy!" I said cheerily, with just a little pep in my step.

I ran my hand along the side of my stomach where the straps from my backpack had rubbed the flesh raw, and tiny blood blisters had popped, oozing red liquid down the side of my stomach. I had reached the Mahoosuc Notch intersection, and as I let my wet shirt slide back down upon the wound, I saw a side trail which would lead me down to Success Pond Road and ultimately aid in slipping past both the Notch

AND the Mahoosuc Arm altogether. This, of course, would leave me without ever having to do either.

I was only slightly conflicted. I enjoyed the thought of going my own way and finding a simpler course over what I found to be a pointlessly dangerous section of trail. Particularly in the torrential rain coming down around me.

But then again, a thought came over me at that moment. This trail was never going to be the way 'I' wanted it to be. It would be tough. It would be hard and more often than not I'd look negatively upon it.

But that would never change it.

I couldn't warp the terrain by constantly whining about it and always trying to avoid it.

All I could do was hike. I could choose to take the trail, or I could bypass it all together and once again find my own way.

But this was too monumental a portion to bypass.

I looked at my old cell phone which no longer had service on it anymore. I used it now to write my blogs and to take pictures or simply listen to music while I hiked. Other than that, it was a paper weight.

I looked up at the intersections sign and took my picture next to it.

It wasn't a happy expression, to be honest, but I also wasn't stopping.

"Let get this over with...Greg." I said, walking into the mist and vanishing beneath its clouded shield.

"Wow..." I muttered out loud as I looked at what was laid out before me in awe. Humongous rock walls on either side of the valley showed exposed granite—more so on my right going north than on my left.

Over the last thousands of millennia, boulders had broken loose and fallen into the valley which was about as wide a football field. You were completely locked in by craggy flat mountain sides East to West that offered NO alternative way out except by going either North or South. Once you were in this gauntlet, you were there to stay.

The boulders had become completely swallowed in neon green moss, trees and huge mounds of grass growing upon them.

Small pine or birch trees latched on to the tops of these along with thousands of years of dirt drifts offering false views of solid earth.

"Solid Earth" that broke away beneath your feet, exposing a long fall and darkness be-tween the boulders should you take a wrong step.

I climbed these house-sized monsters, up and over—or at times from underneath. I felt my arms took the brunt of the strain, mostly because I was pivoting between rocks or pulling myself up over awkward diagonal angles.

Other times I was launching myself by precariously hopping from boulder to boulder over thirty and forty foot drops.

I paused when I came across a section I wasn't too sure I knew which way to go through. There were multiple routes to take through the notch at any given time based upon your size and physical abilities. I found that I most often chose the higher ground as opposed to going into the small, wet, dark caves beneath these massive granite buildings.

I started off slowly by gripping knife blade rock ledges with both hands and monkey crawling along the rock slab wall; while my crumbling, utterly cheap Keen boots...frantically scraped against flat stone surfaces that offered no grip.

I looked down to see the fall was quite a radical one. Doing this only strengthened my grip on the rock momentarily as I shimmied across.

Meanwhile, Greg continued to hang lifelessly to my back; pulling me down. Almost as if WANTING me to fail.

Willing me to fall.

"Dude come on. Can't you like...make yourself lighter or something?" I said to Greg, with beads of sweat dripping down into my eyes. I suddenly imagined my backpack flipping over and purposefully dumping all of my things out, to make itself lighter as I had requested.

"Scratch that, actually."

When I glanced back halfway through the scramble, I saw I had gone the wrong way.

It was only slightly foggy in the area, but I didn't know what the hell I was doing. At times I wasn't even sure I knew where the hell I was going anymore either since the rain had started to fall harder and was only accomplishing blinding me, and assisting in the defeat of my grip on the stone slab before me.

But I've always been the type that's too stubborn to turn back, even if I know I'm going the wrong way.

I purposefully find that I choose to want to stay in forward motion, even should that prove to take longer. Or even if it meant carving out my own way where one didn't actually exist.

I came to a point where I needed to make a decision.

When I reached out for an adjacent root...I put far too much strain on one hand. I'm not a strong upper body strength sort of guy. So as I reached out for the exposed root of this miniature pine tree, I knew I had just this one shot at grabbing on to something. On to ANYTHING actually because the grip in my right hand was failing rather quickly as well.

I stretched, and my left middle and forefinger scraped the roots surface...

...no.

But I was almost there.

I rocked back, as fear shot like lightning through my core.

I made one last lunge forward...but grasped nothing. I was too eager and closed my fist early and too short of the root.

My grip on the granite slab broke free and suddenly I was falling.

My descent was fast, but the shock was faster.

I thought to scream out, to call out to something, some higher power or to anybody. But more importantly, the thought to brace myself for the impact came first.

Besides, there was nobody around to save me.

I shot my hands up behind my head almost without thinking. I'd have wrapped my entire arms about my skull had I reacted faster, but I didn't, and it's far too hard to think when you've only got seconds to do so.

The backs of both my calves struck a jutting rock first, causing my fall to become more "headward bound" towards the earth. In the second I had before striking the crumbling granite slabs beneath me, I knew I was about to die. And no, time didn't slow down like it does in the movies. There was no "light at the end of a tunnel" and there sure as hell wasn't enough time to reflect on my existence from birth up to that moment before I violently struck the broken, stony earth beneath me.

I had landed more on my pack than on my spine; puncturing one of my water bottles in the process which shot out from the rear pocket like a rocket. This was as I partially slid down the angled rock wall, and my body flipped over backward.

As I hit, my left hand caught the snap back of my neck and rear of my skull. There were a couple of small cuts and skin punctures on my knuckles as they crushed into rough marble sized stones and pebbles beneath my weight and immediately began bleeding. The back of my hand would be rather bruised, but ultimately my skull was excellent aside from the jarring palm bounce it had recovered from. My neck, on the other hand, felt as if it had been strung out like a rubber band until the point of snapping and then let go. It left a sharp pain in the torn muscles it garnered from the fall that would last over a two-week time span in the days to come as well.

The air in my lungs rushed out harshly, but not enough that I was gasping immediately for more.

My backpack shot free from one arm, and its weight tugged me down with it causing my arm to jerk violently with 60 pounds of force tearing off of me. It left a huge nylon burn along the inside of my arm that would later blood blister over and then scab.

In the seconds to come after I had fallen, I was so surprised at how lucky I was to not have broken my neck by landing directly on it.

I had landed so awkwardly, I believed it had ended up spreading out the shock of the fall from my pack striking first, to my calves slowing the descent possibly. All as the shock spread to my hands and shoulders and finally the rest into my spine.

I rolled over, groaning because of the sharp ache throughout my body, but mostly radiating in the rear of my legs and where they had struck the rock above me, as well as the violent twist to my neck. I wished I had more than two arms, to hold everything aching, burning and bleeding on me.

I managed a painful laugh, though it wasn't out of hilarity. It was out of surprise...that I was still alive.

"Greg..." I said, breathlessly as I started laughing again.

"Greg, you sonofabitch. You...know..." I said, bursting into a round of chuckles. What the hell was wrong with me? Was I so excited from the adrenaline rush, and the dopamine that had entered my bloodstream during the fall that I couldn't control my own laughter anymore?

"Greg, you saved me again you ol' bastard," I said, as I looked over at my pack.

The scrapes burned like lime juice on an open cut, but I still laughed. I was so incredibly grateful, because I hadn't died and because I wasn't paralyzed.

But the laughter soon died...replaced by anger and sheer awe at my luck.

I rolled onto my side and laid there for 10 minutes before moving again. The rain pitter-pattered around me, and I closed my eyes simply soaking it all in. Something was poking my hip rather painfully. I rolled over, just enough to see my hip was bleeding as well from the jagged boulder my waist had bashed into when I had fallen. It wasn't bleeding that much, though, so I wasn't too concerned.

I stared at water droplets falling one after another on a single patch of ornate moss that had all kinds of different strange blooms, small mushrooms or fungi and white flowers growing out of it.

It was beautiful.

I touched the droplets with my fingertips and brought them to my mouth. Suddenly I was ravenously thirsty, but I was still too much in shock to move. Honestly, I was also too scared to move, thinking that the second I did some busted vein inside me would rip apart and I'd die from internal bleeding. I picked up a relatively fresh leaf on the ground beside me and placed it against the little waterfall forming from the recent downpour. I then led the tip of the leaf to my mouth. Five to six drops a second fell onto my tongue, and I drank desperately before the strain in my torn neck muscles were too painful to bare any longer.

I rolled onto my stomach and slowly garnered the strength to push myself to my knees. It was painful, but to stand was ruefully excruciating on my gashed-open calves.

I wanted to go home.

At that moment I'd had the urge to leave Greg right there and simply walk away from everything.

You're doing it again, John. Sinking into self-doubt. I tried to tell myself.

"Just quit then..." I said to myself, almost sarcastically out loud but angrily all the same. There was a hint of disgust in my tone.

"Quit, like you've quit and given everything else up that's ever been hard in your life, you loser," I said, this time cutting myself deep with the sharp words.

Show everybody out there that you're a failure. Like you've always been. I thought to myself.

My words and thoughts of self-deprecation vanished into breathy huffs, rising into the cold air before me.

They dissipated, into nothingness and offered no comfort or lasting effect in doing so.

Gregory had been canted at an angle and was slipping slowly enough down an angled rock slab from the rain that I hadn't noticed. It now fell over and slid down into a deep gulley where it disappeared from sight into a dark hole. I followed its fall with my eyes and saw it tumble under the boulders and beneath a house-sized chunk of granite with a white arrow painted on it—pointing towards the trail.

Almost as if giving me a sign of some sort.

"I really am, losing it," I said, shaking my head from side to side as I smeared streams of rain from my face. I thought of my new found backpack friend and his inaudible way of telling me to go on.

As I slid down into the hole to retrieve Gregory, I took a moment's reprieve from the downpour above.

I sat on my pack and surrendered to the trail. I surrendered to the fog as I breathed in its cold, eerie existence into weak lungs.

Exhausted and sore, in the middle of nowhere, I realized I had nothing.

I...had...nothing.

I was but a featureless silhouette sitting in a forest, thousands of miles from home.

It had taken 2 hours and 18 minutes to finish that 1.1-mile section.

I shouted happily upon reaching the end, turning and giving the path I'd just walked both middle fingers in defiance. A smile ran across my face as I excitedly jumped up and down.

I even started to do a little victory dance, which consisted of a poorly constructed robot followed by a little pop-n-lock action.

I couldn't believe how built up the notch had been. It had been a path I had feared. Something I had dreaded, I wouldn't ever be able to complete.

Suddenly I remembered back to Neels Gap in March, when I had first started out with Torry, and the hikers that had built up the White Mountains to be so incredibly hard that some rookie like myself would have never been able to tackle such an enormous task.

It was quite true that often places along the trail could be built up to mythological proportions by other hikers. You could sometimes begin to doubt yourself so readily before ever even attempting it.

Thinking about my earlier tantrum, I didn't have an answer for my thoughts.

However, I did have an apology to make.

I gently patted my backpack.

"Thanks for saving my life back there Greg. And I'm sorry about the whiney little breakdown I had."

Greg didn't feel much like responding I suppose, so I decided he was probably just as tired as I was.

I looked up at the Mahoosuc Arm before me.

It was said to be harder than the notch by some.

But my new found confidence awoke a fire in me that I didn't think I had ever felt before in my life.

I continued my journey.

There would be no giving up that day.

The Mahoosuc Arm was made up of brutal rock slabs with no ladders.

No rebar hand holds like I had seen along the trail the days before.

There was nothing to walk you through this section of the AT, with baby steps or to forewarn you and gradually make you see what was to come. Instead, from the first phase in you were thrust straight into this world of terrain grades so terrifyingly straight up that at times it felt I needed a fall protection harness and an OSHA observer nearby just to clarify I was traversing it safely.

Mentally, nothing was going to stop me. If my body failed me, then that was a whole other story. I'd crumble down the mountain, dying, knowing that I had tried.

"I know Greg..." I said out loud to my backpack.

"I tend to dramatize things too much for my own good. I'm not gonna fall to my death." I said more to calm my own fears than those of an unresponsive, non-conscious backpack with no intelligent thought or mouth with which to assure me.

I jogged up the summit in the few spots that I could, though I didn't have the strength and stamina to last that long, nor did the trail readily support that action. The grade was simply too strenuous. Still, I had subtracted all limits. I didn't care about blowing out a vessel in my heart despite the sustained arrhythmia I felt inside my chest. I didn't give a damn about my throbbing skull, exploding in pain or my stiffening neck and aching body parts from the fall that I had endured just an hour before.

I ran with no oxygen in my lungs, gulping air and reaching blindly for anything and everything I could claw and dig my fingers into. To reach the top, like some muddy, sweat covered beast with clenched teeth and wild eyes.

Sparks of white spots lived and died in my eyes, popping and appearing in my dizzying vision. I had to stop. I should have stopped.

But I kept going.

I met opposition through wet rock slides that sheer luck didn't have me slipping off of to my death. I climbed these sections, probably looking a lot like Spider-Man clinging to the glass sides of a skyscraper.

I crossed obstacles of slippery slopes, but courage raced like lava throughout my veins as I did.

And when I fell, I bashed my knees and gashed open my shins.

Furious, I kept on because I had no other choice.

"We have to..." I said breathlessly, as I pulled myself up on the massive tree root dangling above my head.

"We have to do this, Greg," I said, strenuously hefting both myself and my backpack weight up along the side of the trail. The wet earth crumbled from beneath my feet as the soles of my boot left the soil. My hands shot up and gripped a slick hunk of granite; clinging instantly to it. When I turned to look down at the earth sliding away from beneath my feet, I knew that if I were to let go, I would easily continue sliding down the mountain the rest of the way to the bottom.

After climbing atop the root, I sat back against the wet earth and the streams of rain passing down the mountain beneath my dangling legs.

"We have to try, because we were meant to succeed," I said, brushing the mud off of my hands against my pants. I inhaled huge gusts of wind, feeling light-headed and nauseous all at once.

"We have to succeed...because I have to show my parents, just how much I love them." I added, exhausted and broken.

Carefully, I got to my feet and felt the tired burn, of painfully strained calve and thigh muscles. I felt the joints in my knees popping and grating together with sharp jagged pieces of metal lying snuggled between the bones.

"This is all I have left, to give," I whispered, as I brushed the rain from my face and watched the waterfall the trail had turned into cascade down upon me.

It was picking up in severity, as the downpour increased around me.

When I finally rounded the ridge at the top of the Mahoosuc Arm and hit that last fifteen-foot bald climb, I shouted out in triumph.

"Oh, thank you, God. Thank you so much!" I said, smearing streams of sweat from my face and from the corners of my eyes. I had replaced it with mud instead.

I felt amazing because I had finished the Mahoosuc Arm in under 30 minutes; having surged my way up to the top. Ultimately as I stood there, gasping for air, I wondered if I had tackled every mountain like that—how quickly I would've already been done with the entire trail.

At the summit, somebody had spelled out "Legs Day" with rocks on a smooth granite boulder only slightly erecting itself from the earth. As I took a couple steps closer to view it, I burst out loud into exhausted laughter and appreciation of the message.

It would be 4 P.M. when I reached the area I had designated as my camp for the evening. My clothes were drenched, and I removed everything from my body as I stood—shivering in the cold.

I crawled into my sleeping bag, but the wind was cutting through the thin material of my bedroll. It was blasting throughout the shelter as well, with all of the many gaps in the walls. Much like I had learned back at Sassafras Gap just outside of the NOC in North Carolina; I boiled water and poured it into a Powerade bottle, which I then threw into the bottom of my sleeping bag. Boy did it help. I was warm throughout my sleeping bag in no time as the heat radiated and bounced off of the walls of the sack.

"We made it, ol' buddy," I said, patting the side of my backpack. And though Greg didn't bother to respond, I sort of felt as if he kind of agreed with me.

I turned the sweat soaked, smelly side of my pack around and propped myself up against it as I rehydrated some pre-packaged apples I had vacuum sealed over a year before. I put 2 cups of water in, with 2 strawberry cereal bars and two apple cereal bars as well. I then proceeded to smash the ingredients all together within the vacuum sealed bag.

The concoction had turned into a warm, fruity oatmeal, which I hungry spooned mouthfuls out of.

It had served two purposes. Filling me up, and warming my shivering, half-naked body from the inside, out.

Having connected all of the northern portions of the trail, and having finished out Maine as well—we now had the next 80 miles of the White Mountain range set out and splayed before us in the days to come. Our plan had been to continue to park our car at road gaps between each of the various sections of mountains and continue on south like we'd been doing thus far.

After our achievement and having finished the "toughest portion of the Appalachian Trail" as it had been called, we were now zeroing for the next couple of days before we began our ascent up Mt Washington.

That first zero day, we stood at the Pinkham Notch visitors center watching with hungry eyes as people inside gathered and ate from a $14 dollar per person buffet.

"What the hell do you think could be so expensive about that breakfast that it costs so much?" I asked Woodstock, as he stood beside me with his face pressed against the glass of the window; staring in.

"Maybe it comes with delectable desserts like Crème Brulee, or Flan, or…" Wales trailed on before I cut him off suddenly.

"Or maybe they just overprice everything because of lack of available options elsewhere out here." I spat, rather cynically.

Wales gave me an apologetic look, as I shook my head with disdain and turned away. I had no interest in staring at what I couldn't have.

Our intent had been for the three of us to ditch the associated $30 per person fee and to illegally hitch a ride to the summit of Mount Washington, via the Washington Auto Road instead. We would then hike down the mountain with slackpacks on along the Appalachian Trail for thirteen miles that went by the Lake Of The Clouds Hut and over Mount Madison. Had we been able to accomplish this,

Woodstock and Wales wouldn't have to hike that portion of the AT uphill once we had finished our zero days. Thus still maintaining their purist, thru-hiker status.

Unfortunately for us, the three of us had taken the wrong path towards the Auto Road and found we had been walking the wrong way.

We didn't realize this though until we were 2.4 miles up the Tuckerman Ravine Trail which had nothing to do with the mileage we still had left along the AT.

At this point, it was imperative that we stopped at the Hermit Lake Shelter and re-access our situation.

"I suggest we go back down. Either call today a wash or attempt to hitch again up the auto road." I offered.

"I think we should go all the way up. We're only 3 miles from the summit." Wales exclaimed, however.

"I'm all for either going South to knock out some other slackpack options or hanging out back at Pinkham's Notch and using their free Wi-Fi all day," Woodstock said.

"Eh....I don't know. I don't really feel like breaking up any more portions of the trail and driving back and forth anymore. Honestly, I just want to get this section over with and get to Vermont where the trails are far easier." I said.

Finally, I thought about it like this.

Now the 26-mile segment from Pinkham Notch to Crawford Notch was almost exactly 13 miles North and South from the Mt Washington summit while following the AT.

I knew the way I hiked.

Had I known this "Tuckerman Ravine" trail existed come the day it came to walk this portion of the AT—I would've taken it, with it being the shorter route up to the summit. UNFORTUNATELY, Woodstock and Wales were both purists, however; locked to white painted stripes on trees and rocks. This day, should we even summit would be a wash for them all together.

"I guess I'm with Wales. Might as well call today a fail, and just hit the summit of Washington. Then we can either hike down the Auto Road or we can hitch from the parking lot." I suggested.

The day was beautiful and despite the fact that this specific trek had meant nothing to the mileage Wales and Woodstock had left; we were going to make the most of it.

Tuckerman's Ravine would climb 4,000 feet in over 4 miles. It was a steep run that would take four hours to complete, but the views were what sold it. Crumbling exposed rock faces and a trail that followed a natural spring and waterfalls all of the way up.

The water appeared to be so clear and fresh, I cupped my hands beneath the tumbling flow and drank as day hikers eyed me like I was some kind of freak. I splashed large handfuls of water into my bearded face which was coated with a week's worth of dirt, sweat, and grime.

"Is that even safe? Do you know what you're drinking?" A woman asked me as her teenage son looked up at me with distrusting eyes.

I ran a hand over my face and pushed the cool spring water from my eyes.

"Well..." I said, standing slowly.

"Haven't died in the months I've been doing it yet," I replied, splashing one more handful of water across my hot face. When Woodstock stopped alongside the same waterfall, he too began to splash water on his sweat covered face.

This time, the lady shook her head as if we were both absolutely looney, and turned to continue on up the mountain.

The wind was harsh, and there were reports that the gusts up on top of Mt Washington were as fast as 70 mile per hour that day.

It was so intense, that at times it literally lifted us from our feet, causing us to stumble. To hold our arms out as this happened quite often made us feel as if we were going to fly away.

I yearned to hike the AT now that I was up here.

The beauty up here was so awe inspiring, any physical limitations I felt I'd had on my way up had evaporated. Mostly because I had never been upon terrain like this before in my life. I had lived such a sheltered existence up to the last year, that had I not left home I'd have never known such incredible places of beauty actually existed.

The final 300-foot climb brought us to a parking lot and a thoroughly corporatized summit. Food, gift shops and fat, bloated tourists shoved us out of the way for photo opportunities by the summits sign.

After eating a quick lunch, the clouds of an afternoon storm began rolling in. Wildcat Mountain was a tiny blip in a white rushing tidal wave of incoming rain accumulation.

We sought shelter in the hiker's basement of the main cafeteria as the wind had picked up so greatly, that it had literally started blowing people away. Small children were screaming and holding on to their parent's hands as the wind gusts took to violent speeds and huge gusts.

It was there in the basement, we got to interact with stuffy, snobby French Canadian day-hikers that had driven up Mt Washington on a tour bus. We were sitting at full tables in the basement as these people mumbled or whispered under their breath while watching Wales and I eating leftovers from lunch. Some pointed and laughed while covering their mouths.

One confident guy came over and threw his coat and a backpack completely on top of my hands nonchalantly as I sat at a table looking at my phone.

Woodstock looked at the guy and then me as the French Canadian walked off towards the bathroom, speaking to his friend in French.

"Well, *that* was rude." Woodstock said, with wide eyes.

"It was, wasn't it?" I replied, with just a tinge of anger. I quickly bucked the items off of my hands and onto the floor.

I garnered a few looks from the other group members as they whispered to each other and continued to point at us as if we were the odd ones out.

"Am I missing something? Do I have shit on my face?" I asked Wales suddenly. Wood-stock looked down at his phone with a mischievous grin.

"I don't think they like you, Morris," Woodstock said, looking up at me with an instigating expression.

"Ils sont sans-abri?" one of the teenagers muttered quietly in French, which caused a flurry of laughs amongst the group.

"Only cowards whisper under their breath..." I replied, loud enough for every one of them to hear me.

We finished our lunch and left.

As it was getting to be so late, the three of us stood for half an hour as clouds swallowed the entire mountain. The storms that had been rolling in had finally reached us, and suddenly lightning started ricocheting through the clouds around us. I didn't feel so safe being atop there anymore. This said nothing to the deafening blasts of wind that had all but completely crippled us on an audible level as we yelled at each other to talk.

We stood undeterred by a sign reading "No Hitch-Hiking" and proudly presented our thumbs. We garnered a few laughs from tourists heading back down the mountain and even some photos from people asking us to pose next to the signs. It was finally when a nice man and his wife drove us the eight miles down to the base in the back of his pickup truck, however, that we finally got to get off of Washington before lightning and rain enveloped the summit.

Upon reaching Highway 16, we stuck up our thumbs again, and this time, we got a ride from a Washington Auto Road Forest Ranger to Pinkham Notch.

"I'm gonna guess you guys illegally hitch-hiked down Mt Washington, huh?" He asked us as we sat in his forest service truck.

"Is it actually illegal? Or just an un-preferred action?" Woodstock asked, from the backseat. The ranger looked up in the rearview mirror at him and then over to me without answering.

It was September 22nd, and the valley of Pinkham Notch was cold, and wet. A steady drizzle had started coming down as the three of us hiked north into the wood line, to find a campsite for the evening. As we scoured the woods, our breaths dissipated into small clouds blinding us even more than the night and absent moon already had.

"We should so, be in a hotel room right now." I muttered in a depressed tone.

"Believe me, I wanted to be in one. But *that* crybaby wouldn't let us." Woodstock said, jutting a thumb over at Wales who had a sheepish expression on his face.

"Just think about how happy you'll be when you realize you have enough money to finish the trip. You won't have blown it all on motel rooms." He tried to offer.

I stopped in my tracks, as the wind picked up. It had to be no more than 50 degrees outside.

"Maybe I should go back..." I said, tired and not really inspired to hike anymore.

Woodstock had convinced me that despite the rain coming down, I'd sleep better in my hammock.

"I'm not trying to make up your mind for you, though." He had reassured me.

"No, you're right. I'd probably hate it in that car." I had replied, grabbing my things.

Sadly, as I led the way through the night, I felt like I had spoken too soon.

We walked along slippery planks and slick rocks or roots headed North through the White Mountains along the AT.

After a 10 minute walk, I was stringing up my hammock tent near Woodstock who had set his ground tent maybe three feet away from mine.

I slowly settled down into my hammock and slipped into my sleeping bag. I then closed my eyes and felt darkness start to overtake me.

Wales (left) and Morris the Cat (right) take a picture atop a Maine mountain summit.

CHAPTER 6

A Friend, Says Goodbye

IT WAS THREE HOURS LATER when I awoke in all-around shock, unable to breathe and gasping for air. My back had hit the earth first, and then the back of my skull which had violently bounced off of the ground. There was the sudden crashing followed by a loud thud less than an inch from my head. Everything was happening simultaneously and caused my heart to practically tear from out of my chest. I finally managed a cough and took a large heaving breath as my hammock fell back against my face, smothering me. I struggled to move, but something heavy had pinned me down in place. I had to shove aside something heavy, possibly a branch or a two-ton stone pillar of some sort just to unzip the tent door.

After managing to crawl out of my sleeping bag, I looked down only to see from outside of my bug net that my tent was sitting in a puddle of water that had started dribbling into my hammock from the bottom. Black muck had begun to push through the bug net screen—pouring along the side of my sleeping bag.

"Jesus Christ, what the hell is going on!" I shouted out loud.

I groaned, rolling over slowly as rain poured down harder than ever outside of my tent. I called out, not sure I even knew what I was saying.

I felt dizzy and disoriented, and the back of my skull was throbbing from where it had bounced off of the earth. It had left me with a nauseated feeling as if my brain was bruised on all sides.

I began to notice a bright light shining on my face suddenly.

That's when I heard Woodstock call out to me.

"Morris, are you okay?"

I hid my eyes from the brightness of his headlamp. At that moment, I didn't know what had happened to *him*, nor the severity of the incident that had just occurred and how it had affected his welfare and the future of his hike. All I cared about at that moment, was *me*.

"Please, you're blinding me..." I said, shielding my eyes. As the light fell, I noticed blood on his bottom lip.

Woodstock had been awakened himself by the commotion happening in the monsoon taking place around us. He had awoken in far worse shape than I had, spitting up blood and splinters of his own broken teeth.

I fumbled around in the dark until I found my headlamp sinking deep into the mud puddle I was now lying in. Even more black muck and muddy rain water had started pouring into my hammock from a large rip across the bottom of my tent. I slowly unzipped it, only to find I was still trapped.

"I can't get the hell outta here. What's going on?" I shouted, jerking angrily at the ruined hammock. Something heavy was keeping me from getting out from beneath the rainfly and tarp I had thrown up and over my suspended tent during the night. That was when I noticed what had actually pinned me in place.

A birch tree about 10 inches in diameter had fallen during the night. It had struck my hammock tent first, at an angle and ripped the bottom of my rainfly in half as well as a small portion of my bedding. The bug net had been destroyed as well, leaving only a flap blowing wildly in the violent wind. But the damage hadn't been done there. The force of the weight had also torn a gash from the stress of the tree, snapping my hanging cord in half; and pinning me in place as I had fallen towards the wet earth.

The weight of the widow maker had then caused the support rope to snap into shreds as well which brought me down with it from the other side after it had crashed across the base, only narrowly missing my feet and possibly breaking them.

"Are you hurt?" Woodstock asked, helping pull the sodden material that once housed me from my path.

"I'm fine..." I muttered miserably, finding my way out of the tattered and torn fabric maze of rain and mud that was now my hammock.

As I sat up in the rain, my weary eyes followed the fallen tree where it had grazed the top of my skull, hadn't landed on my chest or body; and then narrowly missed my left foot on its descent. As I continued to follow the length of it, I found it had fallen completely atop Woodstock's tent as well, snapping his support beams in half.

My daze vanished instantaneously.

"Jesus Christ dude, are you okay?" I asked worriedly.

"Wales! Wake up!" I shouted.

"What's going on?" He mumbled in a weary response from within his own tent. Moments later he unzipped open the window on his door and looked out into the rainstorm at us from the safety of cover.

"Guys, I'm fine. The tree just landed on my head." Woodstock said. He followed this up by spitting a few chunks of shattered teeth out into his hand. I thought it was probably the most ironic thing I had ever heard before in my life. There was a large knot forming across his forehead, and he no longer even sounded like himself. As if something had crushed his nasal passages.

"Open your mouth," I said, as I approached him.

I flashed my headlamp into his maw to see his upper row of teeth shattered and broken. A couple splinters of his teeth had even torn up and through his gum line. It was a massacre of blood and bits of broken bone and torn flesh.

"Christ man, we need to go to the hospital, now," I said as I glanced back at Wales' tent. He was getting his boots on.

I already had my phone out, and was searching to find a signal and possibly call for an ambulance.

"I don't think we're gonna find anything open this late," Woodstock said, standing and looking around himself; confused. I ignored him, though, as my phone battery flashed a low power warning and I cursed technology and its flaws with everything in me. Why was it I never found myself prepared for when these kinds of situations arose? How efficiently was I utilizing the technology afforded to me when I waited to refill my battery life only at outlets or when my phone had been dead for two or three days.

"Then we'll drive around until we *do* find something. Wales! Let's go, now!" I shouted.

We threw everything including both my ruined hammock and Woodstock's shattered ultralight tent into Wales' prior domain that evening before the turn of events had taken place.

As I looked upon all of the damage done by one lone rotted tree, I was once again awed at how quickly a situation could change on a dime in the wilderness. The birch tree had apparently broken at the trunk of the tree during the down pouring and with the gusts of wind whipping about wildly; obviously rotted through.

It was unclear if as it fell, it split above or actually across Woodstock's face upon impact. Regardless, the force of the blow had clearly been lessened by first hitting my hammock and tearing it to shreds upon its descent.

We guided Woodstock back to the car as he apologized profusely again and again to either of us as if the whole turn of events had somehow been his fault.

"Guys, I'm sorry this happened." He said with shame in his tone.

"Why are you apologizing? You didn't do anything wrong! It's not your fault a tree randomly decided to smash you in the face." I tried to emphasize to him.

But Woodstock still felt bad for something he clearly had had no control over. And it immediately showed insight to his humble and modest nature.

As we walked through the pouring cold rain, with no cover to keep us warm from the elements, I thought about his absolute selfless attitude. I had been missed by the tree altogether and found that I was incredibly enamored by the fact he had first asked if "I" was okay before showing his own casualties.

After a half-ton tree had landed on his face.

As he continued to apologize, I patted him on the back—wanting wholeheartedly to hug him at that moment as not just a fellow thru-hiker or only an acquaintance; but as a best friend.

Rain continued to drizzle as we crossed a surprisingly busy Highway 16 in the middle of the night. Just three headlamps cutting through the darkness along a rural road in the midst of nowhere. The world was completely oblivious to the drama and the horror that had taken place only moments before.

Woodstock took shotgun as Wales drove through the pouring rain and I navigated our route from the back seat over Wales smartphone—the only one with a decent Verizon signal with which to utilize Google Maps and Navigation.

We kept conversation jovial and funny if for no other reason than because I had become concerned of the concussion Woodstock had possibly sustained, and I didn't want him falling asleep.

"Just think man, we're finally going to get that hotel room you wanted," I said, patting him on the shoulder.

Woodstock's head rolled slightly, almost as if he had momentarily fallen asleep.

I patted him harder.

"Wasn't that funny?! Ha ha ha! Laugh Woodstock, laugh! And for God's sake don't fall asleep."

We pulled into the nearest hospital where Wales and I guided him into an empty emergency room lobby.

In the corner sat a bored, unarmed, Securitas Security Guard staring at his smartphone with a lazy expression upon his face from behind the receptionist's desk. Beside him, a woman who appeared devoid of any emotion at all. Almost as if she hadn't seen many conversations during the last few years of her life.

She scrawled signatures onto forms and filled out paperwork of some sort with a blank face.

We stood there momentarily, as she slowly looked up towards us.

"Can I help you?" she asked.

"A TREE FELL ON HIS FACE!" I blurted out, with no other help at all to offer in regards to his condition.

The woman gave me an odd look, and the security guard cocked an eyebrow up at me from his smartphone as well.

"Morris, calm down," Wales whispered, patting my shoulders.

Woodstock proceeded to give the woman all of the pertinent information, with my occasional additions and details of the incident. Yet as I stood there, I was in awe that this lady was asking him rounds and rounds of questions after he had possibly sustained a brain injury from the tree that had just bashed into his face.

"Okay, can you give me the name of your employer? And a contact number?" she asked.

"I...I, don't...have one..." He replied.

"We're Appalachian Trail thru-hikers!" I spat impatiently as if I had expected her to have any idea of what that meant.

For God's sake GET THE DAMN DOCTOR! I thought angrily as the disinterested look on the tired woman's face only deepened my anger.

Did Woodstock have to fall to the ground unconscious, from a possible brain hemorrhage first, before he could be considered important enough to receive immediate care?

"Before we go any further, I'm gonna need your insurance information." She said, smacking loudly on some chewing gum. I rolled my eyes and threw my hands up into the air impatiently. As Woodstock tried to fumble through his items for his insurance card, he eventually began to lose concentration and had a hard time focusing.

"Help me please." He said, gripping the edge of the counter. He handed me a jumbled bunch of business cards, old receipts, credit and ATM cards to help him search through.

"So I was curious," I said, with obvious anger in my tone as I rifled through his cards. "What's gonna happen when he dies from brain bleeding?" I asked the lady, as I handed over his insurance card to her.

"Sir, calm down. He'll be just fine." The security officer started, acting as if I was exacerbating the situation.

"I wasn't talking to you!" I said, feeling as if I'd lost myself.

"Okay, you need to drop the attitude. We're only trying to help your friend out." The receptionist stated, smacking her gum even louder. The security officer had started to stand up slowly.

"Morris, calm down," Wales said. This time Woodstock looked up at Wales and then to me before he said: "Take him out of here."

"No! I don't need to go anywhere! I just said a tree smashed into your head and that you can't feel your face right now and these guys are more concerned with getting paid than they are saving your life." I said shrugging free from Wales.

"Sir, we have other people here with other illnesses as well that are in just as bad a condition as your friend here is, if not worst." The security guard tried to explain.

"Oh, I'm sorry *Doctor*. Did you go to medical school for eight years? Are those telescopes you have for glasses, equipped with x-ray vision? Can you perform a CAT scan on Woodstock with those bifocals of yours?"

Wales was leading my away now.

"Who are you again? Why are you even talking to me?" I said to the security guard as Wales led me outside.

"Unbelievable. Our healthcare systems asks for a paycheck before they offer to save your life." I said outside in disbelief. Wales looked at me solemnly, as I paced back and forth trying to calm down. Eventually, I walked away, as he went back in to check on Woodstock.

As red, yellow and orange lights from an incoming Ambulance, glared against the wet glass of the Emergency Room Entrance; I thought about how I had let the very things I had established as "reason" to complete the trail, drift away. I thought about Woodstock lying on the hospital bed in the other room down the hall, and wondered what his thoughts were on ending his trip.

Because this was it. It was all over now. And while I was angry, it wasn't just the receptionist and the security guard I was languishing over. It was the fact that I knew Wood-stock would *never* be able to continue the hike having sustained the injury he had. Now it was down to Wales and me.

I walked through the ER parking lot, smoking until the security guard from inside came out and told me I had to leave the hospitals property if I had wanted to smoke. I shook my head from side to side, took a final drag and crushed the cigarette out in the trashcan butt tray on the way back inside the building.

After an additional 20 minutes of questions, filling out more forms and then leaving Woodstock to sit in the empty lobby for an additional thirty minutes, they finally took him into the back where he received a chest, a neck, and a spine x-ray. They also proceed to give him a CAT scan as well.

In the lobby, Wales and I sat in bacteria laden hospital chairs, with no conversation passing between us—watching an audibly muffled and pixelated Saturday Night Live episode on the lobby's television. Kanye West was the musical guest, whining in some stupid song about "racism" and how bad he had it in his life, through his stupid lyrics.

"Millions of dollars, and millions of stupid fans that follow him. He can write a song with little to no words that sell millions because of nothing more than its beat—bang all the hot women, and or men that he wants and never has to worry about a thing again for the rest of his life. Except the next million, he's gonna get to add to the hundreds of others he already has. But he's got it *so hard* doesn't he?" I asked out loud in awe.

It would've been amazing to watch a tree fall on *him*.

It was 2 hours later when Wales and I were both allowed into the hospital room with Woodstock.

"How are you?" I asked, as Woodstock laughed and shook his head from side to side.

"Crazy night. I'm ready for bed." He said as I leaned back against the counter. Wales sat down on the doctor's stool and looked oddly out of place doing so, being the giant that he was.

The thought was already running through all of our heads, but I still didn't want to ask Woodstock the question. He was in bad shape, and it was clear as day to see it. And what he had suffered through wasn't really something he could choose to ignore and hike on with. The poor guy could barely chew anymore, let alone keep up with the elements of the cold with a constant low immune system and possibly end up getting worse or having infections from the mouth injury.

"Maybe we should get that hotel now?" Woodstock offered, trying to lighten the mood. I smiled, and Wale's looked quietly at the ground. There was a silence that came momentarily before Woodstock broke it.

"Come on guys. It's not that big of a deal. I mean I had fun out here while it lasted." He said.

"Sorry, we're not cheering the idea of you going home, Woodstock," I said sadly.

"Yeah, I know because you want to use the car…" he began before Wales cut him off.

"No, because we're going to miss you." He said flatly.

I nodded my head slowly, thinking about everything. In some small way, this was all starting to feel like the beginning of the end. Not because Woodstock would be taking his vehicle and driving back home to Minnesota, but because he was leaving all together. Down to just Wales and I, I wondered partly what I was to expect next.

"Well Morris, at least you still have Wales with you," Woodstock said. I nodded, feeling a little comfort in that. The chemistry between the three of us had been so strong, I didn't want it to end any other way than with our completion.

While we talked about the times we had all shared together, it felt like we were doing this more to ease the pain of what was ultimately to come.

Woodstock looked up nearby hotels on Priceline via his phone, while Wales and I awaited the doctor to release him. Unfortunately for us, the inclement weather outside had caused people to take the same route we had thought of, and this was to include hikers as well.

Everything was booked.

Nowhere in Gorham or North Conway had any rooms available, whatsoever. The one place that *was* open (Green Granite) wanted $139 dollars a night, despite the fact it was now 4 A.M. and we'd have to check out by 10 or 11 A.M. that same morning. To top it off, they didn't even offer breakfast either.

"Remind me next time I bust my teeth out after a tree falls on my face and I'm laid up in the hospital looking for a place to stay overnight—to avoid Green Granite," Woodstock said with a small chuckle. I looked at Wales who looked back at me, with tired, bloodshot eyes. I shook my head and walked out of the room.

After he had been discharged, Woodstock was given a prescription for antibiotics for what the doctor thought was a sinus infection found in the CAT scan, and for the possible inflammation from the tooth trauma.

Later, when we arrived back at Pinkham notch; Woodstock and Wales reluctantly headed back to the camp in the pouring rain, while I opted to sleep uncomfortably in a smelly, cramped car. My decision wasn't made exactly by choice, but then again it truly was.

That's because my hammock tent had been decimated.

It would be maybe 30 minutes later when Woodstock would return to the vehicle, and take up residence in the driver's seat as well.

"My nose started bleeding for no reason on the left side of my face." He explained.

"That's because the sinus infection that doctor spoke of was probably blood in the sinus cavity from the tree smashing against your face," I replied.

"Maybe..." Woodstock said, blowing a clotted mixture of mucus and blood from his nose into a napkin.

"That hospital, man. What a joke." I said, with an unbelievable laugh.

"Didn't mean to take up your space in here, by the way." Woodstock apologized.

"I admire you, Woodstock," I said, suddenly.

"Why?" he asked with a laugh and a smirk on his face.

I had tears he couldn't see in my eyes when I replied.

"Just cause. Just cause."

We celebrated the event that had taken place the night before, by eating the Pinkham-Notch-Visitor-Center-$14-AYCE-Breakfast-Buffet the following morning, before booking a motel room and deciding on taking a zero day.

This was done so that Woodstock could rest up from his ordeal the night before and make preparations to return home. Wales and I could also begin to consolidate our items and figure out our plan of attack now that we no longer had a car to transport our extra changes of clothes and extra food items.

"My parents are coming to visit me in October," Wales said to me suddenly, as I removed an old drop box sent from my parents out of the rear of the vehicle. I looked at him.

"How long you gonna be off of the trail?" I asked.

There was a short pause, and then Wales replied almost as if he was ashamed to answer. "Maybe around 2 weeks or so."

I nodded, knowing my response appeared distant.

"I'm still gonna finish the hike…" he added.

I was trying to figure out how I could schedule *my own* hike into that scenario. Wales always was a far faster hiker than I was. Maybe I could take it easy, by only pushing out 10 mile days during his absence while he went on 15 or 20 mile days himself upon his return. Eventually, we would surely meet up again.

All the same, he seemed worried by my expression on the heels of Woodstock leaving.

You've started to regress, haven't you? Something suddenly asked, within the privacy of my own mind.

You thought that when Melody left you, that was the only heartache you were going to have to suffer on this trip. But then you lost Torry as well. The voice went on, almost in a mocking tone.

"And now Woodstock…" I muttered out loud.

"What was that?" Wales asked me, but I was a million miles away from him in those following moments as I turned away.

Piper left the trail for a woman back in Virginia. Krystal and you, well we all knew that was just a fling. She's gone now. Tell me, did you notice how your parents and sisters have never once visited you along the way? The voice pestered on.

"They have jobs. They were busy." I found myself whispering to myself, as I walked away from the car.

What was wrong with me?

Was I losing my mind?

I knew I was only talking to myself, but this absolute sense of "self-doubt" came on so suddenly and forcefully, it almost felt *real*. As if some parasite had worked itself into my brain and was suddenly telling me or giving me reasons to give up.

"John, are you okay?" Wales asked. I didn't respond.

Tell him the truth. You aren't OK at all. You can't finish this hike because the only thing that's carried you along this far was the company of others. That's carefully starting to diminish now, isn't it? The voice spat, almost with laughter in the tone.

I took a deep breath, choosing not to respond.

Wales went back to packing the remainder of his things after separating what he'd planned to throw away and what he planned on shipping back home.

I knelt down next to the food box my parents had sent me, and read a note my father had written. I had been so concerned with food, and the contents of the box I had completely overlooked the message my father had placed at the base of the cardboard container.

It read:

Richard, you have four more food boxes left before you run out. If you need any more food along the way and you can't afford it on your own, you can always overlook your pride and ask your mother or me for help. You have a lot of people out here at the plant that are following your journal entries, and that believe in you. Each day you post your journal, your mother and I are living vicariously through your words. You've made it so far, and I have no doubt you'll make it the rest of the way. Always know we're proud of you.

I blinked tears away and folded the letter back up; placing it back into the food box as I stood and took a deep breath.

That message had all the confidence I needed, to continue on.

In my three months of having hiked with Woodstock and Wales, while using a vehicle to transport us from spot to spot along the Appalachian Trail; I had walked over 300 miles with them. I had completed all of West Virginia, Maryland, and Maine. I had walked a small chunk of Pennsylvania up to the official halfway point of the Appalachian Trail as well.

During our adventures together, we had dabbled in the outskirts of New Hampshire's border around Mahoosuc Notch. Having hiked past the state line, I was now looking ahead (south) at one of the most memorable sections of the entire trail.

The White Mountains.

So much of that time we'd spent in those three months together had been zero days, chore days or going to places we'd never been to, such as Manhattan, New York. It had included hiking a 30-mile portion in Vermont, along the southern border of New Hampshire. We did these things while either waiting for weather conditions to improve along the AT or while waiting on reservations for campsites to open in whichever state park we were closest to. We had used the vehicle as an excuse to explore Gettysburg, and Washington D.C. and all while regularly (and maybe a bit purposefully) forgetting the real reason we had come out there, to begin with. It had become apparent that the use of a car had complicated things more than it had helped the three of us ultimately. It had given us far too many options or reasons to sneak into the city for *real food*, or to pine over and eventually cave in to staying in a motel, or a hotel where we could find a washing machine, hot showers, and a soft bed out of the elements.

In the period we had spent together—I concluded that I had lost track of time, and the great sense of completing the journey had started to drift away from my thoughts.

We went to hookah bars, smoked and drank alcohol plainly dressed out of our elements within night clubs as we stumbled into these establishments in our ragged trail clothes.

Yet together as a trio, we were unshaped and unbothered by the looks of condemnation and ridicule from the rest of civilization. That is because we were within our own culture. We had gotten used to being in an environment out in nature where it was normal to smell bad amongst other people. Because all of the other hikers expected you to stink just as bad as *they* did. It wasn't unsightly that you were wearing crocs, zip off pants-shorts with stitches all over them and a darker shade of "dirt" coating your skin.

At times, it was odd to exist as that kind of person. Entitlement sometimes came from this abstract point of view. You would think the disparaging looks would cause distress and discomfort and at times you would be right. But more and more you found, that you didn't care what others thought about your appearance as time went on. I could look at a homeless person now, and on some low and very basic level understand both their needs and ultimately maybe even their potential detest towards society as well. Their unbothered attitude towards their own appearance was understandable—not just because they didn't have a choice, or because they didn't have a place or a way to clean their selves or their things. But because if the world and the majority of our society were going to view them as monsters, why try to refute or argue every day to be anything, but?

Wales and I had been dropped off at Rattle River, where we both would be crossing Wildcat and Middle Carter Mountain within the next 21

miles until we had reached Pinkham Notch. We had been camping there, the night of the storm just days before and it wouldn't take long for us to connect this portion of the AT on our journey south.

In the gravel parking lot, I glanced down at my phone; momentarily blinking out of my own thoughts. I was reading the current conditions atop Mt Washington. It was now 23 degrees with 40 mph winds that with a wind chill, brought the temperature down to just 3 degrees Fahrenheit, according to the website.

There were pictures of snow and ice, caked across the summit in thick blankets and drifts. Meanwhile down in the valley, all you saw when looking up at Mt Washington was the cloud cover it had become submerged in. It was like looking up at a gigantic monster or beast you knew someday shortly you'd have to eventually slay. Haunted continuously by its ominous and enormous presence which was always within eyesight as you hiked towards it over the course of several days.

Climbing out of the vehicle, I removed my backpack from the rear seat and put the heavy contents back atop sore shoulders. Woodstock smiled approvingly as Wales got out with his backpack and stood beside me. Woodstock looked us both over, and in a sense, it felt as if we were waiting for him to dismiss us on our march south, towards the completion of our 2,188-mile hike.

"This is the part where I say *just kidding*, and grab my gear and join you guys on the trail," Woodstock said, as Wales and I only smiled knowing there was no truth in those words.

Woodstock's smile faltered, and he cleared his throat knowing that this was going to be just as hard for him as it was for us.

"You guys know we're gonna meet up again someday, right?" he asked.

"Are we?" Wales queried, with noticeable skepticism in his voice. He also appeared very hurt in his expression.

I looked to Wales, who looked back down to me for confirmation if only to see if I felt the same way he had. As if this really was, the last time we'd ever see Woodstock again.

"Morris seems optimistic," Woodstock said, as I smiled and hugged him.

"Get over here, you jerk," I said, tugging on Wales and pulling him into a hug with Woodstock and me.

The three of us posed for a final picture together there in the parking lot of Rattle River.

We were able to elicit smiles, only after pinching each other's ass out of sight from the camera lens. It was an image of us laughing and having a good time to memorialize the incredible moments the three of us had shared together in days now passed. All captured within the 3.7 megabytes of information stored upon my cameras flash drive.

The 1.7-mile trek to Rattle River Shelter was comfortable and flat enough that it went by in less than an hour.

The 2,700-foot climb beyond it, however, was steep and unforgiving.

I was making excellent time despite the slick rock inclines and the misting rain that drizzled upon us at every moment. On my way up I noticed that there were patches of snow along the sides of the trail. Eventually, I passed a hiker who explained that there had been a blizzard on the range during the night and that it was going to be very hard hiking from there on out.

I thanked him for the sobering news but was slightly perplexed as I hiked on.

Maybe it was because I had been used to the terrain in Maine and this was just another steep section of trail to me.

But what I did know, was that it was just as rugged as anything and everything else I had already encountered north thus far. As I continued hiking, I began to realize that indeed I had already hit the hardest portions of the trail. I remembered the topographical map of the AT back in Harpers Ferry, West Virginia at the Conservancy. I remembered the jagged lines in AWOL's guide book. What was I so fearful of anymore? The White Mountains?

I hope you're prepared. That cynical, self-defeating voice muttered in my mind.

"I am," I replied, continuing on.

At the summit, I walked along soggy wooden planks and passed by the intersection marked to climb up to the nearby Mt Moriah peak.

It was dusk as I walked down the other side of the mountain along exposed ridgelines with massive granite outcroppings. The occasional iced over trees glinted and sparkled in the distance beneath benevolent and ethereal skies. I could see Gorham in the distance as it existed only as a long stream of street lamps, head lights on cars and businesses in a deep Valley far, far away.

Upon reaching the Stony Brook Trail intersection, a weathered and tilted sign stated that I was only 3.8 miles to Pinkham Notch Route 16.

I was also .7 miles from a place called Imp Campsite and I texted Wales with an update since he hadn't planned on making it there that evening.

It was dark when I reached the site at 7 P.M., and already I knew I wouldn't be sleeping alone.

You could smell marijuana from over a hundred yards away, drifting up the trail of broken stones and wet boulders I had traversed downhill to reach the campsite.

Sure enough, as I walked into the shelter, there were three other individuals all taking hits off of a pipe.

"Uh oh, Spaghetti OH's." one of the hikers said as soon as I stepped inside.

"Better hide the weed, unless this isn't a narc." the bearded fellow said to the other two hikers. The couple immediately passed a paranoid look between each other and then handed the pipe back to the "talkative" one as if apparently ashamed of having indulged in the festivities their selves.

"Where'd you come from today?" the mouthy one asked me.

"Route 2..." I replied, setting my bag down in the far corner.

"Was it Route-Tootylicious?" He asked, bursting into laughter at his own joke. The couple, still uncertain of my attitude towards their smoking, watched me carefully.

"Yeah," I replied quietly as I began to break out my things from my wet backpack.

"Well damn dude, you sure are depressing, and you're kinda bringing things down in..."

"Could you please *shut the fuck up*, and leave me alone?" I suddenly spat so bitterly, and with such anger in my tone that I was surprised at my own reaction.

Now would you look at that? The pestering voice inside my mind muttered with amusement.

There was silence from that moment on within the shelter, as the chatty-hiker with the red tinged beard took a few more hits from his pipe without saying another word to me. That is, until I broke the tension.

"I'm sorry..." I said, lying down on my rolled out sleeping bag, as I turned my back toward the three of them.

"A good friend and thru-hiker I'd been traveling with had to get off the trail today, and I'm just not in a good mood because of it," I added. There were no replies, from the other three individuals and I was content with that.

As I laid there, I took bites from a cold dinner and stared at the wall in silence.

I got up around 10 A.M. but didn't leave until 11—long after my fellow hikers had already vanished. My anti-social outburst towards them the night before hadn't come about out of malice. In truth, I had just been bothered by the fact that Woodstock was now officially gone and I had callously taken my anger out on *them*. Each time I thought of Woodstock being gone, I kept hoping that upon reaching Pinkham Notch in the days to come, I'd find him there as if the whole incident with the fallen tree had only been a bad dream.

But deep down, I knew that would never be the case. Miracles seemed to be far and few between out here in the wilds which made them so incredible once they had been experienced. I could understand the term "Trail Magic" now with a little more clarity.

Small pieces of kindness from other human beings that broke you out of feeling anger or disassociation towards the rest of the world and society. Proof that while you had come out here to "escape civilization," some part of you always came crawling back to receive a handout or an act of kindness almost hypocritically from them in the form of food, money, a free place to sleep or a hitch-hike into the local town.

Once again, that sense of entitlement could quite often prove to be quite detrimental to hikers as it warped their mindsets into thinking: "Why didn't that asshole pull over for me!" or "All I asked for was a dollar for a drink!"

I was weak in this sense too, and quite often found myself trying to retreat from that sort of attitude. And I had felt that way when the other hikers tried to engage me in conversation, and I had expected them to give me solace and comfort for an incident they knew nothing about.

I smeared sleep from my eyes, as I crawled out from my sleeping bag and looked towards the gray morning awaiting me outside. Thick clouds and fog made anything viewable more than 15 feet away—damned near impossible. It was hard to believe that it was nearly noon and that the sun hadn't even minutely burnt away the least bit of fog yet.

I set out, with creaking knees .7 miles back uphill to continue along the AT in a forest bound by dampened, faint sounds, and foreboding omnipotent silence.

As I made a 1200 foot ascent up Mt Carter, I came to notice ice collecting on the trees like glass, and rock slabs and boulders that you were expected to climb—glazed over in clear, glimmering crystals. I wiped perspiration from my eyes and felt the undulating burn in my worn out calve muscles telling me to hold fast as I caught my breath. It dissipated into the fog surrounding me or collected into droplets against my beard as I searched for any sense of a "sky" above. There was the lone chirp of a bird far away for a moment, and then utter solitude. Looking down, I found Wild Mint growing within a bed of moss by my feet with beads of water decorating the leaves. I knelt down upon the wet, stony earth and picked two leaves.

There was the sudden sound of a branch falling somewhere far away, as I stood and placed both fur covered leaves atop my tongue and continued on.

When I had reached an intersection that notified me of a blue blaze headed southwest towards Route 16—I felt the pull of spontaneity, just a little too much to bear. To capture a bit of adventure without knowing what to expect ahead.

The sign had claimed Route 16 to be no more than four miles down the mountain, and ultimately I wanted to get to Pinkham Notch, and then head up Mt Washington and start hiking my way out of the White Mountain range as soon as possible. Even more so now, with the earliest signs of ice and snow already collecting upon the summits.

I wanted to put so much distance between myself and "memories" that I wanted my whole world to be nothing but new adventures. This way I was no longer languishing over "the past" and *what could have been* if friends hadn't left, or others hadn't gotten hurt.

As I rounded a corner at about a third of the way down Carter Mountain, suddenly I heard something running up the dark, cloudy trail rather swiftly. There was ragged breathing attributed to the scampering of paws upon the broken stone path I had been traversing.

I stopped my forward progression momentarily as the patting of the feet got louder, and the breaths raspier.

The sound suddenly stopped, and I held my breath. The fog made it too thick to see anything of detail—but then the figure of the silhouette was there. It's broken, sauntering gait pushing through the damp air.

As I slowly rounded the corner; I peered past two conifer trees dripping from the fused glass coating of their needles, in ice.

I saw matted fur and mangy, bleeding flesh pustules on a giant creature. I held my breath and looked around for a weapon out of fright, but there were only small stones at my feet.

I grabbed a handful regardless.

I slowly crept around the narrow outcropping of trees acting like a peninsula in the middle of the trail, and that's when I saw it entirely.

Dark brown and grayish clumps of fur, with hollowed, black parasitic eyes piercing through me. The creatures gnarled lips, exposing two rows of rotted teeth.

There was a collar around the things neck, but it looked to have been there for so long, it appeared as if the flesh had grown around it and had even partly consumed it over time. It had become less like a choker on the creature now, and more like a tightened noose. The hair around the underside of the throat looked to be missing or rubbed raw over time—now just a large mass of infected, bubbling flesh.

Later I would come to think it was some kind of German Shepherd mixed with a larger breed of dog of some sort.

But at that moment it looked more like a mutated wolf to me, than anything else.

The creature's ears were perked up at first with a look of concern on its starving face after I had come around that corner. When it saw me, its lips peeled back as the animal growled in warning.

I couldn't move and felt my heart beat pounding. I felt the throbbing of my jugular vein pulsating beneath my neck and had images of the beast pouncing atop me, and tearing the flesh out from my throat in horrific fountains of blood.

While hiking, I'd always imagined during my daydreams that should I ever come across a wolf out here trying to attack or even kill me, that better chances than not—I would be able to kill the beast first before it took my own life.

But I was now devoid of that egotism and thought altogether.

There was some innate hidden fear that arose within me as if we had been primordial enemies over the course of time. Something ingrained biologically TOLD me to fear this wild dog. In a fight or flight moment, my brain was telling me to run while my muscles began to tense up and my fists tightened in preparation should I have decided to stay.

The dog by all visual accounts had won already because I was backing down with my head lowered in visible submission.

As I slowly stepped backward, the thing stepped forward as if slowly pursuing me or challenging me regardless. I had a hand full of stones in one hand, and my other was trying to unzip my waist pouch on my backpack to remove my Leatherman Multi-tool.

"Hey, buddy. Calm down." I tried in a soothing voice. The dogs' eyes rolled backward with insanity as it proceeded to erupt into a flurry of loud barks in response. Its head then shook maniacally from side to side as if something was digging into its eardrum, and its rolling emotionless eyes fell back upon me as the barking ceased.

I had retrieved my multi-tool during its fit of rage into my left hand and slowly unfurled my blade as the beast sniffed the ground—eyeing me as it continued to approach. Its head bobbled corruptly, and completely wrong. This poor animal was suffering from a lot more than I initially thought—and suddenly being killed by it seemed like a very real thing that could happen. Whether the creature was conscious of its actions or "persuaded" to do so by something else currently consuming its mind. As I looked at the infected collar festering with decaying flesh, spoiled blood and bacteria, I wondered who could be so cruel as to let their dog go out here in the wilds and leave it to survive alone with this buckled piece of nylon and polyester webbing slowly and quite horrifically decapitating the creature.

I wondered then if the dog had any memories of a former life where someone had apparently once loved him enough to put a collar around its throat and to take ownership of him. Were there any happy memories, of being held and loved as the hands of its master softly smoothed their palms against its once beautiful fur?

I also wondered if the dog felt any apprehension towards humans, or loyalty, or devotion within its parasitic ridden, diseased mind. Or had those memories been eaten away long ago?

The dog continued growling while indirectly looking up at me. Yellowish frothy drool dripped down from a broken bottom canine tooth onto the ground. I started to pick up pace, as I backed up and noticed that the creature was still trying to keep up with me. Some part of me knew that if I had turned my back to the dog and had taken off in a sprint up the trail, he would've been upon me in moments.

"Back!" I shouted suddenly, which surprised the dog and brought about a challenging response. Immediately, he snarled his lips, exposing its jagged, splintered and browned upper row of teeth. The dog then began a series of barks so piercing and loud that my stance began to falter.

I gripped my Leatherman tighter.

"NO! Get back!" I shouted, trying to sound louder and angrier than the dog. This time the beast snapped its teeth threateningly towards me and in mid bark and I threw my handful of stones at him hard enough to make him yelp and skip back. The rocks bounced off of various places like a shotgun blast of bird shot across its body.

"Get back!" I shouted again in warning.

He immediately stopped his racket after having been hit with the stones, but still stood in place growling.

I didn't want to hurt him. I actually felt sorry for him. His ribs were badly exposed, and he looked malnourished. As if a freshly skinned pelt had been thrown over atop bleached bones, to complete the "ensemble" that was him. I knew the animal had to be suffering from heartworms and possibly even Lyme disease with the way his head jerked to and fro, and his eyes continued to roll back into his skull periodically. But I wasn't in a position to find him help out here in the middle of nowhere and I didn't know what else I could do at that moment to protect myself—other than run.

A couple strands of drool were hanging from the left side of his mug, as his ragged breathing became more adamant. I slowly took off my backpack, setting it as a barrier between me and this feral animal. I opened the brain on my pack and removed six beef sticks.

I tossed one, which bounced off of the dogs' right paw, and landed directly in front of him.

He sniffed it.

"Good boy. Eat it. Go on." I whispered calmly.

The creature began to growl again, ignoring the food.

Just as he started barking and snapping at the air viciously again, I angrily beamed him in the nose with another beef stick I'd been holding. The dog winced as the chunk of meat arced into the air and then plopped to the stones directly by its left paw.

"No! *Bad dog*! Eat it, stupid!" I shouted. I was terrified because it now appeared that even food couldn't tempt this creature into submission. I was almost confident that instead, the beast would have been far happier lapping up my blood as I lay lifeless on the trail instead.

The dog looked around and then began sniffing the beef stick again while growling in concern. He shook his head as if trying to get some evil inner voice out. Each time he did this, though, he'd glance up in my general direction with his rolling, lunatic eyes, and growl again.

"You're insane, you miserable creature. Do you know that?" I said, taking a bite from another one of the beef sticks and tossing it at his feet. I was attempting to show him it was food. The growling stopped momentarily as he sniffed and then licked it.

He then began to chew it slowly; doubtful and careful.

"Good boy. Here you go." I said, tossing him two more which he ate as well. I didn't dare approach him or try to pet him at this point despite the fact I felt that I could have eventually fed him enough to do so.

The last thing I needed was to tempt fate and get rabies or suffer some kind of hospital visit I couldn't afford for an infected dog bite.

I tossed him the last beef stick I had, then broke out some crumbling cheese and peanut butter crackers from my side pocket. I stacked 5 of them in a pile at my feet after I tossed him one to show that these new items were in fact, more food.

He ate it, as his eyes rolled and his ragged breathing continued to get louder. His head shook and lobbed from left to right before centering upon me again with a violent and jerking rhythm.

I put my pack on slowly and began to walk into the forest on his right, far from his immediate area. This was hard, though, due to the steep terrain filled with rocks and boulders that over time, had become covered in slick, crumbling moss.

The German Shepherd hybrid eyed me with his ears still perked up as I slipped and fell more often than not, or twisted my ankle on rolling stones the size of basketballs; all tumbling out from beneath my feet.

There were more growls, and groans of concern that sounded almost a bit like whimpers and whines of fear. I genuinely felt as if the dog actually feared ME more than I did him. The dog sniffed the air and then slowly approached the stack of peanut butter and cheese crackers I had left for him.

It was a working distraction and all I needed.

He shot a wary glance back at me as fallen twigs snapped beneath my feet while I passed him by, a good 20 feet away.

As he ate, I circled back to the AT and grabbed the beef stick on the trail that had bounced off of his nose and tossed it to him.

He ate that as well.

I continued down the trail, only now I was running. My ankles and knees were in intense pain and the joints in each, protested. But my mind shouted: *"TOO BAD! Get over it and run!"*

I was terrified, thinking this dog could come at me from behind at any moment and take a chunk out of my calves. My feet dodged stones, and I jumped over large gaps in the trail that might have otherwise spelled my doom. My knife blade protruded between sweaty fingers and a loose grip as I kept glancing back, expecting the dog to rush towards me at double the speed I was running.

Perspiration poured down my face and stung my eyes mostly from the pain in my joints, as opposed to the exertion of my run.

There was a small downed tree in the path ahead, and I took a running leap over it. When I landed on the other side, my foot slid on a small apple sized stone that rolled out from beneath my feet. I tried to fall backward but the force and weight of my 60lb backpack careening downhill shoved me forward instead as I over corrected and collapsed face first into the earth. Immediately I thought of the multi-tool in my hand and the unfurled blade—just as something sharp penetrated my shirt and tore into my stomach. It was only a passing nightmare though as I purposefully tossed my knife in front of me as I fell; to keep it as far away from impaling me as possible.

I skidded painfully for a good six feet across the broken surface of rocks and jagged stones. I watched, as the shiny blade skittered down the trail into a crossing stream in front of me. I had slid to a stop into a small stream of water and looked back behind me, waiting for the dog to pounce on me from behind, and tear my throat out.

Instead, I only heard silence. I watched my breath dissipate as I looked desperately upon that trail and where it vanished behind curves and corners in the path; waiting for death to come sprinting my way at any moment.

Nothing.

I gripped a baseball sized stone and stood slowly, readied for anything as adrenaline burned like lava through my veins. I was still listening for any deviation of silence in the air. I thought I had heard running several times downhill towards me but eventually came to believe it was simply nothing more than my own paranoia and my thudding heartbeat rapidly thumping within my head.

I quickly dropped the stone and grabbed my Leatherman from the stream and listened a final time.

Once again, nothing came.

I folded the blade to my multi-tool and slipped it back into my waist pocket before continuing my descent down North Carter trail; towards Pinkham Notch.

Once I had reached Route 16, while my phone danced upon a waning signal, I managed to find that I was actually between five or six miles from the Pinkham Notch Visitor Center.

It was 2:50 P.M. and a lot warmer in the valley than it had been in the clouds further up in elevation. The wind was pushing clumps of marshmallow pudding across the skies, completely enveloping anything more than 200 feet up.

Every now and then the wisp of a stiff breeze would send the puffs of clouds scattering by; only to recollect and flow slowly on once again minutes after.

Never giving those summits a break from the suffocation and blindness they endured.

I crossed the road and stood with my thumb out, almost demanding a ride after suffering what could have been a more dangerous ordeal than I had bargained for only a couple of hours before.

In my time hiking the Appalachian Trail, or avoiding it and finding a different way through towns or down roads and using it as a marker instead—I had definitely learned how to hitch. It had been my intention and desire to include some words of the wise, from various sources. This is because everyone had their own theory on hitching and how to do it effectively.

Woodstock:

1. *Set your pack down at your feet in front of you so that they can see it as they are driving up.*
2. *Take off your hat/beanie so people can see your face clearly.*

Torry:

1. *Stand in a place that gives the target (car) plenty of room to stop.*
2. *Smile, to show that you aren't a threat.*

Morris the Cat:

1. *Finally, offer them a friendly wave as they pass you by, as it shows you're not angry about their decision to continue on. A guilty driver will always look in the mirror at you one last time as they drive by. This last moment gives notice of your peaceful nature which in turn, tugs on their heart strings.*

I had been holding my thumb out for an hour when a woman passed me in a white Volvo Station Wagon. I had been feeling hopeless and thought that if I didn't snag a ride within the next 30 minutes, I would definitely be walking the rest of the way back.

As she drove by and proceeded to pretend as if she was playing with the dials, knobs, and buttons on her dashboard—I gave her a sad smile and a gentle, exhausted wave as I continued on foot towards Pinkham Notch behind her passing vehicle.

The wind picked up and blasted me rather hard as I looked down the empty road behind me. Another storm was coming in from the west, and I was maybe 8 or 9 miles away from it. Unfortunately, I knew that at my walking speed it would reach me long before I found shelter inside Pinkham Notch Visitor Center, and maybe even possibly reach me within the next hour.

That's when I picked up the red brake lights in my peripheral vision from the woman's white Volvo. I threw my pack over my shoulder and ran towards the car as a massive logging truck blasted by me deafeningly. The wind almost felt like a vacuum—sucking me beneath the passing semi, but I held fast.

As I approached the vehicle, I found the driver was clearing her front and back seat out from notepads, and school textbooks.

I leaned down to her driver's side window.

"Hoping to catch a ride to Pinkham Notch if it's not too far away," I said, shivering only slightly in the cold gray wind.

"Sure, get in. I'm on my way to work and pass right by there." She replied with a kind smile.

"Well, as long as this doesn't make you late..." I said pausing momentarily.

"No, no, not at all. Get in!"

I set my backpack in her rear seat and then hopped shotgun on the front passenger's side just as she took off.

"I apologize for the mess." She said as I closed the door.

I laughed.

"You're fine. This is heaven compared to out there. I'm the one who's sorry for my smell. It doesn't take long from hiking out here to start stinking. Thank you so much for the ride." I replied as she laughed and replied that my smell wasn't that noticeable. Still, I wondered if she was just being kind.

The woman exclaimed she always picked up hikers through here despite the fact her children were so adamantly against it. I, in turn, told her that I could understand her children's perspective, especially when she stated: "You never really know, which one, will be the crazy one."

And I sympathized with her completely. Here I was hitching and looking like a complete maniac and serial killer that hadn't bathed in days. I had wild clumps of something amounting to what one would call *hair*; formed and matted by grease and body oil over the course of a couple days. I was 6'2, and my chest and shoulder width was 55 inches wide. I knew I looked intimidating.

And she was exactly right. You never knew if the people you picked up were secretly up to something or had bad intentions or not.

"I think a good way to have a partial filter of the crazies out there, is to keep your doors locked, ask where the hiker is going and try to feel out any strange vibes or mannerisms in conversation first before letting them in," I explained to her.

"If your gut tells you something is wrong. Simply drive off with no explanation. You don't owe them anything, and you made no promise to carry them along either. Even by only stopping, you're still giving consideration which is a lot better than nothing." I added.

"Okay, so then I have to admit something." She said as she glanced over at me with regret in her eyes.

"You didn't want to pick me up, did you?" I asked, immediately chuckling afterward.

"I'm so sorry! You just…and I don't want you to take this the wrong way. But you're *scary-looking*."

"It was the *wavy thing* I did, wasn't it? That was the hook; waving at you with a sad smile as you drove away." I said, with a pitiful voice.

"Are you kidding me? You planned that all out?" she asked incredulously.

"Hey! It worked, didn't it? I mean it got you to stop, and look at it like this. I gave you some very helpful information for future hitchhikers you come across out here."

She smiled then.

"You did. What was your name again?"

"Morris the Cat. It's nice to meet you."

"I'm Louise, and it's nice to meet you too—*Morris, the Con Artist Cat.*" She sneered with a playful smile.

Louise told me as she drove that her daughter had worked at the AMC and was an avid hiker. She also explained that her daughter had always wanted to thru-hike the AT someday as well, but that as her mother; she didn't like the idea so much. I tried to put her fears to rest by explaining there was a 14-year-old hiking the trail that year on her own, as well as a 9-year-old who was thru-hiking with her family.

"Oh really?"

"I have my good days and bad days out here. It's tough, and a lot of times I don't know what I want. But I think I feel better for having come out here and experienced all of *this*." I said with reflection.

"And what about your parents? Do they know you're out here?" she asked.

"Yeah. And they believe in me. As do many friends and family back at home." I said with a confident smile.

She dropped me off at the visitor's center and wished me luck as she drove away.

I glanced up and immediately found the storm continued rolling east towards my direction. I instantly felt reminded of the events the days before with Woodstock.

I had to get inside.

My stomach growled, and I felt the urge for some steaming hot clam chowder as I walked into the center. The place appeared empty and abandoned. There were no staff or workers, nor were there the average nominal amount of perusing tourists. Instead, lights flicked eerily, and I sat in the main dining hall alone and watched the winds whipping the trees outside, back and forth in huge gusts. Eventually, as the storm picked up in ferocity, I felt the need to get away from the huge glass windows I had surrounded myself with by sitting in the dining room. So I walked down the stairs to the basement of the facility where they had a backpack preparation area and a hangout for thru-hikers with maps and local mountain summit information on the walls. There was also a hiker box down there, littered with items Wales, Woodstock and I had dumped into it two days before when we had been consolidating the things left in his car.

The Pinkham Notch Visitor Center offered four-minute showers in its basement at two dollars apiece. Each additional minute was another twenty-five cents. To borrow a towel to dry off with was another two dollars as well. As I set my backpack down in that basement, I suddenly realized with fear that I didn't have a place to sleep that evening.

I remembered my wet and now mildewed, mud covered hammock tent that had been torn and ripped apart during the rain storm three days earlier.

I looked around at my surroundings and was aware that this basement was kept open all night for hikers coming in from the cold. And while I was certain it was against the rules to sleep down there—I partly wondered if I could, in fact, get away with it as well?

Morris the Cat stopping for a moment, and looking back north towards Mt Washington; before he continues hiking south.

CHAPTER 7

The White Mountain Range

THEY HAD PERFECTED THE ART of making me feel like an outsider and a black sheep of some sort.

As I quietly spooned warm potato and leek soup into my mouth, I was oddly aware of the looks I was receiving from the visitors—some of which had decided on staying in the rather expensive cabin and bunk rentals that were offered there in Pinkham Notch.

I was garnering distrustful looks and walking as slowly by people as humanly possible so that they weren't caught up in the draft of my hiker stench. I had already heard the comment from a mother pulling her child away from behind me as I had ordered my food.

"Honey, let's stay away from *him*. He hasn't had a shower in a few days."

The woman had said it so callously, and without a hint of sympathy in her tone, that I was surprised by it. In fact, I was probably sure I had in some way shape or form, ruined her entire day just by my living presence there alone. After I had looked back at the woman who had made the comment about me, she offered an unapologetic smile and continued along.

These visitors were rich folk, wearing expensive four hundred dollar Patagonia coats, hats, gloves, and winter spandex with $200 fur boots that climbed halfway up their calves. With their rosy colored cheeks, fair pale, smooth skin, blue eyes, and golden hair—they looked down upon me much like you'd expect they'd look upon a homeless man.

"My wife was wondering if you were going to take a shower." A man sitting next to me asked suddenly. I blinked away from my thoughts and looked over at a woman pinching her nose in an apparent act to make me feel ashamed.

"Excuse me?" I asked, with bothered confusion.

"If you need a couple of bucks, you can have *this*. For the shower downstairs that is. Not for alcohol or drugs." He said, offering me a five dollar bill.

Was this real? Was this happening to me right now? I wondered what made these finicky wealthy people so brazen in their approach, that they could so indirectly or purposefully insult me and feel no shame or reserve in doing it.

"The showers downstairs are..."

"I don't need your money. I have my own. And I know where the showers are." I replied angrily.

"Honey, the smell is awful. We're not trying to embarrass you or anything." The wife said. I felt my face turn red and was on the verge of an outburst, however the flames of rage were quickly quelled as the eyes of others in the vicinity looked at me.

The man slipped the five dollar bill on the table in front of me.

I quickly stood up, grabbed my food and left. I left the money he had tried giving me as well and walked away to eat the rest of my meal in the basement of the building, alone.

I looked longingly upon the $2 dollar, 12oz cans of soda from the late eighties and early 90's era—decaying in ancient vending machines left abandoned in the basement of the visitor's center. The glass screens were coated with dust, and dead bugs lined the lip of the bottom.

"Too rich, for my blood," I muttered, making my way towards the hiker's area and sitting against the wall there.

I had managed to stay there throughout the night before, by walking in and out of the facility occasionally so as to not appear to be sleeping to any site staff.

The picnic table residing in the hiker's room, would also have to double as my bed for the night, unbeknownst to the Pinkham Notch Visitors Center staff. The only other option available, was to rent a bunk bed from the AMC for an exorbitant $80 a night, which seemed a bit impractical.

There in the basement, I continued to make repairs to my equipment, and partially to my hammock tent as well until it was usable enough to hang once again.

I utilized their free Wi-Fi to listen to music over Pandora Radio while charging my batteries and electronics entirely for the 8 to 10 day march through the Whites without the [possibility of power.

I also took the spare time get some other chores completed as well. I grabbed a trash bag from the janitor's closet and made my way into the showers with a handful of quarters I'd gotten upstairs. Unfortunately, I hadn't had enough money to spare to buy soap or body wash. Instead, I took my cooking pan and pumped antibacterial hand soap into it from the bathrooms supply when nobody was looking. I then hopped into the showers and washed myself using the hand soap, from head to toe. I took this opportunity to wash my filthy clothes in there as well.

Afterward, shivering—I used the two dollar towel to dry off and then wrap around the lower half of my body as I wrung out my clothes into the showers drain. Filthy, and almost black water came out of them. They weren't going to be perfectly clean, but they'd be a hell of a lot better than they had been before.

Wearing my trash bag as a shirt, and my rented towel as a kilt—I walked back out into the basement lobby area with my crocs flapping upon the cement floor. I kept looking at my backpack while stretching my clothes out on a table to dry.

I couldn't delay it any longer, and ran my hand across my forehead in disdain.

"Let's just get it over with..." I muttered, as I then proceeded to remove my destroyed hammock from my pack again.

Well, I will be the first to admit, that I was no dress maker. I had no idea how to sew anything that well. So I had decided to start off with the small, easy tears and worked my way up. I had found some eight-pound fishing line somebody had left in the hiker box to use for a string. I was glad I had kept a large needle in the event this kind of thing had happened. This had become one of those 'worst case scenarios' I had prophetically envisioned occurring at some point along my journey.

However, I was barely able to shove the line through the needle's eye because of how thick it was. This called for some ingenuity on my part. I had to use my teeth to bite and flatten the end of the fishing line enough to cram it through. Even after though, I was still having a rather hard time trying to keep the fishing string tight and cinched together without bleeding back out and loosening up when tension came off from the stitching.

"This is hopeless..." I muttered. I had decided after using the fishing line on the ripped out bottom portion of my hammock tent, to abandon all other areas needing repair with it. Besides, I had mostly been concerned with the hammock being able to support most of my weight, and now that the problem had been solved, I was looking towards the black cotton sewing string in my backpack to finish the rest. Two hours later, I had completed the largest and most detrimental of the tears and had moved on to the torn bug net at last. When trying to pull the screen tight and cinching the hole—I found that I was causing new sections of the fabric to rip, thus making my sewing attempt of it just a tad moot. It made sense. The material anchoring the stitch in place clearly wasn't going to be robust enough to support stretching when it came time for somebody to sit or lay down within it while suspended.

As I continued to work with subpar materials, I thought about the weeks I had ahead of me for the use of the thing.

I had 710 miles to go before my journey was over.

If I was able to push out at least 300 miles a month—I could get done sometime around the end of November and early December. It seemed easily achievable, especially if I was to hike at least 10 mile days for the rest of the trail.

I awoke, slightly scared within that cold, damp forest. I had set up my tent at the scene of where Woodstock's face had been smashed into by the falling tree. The same tree lay in pieces on the wet forest floor.

I had fallen asleep within my sleeping bag against the wall in the basement of Pinkham Notch Visitors Center, but had been run off from the warm inside and told I had to find somewhere else to stay by the staff. When I protested and asked what the big deal was, it was explained that my being there was considered a *liability*.

It had dropped to the low 30's during the night in the valley, which made me wonder how insanely cold it had been atop Mt. Washington at that very moment.

As I struggled to find warmth within my recently repaired hammock, I heard birds or chipmunks stirring in the leaves along the forest floor.

I kept envisioning the starving German shepherd dog mix from the day before, snapping hungrily at my throat. I could see its brown, rotten fangs and bulging parasitic eyes staring dead at me, eating away at any reserves of strength or courage I felt within. I continued to imagine the creature lying in wait until I had stepped out from my hammock. At which point, the beast would pounce and sink its infected teeth into my jugular vein and tear its head back in bright, colorful displays of pulsing blood; all as it arced from out of my throat.

"Disgusting..." I muttered as I turned away from the image and shifted sides within my hammock.

The following day, Wales would finally catch up to me which I found quite odd as he had always been a faster hiker than I.

"There you are! I thought you left the trail too. Where you been?" I asked, smacking him on the shoulder.

"I've been hobbling along. That's all. Taking my time and enjoying the nature and reflecting on things." He said in a very pleasant tone.

"Well excuse me, your majesty."

"There's no excuse, for you." He said with a smirk.

"So I was wondering..." I began slowly. Wales tilted his head to the side as he listened.

"Five or six days ago, we reached the top of Mt. Washington via the Tuckerman Ravine trail, right?" I asked. Wales nodded his head in contemplation as he thought over what I was saying.

"Yes," he replied.

"And I was thinking; we've already hiked up there and came back down. We've done the mileage by foot so why not just catch a ride via a shuttle all the way back up and pick up where we left off?" I suggested.

Immediately Wales' face dropped, however. He was a *purist*, as was Woodstock and any workaround I ever found or brought up and offered to shorten the distance or mileage between two points along the trail seemed to turn him off from the idea.

"I can't do that...I'm-" he began.

"*'Hiking the Appalachian Trail'*, I know Wales." I finished the sentence for him.

He nodded his head with an apologetic face.

"Don't be upset. I'm not. I'm proud of you for sticking to your convictions." I said, patting him on the shoulder.

"How about you? You would rather just take the shortcut we did up Tuckerman Ravine as 'mileage' for the AT?"

"Wales, I was almost attacked by a feral German Shepherd someone left to die in the wilderness just yesterday. Wanna know how I came across the animal?" I asked.

Wales smiled.

"I get more experiences, and more interactions with people and dangerous situations when I stray away from the AT. Don't get me wrong, I was scared yesterday and still have nightmares about it now," I said.

"But if I stuck solely to *one single path*, there's no telling what other adventures I'll miss along the way. I'm not willing to narrow my view to one single two-foot wide path over the course of 2,188 miles. The world's bigger than that. And I want to see *all of it*."

The driver was very curious about my hiking adventure thus far. And while it was not my intention to be rude, truthfully I was always asked the same questions about my hike. So much so that my responses had become scripture and rehearsed, within my mind. In fact, I had become so sickened with the words "left it all behind" that I had started to say "I abandoned everything" instead, which I knew mostly meant the same thing.

So you do what a good hiker does. You smile, nod your head and tell them a story. The same one you told the last 900 people that asked you the same thing.

"Please say you have a gun or a weapon I hope." She said.

"No weapons. You don't need them." I replied, before exhaling a sigh. Why everyone thought you needed to have a weapon out here, I wasn't so sure. In fact, I had quite often felt like if I had actually had a gun, I'd have been worse for wear than better.

"What if a bear attacks you?" She asked out of concern.

"Well, I haven't actually seen a single bear this entire trip," I replied as I watched ridges and valleys stained with the beautiful dark reds of maples, and the orange and yellow hues of dying leaves intermingling in with those as well, on distant mountain tops. The shuttle puttered along up the long, twisty road that ditched and dodged in and out of cloud cover.

"Really?" she asked. I saw her eyes lock on mine in the rearview mirror. I only nodded my head again looking back outside the van's window.

The clouds were so odd to me; the way they sat perfectly level with each other at varying heights.

They looked like foggy ships atop an invisible ocean layered atop an unseen surface. And the van we were driving in cruised right through them.

After we had reached the summit, I looked down the road from the way we had just come up and found were above the entire world. In fact, the portal in the wall of clouds we had driven out of had closed behind us. I stood in awe as I looked down upon a vast white ocean of fluff surrounding me for as far as the eye could see on all sides of the mountain. There was no world beneath us any longer. No color of earth, no cut of roadway nor distant mountains. I was living in a physical cartoon representation of "heaven" where everything was a cloud and vast expanses of blue skies.

The air was fresh and clean, and I took huge breaths filling my lungs and getting a natural high off of the intake. I felt alive and energized and as I stood there it still felt like a whole new place I had never visited before.

In the distance, beyond the cloud cover, I kept seeing bright gleams of light towards the east; refracting off of the surface of something hundreds of miles away. It kept pulling me away from my euphoric moment. When I asked the driver about the twinkling lights in the distance, she told me that what I was looking at was the ocean. She stated we were looking into Maine and at the Atlantic Ocean beyond it.

"Amazing, isn't it?" she asked.

I nodded in surprise.

"So how far did you think you were going to make it today down the Appalachian Trail today?" she inquired.

"Hopefully I can reach the Mizpah Hut and camp somewhere in the vicinity."

"Gonna do some Work-For-Stay?" she asked.

"Do they offer it? I don't know much about the process." I replied.

"Yeah, the staff are pretty good about helping you guys out. Do some dishes, mop and sweep some floors in exchange for a place to sleep and some leftover food scraps from dinner."

"Wait, scraps? Like I'm a dog?" I asked, just a tad insulted.

The driver shook her head from side to side as if I didn't understand her.

"Try not to look at it so negatively. The hut staff are doing thru-hikers a favor by even letting you guys stick around." She explained.

I guess I had come off sounding a bit rude and was immediately apologetic for it. I just needed to see the situation for myself to try and get a better understanding.

After thanking the driver for the ride, I took my time at the corporatized summit that was Mt Washington. I bumbled about, reading a little on the history of it.

Apparently, the Auto Road itself was owned by a private family whose hands it had only changed with once, since it first became a business back in 1861. The US Forest Service owned the land everywhere else around the road.

Back in the day, a stage coach took you up to the summit where there was a hotel called Tip Top House. Food and alcohol were served there. Even back then, it had been rather expensive to stay up there, and the accommodations weren't exactly that spectacular.

It would cost you a dollar to stay the night and another dollar for a meal. This was at a time when most people only earned a grand total of one dollar a week.

After buying a soda for two bucks out of a vending machine inside the visitors center, I suddenly realized how much had changed in time, and how very little as well.

The crowds were thick, and I had started to feel claustrophobic as I waded through loud children and fat parents with ice cream stains on their T-shirts.

Bloated, impatient tourists and day hikers, shoving their way through the crowds as if their particular existence was somehow more important and meaningful in this world than anyone else's. Suddenly I found myself almost isolating and differentiating myself from the rest of them. As if in some way I had better deserved the sanctity of the mountain summit myself alone, than those I believed had no real appreciation for the beauty of it. How hypocritical I could find myself being.

"Excuse me, sir?" I was asked suddenly, by a young man who looked to be about 8 years old.

"Are you hiking the Appalachian Trail?"

I looked down at the kid behind me, wading through the crowd with a lost expression upon his face. I immediately looked for parental units attached to him nearby.

"Yeah, why?" I asked, just a tad bothered.

"Just wanted to say good luck, and I wanted to give you this." He said, holding a king sized snickers bar up towards me.

My expression was confused, as I knelt down to one knee and took the candy bar in hand.

"What's this for?" I asked. It was such a kind gesture, I was momentarily struck with awe.

"I just thought you might need something to eat since you're hiking so far." He explained.

There was the sudden feeling of guilt that overtook me as I looked at the kid's outfit and saw how he was dressed in day hiker's clothes. I had been so judgmental of the tourists atop the summit just moments before and self-absorbed in my own journey that I had started to feel it was far more important than anything *they* could have had to experience that day.

"What's your name, kid?" I asked.

"Kyle."

I reached into the waist pocket of my backpack and removed a bracelet that Nomad had made for me back in Hampton, Virginia when I had been officially "nomaded" by her just before hopping into a van set for Damascus, Virginia with Torry.

It all seemed so long ago.

"What's this?" he asked me.

"It's good luck. It'll help you hike long distances." I said with a smile.

The bright colors had started to fade with wear and weather over the past six months, but it was still a beautiful handmade bracelet all the same, for consisting of nothing more than brightly colored sewing string.

The kid smiled in return and then turned and ran to two adults standing just outside the visitor's entrance and leaning against the wall, to show what he had gotten in exchange.

Both men waved at me, with thick beards, shorts, ragged shirts and sandals on. They looked like former thru-hikers their selves. I waved the candy bar in the air, to show my appreciation and turned to head south, off of the summit.

However, I was appreciative of more than just the candy bar.

I was thankful for their helping open my eyes.

The trail was nothing but boulders that had been encompassed by browned grass, several different types of spongy moss and more rock outcroppings.

I made my way down along the crooked path, coming across the Lake Of The Clouds Hut.

It had been erected between two side by side summit ponds that were so incredibly clear you could look right down into their depths like glass. From where I was standing, the house appeared as if it was sitting literally on the edge of oblivion as behind it, nothing but a drop off and white clouds existed to the west.

As I arrived, I walked around the structure to find the windows had been sealed shut. I touched the door and then pushed on it.

Locked.

The AT followed Crawford path, which was called the oldest trail in America.

It curved along the bottom side of Mt Monroe. I stood, looking up in awe at it. I was anxious to go up and over it, and would have, had I known that it reconnected with the AT on the southern side. Looking at a trail map of the Whites back at the AMC, so many paths went *this way* and *that way* that I'd gotten scared of getting lost. And up here in the Whites was the last place in the world with its unpredictable weather that I was looking to go orienteering off of.

Even if I had been in search of adventure.

I made my way along mountain ridgelines that were no more than 50 feet wide at times in some areas. Moreover, the trails had been cleared of rocks and boulders since this was such a popular range. Easily made simple by hand bars over small two-foot rock scrambles you could have STEPPED over.

As I passed by them unassisted, I wondered where these same pieces of rebar had been while hiking through the Mahoosuc Notch.

Not too long later, I was passing beneath the base of Mt Eisenhower and walking along a narrow ridge which overlooked distant rivers and forests that appeared untouched by man.

And hopefully, they would forever stay that way.

As I hiked along the broad shoulders of Pierce Mountain, I looked up at clear blue skies and a shining sun. Far from the misinterpretations of the meteorologists that had promised, we could expect clouds and rain all day.

Not here though. All that was here was sun, and silence.

Upon reaching the Mizpah hut, I walked inside and looked around, wanting to see how this whole "Work for Stay" thing worked.

Stated on a plaque that had been nailed next to the entrance door; a sign read that the building had been erected in 1966 and that it was rated to withstand wind speeds of up to 200 miles per hour.

It had a modern, angular look with a roof that almost skirted the boulder ridden earth around its yard in sharp triangular shapes that reached towards the ground.

It took a second for my eyes to adjust to the darkness inside, and then I found I suddenly was looking at a guy in a white apron, wearing a chef's hat.

The kitchen cook strummed on a guitar and sang to another man who tended the nearby Nauman campsite as an AMC staff member.

I slowly set down my pack; propping it against the wall.

Finally, when I assumed the huts staff were not going to acknowledge me; I asked if they had a work for stay program there. I felt stupid for inquiring, only because the response seemed a bit labored.

"Well, I personally don't really have anything for him..." The man tending the tent pads said, passing a sideways glance towards me.

"Uh...give me a few minutes, and I'll find something for you to do." The Cook said, disappearing into the basement.

No rush, really. I thought to myself, as I looked around.

I wandered about, looking over the almost 50 year old, solid wood structure. My feet creaked across the polyurethane coated wooden floors as I explored. I looked at the ground, specifically at the corner that I figured I would probably be sleeping in.

Far cleaner than a shelter. I thought to myself.

When the cook came back with a bucket of hot soapy water, and scrub pads inside it; he told me to follow him.

He placed the bucket on the 2nd floor, and in bunk room seven.

"Oh yeah, almost forgot. Lemme, get you a dustpan." He said, taking off again.

I looked around the room. There were three levels of bunk beds stacked on top of each other. This particular room would hold nine people.

The bunks looked to be rather old, but very sturdy with a cherry colored polyurethane finish.

It seemed to be rubbing off though in age, as I chipped a small worn piece off with my fingernail.

I turned and looked out of the window behind me. The view overlooked propane tanks and a boulder filled yard fenced in by tightly compacted conifer trees. I believed the tanks were how the Mizpah Hut powered their facility.

As the kitchen cook came back in, he went over what he wanted to be done.

"So, you'll need to spend about three to five minutes on each bunk. I'd like you to take these rubber mattresses off," he said, grabbing one that was eye level with us both and pulling it to the ground.

"And I want you to scrub them down. Sweep each bunk and then scrub those down as well with this soap and water."

"When you've done that it should almost be dinner time. During dinner, you can hang out in the library upstairs. We typically don't let you guy's hang out in the dining room area while our guests are eating. Most of our paying guests end up feeling sorry for thru-hikers... or uncomfortable with being watched. Which can sour the mood, or make things a little awkward." He said with a thoughtful expression.

"Yeah, that makes sense. What, with us, hikers just being A BUNCHA PIECES OF SHIT! Eh?" I laughed out loud rather obnoxiously while clapping him on the back. He eyed me cautiously, offering a nervous smile before returning a confused laugh.

"Uh...okay. So anyways...I know you're going to want a shower but..." He began as I promptly cut him off.

"Probably not allowed. Maybe you don't even have one? No clothes washing either?" I asked with a sarcastic tone.

"Right, but you DO get a place to sleep, and whatever the guests don't eat, you can have." He said as if it was a blessing.

And you know what? It was. As cynical as I was acting and as insulted as I felt about being treated like a lower class citizen—how could I complain about something I didn't even have the right to receive, to begin with? I'd come in here slightly feeling justified in my existence, yet now as I stood here humbled by the fact that I was going to be earning my stay—I felt very appreciative.

"Look out for used condoms beneath the mattresses by the way. Yes, we've found them before." He stated before leaving.

I nodded and then proceeded to pop in my earbuds and jam out to music as I swept and scrubbed everything down. I spent about 45 minutes to an hour cleaning and had gone above and beyond what the kitchen cook had originally wanted me to do.

I picked out old snot rags and scraped gum off from beneath mattresses. I threw away socks left behind and the empty plastic wrapping for old Sudafed caplets or toothbrushes.

Of course, there were some band aids as well. Quite of few of them, to be honest.

One of which had been sticking to the bottom of the mattress and fell, as I hefted it over the ledge.

It landed against my cheek, and my response was immediate.

I freaked out, smacking wildly at my face and dropping the mattress to the floor in the process.

"Are you okay?" One of the female staff asked, as I flailed my arms back and forth like a maniac. She was looking into the room with a rather bemused look on her face.

"Oh my God...I'm gonna die," I whined over dramatically.

"What happened?"

"Some bodies' nasty band aid touched my face. Now I'm diseased." I cried, shaking my hands in the air like a wussy.

"I'm sure you're going to be fine. The bathrooms at the end of the hall." She said, walking off and laughing.

I fought dry heaves in the bathroom once I thought I had seen somebodies scab dangling off of my beard. I scrubbed my face with hand sanitizer first and then foam soap, then more hand sanitizer before I was thoroughly satisfied. Though truthfully, even *then* I wasn't very pleased.

After my chores had been completed, I came downstairs and asked the cook what else needed to be done.

Once he had exclaimed that was all he had for me to do, I headed back up upstairs into the library which was actually a loft overlooking the dining room area. As 6 P.M. rolled around, the delicious smells of food filled the air as well as the chatter and gathering of hungry guests.

These were day or weekend hikers usually making a short trip to Crawford Notch, and Pinkham Notch while staying in the huts along the way. For a small fortune, backpackers got three meals and a bunk bed to stay in as they continued on foot either north or south. Upon arrival at either place, there were shuttles available to bring them back to their vehicles.

I was envious, knowing that this would have been a great past time to have shared with my family growing up. To have this memory with my parents and siblings, would have made for an incredible pastime to talk about. And it was at that moment that I actually longed to see them all again.

There was a ringing of a spoon against a glass, and then I heard the leader of the Mizpah Huts staff speak.

This would be the first time I had heard her say anything, let alone see her with my own eyes. I assumed she'd been sleeping most of the day by the blasé expression on her face and the noticeable bags beneath her eyes.

I sat in the loft looking down at her and all of the paying guests, at their rows of picnic tables within the dining room.

It seemed as if I was the only thru-hiker there...hiding out of sight like a bad dog while they all ate their meals.

Soft orange afternoon sunlight spilled in through ceiling skylights, as I drooled over the smells of their dinner.

"My name is Emma, and I am the House Master. Our food is served family style. You will be full but make sure before you take seconds that everybody has had firsts. Ladies and gentlemen, I wanted to thank you all for being here. With your support, your money goes to the conservation of our trails and huts as well as our paychecks." She said, as there was a light laughter by the guests over this little blunt jab.

I looked on, hungrily.

"The AMC has a 125-year tradition of treating its guests with the utmost care. Should you need anything at any time, please do not hesitate to ask. We do have a few rules before we begin serving your dinner. If you are going to eat, eat all of it. Whatever you don't eat has to be carried down the mountain...because our compost is full. You'll see we don't have napkins at our tables. That is because we also carry out our own trash. If you were to spill anything, we ask you use your sleeves or shirts to clean it up." She stated. There were a few disconcerting whispers back and forth. I didn't think the guests liked the way that sounded for the prices they were paying to stay up there overnight.

"If the spill is too grand for a sleeve, let us know, and we will try to find a towel. Tonight, your first course will be a Tomato bisque soup with buttered honey oat and sunflower bread." There were Ohhh's and Ahhh's before she went on. I'm pretty sure that I was one of the people groaning in hungry anticipation.

"Your second course will be our house made salad. Your main course will be Honey Dijon chicken breasts with rice and green beans. And as for dessert...well....that's a *surprise*." She said with a perfected Oscar Award Winning mischievous smirk.

The guests began clapping after she was finished.

Meanwhile, I rested my head on the lofts overlook railing and sighed.

Boy, was I hungry.

When I could take no more of the guests eating and conversations about where they worked or which countries they'd been to, I turned around and began reading the Mizpah huts old logbooks.

I was amazed! These logbooks went back as far as 1968! I was reading journal entries much like those you'd come across today within an Appalachian Trail journal. Crude dirty pictures, pop culture of the time or familiar phrases and jargon of that era.

Peace signs riddled the 1969 log book as images of pot smokers littered the pages as well.

I read the logbook for 1983, the year that I was born. I was surprised to learn about thru-hikers from way back then making the trek from Georgia to Maine before it had become so mainstream. It forced me to wonder how they had even heard of it, to begin with back in a day without the internet or smartphones.

Some people were my age at the time they were thru-hiking. Thirty years later, they were in their 60's, and now I was partly re-living what they had once done their selves through the words they had written 3 decades before.

I wondered if they remembered the things they had written and the dirty limericks and poems of a perverted clown. A picture of a man asking for a cigarette. Old stickers pasted to the pages from those years so long ago.

It was rather intriguing.

Moreover, I wondered how many of those people were still alive.

"I love you, Mike!" Somebody had scrawled into the back of the 1968-69 logbook. I started thinking about the names I had seen carved into old wooden planks or signs at Albert Mountain back in North Carolina.

The puppy love written messages of two people that probably no longer even remembered each other anymore.

Mike had grown up.

Maybe he had become an office clerk for 25 years at a job he hated. The morning routine of cigarettes at break time and a coffee kick start whenever he could buy time wore lines into his weathered face over time.

Across the next few years, he may have become a manager and had himself a couple of kids he put through college. He probably had a mortgage, a car payment and a marriage he'd grown bored with long before. But Lord only knew he was too bald and too fat to find anybody he felt was better suited for him.

And the mess of a divorce and the complications that arose from it were too much a hassle than just living out your days on a couch, watching your favorite football team with a beer in your hand. Even if it meant a lacking sex life, and the occasional nagging from time to time.

What happened to Mike? What happened to that youth he had so willingly given away?

How many others in these journals had probably lived out the same fate?

I sighed, and slowly closed the book.

After this journey, I knew I could never go back to a normal life. All I'd ever be thinking of was the money I'd make to fund my next grand adventure and a great escape.

I never wanted the 9 to 5 lifestyle again. Or what had been in my case, the 12-hour graveyard shift.

Emma, the head of the staff shouted suddenly, drawing me out of my daze.

"How was dinner, everybody?!"

Her loud voice was a bit screeching and jarring, like nails on a blackboard.

Everybody began clapping and cheering in response to her inquiry. I added in, clapping as well despite the fact I'd had nothing to eat at that point.

"How many of you would like coffee with your dessert? Five?" She asked, looking everybody over who had raised their hands.

"Which of you would want regulars?" she then asked. Two guests raised their hands.

"Two reg-u-laaaar's..." She shouted out in song with the other servers in tandem joining in and repeating to confirm the communication.

"How many decafs?" She asked. Three guests raised their hands.

"Three ir-reg-u-laaaar's!" The crew all shouted out in song again.

It all felt a tad bit cheesy and cringe-worthy, but I kept silent all the same and watched on.

"Evening time rules." Emma began.

"No open flames around the hut for you cigarette smokers. Pack out your trash. If you have brought your own power bars, coke cans or bottles—please take that trash back out and down the mountain with you. Lights out at 9:30 P.M. and we're strict about this." She then went on to introduce herself and added personal things about herself which weren't really that "personal" at all as much as they were average and only awkward because they'd been brought up.

"One time, I gave myself a buzz cut hairstyle," Emma said.

Then one at a time, the other staff members did the same.

"One time I locked myself in my bedroom by accident for 4 hours." This got a barrel of laughs from the guests.

"I'm scared of spiders." The kitchen chef that had delegated my job duties earlier that afternoon said.

"I want to eat..." I muttered out loud. Maybe a little TOO loud. I quickly ducked behind the lofts railing after saying it, and covered my mouth.

There was a bit of silence, and suddenly I felt my face turn about a thousand shades of red.

So the guests had then decided to join in their selves to the introductions. One guest had even explained he had received a 2.4 million dollar severance pay after retiring to which he received claps and cheers over.

I thought about the empty bank account I had myself in comparison, and immediately felt sick to my stomach.

After cringing over corny jokes that were being passed back and forth between the Hut Staff and the guests, ("Once upon a time, a blind man picked up a hammer and saw." Hyuk hyuk hyuk) it was time to eat dinner. I sat in the corner, hunched over my food like a criminal as I crammed it down my throat as if in fear that it would be suddenly taken away from me.

The food was heavenly, to say the least, having been starved for so long while everybody else had gotten to eat.

I mostly filled up on the oat and sunflower bread that had been made from scratch, with large globs of salted butter smeared across the top.

When I was done, I helped the crew clean up the dishes and pots and pans that had been used during the evening.

The sky had darkened relatively quickly, and I had retreated to a boulder outside to watch the last few moments of the sun and think about the trail ahead.

"I believe that this is the hut. Come on and let's go in." I heard a man say, with a woman following close behind him.

When they saw me, however, the man stopped in his tracks.

"Hey, are they still accepting Work-For-Stay inside?" He asked me. The guy had an attractive girlfriend that I had been too busy eyeing, to have heard him clearly.

I shook my head and snapped away from the flood of naughty thoughts running rampant through my mind, just having seen the woman.

"I uh…yeah. I believe so…" I answered.

"Oh thank God." The woman said.

"I'm Morris the Cat. Guess since you're both asking for the "free option" you guys are both thru-hikers as well." I said.

"Yeah, dude. My trail name is Lucky, and my fiancé here is Double Take. What about you?" he asked me.

"Kinda. Started March 17th, flipped at the halfway point at Pinegrove Furnace State Park, and now I'm hiking back south to finish the rest of it." I replied.

"Wow, you've been out here quite some time." The Double Take said with an impressed tone.

"I encourage myself daily, by telling myself I'm essentially walking back home to North Carolina, where I'm originally from," I explained with a smile.

My morning alarm clock had been a series of ragged coughs, followed by shallow breaths as I tried to take in air.

I muttered gibberish, as I rolled over onto my stomach and continued to laboriously breathe from filth-filled lungs. As I hacked, I tasted black exhaust, dirt, and mildew on the back of my tongue—along with grainy bits of sand that had collected on the inside of my mouth during the night.

I had slept next to a floor vent.

If smelling my own death breath hadn't been enough, I more than got the whiff of my own stench as I rolled over onto my side. A huge waft of body odor, with just the right amount of heat during the night to incubate the bacteria growth process, blew up into my face like smelling salts and left me wide-eyed and clamoring to get out of my bag.

I know there's gotta be a shower here I thought to myself rather pessimistically, almost sure the staff had been hiding it somewhere in the basement for their selves, behind a secret door.

Suddenly, I imagined the "croo" as they called themselves, laughing as hundreds of thousands of gallons of hot, steaming water rained down upon them and they danced, covered only by mountainous globs of suds in a large underground shower room kept hidden from public knowledge.

Okay, okay. Just stop it. You're only making yourself needlessly angry. I tried to tell myself as I looked around the large open dining room.

I sat at a table in the corner of the dining area and watched the staff of the Mizpah Hut as they stirred about and started getting ready to serve breakfast by lighting the stove and boiling water. One of the croo actually brought out a guitar and began to play "Wagon Wheel" which had been recently popularized from the past 40 years earlier, amongst hikers this year; by the former Hootie and the Blowfish lead singer—Darius Rucker.

Soon after, the rest of the staff had joined in on the caroling.

"Rock me momma like a wagon wheel, rock me, momma, any way you feel….heeey…momma rock me." They sang while Lucky, Double Take and I looked on from our corner. The four-person staff walked up and down the hallways, singing loudly.

It was as if they were acting like an alarm clock. Some of the guests had started joining in, singing as well and there was suddenly for a moment—this feeling as we all joined in and sang together of a "community" type of setting taking place between staff, Appalachian Trail Thru-hikers and these weekend day hikers. We all started dancing or stretching notes of the song as far as we could audibly take them.

The truth was, I had gotten so sick of hearing every hiker with a ukulele, a backpacker's guitar or banjo trying to play the song at campfires over the last six months that I could no longer stand to hear it. But still, I sang along with everyone else while caught up in the moment.

After the song was over, everyone clapped, and we all generally felt involved and a part of everything.

"That was awesome guys, really it was. Thank you for joining in! If you wanna go on and head upstairs now until after breakfast, that would be fine." Emma, the director of the staff, said with just a tad bit of condescension and authority in her tone.

For a second I was a bit confused as to why I was suddenly being shunned away after the great sing-a-long I had just participated in. I had felt so close to everybody for this small moment in time, and now suddenly I was being put back into the corner as if it was a travesty that I had ever even been a part of the chorus, to begin with.

Lucky looked over at me and shrugged, as I hung my head. Him, his partner Double Take, and I slumped upstairs and out of sight as the staff went back to singing other songs the morning guests had now become less enthusiastic about singing.

As I sat upstairs, Lucky glanced over at me as if he'd had a question and then looked away again. The second time he had glanced over at me however I decided to engage him.

"What is it?" I asked, lifting my head from the balcony railing I had been resting it on.

"How'd you get you name?"

"Well, actually....I gave it to myself." I replied.

"Aren't you supposed to *earn* the name?" his girlfriend asked.

"Well, how'd you get yours?" I returned.

"My boyfriend gave it to me." she replied.

"Isn't that cheating, a little bit?" I asked. She frowned and then shrugged. Apparently no longer interested in engaging with me in conversation, she looked away.

"What about you, Lucky. How'd you come by that name?"

"I snapped my C1 and C2 vertebrae in a mountain biking accident. Just at the base of where the spine connects to the skull. Luckily, I didn't become a quadriplegic." He replied.

Well, it was now a fact, that Lucky had a much better story than I—whose name was based upon an already existing last name. As much as I had tried to attach different events that had occurred during my 2,000-mile hike thus far to my moniker, it ultimately felt a bit cheap to do so. I had caught a small sparrow in mid-flight in Virginia, and I had been attacked by mice at Low Gap Shelter back in Tennessee. I chose to be finicky with my food preferences much like the 9 Lives cat food mascot; however, ultimately the truth was, I had still given myself the name.

"What'd you use to do before you came out here?" Double Take asked me suddenly, without looking over towards me. Instead, her eyes hungrily washed over the breakfast food being prepared by the croo, below us.

"Overpaid, Security guard," I replied.

"Well, that's cool. I guess..." Double Take lied. There had been nothing *cool* about the job at all, and even I could admit it.

"What made you decide to come out here and hike 2,000 miles?" Lucky asked.

Down below, the staff had called the guests together into the main dining room, and they were getting their first round of baked biscuits, cold salted butter and honey, coffee or tea and oatmeal energy bars.

Oh, how envious I was of them as they chomped happily and slurped their piping hot black liquids.

I thought about what Lucky had asked me, and felt with certainty I knew a canned response. One almost exactly like the thousands I had seemingly given before, when asked by other people, or thru-hikers.

"I wasn't happy anymore," I replied, looking over at them. They both nodded agreeably, as they waited for me to continue. They were also a decade younger than I, having been born sometime in the mid-90's. I found it hard to relate to them. Their youth ultimately betraying their agreeable nature as if in understanding.

"But it's also not that simple either. You see it's never just *one thing*, is it? It can't be…because over time it morphs into a hundred or thousand other reasons. Suddenly one day you wake up cold, freezing, maybe hypothermic and you no longer understand why you're out here anymore. You start to feel like you're just walking around in the woods to either prove yourself to the world or to end up dead. Whichever comes first."

"That doesn't sound like reasoning at all. That seems like suicide." Double Take replied, looking up at me with her large blue eyes. I immediately thought of my mother then, and the fears she had expressed over the phone in what I had ultimately found to be so funny and over-dramatic of her response. My mom had been convinced that the only reason I had indeed come out into the wilderness along the AT, was to in some way end my life.

"Well, you can only sit on your couch in an alcoholic haze…watching Netflix with the curtains drawn for so long before you begin to hate what you've let yourself become. Before you despise your very own life. I was killing myself in other ways back at home." I responded in a flat tone.

"Maybe you came out here to get a change of scenery while you found another way to do it?" Lucky offered, in a playful tone. The three of us chuckled lightly over the comment.

"I think I figured that by giving my father something to be proud of, I would somehow find something good in myself worth living for. I wanted my friends and family to see that I was something other than just a security guard, left to scrounge out my life paycheck to paycheck and knowing how everything was going to end." I said, taking out the pinkish granite stone from my pocket that I had taken from the summit of Katahdin.

I kept it on me more often these days, when looking for strength.

"I gave up a lot, just for this stupid little rock. I had thousands and thousands of dollars of *junk*. From expensive 60-inch flat screen televisions, blue rays, Bose Surround Sound speakers, PlayStation and X-box consoles, computers. I even had a dining room table, I hadn't once eaten at after spending $300 dollars on it. My ex loved that kind of lifestyle..."

"Is she still waiting for you back at home? Your ex?" Double Take asked.

I was rolling around the rock, within the palm of my hand before setting it down onto the table between the three of us.

"She's gone," I replied.

Both thru-hikers had picked up on the tone change in my voice. It was evident they had heard the hurt through the words more deeply than even the memory of her walking away back at Stecoah Gap, could inspire or create in my own mind.

"Maybe it's not that rock that matters, though. Maybe it's the journey and the hardships we face out here," I offered.

"So many people come out here to find something in their selves that they didn't believe existed before. And at times through my flailing resolve..." I said, stopping short and offering a chuckle out of reflection.

"I see something in myself that tells me to keep going, even after all that has happened. Even after my friends leave the trail or even when stumbling upon hopelessness and doubt, one step at a time."

"Why don't you just go back home? I'm sure you have family and friends waiting on you that love you." Double Take added.

"I do. But I'm not out here solely for myself anymore like I was in the beginning."

Torry had scolded me, by saying that I wasn't out here hiking for myself. But that I was instead, hiking for the enjoyment of *others*. My ex-girlfriend Melody had ridiculed me in the beginning by stating the very same thing while I had always tried to deny it. And while it could be seen as noble, by hiking for my mother and father's pride, I found that I was also walking for the friends back at home. The people that wished every day they didn't have the responsibilities or work and mountains of bills to hold them back and bog them down from living out their own dreams. I had felt bad for so long, thinking and thinking of what a failure I was and how weak I had become. But I was still out here, doing it. Hiking my own way.

NO WONDER, Torry couldn't stand my whining. Because that's all, I've ever done. But that's also always going to be a part of who I am, and I have to accept that. Am I hiking for myself? You're damn right I am! But I'm also hiking for everyone else at home, living vicariously through my day to day journals. I thought to myself.

Those experiencing my adventures and getting a taste of life, through my words.

"And..." I said out loud to myself, laughing at the feeling of a tangled knot of confusion and depression having suddenly worked itself free.

"And...I'm okay with that." I ended.

While I smiled after my internal rant, I felt Double Take and Lucky were just a little bit befuddled by my random comment.

I swallowed and felt an embarrassing click in my throat.

"It's uh..." I began a little awkwardly.

"It's time to eat soon." I finished.

"Yeah, I wanted to ask the staff if there was anything they needed us to do since they let us stay inside last night." Double Take said as she stood up.

After they had left, I felt so much more free and excited that it was hard to find any sort of depression or anger in anything anymore. Sure, I was a pessimistic, and cynical asshole.

Yes, it was true that I was typically looking for sarcastic responses out of a personal sense of negativity, but it still felt so good to finally come to terms with myself at that moment.

As I stood up, to head downstairs and see what food had been leftover for breakfast—I glanced back at the rock I'd taken from my pants pocket.

I held it before my eyes, pinched between my thumb and forefinger. Deep down, I partly wondered how much lunacy had driven me each and every day or if I was finally growing up.

I slipped the rock back into my pocket.

If lunacy were my sole driving force, the next two months would drive me closer to the edge than I had ever been before.

Breakfast consisted of leftovers and scraps from the plates of the guests. Food that was otherwise going to be thrown away.

I had made off quite well. I'd managed a tablespoon of oatmeal from a bowl split three-ways between Lucky, Double Take and I.

I was also privy to the last tablespoon of canned peach filling for the topping. Beside that sat two small sausage patties about the size of half dollars, and a palm-sized pancake. I topped it off with three cups of coffee for good measure.

After breakfast, I had asked the cook if there was anything else he had for me to do before I left.

He gave a quick look around and then said "Shhhh, just go ahead and get out of here while you still can before the Hut Master finds something for you to do."

"Really?" I asked.

He nodded his head, ushering me along.

Well maybe this whole "Work-For-Stay" thing wasn't that bad after all?

As the three of us started to turn away, he stopped and called out suddenly.

"Not *you two*, however. Morris the Cat did his work yesterday, so you guys gotta help us take care of the dishes this morning."

I could swear I almost saw both of their faces drop immediately. Lucky even brashly said: "Well, I can do a *little work*, but I'm not gonna be here all morning. We need to get hiking."

I smiled and waved goodbye as I headed on out into the crisp morning sunlight.

I took a deep breath of fresh air and set one foot out in front of me before the door to the Mizpah Hut opened behind me.

"Hey, you gonna be at the next hut?" Double Take asked me. I shrugged, though truthfully I knew I didn't have many other options.

Stealth camping wasn't technically allowed within the Whites. You were supposed to hike down and camp either below the presidential line or stay within the huts up along the ridgeline.

"I don't know. But I'm sure we'll see each other again soon." I replied finally.

She gave a wave, as I walked off into the morning.

Ethereal rays shot down between gaps in the trees, casting small spotlights across my face and occasionally into my eyes, as I walked the 6.9-mile path towards Crawford Notch. The wind brought the firm scent of red and white pines, as well as balsam firs. I took a deep breath, and looked upon glistening sap, colored burnt orange in the sunlight cast down upon it.

I knelt down and dipped my hand into the stream crossing my path as I eyed it. The hue reminded me so much of a North Carolina summer sunset, from back home in my youth.

Carefree Friday afternoons after school, where the coming weekend meant we could all stay outside and play, just a little bit longer than usual. Our feet bare, and the soles black like tar as we ran through the centipede grass of my parent's backyard. At dark, we were all shuffled back into our homes under the command of our parents. But between that existed this last bastion of hope. This last little sliver of freedom that existed within the gray margin.

It was strange that such a small piece of sap, glowing and twinkling radiantly upon the side of a tree could remind me of those last brilliant bursts of fire scarring the skies from my childhood. Those last moments as the heat of summer turned cold—just as dusk rolled in, and we children rolled down the hills in our backyards, through thick patches of cool clover and grass just a week overdue to be cut.

Sucking nectar out of honeysuckle growing wild in trees along our property line. Jumping and doing flips on the neighbor's trampoline, or climbing on top of the garage and my father's tool shed and daring each other to jump off of the roof.

And not one damned care in the world, or worry of ever growing older. No sense of responsibility, nor the death of the imagination that tends to come with age.

I looked away from my moment of reverie and wondered if it was true that those moments no longer existed for us as parents, as adults, as business men or women. That ignorant bliss could at times, seem so very wasted now that I was older.

My phone buzzed suddenly, and I blinked out of thought as I slipped my hand down into my pocket.

I had received a text message from Wales.

Apparently, from the message and his location update, he was somewhere in the vicinity of 18 miles behind me.

We made plans to meet up at where the AT crossed Route 302 further ahead. At my first intersection that day, however, I came to a side trail that would have blue blazed all of the way down to it in as little as 3.4 miles. The terrain along the ridgeline through the Whites wasn't that bad, to be honest, and there was no way to justify shortening my day and losing out on such incredible views from Mount Jackson and Webster just up ahead.

Each step forward had me traipsing through ridgeline and summit swamps and small boggy areas with sinking plank bridges, many of which were broken. Sometimes my only protection from walking through six to eight inches of mud, algae, and scum was trying to balance upon these sinking bridges.

Each step forward had me always looking back at how far I had come. The Mizpah Hut was nothing more than a glint of light in the side of a mountain far away. Each outcropping or bald knob had the monolithic Mt Washington looking more and more like a dot on the horizon as it vanished behind a blue and white haze of clouds.

Descending down Mt Webster, I was very surprised at how vicious the trail had suddenly become. Looking back on it, I was actually very glad I hadn't had to climb it going north because it was very much hand over hand hiking in some sections. At one point, a chunk of rock had broken free from underneath my foot and clung momentarily to the gap it had just fallen out of. Meanwhile, I slid on my butt down a forty foot section of granite slab and managed to land perfectly on both feet.

Though I had raked a small hole in the seat of my pants, it wasn't enough to be much of a big deal after having survived the slide.

That's when I heard the tumbling of something large rolling down towards me. I glanced up in surprise, and just barely managed to sidestep a basketball sized boulder that would easily have broken my ankle upon impact.

Trails of smaller pebbles and stones came down behind the boulder along with a cloud of red dust.

A couple of hours later, I sat on the edge of a cliff overlooking the AMC Visitors Center several thousands of feet below. I had a pair of Oakley's sunglasses I had found in the rear of Woodstock's vehicle that he had told me to take with me just before his departure. They looked and felt expensive. However, they didn't seem to shield my eyes very much from the brightness of the sun.

I had a granola bar in one hand, a bottle of water in the other and I had found the perfect little crook to wedge my body into—almost like a recliner with my feet dangling off the edge of the cliff. Doing this, sent little tingles through the bottoms of my feet as I imagined pivoting my weight off of my hands and launching myself over the side of the mountain with no real reason or understanding. My earbuds were in, and I was blasting music as I soaked in the sun and enjoyed myself.

"Eh bien, je voudrais qu'il sortir de la voie!" I suddenly heard from behind me. It was low, and thus I didn't make any quick movement nor did I share any desire initially to move.

"Il a besoin de quitter!" I heard again. This time it was far louder.

I removed my earbuds to hear a woman arguing with a man in what clearly sounded like French.

I hadn't noticed, but after turning around, I found that a group of French-Canadians had swarmed the cliff and were looking down at me.

I started to sit up. The man was incredibly short, wore a safari hat and had a rather large and expensive looking camera dangling from around his neck. He most honestly looked a lot like a Keebler Elf.

I waved at him, and only received a glare back. So as I shrugged and started to turn around again, I caught him throwing his hands up in the air as if having a tantrum. His face had turned almost blood red.

The woman that had been arguing with him noticed the concern on my face.

"Are you okay?" I asked the man.

"No, No. Do not worry," the woman replied with an apologetic smile.

At this point, the short, angry little man had stomped off, and I suddenly felt as if I had accidentally created this situation somehow.

Just as I had started to reinsert my earbuds, the irate little man had sped back over towards me, leaned down close enough to kiss me—with his forearm literally millimeters away from grazing my face.

"Can I help you?" I asked, irritably.

When he was done taking a bunch of pictures, he then began shouting at me with a face that appeared to express angry satisfaction. At this point, I was oddly aware I had done something unconsciously to spur rage from this individual but still, what that exactly was I didn't know.

Finally, I decided that I wanted to leave the area altogether. I was able to understand eventually, if through nothing else than the guy's overreactions and expressions that he had wanted me to get out of the way and possibly even out of the area completely. But to have been so rude about it had been astonishing to me. As soon as I had stood and put my backpack on, the man once again approached me and placed his hand upon my shoulder.

"Yes, Yes," he said, pulling at my shoulder strap slightly.

I quickly shrugged his hand off in anger, while glaring down at him. He didn't keep eye contact with me however and only continued to pull on my arm now.

"Yes, yes," he said again.

"Get your fucking hands off of me," I said, shoving him away from me. I was only mildly aware of how far I had sent him stumbling backward with the slightest of force. Suddenly, I felt immediate guilt. The look of shame on his face, from the lack of physical strength with which to engage me, had made me instantly sympathetic to his size.

Something he'd probably been bullied for his whole life.

After becoming aware of the intonation in my voice, he along with everyone else had stopped talking and taking pictures. Instead, the others had decided to watch the drama unfolding before their very eyes. Some of the guests walked over to us both, speaking in French as they tried to grab the man by his wrists and pull him back from me. Instead, he only jerked his hands-free and made gestures, fussing right back at them.

Apparently, this type of behavior was typical for the man because as another French Canadian was guiding me away when I asked what the guy's problem was all I received was a laugh.

At the base of the mountain, I knelt beside the stream, watching millions of diamonds glittering across the surface of the clear water within the afternoon sunlight. I had built a small reservoir and dam utilizing huge boulders in the area and had managed to pool a sizeable portion of water with which to bathe in.

I removed my clothes and gear and sat in the cold, outdoors bathtub I'd made for myself. My breaths immediately seized up within my chest, into stiff jerks.

"God...Oh God th..t..thats s...s..so co....cold." I stuttered in slight shock as I leaned back into the water. I had wanted to wash my clothes with soap but feared after seeing the many crawfish skirting across the bottoms and the minnows that were picking at the bottoms of my feet—that introducing a substance they'd never encountered before like soap, might end up harming them.

I had taken to boiling water instead and then utilized my waterproof compression sack as a "washing machine". I put a bar of soap into the sack, poured the boiling water into the bag and finally stuffed my filthy, sweat and b/o covered clothes inside the concoction.

I cinched the opening shut and proceeded to shake the thing like crazy for about 10 minutes until the sudsy piece of clothing no longer resembled the black, moldy, mildew covered, sweat crystal enveloped fabric it had once been adorned with. I stretched the sudsy clothing across a hang line and proceeded to pour stream water atop the clothing. I watched with mild amusement as the suds dropped to the forest floor.

"Nice," I said appreciatively.

When Wales had arrived four hours later, he had caught me while I had been engaged in a game of "sink the leaf ships."

Basically, I had taken to tossing pebbles at passing leaves drifting down the stream in an attempt to send them spiraling beneath the water's surface to the muddy bottom.

"Well, I was curious if you were ever going to show up today," I said with a grin, as I shot up and walked over to offer my hand.

"I thought for sure you'd be at Zealand Hut by now." He replied, shaking it.

"I sent another text about a day ago. I said that if I'd have gone on, you'd probably never catch up with me." I explained as he nodded his head and stepped onto the small arched wooden bridge overlooking the water.

"I saw on the map that there was a General Store just down the road." He said, gripping the railing as he watched leaves I hadn't yet destroyed passing across the surface of the creek beneath his feet.

"Well, I've got some good news. About a quarter of a mile down this way," I said pointing east "Is a great place to set up for the evening. It's quiet, there's lots of water, and I built a small bathtub to wash off in the creek." I explained rather excitedly.

"Okay then. We'll set up and then what?"

"Wales..." I said, shaking my head from side to side.

"This is *me* you're talking to. What do you think we're gonna do? We're headed to that freakin' General Store, for hotdogs, hamburgers, submarine sandwiches and huge bags of Doritos."

"Oh no, stop it!" he said, laughing and shaking his hands excitedly in the air as he kicked his feet excitedly.

"Ice-cold sodas, probably beer as well and Zebra Cakes, or HoHo's! I bet you could even find all the ingredients you needed for us to make some s'mores tonight!"

Well, this was definitely torture because now I was drooling myself as Wales did an excited running man dance, shaking his hand's thigh level and his head from side to side.

"I can't stand it! We have to go!" he insisted excitedly.

It was good to see Wales again, and I didn't feel so alone anymore, now that he was there. To relive those moments with his oddball personality traits and mannerisms was welcomed, and fun.

After Wales had set up, we walked out to Route 302 where we discussed which way to go a final time. West was Twin Mountain which hadn't been mentioned in AWOL's Guidebook. Meanwhile, east was the town of Bartlett, and a place that had been listed in his guide called "The General Store."

We had visions of deli sandwiches and huge bags of chips. We thought of Coca-Cola and ice cream sandwiches. Having been so close to the AT, it was hard not to imagine all sorts of things for a hikers resupply.

However, we were sorely disappointed as we stared into the cold food and freezer section upon arrival. Most of the items appeared not only old but nearly out of date as well.

A pack of Oscar-Meyer Bologna was five dollars while a loaf of Wonder Bread was $3.59! To make it a full sandwich with cheese, seven ounces of the stuff would run me $4.79.

I couldn't hold back my anger any longer however after seeing a UTZ chips bag with a pre-priced $.99 cents printed on the sticker. The General Store had doubled the price with a sticker of their own pasted over the top of it. The new price for the sack of salted, oily air was now $1.99.

"Would you look at this shit? These $.99 cent Walmart hotdogs are seven dollars, for eight!" I growled, slamming the door to the wall fridge.

"Shhh!" Wales replied, glancing over at the woman behind the counter as she looked up at me.

"I don't care! It's absolutely incredible how much they are ripping people off!" I replied in a hushed tone. Wales' tried to smile at the woman despite her prominent notice of my angry outburst.

I walked out of the store with a snack-sized bag of chips, a 20oz bottle of soda, a loaf of bread, a seven-ounce block of cheddar cheese, two packs of skittles and a 6-inch pepperoni stick FOR $23 dollars.

I couldn't remember the last time I had spent so much on ONE DINNER, for myself. Because however hard it might have been to believe it, this was more than likely going to last me no longer than 24 hours.

There was no ice cream, and there was no resupply other than three dollar pasta sides you could get for eighty-nine cents each at a grocery store.

After we had overpaid for our food, I was livid. This is what I hated so much about the trail and hiking along it at times. Businesses like this place, which ripped hikers off and took advantage of the fact they were so far from civilization to seek out other choices.

When we got back to camp, Wales began to jump and laugh excitedly while clapping his hands together like an excited school girl.

"The hell's got into you?" I asked, looking over at him with a bemused expression.

"I'm excited to eat real food." He said, clapping his hands louder and throwing his head back in laughter.

"Yeah, but your meal was $24 bucks...and that jar of salsa was $6 bucks by itself," I said incredulously. I wasn't excited about eating a dinner that could have consisted of two or three large pizzas back at home for the same price.

"Yeah but...I don't know." He said thinking about it. He shrugged, and his smile started to falter as he looked at my expression.

I certainly didn't want to rain on his parade. And as I looked at him, I remembered so many times that Torry had tried to change my negative outlook in the past—always interjecting a definite and positive point of some sort.

"Well, to be honest with you. It's sure as hell going to be the best $23 dollar meal I've spent in the last 7 months." I lied with a passing smile. Wales bought it, and the comment had got him laughing again.

I opened the bag of UTZ chips, took a bite and immediately collapsed into my hammock as burnt orange skies lit up our evening meal and the wind from the top of the mountain had started rushing down to greet us for the evening.

Stars washed in upon a pink sky, barging into view between colorful fall leaves, with a bright moon and a lonely ambiance that made me think of laying in the grass of my backyard and staring up at the skies with wonderment and awe of God's beauty.

We ate our food in a world far from civilization, remarking just how happy moments like these made us.

"Wales..." I said, in mid-yawn, from my tent.

There was a light stir from his giant's lair, but no answer. He was such a tall guy that I had always wondered how he had managed to fit into such a small little tent.

That morning, however, it had made perfect sense that maybe he didn't—without curling into a fetal position. His legs were stretched out the front door to his tent, and he was snoring very subtly.

Morning fog drifted like ghostly wisps—wetting not only everything in the forest but the tops of his toes as well. They glistened with a coating of morning dew.

"Hey. I'm getting' outta here." I said, kicking the bottom of his foot. Wales coughed and muttered something indiscernible before responding.

"I uh…sure. Catch up later. You got…phone….number…" he replied, trailing back off into sleep.

I was out of camp and hiking by 6 A.M.; across Route 302. As I climbed out of Crawford Notch headed south, I tried to determine where my next stay for the evening was going to be. I wasn't far from Zealand Hut, but I didn't want to end the day so early either when it was only eight miles away.

"Fourteen miles it is, then!" I said to myself out loud, as I stopped long enough to hear something scurrying through the brush by my feet.

I looked down and didn't initially see anything.

Instead, I looked back to my guidebook and read up on any information regarding Galehead Hut which was where I was seeking to have ended my hike for the day.

There was an odd scratching sound, and when I looked down, I found a pale grayish creature that appeared to be a mix between a chicken, a turkey, and a quail. These little guys were strutting along like I wasn't even there. Sometimes no more than 3 feet away. They made chirping sounds and scratched at the ground, pecking at random things only they noticed with their keen eyesight.

"What the hell are you supposed to be?" I asked the creature, as I knelt down. Once I had, it appeared the others in the group were less threatened by my presence and over the course of 10 minutes had actually started to surround me in their own curiosity.

I sat with my backpack between my legs. I had leftover potato chips that I had crumbled in my hands and had begun tossing to them like chicken feed. The creatures gave cautionary pecks.

One even strutted right up to the base of my boot, took a tap at my heel and then took to the air like a helicopter blade. Partially scaring the others.

After a few more minutes, however, a brightly colored male came waltzing in on the scene. He was discouraging to the other females eating anything I had tossed out to them. Even going so far as attacking the other six to seven females within the group.

I grabbed a pine cone and scared him away which allowed the females to resume their potato chip consumption in peace.

Not to sound brutal, but I had actually gotten the urge to catch one, kill it, clean it and then eat it after spit roasting it over a fire. This was all while brushing it with honey, rosemary, and butter while flames of the fire danced demonically within my night eyes.

Truthfully, however, I didn't know how to kill or clean a pheasant.

Besides, I didn't know the laws of New Hampshire regarding these birds either. I wasn't sure if they were protected, endangered, or if you could only kill a particular sex or size, so I had no intention of breaking the law.

Still, it didn't stop me from glancing back as I started hiking south again.

It didn't keep me from thinking of licking those spit fire roasted juices off of my fingers.

"LET'S GO!" I finally shouted at myself, which scared the group of pheasants off.

They took to the air with wings so loud I felt the air reverberating around me. Truly marvelous creatures.

It was flat plank walking for most of the day, but regardless of that, it was pleasant. The trail went mostly over swamps and bogs. I could only imagine how miserable summer was here, with blackflies and mosquitoes.

As I looked at my surroundings, I noticed blonde orange grass had choked out the nearby ponds in this area. The morning sun so radiantly complemented the golden trails in every shade and hue of 'campfire.'

Red maple leaves that had already fallen for the season coated the earth like rose petals.

The trail followed a broad stream with tiny waterfalls that bragged loudly of being larger from further away than they truly were upon seeing in person.

Once I had reached the base of Zealand Falls, I looked over a boulder strewn stream that looked as solid as ground; solely because it was clogged with red and yellow fallen leaves.

I made my way up to Zealand Hut and bought a bowl of bean soup and a slice of homemade loaf bread for a three dollar lunch.

As it was 1 P.M. and I'd already knocked out 8 miles. I couldn't justify ending there for the day. So I wrote Wales a note in the logbook they had available, explaining to him that I was headed towards Guyot Shelter (12 miles) and maybe even Galehead Hut (14 miles). This meant I would have been completing a 21 – 22-mile day. Something I hadn't done since Troutville, Virginia across Tinker Cliffs and McAfee's Knob.

Once reaching the Mount Guyot summit, I glanced back north behind me, to see the twinkling of the Mt Washington Observatory. It was incredible how far away it actually was, but how it still remained so vast and omnipotent in the background when compared to every other mountain along the range.

I could imagine seeing the monstrosity coming from the south for days, before ever reaching it. Much like you did Katahdin when northbound hiking. It must have led to quite a bit of forethought and daydreaming.

Once I had finally reached South Twin Mountain, it was sunset. I took pictures of a sleeping sun as it nestled into the notch of two distant mountains far away east that I would never be traversing.

I stumbled down the mountain in the burnt orange glow of our brightest star, as it seared the breaks in the trees like thick streams of fire. Red beams from a purple, scarred sky tore across the earth; scorching it and surprisingly never setting the fallen pine needles aflame.

I had reached the hut with maybe 20 minutes of daylight to spare and looked inside only to see a bunch of guests already eating.

I knew instantly that I had arrived too late. I wasn't allowed to be around the dear day-hiking guests.

And though I'd never do it, I still had visions of kicking in the door while the hut staff were in the middle of serving dinner.

Maybe, I just DIDN'T CARE! Maybe I could actually be a brash, bold jerk if I truly wanted to, especially when tired and hungry?

I could see myself barging right in and walking straight to the kitchen. As the following scenario played out:

"Excuse me sir, but you can't be in here during..." One of the male, bearded staff members, would begin.

"Shhhh..." I'd say, palming the guy in the face and pushing him aside, as he stood there with a frightened expression.

"You just feed me. And everything will be all right." I would whisper gently, as he nodded his head slowly, apparently hypnotized by my Alpha Male-like aggressive approach.

I'd grab an apple out of a fruit bowl that was usually priced at a dollar each, and take a generous bite out of it, smacking my lips loudly like I owned the place.

"Hey! Get him out of here!" Another staff member would shout.

That's when I'd beam that crybaby in the face with my half-eaten apple; shattering his dorky 1960's horn-rimmed glasses. He would probably proceed to fall backward into a garbage can with his feet kicking back and forth in the air.

The female staff would be swimsuit models, decked out in bikinis, giggling at the whole turn of events.

"I didn't pay good money to eat next to this piece of hiker trash!" Some stuffy Investment Banker would whine as I plopped down next to him.

"You going to eat that?" I'd ask, dipping my fingers into his mashed potatoes.

"Actually I WAS!" He'd shout, red-faced. I'd proceed to take a bite from his bourbon chicken breast as well.

"Mmmph. Thathhs goodff. Wha 'bout thatff?" I'd ask, food flying out of my mouth rudely into his face.

"You worthless piece of garbage! Stop eating my food!" He'd shout, pulling his plate away out of reach as I stood up.

I'd wipe my mouth.

"That your wife?" I'd ask.

Before he could answer, I'd dip her back and passionately kiss her.

She'd blush, maybe even giggle bashfully and proceed to give me her phone number.

Ah, but that's not the way the world works. I could only dream of being that cool when in reality, I was born to live out these dreams ONLY in my head, without the guts to ever truly act in such a manner.

As I reached the porch, I saw Double Take and Lucky. I stopped my head ward charge and smiled, waving cheerfully at them. I asked how they'd been and if they were offering work-for-stay inside.

"Yeah, I mean, they're letting *us* do work for stay...at least. Don't know about *you*." She replied.

"Thanks..." I said, before turning, putting on my stern face and continuing my march forward.

"Hey, we're not allowed to be around the guests when they're eating. Remember?" Lucky asked as he saw I was set on going inside and securing a place for the evening.

However, my mindset had changed having just dreamt out that scenario in my mind in the minutes before. I was no idiot to be expecting swimsuit models waiting for me with open arms inside. However, I felt that exhibiting an alpha male sort of attitude was bound to work in my favor.

"Don't worry. I got this..." I said strutting inside confidently.

"I'm not sitting out here in the cold like a dog, anymore."

It was three minutes later after my bold statement, and I was sitting outside in the cold, like a dog while the guests ate inside the warm structure.

My clothes had become drenched from sweat throughout the day, had chafed the inside of my thighs raw and felt rather uncomfortable as the air turned chilly—so I had decided to remove them. I snuck around to the backside of the house to change. After having just dropped my pants, an older woman that had been dressing in her bunk room happened to look outside at me just at the same moment she had removed her shirt and was standing in only a bra in front of the window. Despite it being dusk, with only minutes of light left in the skies above, I could have sworn I saw her turn at least fifteen different shades of red.

"Shhhitttt!" I uttered in a hushed whisper, as I attempted to dive completely out of sight.

Christ sake, she's going to think me to be a peeper or a pervert! I thought to myself, with sudden fear wildly racing through my mind. I balled up, the sour smelling pants I'd been wearing for days without washing and stuffed them into my compression sack. It seemed reasonable by all means to contain the stench coming off of them.

After slipping on a fresh pair, I returned to the porch and looked in to see the old woman I had accidentally caught dressing. She was returning to a table in which she immediately started in on some discussion that I knew had probably involved me.

This was because she had turned several shades of red again, and with a nervous smile and chuckle had decided to point out at me as the group of guests inside sitting around her all turned to look back at me through the window as well.

I smiled weakly and gave a quick "hello" of my own.

"Had to tell them, didn't you?" I muttered between clenched teeth and a false smile.

"Had to let *every one* of them know, eh?" I said, squeezing my fists until the nails dug deep into either of my palms.

One of the staff members overhearing the story approached the door and opened it.

"You aren't trying to peep on our guests, are you?" she asked with a joking expression. Some of the guests that had overheard the inquiry inside had found it funny and started laughing.

They'd have to be a whole lot hotter, and at least a hundred years younger than her I began to say, but instead I chose to keep my mouth shut.

While some of the guests laughed, others looked scared and seemed by facial expression alone to presume I was a sexual predator of some sort. The staff member went back inside and closed the door behind her.

"What is she talking about?" Double Take asked me, looking rather confused.

"I was changing on the side of the house and accidentally saw Ol' Granny Jenkin's in there in only a bra. She caught me in my boxers." I replied, a bit shamefacedly.

"Calm down bro. Don't be lookin' at my girl now to take off her shirt too." Lucky said while pulling Double Take closer. They both laughed at his comment. It was evident he had been kidding around, but I chose not to acknowledge him at all.

I would say that I had then proceeded to remove my socks next, but that would be a gross understatement. Instead, I peeled them off like velcro. The fabric inside had become so matted, the fibers felt almost like plastic scales.

I tossed the pair of socks to the furthest corner of the back porch. Secretly I'd hoped I would forget them there, or that an animal would carry them off into the night—thinking they were a dead rodent of some sort.

After the guests had finished eating, I did the dishes while Double Take and Lucky removed pots, pans, herbs, and spices from cabinets in the kitchen and cleaned the shelves they had once sat upon.

For our reward, we were given leftovers which consisted of:

- The two end pieces of a loaf of bread split three ways
- One piece of cornbread split three ways
- All the canned green beans we could ever want
- Three tablespoons of green peas with half a cup of pesto and rigatoni thrown on top

When I had finished my dinner, I was still hungry and went out to the back porch to rummage through my pack.

As I sat down on the back step, one of the female crew members came out and lit up a cigarette.

She looked down at my things and said nothing. Eventually, however, she became curious to see me eating a granola bar after having witnessed my devouring of the plate inside.

"You guys sure were hungry, weren't you?" she asked.

I smiled back at her and nodded.

"They say you burn 5 to 6,000 calories a day out here," I replied.

However, the woman looked down at my stomach and raised her eyebrows up. Immediately, I knew what she was getting at.

"I tend to eat more than I walk, I suppose," I added, sheepishly. She nodded her head, snubbed out the cigarette on the edge of the porch and put the butt into her apron.

"Have a good one." She said, disappearing inside.

I suppose it made sense, if you were friends with the Hut Master, you could get preferential treatment.

I say that because, at around 10 P.M., four young college students came into the hut, laughing and giggling as they stepped into the front entrance.

Double Take, Lucky and I all sat up at once and looked towards the people that had awakened us from our slumber, with murderous eyes.

"Sorry," one of the guys said, and the other three burst into immediate laughter.

"Is Emily still awake?" one of the girls asked.

"I don't know who Emily is," I replied, laying back down.

From the stairs, one of the male staff members of Galehead Hut came down.

"Hey guys, we're all in Jacobs's room. Did you bring the alcohol?" he asked the new arrivals.

"Yeah, lugged it all the fuckin' way up the mountain bro." one of the intruders replied.

"He only fell like fifteen times." A girl in the group added with a chuckle.

"Shut up Christy, that's only because you can't keep the beam straight on your damn headlamp."

I rolled over, collapsing my arms across my ears angrily until the headmaster came into the room as well.

"Guys, these people are trying to sleep. Let's go into the room." She said, and then the five of them were gone.

Sleeping on the floor was no longer even possible, however, with all of the laughing and drinking and noise taking place in that room; even behind closed doors. I was surprised that some of the guests that had paid to stay there weren't angry about the gross amount of negligence and lack of sleep taking place because of the racket.

Late into the night, the sounds of music and laughter had finally calmed down.

It was then, we got to be treated to *other sounds*.

These sounds were the kind usually made when two people were screwing. A bed somewhere was creaking, and moaning was taking place. Soon after, it was joined by another couple of the croo members doing the same thing.

"I'm so close to just going and sleeping on the damned porch!" Lucky whispered to me.

"This place sucks. God knows!" Double Take chimed in.

I reached into my backpack and retrieved some earplugs I had been given by Woodstock when we were cleaning out his vehicle just before he'd said goodbye. I knew that at some point I might have needed them, and sure enough—now was that very time.

I handed both lucky, and his partner Double Take a pair.

"Don't worry. They're clean. Never used them. Besides, I have these." I said, shaking out a pair of earphones. They thanked me and not many minutes later, I was fast asleep.

Double Take and Lucky had decided to bail on breakfast and headed out early enough before anyone else had gotten up. When they looked over at me and asked if I was coming, I waved them away with a lack of sleep obviously making the judgment call. Initially, I was sort of happy with this, because I knew it meant more food for me.

Having experienced my first work-for-stay situation at the Mizpah Hut the day before, I was under the impression that breakfast was going to be free as it had been before. Especially considering the work, I had already completed for my stay.

Unfortunately, I found out the hard way that Double Take and Lucky had made the better choice by skipping out earlier that morning. This was because after a cup of oatmeal with two left over raisins placed on top and three silver dollar sized pancakes—the staff had decided to make me sweep and wipe down the bunk beds after the guests left.

Here's where it got confusing. I had been told the night before that after doing dishes—my dinner and my breakfast the following morning, came along with my spot on the floor for free.

Well, I suppose "the croo" had either decided to say: *The hell with that* or they had simply lied to me.

Emily handed me her boyfriend's breakfast plate and asked me to take it to the kitchen and informed me to ask one of the croo members there for the hand-sized broom and dustpan.

I looked down at the plate with the odd temptation to let it drop and shatter immediately on the floor. Instead, as I walked into the kitchen, I handed a staff member the plate.

"I thought you could go now?" he said to me, with a confused expression.

"I don't know. I mean…maybe you can talk to the Hut Master." I replied with a shrug, hoping that he could convince her otherwise.

"Well, if she told you to do it…I mean, she is the one in charge and all." He replied, not even bothering to attempt asking.

My face dropped, and I took my tools of the trade and headed to the back of the building to start work.

While sweeping, I overheard one of the female staff members that had been getting plowed by one of the men from the group that had hiked in the night before. She was whispering to the male employee in the kitchen after I had already finished cleaning the first two rooms.

"Maybe you should get him to scrub the bathroom as well." She offered.

"I don't think he'll do it." He replied.

"Might as well try." She insisted.

"Yeah, but he already finished his work last night...now you've got him sweeping bunks,"

It was Emily, the hut master. Here she was, trying to exploit my position and use me unfairly.

"So what? We can get him to do it anyways. I don't wanna clean shit off toilets. Did you see the bathroom this morning? Tamara puked all over the sides of it after drinking last night." Emily said.

"Nah, not really interested in seeing that." He replied as they both chuckled over it. I had leaned out of the room I'd been cleaning with my ear directed down the hallway.

"Besides, it's Jacob's turn anyways." The croo member said.

"I'll just tell 'Morris-The-Whatever-His-Name-Is,' to take care of the bathroom since you're a pussy, and then Jacob can help you and me later with dinner."

I had been in the last bunk room on the left...when I had stopped sweeping and crept up to the doorway to listen in on their conversation. The door creaked, as it started to drift open.

"Is that the hiker?" she asked in a hushed tone, hearing the noise.

I quickly retreated back into the room, as I heard her footsteps coming from the kitchen down the hallway.

I heard her calling "Morris" and quickly climbed to the top bunk, having ditched my broom and dust pan on the adjacent bed behind the door. I laid back as far as I could against the wall closest to the door. This had provided a partial blind spot as the top bed was so high up. I had also pulled the rubber mattress corner up just enough to lay down beneath it into the four inch well of the gap. I'm sure upon more than a second's closer inspection, I would've been seen. However, a quick glance wouldn't bring much attention if I was still.

When Emily opened the door to the room I was hiding out in, the guy from the kitchen had approached her from behind, just in time to distract her and draw her attention away from the room.

Good boy I thought to myself.

She closed the door and proceeded to finish scanning the other bunkrooms while calling out for me. Just before she got to the door of the room I was in again; she said: "Where the fuck did he go?"

"Is he out *there*? On the porch?" She asked another staff member as she walked away. Her subordinate's response was inaudible, though.

"Who are you looking for?" I heard her boyfriend call out to her. I watched him walking by the window outside, before he made his way up the stairs to the side entrance of the house, where he entered.

There was some stomping around by her croo for a while as I laid there...and more indecipherable conversations. Finally, two people walked back towards the rooms and one opened the door to the one I was in again.

"He was working around here a second ago. I don't know what happened." The croo member that had been working in the kitchen said.

There was a: "Hmph. Well, that's strange...." response, and then more inaudible chatter as they scattered once more throughout the house.

Five minutes later, I watched from the window after having crept down from my hiding spot. Two of the staff walked around the building outside, and one ran towards the direction of the Appalachian Trail.

"Did he steal the broom and dustpan?" Someone asked in a muffled voice outside of the building. A girl with black hair, presumably one of from the group that had come hiked in the night before; responded that she could check the bunk rooms again.

That was my cue to leave.

I opened the door to my room and canted my head down the hallway. I withdrew it just in time as someone came around the corner from the kitchen and dining room area. They walked into the first bunkroom, and I used the opportunity to slip out the side door. I crept around towards the front porch as Emily walked back inside, having snubbed out her cigarette.

"His backpack is still here unless it's one of the guests. But I don't think anyone said they were staying over!" I heard her shout from inside the house.

I ducked down, crawling on all fours out of sight along the front of the porch. I looked up at my socks in the opposite direction I had just come on the edge of the porch.

"Forget em'," I muttered. They had two holes, one in each foot anyways and the once soft wool lining inside them had turned into rock, over the course of thousands of miles without proper cleaning.

I got to my backpack which I'd left propped against the front bench and quickly dragged it off of the porch.

After throwing it on, I took off running without ever saying a word.

I was in a hard sprint, as I heard someone come out the front door onto the porch behind me. I didn't look back, but nobody had called my name either.

My foot struck a rock jutting out of the grass, and I stumbled forward, regained balance, and kept on until I was far out of site.

I had reached Greenleaf Hut, shivering from the cold winds blasting about outside the structure. I was dizzy and tired, feeling quite dehydrated from the day as well, having run out of water two hours back.

Still, I had managed to climb Mt Lafayette somehow, as my dry throat begged for anything remotely wet. My mouth had become so arid in fact, that it had started to hurt just to swallow at all.

I collapsed on the rear deck of the structure, lying face down against the floorboards with my two-ton backpack crushing me beneath its weight. It made things just a tad harder to breathe, so I managed to roll onto my side slowly and take huge gulps of air.

"You gonna make it?" a young woman asked me. I couldn't bear to lift my head though to see where the voice had come from.

"Shoot...me," I whispered, hoarse and immediately succumbing into a coughing fit before lying my head back against the floor boards.

A young blonde woman knelt down by my head, setting down the book she had been reading. It was Ann of Green Gables, and oddly enough I had remembered the series having been a favorite of my older sisters when I was growing up.

"Can I get you something?" she asked, as I just lay there. I didn't want to talk. I didn't want to answer. I just wanted to pass out from the sheer pain in the bottoms of my feet, my throbbing headache, my raw throat and my screaming joints.

"Water. Please." I muttered, miserably.

She placed a water bottle to my mouth, and I took a quick sip.

Suddenly, I was like Popeye the Sailor Man having been given a can of spinach. I threw my backpack off quite suddenly which caused her to fall back onto her butt in surprise, as I stole the bottle with shaking, desperate hands and proceeded to drink every last drop.

I immediately regretted my decision and felt nauseous.

"Calm down. You gotta take slow sips."

"I'm gonna puke..." I muttered, crawling on my hands and knees to the side of the porch and dropping my head over the edge.

"Oh quit being dramatic..." she said, kicking me in the butt with her foot.

I tossed back an evil glare as she placed her hands on her hips and cocked an eyebrow as if daring me to contest.

Instead, I just looked away and let the nausea pass.

When my dramatic spell had finally gone away, I got to officially meet the "croo" of Greenleaf Hut. It was comprised of three beautiful young women, all of which were wearing high shorts, far above the halfway points of their thighs.

I looked at the smooth, tanned flesh with dewy eyes as they brought me fresh baked chewy chocolate chip cookies and more water than I could stand. I had become a project I suppose after my dramatics and these three nurses-in-training were bringing me back to full health.

"Come with me." The brunette with ocean blue eyes said.

"Where are we going?" I asked, standing and floating towards her.

"You need to lie down for a little bit. Come lay in one of the bunks." She offered, taking my hand. She couldn't have been older than 20. I looked at her swollen pink lips, to the tight gray Aeropostale T-shirt she was wearing that barely covered her flat stomach below her belly button.

I gulped, feeling my hands immediately turn clammy as I started to fall in love instantly.

"Lana, hold on. Let me give him some more water." Ginny, the blonde Leader of the Hut I'd first met on the porch, said to me.

"Oh no. I'm good. I promise." I replied. She playfully pouted, and her light green eyes mesmerized me as they then sparked to life with mischief.

"I'm sorry for giving you a hard time outside earlier. I was just trying to get you revved up, and your adrenaline pumping so that you didn't pass out on me." She said in what I supposed was an apology.

However, Lana had started to tug on my hand again, and my love lust turned from Ginny towards *her* again.

"You ready?" she asked, looking deep into my eyes.

"It….it's…been…awhile…" I stuttered.

"What?" she asked confused.

"I uh..." I began, shaking my head from side to side.

"I meant...it's been awhile since...I uh...laid on...a bed..." I replied as if that made any sense at all. Clearly, I was an idiot.

She chuckled and pulled me towards the bunkroom where she showed me to my bed. Just before she turned to walk out, however, I stopped her.

"I uh...I can just sleep out on the floor. I don't want you to get in trouble or anything." I said.

Lana gave a concerned look.

"Honey, we're only going to have about seven other guests tonight. We've got more than enough bunks to share. You just relax and get comfortable, okay?" she asked, brushing the hair from my eyes.

I nodded, feeling the tad bit of guilt I'd had, suddenly dissipate within the dimples of her bright smile.

Yep, I was definitely in love again.

"So then this guy is running from Torry and me, screaming at the top of his lungs 'Help Help' and suddenly we stop in the middle of town with all of these other hikers and locals looking at us," I said as the group listened intently. We were eating a dinner of vegetarian burgers that sat upon a bed of southwestern salad mix, bowls of turkey soup and homemade dinner rolls.

I paused and took a sip of water.

"Well, then what happened?" Tina asked, clearly deeply drawn into my story. Tina had been the third Greenleaf Hut Goddess/staff member that had offered to wash my clothes with hers upon my waking from an afternoon nap.

Her brilliant fiery red hair contrasted against her speckled freckles.

"The guy makes such a racket, me and Torry decide to head to our campsite on the side of the French Broad River, and it's there the local cops decide to make an unannounced visit during the night. Kicking our stuff over and rooting through our campsite trying to find drugs or any reason to pull us into the station."

"I hate pigs…" Jessie says, shaking his long, curly hair from side to side. He sits in a bright blue Hawaiian T-shirt opened halfway down his bare chest. With flip-flops on and a thick beard on his face, he appears to be just another thru-hiker. Truthfully, though, he was only up for the evening having done a day hike with his father, Timothy.

"Morris, you said you've walked how many months so far?" Yuna, Jessie's girlfriend, asked me suddenly.

"Well, I'm at mile 1500 or so. I've got around 700 to go, and I've been out here since March 17th." I replied, dipping a hunk of the bread roll into the turkey soup and taking a bite.

"Hey, tell them about the Shenandoah River, and how you and your friend Torry went down it in an inflatable raft for 10 days," Lana, the hut leader said excitedly.

I want to kiss your mouth I almost said out loud, having fallen under her spell again the very moment I looked over at her.

"I want to kiss…" I said, before stopping. Everyone was watching me.

What, an idiot I immediately thought of myself.

"I'm sorry?" Ginny asked, confused.

There were a few awkward chuckles as everyone looked from one to another trying to understand my nonsense.

I laughed nervously, as my face turned several shades of red.

"I uh! I want to kiss the lady who cooked this soup." I clarified, trying to recover.

"Well, that'd be me," Tina said, leaning over and offering her cheek to me. She had shoulder length red hair that cupped her perfectly oval face. Her tiny nose crinkled up when she smiled.

Shy beyond belief, I leaned in and placed a quick peck on Tina's right cheek as everyone at the table chuckled and clapped.

That's it! I'm living here for the rest of my life! I'm going to marry Tina, Ginny, and Lana and we are going to live happily ever after up here! I thought to myself.

Tina dropped her fork and bent over to pick it up. As she did, I had to look away from the bountiful cleavage appearing behind the oversized black and red flannel button up shirt she was wearing.

"John, what makes you keep going on each day?" Jude, the older fellow at the end of the table, sporting what appeared to be a South African safari hat asked me suddenly. I was drawn away from visions of lust invading my filthy mind.

Tina looked up, just in time to notice where my eyes had been. Her cheeks turned red and rosy, and immediately I smiled sympathetically. She was a 26-year-old nurse, who took summers off to work up in the huts. God only knew, how bad I had wanted her to be *my* nurse.

"John?" Timothy asked.

I looked away from Tina and then to Timothy.

"I...am...sorry. What was the question?"

"John, I'm sure these beautiful women are already taken," Jessie said with a laugh. Had I truly been that transparent?

The whole table laughed, and I only smiled—feeling as if my head was about to explode.

"I apologize. It's just nice to have been taken in by such lovely women who immediately started taking care of me the moment I collapsed on their porch." I said, clearing my throat.

"Awww..." Tina said, rubbing my hand.

"Keep that up, and I'll probably marry you," I said, as the table laughed and Tina jerked her hand back immediately with a surprised expression on her face.

When the joking had cleared, and we had all started talking again, Jude asked me once again what kept me going each day.

I reached into my pants pocket and removed my stone from the summit of Katahdin and asked Yuna to pass it down to him.

"That little rock. That's about it." I replied.

Jude turned it over in his hands and then cocked an eye up over at me.

"What's so special about it?" he asked.

"I'm bringing it back home to my mother and father. It's the only reason I'm still out here." I replied.

"Couldn't you just hop on an airplane and meet them both at the airport and hand it over there?" Jessie asked.

The whole table laughed, as did I.

"I know. Why walk the thing 700 miles back home? Can't you just get on a train or a bus?" Lana asked.

"I could…I suppose…" I replied with a shrug. Jude had handed the stone back to Yuna who had handed it back to me. I was now rolling it around within my hand.

"But that would be too easy. I think I'm supposed to learn something out of all of this." I replied as I held out the stone, directly in front of me for the whole table to see.

"This is a symbol of every hardship I've faced, and overcome so far. Every cold night I slept in the rain and every dangerous or close encounter that could have ended worse. This is everything I gave up, to be here. This rock…" I said, pausing.

I felt my throat tighten, as I thought of Melody who had driven away back at Stecoah Gap. I thought of her tear filled eyes and could almost smell her perfume as she embraced me one final time there on the Appalachian Trail.

She had wanted so many things, to exist between her and I. There was no telling where I would have been back at home, if I would still be working as a security guard, or if I'd have already started setting up my enrollment for Wake Technical College. Maybe I'd already be in classes as well?

Instead, I kept seeing her turn away and then her Audi disappearing behind that mountain curve.

The room grew silent.

I finally swallowed, and then excused myself from the table.

I sat in my room for a while later that evening, missing my family and friends from back at home again. Even those that had turned away from my friendship.

I missed Krystal and the short blip of time we had shared together. It wasn't that I had fallen in love with her, as much as I had craved being adopted by somebody if only for a moment in time.

I had finally come to understand that.

I was changing, and I was no longer scared to be out here anymore on my own. I had grown in a sense, that I no longer felt physically inept and unable to finish my hike.

But the mental ineptitude would take a little longer to overcome. And each day I continued south, my internal, mental and physical strength grew.

The following morning, after a satisfying breakfast and having helped the three beautiful women clean up—I found myself reluctantly saying goodbye to the day hikers and to the Greenleaf Croo.

"You know John if you were coming back down to Route 3 with us, we could take you into town. I just wish there was something we could do for you." Jude said.

Well actually, that sounded VERY much like the plan I wanted to be a part of.

"Well, you know what? I'll just take you up on that offer."

Suddenly Timothy spoke up, however.

"You can't do that. You're hiking the AT. You've gotta go the *long way*."

Ha Ha, Ha! Shush, you foolish old man! I found myself almost saying out loud between clenched teeth, all while trying to express a fake smile.

"Well, I mean…I'd just pick back up…"

"You're right Tim. John, I'm sorry for trying to tempt you to come into town for a shower, change of clothes and real food." Jude said suddenly.

You're WRONG TIM. YOU'RE VERY WRONG! I could go right now! Let's go home, Jude! I almost wanted to cry out loud.

Instead, I hung my head and walked out onto the back porch. I looked up at the 1,200-foot climb I had ahead of me to reach the summit of Lafayette again.

"You are a brave man, sir," Timothy said clasping my shoulder and squeezing approvingly.

"I wish I had your gall," Jude added, shaking his head from side to side as he walked off.

I gulped, half smiling as I looked around at the others smiling back at me with astonishment in their eyes.

Each and every one of them.

"Shit…" I was muttering into the gale-force winds, 30 minutes later with my hands buried deep into my fleece pockets.

The wind snapped wildly as I held on to boulders or shrubs on my way up to keep from getting blown off of the side of the mountain.

The cloud cover had become so thick, one could have cut grayish-white chunks out of it with a knife.

When I had reached the summit, I found myself hopping across a broken trail from boulder to boulder as winds from the valley rose up and over, pushing an unfathomable amount of clouds in a never ending cycle over the gap like an upside-down waterfall of fog.

Huge boulders stood out like featureless hulks or monsters in the mist.

I hopped across a short crumbling cliff to a stone step on the adjacent side of Little Haystack Mountain. As I traversed Franconia Notch, I realized I needed a quick break from the cold.

I sat for a moment, hidden in a crevice between two toppled boulders and while there; I downed a liter of water.

It was noon when I finally reached the very bottom of the ridge, after a 2 mile downhill hike that had managed to eradicate any remaining cartilage in my knees, leaving bone grinding painfully against bone.

Instead of continuing along the AT under I-93 however, I took the White Tail Trail to the Pemi-Trail which led me to the Flume Visitors Center.

I was lost, and looking for Wales who had texted me the following message the night before: "Meet at the bridge at the bottom of Franconia Notch."

Well, that was a bit vague because afterward, he hadn't bothered to reply as to *which* particular bridge he'd meant.

We were supposed to be meeting so that we could hitch together into town and take a day off to wash our clothes and relax.

After two hours of wandering, I was livid.

I called Wales on my phone when it had little more than 5% battery life left. I was lost in the maze of paved recreation trails intertwining within this park and another. My GPS couldn't get a decent fix on me through the trees and rain clouds and had me teleporting all over the 4-inch digital map screen.

Finally, Wales picked up after one of my 20 phone calls.

"Y'ello." He said cheerfully.

"Where are you?" I asked, slightly frustrated.

"The visitor center. *How about you?*"

"Well let's see. There's a tree over *there*. Oh, and another one beside it. And about 5,000 more behind *that one*. Oh, there's a boulder over there across from two others on the adjacent side of the trail. Wait for a moment…is that? Oh yes, it is. IT'S ANOTHER DAMN TREE, WALES!" I shouted angrily into the phone. I had been sitting beneath the I-93 overpass waiting on him for the longest time.

"Hrm. That isn't exactly helpful." He replied nonchalantly, with a muddled tone. I could tell his mouth was full.

"I...I'm sorry..." I laughed, incredulously.

"I'm sorry, but are you EATING, right now?" I asked, feeling my temper rising even more than it already had.

"Yeah, they've got a food court in here. Kinda pricey, though." He said smacking away in my ear.

I tore the phone from my FACE and writhed my hands around it as if it were his throat, with images of strangling him to accompany the actions.

When I calmed down, I gritted my teeth and tried smiling as I placed the speaker back to my ear.

"WELL GLAD YOU'RE ALL NICE AND *FULL*. I COULD SURE USE SOMETHING TO EAT." I laughed angrily into the phone; tears of rage coming to my eyes.

"Yeah, there's like a carriage here...or something...and yeah....I dunno..." he added, in between imperceptible words as he ate.

"Maybe you could, OH I DON'T KNOW...stop eating FOR A SECOND and tell me WHERE THE HELL TO GO?!" I asked as pleasantly as possible.

I can tell you, it wasn't very pleasant.

Wales was then able to talk me to the Visitors Center an hour later. Upon arrival, the sheer amount of tourists within the area made me feel sick to my stomach.

I just wanted to get away from there altogether.

So Wales and I stood on the side of the entrance to the park, where we would hang our thumbs out for 20 minutes before we were able to catch a ride to resupply in the town of Lincoln.

When I exited the bathroom in my freshly laundered clothes, it was almost like heaven. I had taken an hour long shower and felt cleaner than I had since I could last remember.

I collapsed onto one of the two queen beds in the room, as Wales eagerly went into the bathroom after me.

I rolled back and forth, smelling the sweet scent of unsoiled clothes hugging my body, and relished in it. I couldn't remember ever being more appreciative of smelling like flowers before in my life.

Having been nine days without a shower, my scent was quite a bit like spoiled trash, left to bake in the summer sun.

When Wales came out, he too collapsed on his bed and immediately smiled as if the thought that he was going to be sleeping somewhere comfortable that night, had only just now struck him.

"You know, it's beautiful out there in the wild. And I'm appreciative every time I choose to stay on the Appalachian Trail instead of finding some different, random path or road down south. But man, days like today sure are beautiful." I explained, flicking the television on.

We watched an episode of Catfish on MTV, which had been Wales, Woodstock's and my favorite show while holed up in hotels or motels over the last few months. As evening came hand in hand with night, we found ourselves walking into town to resupply and get ourselves dinner. While walking, we saw Lucky and Double Take hiking west down Route 3 as Wales, and I walked east towards the Price Chopper grocery store.

"We were just talking about you! We were like: *I wonder if Morris the Cat made it into town today like he said he would.*" Double Take explained enthusiastically. Her boyfriend was on his phone and waved a busy hello at Wales and I both.

We waved back.

"Yeah, here I am. I stayed at Greenleaf Hut last night. It would have completely changed how you felt about the whole of the huts "lower class citizenship" system. They let me eat at the table and I wasn't made to hide outside on the porch. I wasn't told I couldn't talk to the guests. I even got a bunk room completely to myself! Tonight, we're staying at the Autumn Breeze Inn." I exclaimed excitedly.

"That's so cool! We stayed at Liberty Springs last night up on Franconia Notch. It was nice." She went on. She didn't look too convincing though when she'd said it was "nice." In fact, her face had dropped, and her voice trailed off as she looked away.

It had been cold, the night before. So much so that when I awoke even at a lower elevation than she had slept in—already I could see snowflakes coming down from the top of the storm clouds that had encompassed Lafayette on my hike back up.

I knew it hadn't been an easy sleep for them.

"So this is the elusive Wales you've told us all about, but we've never met. We were starting to think he'd made you up." Double Take said to him while chuckling cheerfully.

"Yes. It appears I'm real." Wales returned, laughing as well.

"And single...right?" I said, making the situation immediately turn awkward.

I elbowed Wales in the ribs.

"Eh? Ehhhh? Single aren'tcha?" I grinned with an annoying expression.

"I uh....don't know....what that has to do with anything...." He said blushing and giving me a confused look.

"So where would you suggest a good place for us to eat around here?" I asked, quickly changing the subject.

"Well, Nick and I...err. I mean Lucky. Sorry, still getting used to calling him by his trail name. We ate lunch at the Gypsy Diner...but it was kinda pricey." She said with an apologetic expression.

I'd have been okay with McDonald's myself. But Wales being a vegetarian knew all kinds of strange secrets about what foods to eat and not eat because while they may have been lacking meat, they didn't lack some sort of hidden meat protein or stomach enzyme from a cow that he wasn't allowed to ingest.

For starters, apparently, McDonald's french fries were cooked in beef lard, since noticed back in 2000.

Parmesan cheese had rennet in it. I'd never heard of it, but according to Wales, rennet was actually curdled milk from the stomach of an unweaned calf, containing substances used in curdling milk for cheese

Wales also couldn't have several types of candy or anything that had gelatin in it because gelatin was typically made from certain parts of animals (hooves, bones, cartilage) that had been boiled down.

And honestly, as Wales started to tell me about these things as we walked—I found myself surprised at how much knowledge I lacked in what I had decidedly put into my body on a daily basis over the past three decades.

However, it was also a conundrum as I didn't taste pig hooves, or cartilage when eating gummy bears or cherry flavored Jell-O. So how effective it would be at stopping me from ever consuming those products again, only time would tell.

"How about we stick to the grocery store?" he asked, looking over at me. I rolled my eyes and then shrugged.

"I don't care. Sure, why not. We gotta resupply there anyways. I'll just get some stuff to last me a few days." I complied.

"Where are you are guys staying tonight?" I asked Double Take.

"We're holding up in The Carriage Motel just across the street from where you guys are staying." She replied.

"We'll see ya on down the trail!" She said, as Lucky who had still been on the phone the whole time waved us off.

However, this would be the last time I saw either Double Take or Lucky ever again. I only hoped they eventually made it the rest of the way.

Such was life, on the Appalachian Trail.

Wales and I stood on the side of the road, beneath cloudy skies as cars flew by us.

"You think Woodstock regrets going back home?" Wales asked me.

I looked over at him, not initially sure how to respond without assuming things.

"It's not like he had a choice," I replied.

"I know, but we're more than halfway done. It just seems like quitting so close to the end would be harder to do than I know how to comprehend." He said, distantly.

I leaned down, stretching my back and feeling the weight on my bruised shoulders straining slightly.

When I leaned back up, I looked over at him and offered a sympathetic smile.

"He'll come back out here someday. He was already making plans on it before heading off." I replied, trying to cheer him up.

"Yeah, but I wonder if he was just saying that," Wales replied, scratching his head.

"Oh, here we go! A red Corvette is coming down the road!" I shouted.

Wales stuck out his thumb, and I rolled up my pants leg, dangling the hairy hunk of meat out into the air as bait.

The lady driving the Corvette laughed and honked the horn as she drove by.

"Bah..." I muttered, disdainfully.

"You think maybe your leg is scaring them away?" Wales tried to offer as insight.

"It's gotta be my beard. My Godlike, manly, unshaven face and your freakish Beethoven-like hair that's scaring them away." I said, shaking my head from side to side.

"So many cars with lots of extra space that just don't give a damn," Wales said impatiently.

"What if we just walked to the Flume Visitor Center?" I asked. Just then, a car drove by, with the driver waving at us.

"Thank you! That's exactly what we needed lady; a friendly wave. Not a ride!" I shouted sarcastically, while waving right back.

My smile dropped as the car passed. We'd been standing there for a little over an hour.

"It would take too long, though..." Wales replied, dismissively.

"Hear me out. So we hike three miles to Flume which takes forever. When we get there, we eat and then sleep the rest of the day since its cold, it's drizzling, and we don't feel like hiking anymore. Maybe use the internet to watch movies all day on our phones, huh? Sound about right?" I asked.

"I don't get...your logic..." He said, passing me an amused, but a confused face.

"How does that help us finish the trail?" He asked.

"Think about it! After walking 3 miles on a flat road. God knows we're gonna be dead tired. I'm probably going to be a lil' bit hungee...I mean, last time I checked I'm not training for the Iron Man competition. Alright? NOT TRYING TO BECOME AN OLYMPIC ATHLETE OUT HERE, DUDE."

Wales sighed, shaking his head from side to side.

"You truly are, *Morris the Entropic Cat.*" He replied.

The cars continued to ignore us as we started walking.

Some of them honking enthusiastically, maybe because it was fun to watch two guys hike in the rain?

One guy even had a P.A. system attached to his truck.

"Hikin' the trail...hikin' the trail..." He sang out as he drove by us.

It was cruel, but I was kind of hoping he'd accidentally crash off of the edge of a cliff when not paying attention further down the road.

Gonna be one of THOSE days today, huh? I thought miserably to myself.

Wales and I kicked rocks along the shoulder of the road, continuing to jut out a thumb to the occasional passing car. After a mile of no luck, we stopped at a picnic area off of the side of the road.

Wales had proceeded to begin making some vegetarian burritos from ingredients he'd gotten from the Price Chopper the night before.

"Here we go again, always waiting on Wales making burritos and sandwiches." I scoffed.

He handed me a wrap with vegetarian refried beans, bean sprouts, spinach and soy cheese crumbles sprinkled inside.

My mouth hung ajar as I looked down at it.

"Is this even food?" I asked with a disgusted expression.

"Try it out. I guarantee you'll like it." He replied with a smile on his face.

I only smiled with my head lowered after seeing his expression.

"Are you *ever* negative or pessimistic about anything, Wales?"

He shrugged and took a huge bite of his burrito.

"Thanks," I said, raising the one he'd given me into the air before scarfing it down. Sure enough, I had been judgmental far too soon. As I ate, my eyes widened, and Wales grinned at me.

"So..." he said, clearing his throat.

"Okay, Okay. It's good. You were right." I said, rolling my eyes and finishing it off. After eating it, I proceeded to make a tuna fish, horseradish cheese and Snyder's Hot Buffalo flavored pretzel wraps for lunch.

I offered him one, which I knew he'd decline.

"Enjoy your grass and leaves, herbivore," I replied as he smiled.

When we had finished eating, we started walking again just as it had begun to rain.

"Now that it's raining throw on your sad face!" Wales shouted to me over the roar of cars and wet tire traction deafening his words.

We both stopped, turned and poked out our bottom lips simultaneously as the cars flew by. Our expressions drooped, and I even mocked bawling my eyes out, by pushing both closed fists against my eyes and twisting them back and forth.

NO more than two minutes later, a guy in a white Ford F-150 pulled over immediately much to the angry cars behind him, slamming on their horns.

"Way to go, man!" I shouted excitedly to Wales, clapping him on the back as he laughed happily. We jogged towards the pickup.

"No room up here, but you guys can hop in the back if you want!" The driver shouted. We thanked him graciously and threw in our packs first, before jumping over the tailgate and into the bed of the truck. Meanwhile the drivers behind us shook their heads from side to side and bitched or complained within the comfort of their warm, dry vehicles at our having halted their forward progressions.

Raindrops stung our faces as the driver continued east. I huddled into a small ball, bringing my knees up to my chest as each splatter felt like a bullet against my cheek.

Still, we had gotten our hitch back to where we had left off the day before.

The driver pulled into the Flume Visitors Center 15 minutes later, and we were quickly on our way once again.

The wind blew, making wet leaf tornadoes in the parking lot. They swirled in fiery red, orange and yellow flames about waist height.

For even such a dreary, ugly day, it was always imperative to look for the beauty in it where ever it could be found in little moments like that.

The trails that day were comprised of old stream beds some idiot had decided to call a "path". We were walking up boulder-strewn creeks and waterfalls that ran halfway up legs. Our boots submerged beneath the current as we walked, occasionally causing the odd stumble and fall.

You couldn't tell where the mud pits or waist-deep puddles were anymore either because they were disguised by the river of fallen leaves passing between our legs.

Wales appeared pale and out of breath. I watched as he slowly sat down, breathing heavily and wiping streams of rainwater from his eyes.

"You okay?" I asked, in the torrential downpour.

"Yeah, I'm probably going to rest a second, though." He replied.

I sat alongside him, and together we complained about the weight in our packs and the crappy state of the trail at that moment.

Then we both commiserated over how that kind of terrain didn't even make hiking fun.

It was always a bit of help, to bitch and moan about the state of things with another person instead of feeling like you were the only one complaining all of the time.

Later in the day, after having passed Wales further along the AT, I made my way past Kinsman Peak, and on to Eliza Brook Shelter which was an additional 4 miles.

I had reached the southern pinnacle at 7 P.M. and took pictures of a darkening sky where the last bastions of light broke through like golden swords stabbing through a vast, black ocean of clouds. Down in the distance, you could see the town of North Woodstock and the electric street lamps starting to sparkle on, one at a time.

The drizzle that had accompanied our hike throughout the day had finally ended.

I retrieved my headlamp from my backpack and started walking down the mountain.

Traversing down Kinsman southbound was a huge pain, especially when everything was soaked and you were night hiking. I slipped and fell so many times, I believed I actually lost count at one point. So many obstacles required you to turn and hold on to the roots of trees along the side of the trail. A lot of the flat rock slabs simply gave no other option but to slide down a wet surface across cold, slick, moss-coated granite.

This was not the best method of traversing this path either because the weight of a backpack made a person shoot down in elevation like a bullet. At times, this had me landing awkwardly and stumbling forward towards my death. One such time, as I barreled towards a four hundred foot drop, the weight of my backpack swung towards the cliff almost as if TRYING to throw me off of the side of the mountain. I spun around and gripped a thin branch that immediately snapped and felt myself in free fall until I shot my hand out the second time. I had only just managed to seize the 3-inch wide trunk of the sprouting pine and steadied myself.

"For God sake," I whispered breathlessly, as I glanced back down behind me and pulled myself forward against the mountain.

"Gregory, you tryin' to kill me, dude?" I asked my backpack.

There was no answer, as I lay my head against the stone wall before me, and took a deep breath before continuing on.

I hiked through the darkness until I crossed Eliza Brook stream that according to AWOL's guide, was only .8 miles to the shelter.

Strange how if that was the mileage, it had taken me an additional 50 minutes downhill to reach it. This told me that it was possible the trail had changed since 2012, and as a result, I was hiking a further distance than what the book had accounted for.

Often, I'd find myself calling "The 2012 Appalachian Trail Guide", the *2012 Appalachian General Direction Guide.*

Upon reaching Eliza Brook Shelter, I found it was empty save for some old cans and a smoldering fire somebody had left behind. I used the cans filled with rain water to put the fire out the rest of the way and cursed the irresponsible person that had left it burning there.

Dinner was more tuna and cheese wraps accompanied by Snyder's Hot Buffalo flavored pretzels sprinkled as a topping. My mouth watered as I rose the strange burrito concoction to my lips.

"Hey…" I heard suddenly which had startled me enough to almost cause me to drop my wrap.

I immediately slipped my headlamp on and scanned the darkness. No one was there, however.

"Hello?" I called out.

There was no reply.

Finally, 15 minutes later Wales arrived with his backpack on.

My headlamp lit his exhausted face, as he held up his hands to hide his eyes from the light.

"How long you been here, stalking around in the woods?" I asked, confused and angry.

"What are you talking about?" Wales replied as I switched my headlamp to a red filter to save his eyesight in the darkness.

"You called out to me but didn't come around until now," I spat.

Wales only shook his head from side to side.

"Dude, I just walked up." He said, stripping his wet clothes and pulling out dried ones from a compression sack within his backpack.

"Are you kidding me?" I asked for clarification as I grabbed his arm. He looked at my hand and then to me again.

"What's wrong with you?" he asked.

"It's…" I began, confused and tilting my head to the side.

"I don't know. I just…I guess I was confused." I replied, letting go of his arm.

"Maybe you're just tired. We had quite a haul today." He said, stretching his bag out over the floor. I nodded, though I was distant in my thoughts.

"There's mouse feces, everywhere in here." He said with a disgusted face.

"Shit?" I called over to him.

He looked up at me.

"I'm sorry?"

"You mean *mouse shit*?" I clarified.

"Same thing. You know people die breathing in toxoplasmosis from mouse fecal matter." He said to me.

"You mean *mouse shit dust*." I clarified.

He looked over, irritable in his expression as I laughed.

I got up from my sleeping bag and began sweeping the shelter out with a broom somebody had left behind, as Wales covered his nose and mouth to keep from breathing the dust from the mouse droppings in.

"You happy now, your majesty?" I asked, giving him a bow.

"Well, I could use a foot massage, now that I think about it."

"Go to hell," I said, as we both chuckled.

As we lay back in our sleeping bags and listened to raindrops tap, tap, and tap some more against the tin roof— we talked about the plans for the following day.

We had 18 more miles to go before we would be done with the White Mountain Range at this point, and would have successfully connected to the Appalachian Trail down into Hanover, New Hampshire on the border of Vermont.

We talked excitedly about whether to split it up into two nine-mile days. However, the urge to just get it over with and be done with the next 50 miles of trail was too tempting to pass up.

When I was a teenager, my father and I looked over the husks left behind of the cicadas that had clasped to our pine tree in our backyard. I remembered collecting them when I was a kid and hanging them around the house, or shooting them with my BB gun when I was younger.

I picked at a discovered bulb of pine sap that was about the size of a quarter. The substance had already hardened white on the outside. I broke it open and touched the amber colored fluid with it.

"Did you know the Native Americans used to chew on pine tree sap like gum?" My father asked me as we both looked up at the trunk of the 200-year-old pine tree behind our house.

Of course, I didn't out rightly believe him nor did the white, semi-hardened substance appear very appetizing at all.

"Really?" I asked, as I dug my finger into the goo and removed a sizeable chunk off that clung to my index finger.

"Yeah, go ahead and try it." He said as I looked unsurely up at him.

"It has anti-inflammatory properties. They used it for burns, and for small cuts. It helped in sealing them up. Pine sap also boosts the immune system which is why they used to make people drink pine resin mixed with water." He explained.

I scrunched my face up. Deep down, I wondered how sweet this stuff had to be, to have been used for so many different substances. Was this sap sweet like honey, just seeping from the tree behind my house my whole life?

Had I never known of this incredible treasure trove of delicious sugary sustenance? And why hadn't we ever eaten it before?

I placed the pine sap into my mouth and bit down on it, immediately spitting out the bitter substance.

Nope, there was absolutely nothing sweet about pine sap.

"Nice one pops. You got me..." I said, almost retching.

"Well, I never said it tasted good. The Native Americans used to pack it into their cavities as well."

"Yeah, why don't YOU pack it into YOUR cavities?" I said, spitting more of the bitter sap out onto the ground. He laughed.

"Well we have dentists now...so we don't need to do that anymore. It's just something to know in case you're ever in a survival situation that calls for it."

"Right and the average age of a person back in the day was what, thirty-five? Forty years old?" I'd asked, before walking off.

As I lay there the following morning, within the Eliza Brook Shelter, I thought about the things my father had taught me when growing up and how much he had wanted to instill life of the outdoors in me.

I wondered now, if that knowledge would ever save me some day, or if it would only exist as a real conversation starter to have with people down the road.

Wales coughed, rolled over and faced the wall.

The water droplets that fell outside the shelter were poetic in their hushed conversations upon impact with the earth. They told stories to the rocks and the leaves that they touched, of how much longer mother earth could expect the rest of their friends to fall from the skies. They brought the dreams of clouds, as each raindrop spattered against the sticks and stones. Telling grand tales of heights, and flying beasts they would probably never see.

It was a calming hum of noise that slowly began to pull me back into sleep.

Shhhhh... The rain whispered to me in its ancient language.

Time slowed as my eyes became slivers, allowing only the minutest fragments of light in. Each drop that fell hit a tree branch and split into four or five more and continued its broken descent towards a thirsty earth willing to receive it.

Shhhhh... Mother Nature's gentle lullaby continued to sing.

My eyes closed, and once the darkness took me. There was no turning back.

I had no more strength left in me.

The boiling of Wales MSR pot was what woke me two hours later. He caught my movement and smiled over at me.

"Would you like a quinoa and shredded cabbage burrito?" he offered, holding it out to me.

"Gross..." I replied, scrunching my face in disgust and rolling in the opposite direction from him.

"I want biscuits. Biscuits covered in gravy with piles of bacon on top. And a three...no...a five cheese omelet." I complained.

"That would be so sad, to know so many animals had to die, to sustain your one breakfast." He replied in a somber tone.

I cocked my head back at him.

"Wales, you know of course I'd only do such a thing if those animals actually had names, and families as well. Right?"

He rolled his eyes at the crude comment.

"And if they were tortured a little. Can't enjoy bacon without knowing the pig suffered for a few hours..." I added.

"You're sick."

"...or days." I taunted.

He had created for himself.

I yawned and stretched slowly, feeling my back pop in about fifteen different places.

"This sucks," I said as I writhed with the tingles spinning their way up my spine.

"What sucks?" Wales asked in mid-bite.

"THIS!" I emphasized by casting my hands out at the gray skies before us.

He nodded, wiping his face and greedily taking another bite.

"I mean, are we still shooting for eighteen miles today?" I asked, in a whiny tone.

"Why not?" he countered.

"You understand we'll be walking through the dark, right?" I confirmed.

"I mean sure. But, you know how bad I want to try that Indian Buffet they have in Hanover." He said, with a chuckle.

I nodded, not really giving a damn about some expensive Indian restaurant food.

I just wanted to be around civilization long enough to shower again, wash my clothes...and eat something other than instant mashed potatoes and more noodles.

After packing my things, and downing a quick breakfast, I slung my backpack on and turned back to him before heading out.

"I'll meet you at Hot Iron Rd..." I said, showing him a point on Highway 25 using the map on my phone.

"So you're not taking the trail?" He asked.

I looked up at the bruised skies and gave him an apathetic shrug.

"It's more fun this way! I never know which way I'm going Wales. Besides, Moosilauke is going to be a bitch of an uphill scramble in this crap. There will be NO views up there, and the only satisfaction you'd get from such a climb is "bragging rights" that you did it on a shitty day. Personally, I don't have the pride or ego to need those bragging rights." I said.

"But this is the LAST mountain of The Whites." He said, shaking his head from side to side.

"I know. And I'll find an easier way to tackle it than you will." I replied.

"Morris, the Entropic Cat," Wales said, with a chuckle.

"Listen, the AT crosses NH 25 south of the Moosilauke summit. When you get there, go northeast along the road for about two miles or so, and I'll meet you at Hot Iron Road. It'll be on your right. We'll hike into this town…Haverhill, or whatever it's called." I replied, showing him the destination on my phone once more.

We stopped and filled our water bottles at Eliza Brook stream before heading out. Wales didn't bother filtering his, so I decided I'd bypass it too.

He looked up at me from the edge of the stream with a question in his eyes.

"Where are you going to sleep?" he asked.

"I'm sure there are woods all over the place," I replied with a chuckle.

"Yeah, on people's private property…"

"Who says I'm staying on their property? What if I meet a hot babe, who lets me stay in her backyard for free?"

"Sure." He said, rolling his eyes.

"Or maybe even her bed!" I said, pinching him on the side. He laughed and swatted my hand away.

"You sure are a dreamer, aren't you?" he asked.

"Only the best kind of dreamer Wales, only the best kind."

The rain had started to pick up rather heavily, falling in fat, cold drops that exploded like tiny little water balloons against us. It didn't take long for the weight of my backpack to nearly triple as a result.

"So what do you miss most about home?!" I shouted out to Wales over the roar of the downpour. He thought it over for a second before turning and answering.

"Video games mostly. I wanna play video games rather badly! At this point I'm even desperate enough to play Pacman or Galaga in one of those $.25 cent arcade machines right now, just to get my fix." He spoke back towards me.

The rain had created rivers along the valleys on either side of his nose and the grooves of the dimples around his mouth.

I shook my head sadly.

"Wales, don't say that. That's like saying you wanna get laid, and then settling on an 80-year-old cougar." I replied.

"You gotta have bigger aspirations than that." I added.

"So what did *you* miss most about home then?" he asked as we clomped along through milky rain puddles that had begun to drown the trail whole. We were sloshing through in our boots through six, to seven inches of pooling water.

"Sitting on my balcony reading, with warm, chocolate chip cookies Melody had just baked and a glass of milk."

"It's always food with you, isn't it?" he asked.

"It's like, my go-to thing when I'm angry, sad, or depressed. In that situation, however..." I said with reflection.

"It's the only time I can feel as if I have no responsibilities in the world and am existing in that moment only for myself. Living vicariously through other people's stories and suffering none of the hardships." I replied.

"Porn is good also," Wales said, with a grin.

I nodded my head agreeably.

"Yes, Wales. Porn is good also." I said with a laugh.

After a mile of hiking, we had reached a sign with the words: *Reel Brook Trail Crossing* on it. It read that 3.5 miles down it would reach Highway 116.

I took out my phone and looked at my GPS and Google maps to scout the way ahead. I found that I could take 116 to Lime Kiln Road which would connect further south with Hot Iron Rd.

Meanwhile, it also read that Wales had seven miles to go just to reach Kinsman Notch.

"Gods, we've only gone a mile?" He cried in defeat while sitting down upon a large boulder on the side of the trail.

"Ahhhh well. Looks like 'Morris the Entropic Cat' finds yet another shortcut. Ahahaha!" I said widening my eyes and rubbing my hands together greedily.

"I take it, you're not going any further along the AT are you?" he asked.

"Two men, locked in a never ending battle...." I began in my movie trailer announcer's voice.

"One man. A purist, locked to the sanctity and sacred chastity of the trail. Banned from seeing anything beyond the borders of a two by four-inch white blaze. The other, a rebel. A ladies man swimming in women. Does whatever the hell he wants. Goes wherever the hell he pleases, in his never ending journey home. Which person will succeed? Which man will fail?" I said just as my voice broke and I began coughing from laughter.

Wales shook his head, envious by the expression upon his face.

"Wales, I've learned one important thing out here if I haven't learned *anything* else. *Hike your own hike*, truly means jack shit to the majority of hikers that look down upon you, when you do." I said, patting his shoulder.

"In all honesty, I just don't give a shit anymore or what anybody else thinks about my hike. I'm not out here for them, any more than I am for you. I'm out here to get this rock home to my parents *my own way*. And I'm really not too far away from completing that goal!" I said, then pointing towards the southern sky.

"It'll be raining harder on you *up there* than it already is down here right now—and you're probably going to be slipping and falling left and right," I said.

"Be careful, bro," I said, elbowing him playfully.

He smiled.

"I'll be headed to the Jeffers Brook Shelter past Moosilauke summit. It'll be a 16-mile day for me. I'm not gonna push eighteen miles all the way to the road. Not in this mess." Wales explained with a depressed expression.

"I'll see you on the other side, buddy!" I called back to him.

"Yeah..." Wales replied somberly, as he turned to look at the trail ahead.

Reel Brook Trail? More like Reel HARD Brook...trail I thought to myself. And while I had known the joke was rather flat, I laughed at it all the same.

I stopped for a moment and looked at my GPS and the chunk of woods to my left and then immediately to my right.

No Trespassing signs ran along almost every other tree until suddenly stopping. I guessed upon their sudden disappearance that this was the edge of the local paranoid "Doomsday Preppers" territory.

I chose to carve off going out of the way and walked through tightly knit trees interwoven between strands of ivy and other vines.

When I reached the road, I turned southeast and started my 18-mile hike for the day.

Bloated skies sprayed down occasionally upon me, but not enough to soak me any more than I was from when Wales and I had first started out that very morning. I threw my fleece on to help with the cold winds whipping about but ended up taking it off as I began to heat up. The basting stink of bacteria covered flesh was too unbearable to smell any longer.

Ahh yes. There was that lovely hiker stink I had so terribly missed. It wafted like rotten roadkill laid upon a hot radiator, airing out deep into my nostrils.

"Ohhhh...nothing smells as bad...as a hiker walking past. Yellow teeth...critters in his beard...dirt under his nails..." I tried singing. Then I realized I wasn't so much singing as much as I was pronouncing the most disgusting things about hikers out loud, that I could think of at the moment.

"Ohhhh, we're poor. Our clothes are shabby. I'm stocked with parasites of every kind...got scabs all over my body! YEAAAAHHHH! JOCK ITCH EATING ME ALIVE! PROBABLY HAVE RABIES..." I started singing louder.

A few birds looked down at me from the powerlines as I walked along 116, cocking their heads from side to side.

"OHHHHH, I SMELL SO BAD IT HURTS..."

I laughed at myself suddenly, unable to continue on.

The wind began to pick up rather roughly, and so as soon as I had reached the 112/116 junction—I took cover in a sliver of woods that ran alongside a river.

I broke out my tarp and wrapped it around me as I hid beneath a maple whose leaves were almost all gone.

I looked up at Mt Moosilauke, thinking about Wales. The clouds had almost entirely erased any proof there had ever been a summit up there. You could actually SEE the rain coming down as well and streams of water pouring off of the sides of the mountain like waterfalls.

"Hope you're alive, and doing good buddy," I whispered out loud.

I took Highway 112 to where it split left over to Coventry Road.

I had taken the scenic route along Windy Ridge Farms. The theme of the property seemed to be apples, with what looked to be a nubile orchard growing.

Everything was painted an awful maroon red. Light blue flannel flags and red picnic tables with matching patterned table cloths, appeared to have been nailed down to the wooden surfaces.

This place was country themed in every way. A "We're Open" flag hung at the driveway entrance waving back and forth in the breeze, despite a chain being up that blocked entry by vehicle.

It reminded me a lot of a southern farmer's market set up, with tables or boxes at obtuse angles with which to hold the fruit for viewing before purchase.

It also touted a "Cafe" that served food. I suppose the picnic tables made sense now.

I imagined real food, like barbecue chicken or pork, and brisket being served on paper Dixie plates there. Potato salad, coleslaw, baked beans and dinner rolls to accompany the meat.

I had become so hungry thinking about a southern cuisine that I hadn't noticed the string of drool hanging from my beard until it had brushed against my forearm.

"Yuck..." I said, wiping my arm against the side of my shirt.

Long fields and farmland open to horses or pigs dotted the horizon. It was cold and gray out, but I could close my eyes and see this same view on a warm, September afternoon at sunset in my mind.

The thick, dark green grass with golden skies and a dying sun that left the world on fire before its departure.

I imagined it was beautiful.

When I reached another split in 112 further south, I stopped at the intersection and looked around for a bit.

Suddenly, somebody called out to me.

"Where ya headed?" the woman's voice asked.

I looked about for a moment, unsure as to where I could navigate my gaze towards the direction of the inquiry. Everyone seemed to have been within their homes or existed only as quick blurs in passing trucks and cars that day.

"Yeah, I'm talking to you!" She shouted again, as her dog ran excitedly around her legs.

She was standing on my right at the edge of her porch and waved me over.

"I guess, *that way*," I said pointing to my left. I confirmed this, by looking down at the map on my phone.

"You one of them hikers?" She asked, coming down off of her porch. I looked both ways and crossed the road towards her.

Before I opened my mouth to answer, I wondered if she'd meant that question negatively.

What if I said yes? Would she remove a steak knife from behind her back and start slicing at the air at me? I thought, cynically.

For some reason, I always felt paranoid when somebody questioned if I was thru-hiker—as if I should feel shame or fear for being one in some weak or pathetic sort of way. All the same, I'd decided to answer her truthfully.

"Yes, ma'am I am. I'm looking to reach Lime Kiln Road." I replied.

"Ayuh. You got good ways to go. You need a ride?" She asked.

Well, ladies and gentlemen, this was the day I said: "Screw this hike, I'm going home!"

I then proceeded to win the lottery, and live out my days on a tropical island I purchased with my winnings. Accompanying me would be a swimsuit model stuck to my side. Maybe two swimsuit models actually, because I could now afford to make both happy. At least monetarily.

Realistically, though, I was standing in soaking wet clothes, shivering beneath gray skies with a pack that weighed double due to the gross amount of rainwater soaking through it.

The urge was there, to hop into her car and alleviate the shin splints I felt...atop of my crackling, sprained ankles. I could get a ride into Hanover that very night, and eat at the very Indian Buffet Wales had mentioned. I could even send a text message with a picture of me gorging myself on the food as well, to shove it in Wales' face.

"Well never mind that, you wouldn't be a hiker then if we did that." She laughed, making the decision up for me.

I could have cried. Right then and there. I could have just broken down and burst into tears at that very moment and replied: *No please. You're right, I'm not a hiker. I'm just a piece of shit, honestly. Please take me to a warm bed, and a shower and dry clothes somewhere. Anywhere! LET'S GO NOW!*

"Thanks anyways, though. I think I'll probably just sit over *there* in that ditch, next to all that trash and eat a granola bar before I get going." I said, smiling sadly.

Ah, the alternative. Never quite as lovely as the first offer, however, I'd also been playing a hook. It was an attempt to maybe tug at this kind woman's heart strings and get some free food instead.

But would it work?

I was searching for a moment of sympathy on her weathered, wrinkled face.

"I just hope I don't choke to death on the thing…my throat is so dry and all." I said with a sad, pathetic shrug as I began to turn away.

"My friend from church has four different apple trees in his yard. I collected a bunch of apples the other day and made three pies this afternoon. Would you like a couple pieces honey, for the road?"

I felt my brain explode. The kind old woman hadn't just said "PIECE."

SHE HAD OFFERED "PIECES"!

That was plural, wasn't it? That meant more than one!

I could have kissed this woman on her wrinkled old mouth at that very moment.

I wanted to grab her and swing her happily through the air while belting out: *AMERICA! AMERICA, GOD SHED HIS GRACE ON THEE!* At the top of my lungs.

"Well...you know...if...if it wouldn't be too much trouble...I uh...I mean sure. I love apple pie." I replied, humbly. If only I'd had a hat to writhe between my hands, while sheepishly digging my toe in the dirt to complete the act. Instead, I offered my shy expression and tried to hold my breath to make it look as if I was blushing.

Inside I was an exploding fireworks factory.

"Unfortunately I don't have any more ice cream. The grandchildren finished that off yesterday." She said, climbing her steps and holding open the screen porch door for me.

I looked down at my muddy boots and thought of how smelly and disgusting I was.

"I can wait out here. I'm kind of filthy." I offered, as she turned slowly and gave me a surprised look.

"Well, if that suits you. How many pieces would you like?"

"I think I'll start with two, ma'am," I replied, smiling. My stomach had begun groaning in anticipation at the prospect of homemade apple pie.

"Oh please. You look like you could eat a horse." She said waving her hand dismissively at me.

She came back out with a hunk of apple pie about the size of 2/3rd's the pan.

I was about to succumb to a diabetic coma, and I didn't care!

We talked as I ate so much sugared fruit and buttered pie crust I felt like my stomach had been on the verge of exploding. The woman had given me a glass of milk with my dessert as well.

I didn't think to ask if she lived alone. I didn't want to seem nosy, so I told her about my adventures on the trail. As dark started to creep a little closer, I took out a five dollar bill and offered it to her.

"I don't want that!" She exclaimed with a purposefully overdramatic face. She shoved my hand away.

"Please, you've been so kind, and that's rare out here at times," I explained. I then told her about the older woman in Tennessee who had offered Torry and me cold water on a hot day back when we had decided to orienteer our way north after leaving Greasy Creek Hostel.

Occasionally people saw the packs and knew what we were about without ever speaking a word and decided to offer us help without so much as a question. However, that hadn't always been the case either.

"I appreciate it sweetheart, but you'll need it more than I ever will." She said smiling and closing my open hand. My fingers tightened around the crumpled bill.

"You're incredible. Thank you so much." I said, squeezing her hand.

Before I left, she said a prayer out loud for me.

"Please bless Mr. John Morris, on his hike back home...to his parents who probably miss him and fear for him every day that he's gone. Shower him with your undying love and devotion. Be with him, and if he hasn't yet—help him find his path through your never-ending light. In Jesus name."

I wasn't outwardly religious, but I added an "Amen" as well.

I thanked her graciously as I walked off into the sunset.

Fresh tears welled on the edges of my eyes for the actions of such an incredibly friendly, elderly woman. I laughed in awe at the sheer generosity I'd received out of complete strangers on the trail.

I had ragged, smelly, filthy torn clothes on, and I was unbathed. Still, my weathered, worn features hadn't frightened her at all. I could have been a psycho or a murderer...but she was so kind she probably couldn't even fathom that possibility within her mind.

It was moments like this that made this experience worth every ache.

Worth every pain.

A couple tears of sheer graciousness rolled down my bearded cheeks as I glanced back at her house and waved a goodbye.

When I reached Lime Kiln Rd, I followed the dirt road for about 3 or 4 miles through your classic country farm setting. The kind you see in pictures that are usually hung in bathrooms or doctors' offices. Cobblestone Cottages in distant, dusky fields with yellow light seeping out from their stone-sill windows.

Sometimes accompanied by orchards sitting atop rolling hills.

Upon reaching the end of Hot Iron road, I found a grass field on my left, about thigh high. On the other side of that was a set of trees.

At the end of the road, however, there was an old bus stop and a weather booth somebody had built for children long ago. It was dilapidated and crumbling apart. I shivered in the wind as I looked up at the gray skies and then back towards Moosilauke that was still covered in thick cloud cover.

The old bus stop smelled strongly of black mold and urine.

"So much for that..." I muttered as I looked across the road. I'd likely get tetanus or a black widow spider bite from staying in there before I would any sleep.

I walked into the middle of the road and looked in either direction. The road carried on for miles without a tree or turn or curve in sight. Instead, it vanished at a point along the horizon.

"Oh, being a hiker sucks! Sometimes you gotta find a place to sleep...and you don't have nowhere to go..." I sang out loud, and with no rhyme or reason.

I awoke to blistering, miserable wind gusts that tore through every layer of clothing I had on.

I peeked out southwest from my hammock tent towards the end of Hot Iron Road, and when I felt it was safe, I stuffed my pack and crossed the field.

I made my way back to the bus stop and stood for thirty minutes before the wind became too much to handle.

I had to kneel to get inside the rotting structure because the opening was so small and naturally made for children.

On the walls inside lay your typical immature graffiti. It consisted of dick pictures, foul language, and crudely drawn naked stick figured women in the middle of some distinct sexual act that the actual artist probably knew nothing about.

I read a sentence scrawled sloppily on the wall.

"Amanda loves Chris so much; I'm gonna fuck him!" It was dated Sept 20th of 2000.

Thirteen years later, Amanda was probably almost my age.

She might have been married with kids now too.

When I looked at this kind of crap, I wondered if the person who'd written it ever saw it again decades later and realized how childish it was to write such a thing on the wall. If there would have been any shame in seeing it all these years later.

Outside, a loud semi-truck passed by, shaking the thin structure as drops of rain started to fall.

"Great..." I muttered looking sadly up towards the skies.

The wind was tearing through the cracks or holes in the wall, leaving me to believe I'd have been just as sheltered from the cold, outside, as I was in.

I picked up and propped the broken door that had been torn from the hinges against the opening to the structure, to keep out as much cold wind out as possible.

Suddenly, I heard someone call out my name.

"Morris!" I heard the voice shout, and then instantly become carried away by the deafening roar of wind outside.

I looked out east and saw a tall, blonde, curly-headed fellow walking along the side of the road and shouting out into the woods.

"Morris!" he shouted again.

I stepped out of the structure and waved cheerfully at him.

"Yo! Over here!"

When Wales arrived, he was shivering rather violently, only clothed in shorts and a short-sleeved cotton shirt.

"We did it, dude!" I said, shaking his hand as he laughed, and nodded his head.

"We're done with the White Mountains, finally." He confirmed, with a weak voice.

"How was that excellent view up on top of Moosilauke yesterday?" I asked, with a smirk.

"I thought about you enviously, every minute you were gone. I must've fallen at least twenty times. I kept thinking you had probably already reached Haverhill on your own, and you were long gone towards Hanover." He said, almost with a relieved tone that his prediction had turned out to be untrue.

"I couldn't leave you behind bro. Though I won't lie, it came to mind in this wind." I explained, holding my hands up in the atmosphere surrounding us.

"You've been hiding in this thing all night long?" he asked, kneeling down and looking into the structure.

"Only for an hour or so."

A car sped by, doing easily twenty, to thirty over the speed limit. We both watched the red Mazda Miata vanish down the long road as a sudden increase in the downfall of rain brought us both back to our senses.

It took us three rides and 2 hours to get from Highway 25 back into Hanover. We managed to snag a ride from a garbage truck for 3.7 miles before we were dropped off at an intersection outside of Oliverian School. From there, we were able to retrieve another ride to Highway 10. We were let off in the gravel lot next to a bridge overlooking a small river.

"Well, these short ass hitches are taking forever, but at least we're on the main strip now. All we gotta do is get…" I had said before Wales cut in.

"Twenty-six miles southwest." He finished for me, while looking at his phone.

I sighed and looked at the endless flow of traffic packed along our route which would make for an inconvenienced walk. We held our thumbs out for at least another hour in the cold rain, before a truck filled with junk in its bed finally pulled over.

"Where you fella's headin'? I'm only going as far as Lebanon." He shouted out his passenger side window to us.

"That's perfect! If you could drop us off at Burnham Field in Hanover, where the Appalachian Trail runs through the center of town—that'd be awesome!" I called back to him.

"Get in the back, that's not too far off track." He called back to us.

The rolling hills of Vermont.

CHAPTER 8

And so, I Hike Alone...

"I'M DISGUSTING. JUST SAY IT to me. I won't care." I said, only not loud enough for the cute girl across the intersection to hear me. She was trying to avoid eye contact of course, and I understood why.

Having lived the life as an overweight monster, I had become quite used to these kinds of looks from women. Even more so now that I let my beard grow out wildly, and I smelled like spoiled parmesan cheese.

Why would she ever look at a slob like me?

"I'm wearing shredded, disgusting rotting clothes. But I have an awesome personality." I offered her inaudibly.

She looked up at that moment. Almost as if hearing me speak suddenly.

"That's right. Look at me. I'm only talking to you." I whispered. A few Dartmouth College students standing beside me overheard my mumbling and laughed at the one-way exchange.

"I...LOVE...YOU" I mouthed. The mysterious young woman was decked out in knee-high brown boots over a scantily form fitting pair of gray synthetic tight leggings. She was wearing a professional looking gray jacket with huge gaudy buttons. Her hair was in a seamless ponytail. She was maybe 23 to 25. She gave me a disgusted look.

The "Walk" sign flashed, and both sides of pedestrian traffic began to approach each other.

"So as I was saying..." I began as she got within a few feet of me.

"You're fucking disgusting. What are you, like 45 years old?" She asked shaking her head from side to side as she walked by. The other college students that had been watching me shouted or howled in laughter with: *"Ohhhhh's"* or *"You just got burned, buddy!"*

One guy even acted out a knife being plunged into his chest and stumbling almost to his knees while everybody else laughed at my expense.

"I'm only 30," I muttered as she sped off without as much as a glance back at me.

I suppose it was for the best anyways. I was in route to the Post Office to retrieve a package anyways, and didn't have time to make new acquaintances.

My parents had explained they'd filled the box with Boars Head summer sausages and some fancy cheeses.

An updated version of my driver's license had come as well, and my parents had shipped that too. Extra food that I had bounced forward from North Conway back before even starting the White Mountains, had arrived as well.

I sat down on a bench inside the Post Office and took a few things. Granola bars, candy, peanut butter packets, protein bars and just your basic trail foods that wouldn't weigh me down too much.

I then bounced the box forward again with the rest of the contents; this time to Williamstown, Massachusetts. It was around 160 miles give or take 20 or so down the AT.

After I had received my things, I looked outside at the storm brewing. There was a wind advisory for the area that suddenly alerted as a notification on my smartphone.

The wind was blowing so hard, that the post office doors were flying open by their selves, and customers were standing inside, looking out and watching the chaos in the streets.

However, my eyes had been trained across the street at a Starbucks. I zipped up my coat and pulled my toboggan down upon my head.

A warm Venti Latte would have been nice to sip on until the storm passed by.

As I stepped up to the door, an older woman grabbed me by the arm.

"Wait, you're going out in that?" She asked me.

Outside a trashcan was rolling down the street and rammed into a guy's car who had stopped at a red light. A woman was chasing her umbrella that had flown from her hands and crashed into the side of a woman's stroller who was parked on the edge of the road and had been hurrying to get her child into baby seat within her Toyota Tacoma.

An advertisement board for nearby businesses and sales events toppled over as well and skid beneath the tires of a passing UPS truck which proceeded to crush the thing into splinters.

"Hell yeah! Look at all that fun going on out there!" I said sarcastically. I opened the door and was immediately greeted with a waterfall of rain to the face that instantly blinded my eyes.

I ran to my right and pounded on the "Walk" button against the street corners pole, jumping up and down with my arms around myself.

"AGH! THIS SUCKS!" I shouted out loud.

A young Asian woman was shivering and gave me a: *Some luck... huh*, kind of expression. Her mascara was also running down either of her cheeks. She was swiping at them fruitlessly.

"Don't cry! I'm sure it will pass!" I shouted, smiling through the whipping wind.

She laughed. "It better!"

We stood there momentarily in the rain together waiting for an impossibly long light. I was a moment away from jaywalking through the crowded intersection.

"Coffee would be great right now, eh?" I asked.

She smiled.

"Yeah, but it would just get cold and watered down in this weather."

"Well, that's why we would drink it in there," I replied, pointing to the Starbucks establishment across the street.

"Oh yeah. Duh." She said, giggling shyly.

I wondered suddenly if it was that simple.

Had I subconsciously just asked this woman if she would join me for a coffee at Starbucks?

I perked up a little.

Well, look at you, Rico Suave I thought to myself.

Maybe this time out on the trail had changed me a little more than I initially thought it would.

I looked both ways, before taking my Dri Down jacket off. I knew I partly was going to regret this. But a side of me knew it was so incredibly bold and such a nice gesture that nobody could refuse a couple of minutes of conversation over coffee afterward.

Let's face it. Let's call a spade, a spade, alright? I was bored...lonely and thought I had a shot for some reason if through nothing else than my charm.

She was cute, and maybe she'd give me the flirtatious conversation I'd so lately missed, being around either Wales all day or just by myself.

I threw my jacket across a small shallow puddle in front of her onto the road. I'd hope she'd understand the reference.

"The hell with this light! Let's go!" I said offering her my hand. The road jam was cleared. Nobody was anywhere near us with a car.

She gave me a confused look, though, then looked at my coat on the ground as the waves of water started to inch it slowly towards the gutter.

"We can't. The light didn't change yet." She said, pointing towards the sign across the street.

Well yeah, I was aware the sign hadn't changed lady. I was saying let's get the hell out of this rain already I thought to myself cynically.

"Why'd you throw you jacket on the ground?" She asked with a laugh, as if I was a complete moron.

"It's for you to step on..." I said with a sigh, as my down coat only got more and more soaked in the dirty street water.

"Oh, okay." She responded as she hovered over her phone to check the time, a text message or to show me she was basically uninterested in my gesture.

Well, I can honestly say at this moment that I had most definitely felt like a complete moron.

Moreover, I didn't know if I should pick my soggy jacket up or if it would appear rude to do so at this point. Maybe after the Walk sign gave her permission to make up her mind, she might want to use it.

I'd probably look like an incredible moron, more so than I already did if I moved it now. However, the thing was starting to drift away, and so I reached down, picked it up and set back in front of her again.

The woman looked confused as to what I was doing and frankly I was confused myself as the damned coat was so soaked it had become pointless for me to have thrown it in front of her at all.

Her eyes went back to her phone.

Well, I wish someone would just shoot me in the face right about now I thought to myself, blushing about fifteen different shades of red.

"Yo." Somebody suddenly said from behind me.

The voice had come from a guy, dressed in unlaced Timberlands with sagging pants below his ass and a white Jersey far too large on him.

He looked to be an Eminem impersonator...with his shaved blonde hair and lines cut into his eyebrows. He had clipper lines in jagged angles on the left side of his skull.

"T!" The Asian girl said. She hugged him, apparently knowing the guy.

They talked for a bit. Meanwhile, I stared sadly at my drenched coat that passing cars continued to splash ditch water on top of—one after another.

"Yo dude. Who's jacket?" He asked me with his arm around the girl's shoulder that "I" had invited for coffee. "Mine," I said, leaning down and finally picking it up. Dark, dirty water poured out from the pockets.

"Why you jest drop yo shit in tha street?" He asked like I was crazy.

You know I was asking myself the same thing at that point.

"He put it there for me to step on or something. Right?" She asked me.

I nodded.

"Fo' reals?" T asked, chuckling…like I had just come straight out of the 1800's.

The "Walk" light flashed, and suddenly the guy picked the Asian woman up and cradled her. She yelped in surprise before laughing.

"Who needs to walk when you can be carried, girl." He shouted, stepping off of the curb. He crossed the street with her in his arms.

I looked down dully at my soggy coat and then watched them walk away.

I was dripping as I entered the Starbucks. People all turned from their books or canted their heads from around their laptop screens to look at me as if I was the creature from the black lagoon. I immediately stalked into the bathroom with a sopping coat dripping relentlessly upon the floor, and dragging behind me.

I spent the next 20 minutes wringing water out of my clothes and jacket into the sink. I patted myself down with paper towels as best as humanly possible to dry myself out.

"Lesson learned. Never be so accommodating to complete strangers, ever again." I muttered to my reflection in the mirror as I exited the restroom.

I was sure I looked just as pathetic as I had felt when I walked up to the cashier. I ordered a pumpkin spice latte instead of a regular latte, which still managed to warm me to my core. When I'd finished it, I ordered another.

I sat down at the one empty table in the place and looked around at the college kids working on their laptops or typing up essays. Doing research on things and writing things.

It wasn't long before I felt out of place.

I hummed a little while looking at local artwork that had been put up on the walls.

I was confused about a particular painting hanging by the far entry way.

"Somebody called THAT art?" I asked the guy next to me who had been glued to his laptop screen before I chose to engage him in conversation.

He passed me annoyed expression and then looked over his Sony Vaio screen at the artwork I had been speaking of.

"I know the girl who painted that piece. She happens to be a friend of mine." He said, with full loathing and detest in his tone.

"Oh…yeah. I…uh, just meant I didn't understand it…" I stuttered, immediately regretting opening my mouth at all.

"Maybe you shouldn't put something down, just because *you* don't understand it." He replied snobbishly, closing his screen and standing.

He sat across the room at another empty table and offered me a bothered look, before blocking me out altogether with his laptop screen.

"Hmph. I wonder what *his* problem was." I said to a young woman sitting on my right, who had glanced up to watch the exchange.

"I'm sorry, but I'm trying to read here." She responded.

"Sorry. Didn't know I was in a library." I whispered.

She didn't answer.

"Hey buddy, if you don't have anything to do. Why don't you just leave?" A yuppie with a bunch of graphs in front of his iPad said to me. His group of friends looked over at me from the high table catty-corner to where I was sitting.

I sighed, offering neither a response nor anything else to say.

I simply walked out, not wanting to be a bother to anyone.

I navigated through the darkness with only the light from my cellphone illuminating the way. Two huge trees had fallen in the three hours I had been gone, during the storm. They'd fallen across the path and directly into our campsite where Wales and I had been set up just outside of the ballfield.

"Wales!" I shouted, almost immediately thinking back to the recent incident with Woodstock at Pinkham Notch.

I got no answer and began jogging down the trail.

"Wales, are you okay?" I shouted again. I tripped, falling over a downed branch, but quickly recovered and got back to my feet after feeling around for my phone.

I had resumed running and pushed through the branches of another fallen tree.

"WALES! ARE YOU OKAY? WHERE ARE YOU?"

Only silence met my calls.

"WALES! I shouted at the top of my lungs. Finally, I saw a light turn on in the darkness.

"Morris..?" The response was weak. It sounded exhausted as if he had been calling for help, for hours and nobody had responded. I knew it then that a tree had crushed him. As I ran towards the light, I saw images of gore from the weight of the tree having pushed his intestines out from his mouth.

Huge pools of blood, and…

"Dude, are you okay? There's fallen trees all over the place out here!" I shouted.

Wales popped his head out from behind his tent door flap. In doing so, a small leafy branch that had fallen atop his tent tumbled down to the ground as I looked up with a bothered expression at the rain.

"I'm all right." He mumbled. I might've woken him up.

"Jesus Christ dude, I thought you were hurt or something. I'm sorry." I replied, falling to my knees. The images had seemed so real, though I had only imagined them. I realized I had expected that the worst had happened.

And in doing so, I realized with disdain that I was doing it all over again.

I was clinging to Wales now, as I had Woodstock and to Torry before them.

I sat down on the fallen tree, ten feet in front of his tent, with light, breathy clouds coming out from my mouth and then vanishing before my eyes.

Nothing about me had changed. In all the time I'd been out here, I was still just as scared as I'd always been. Afraid to hike alone. Afraid that if no one else were with me, I would somehow fail.

It's a sad thought when you come to realize how incredibly weak you are. To sit back and think that the only reason you kept going were because of *other people*. Never because of yourself.

Torry had been right, so many months before in a sense when he had shouted angrily at me: *So it's true then? You are hiking for everyone else, and not for yourself!*

I had been so adamant about exclaiming he was wrong. But still several months later, I realized he'd been right all along.

"Did you have your earphones in?" I asked, quietly.

"Yeah, I haven't heard anything."

"Not even this enormous tree, crashing down directly in front of your tent?" I queried with a dull tone.

Wales's eyes went wide when he looked out at it as if the whole thing had suddenly just appeared before his eyes.

"Guess I might have thought it was thunder when it fell." He said, smacking at a mosquito that had landed on his knee.

I found that the popular tree had fallen across the support rope of my tent. However, the line hadn't been broken and instead, it had only tugged my hammock tent down to ground level instead.

"Lucky, I guess," I muttered to myself, still slightly upset at my initial reactions when running into our camp. I'd also felt very awkward and stupid for reacting the way I had even though Wales' expression seemed thoughtful in that moment and unbothered. I guess that was something.

As I started to stand up and make my way towards my devastated bedding, Wales erupted into a series of wet coughs.

"You okay?" I asked as I turned to look back at him.

"Think I may be getting a cold. Or maybe even the flu." He said weakly.

I nodded and replied:

"Maybe we'll get a room or something tomorrow? On me." I offered.

I took down my hammock and stationed myself farther away from the fallen tree and our campsite.

"Morris, thanks," Wales called out suddenly.

I turned and looked back at him.

"For what?"

"Caring. Being scared for me, I guess. You're a good friend." he said, a bit sheepishly.

Maybe my fear hadn't been so much out of losing someone to drive me on each day, and instead, it had been miscalculated altogether.

What I had feared was my friend potentially being hurt, and immediately I had gone to cursing myself for giving a damn.

"It's no problem, bud. We gotta look out for each other..." I said, untying my tent.

Upon rehanging my hammock and climbing in; I found my sleeping bag, fleece liner and everything else to be soaked. In fact, I found that if I could get no other use out of my hammock regarding a sleeping spot—I could always use it to capture water at least. It seemed perfect at doing that.

I sat quietly at a table alone, in the dining room. There were tons of people around me, bumping into each other, complaining, talking about day plans or speaking in French.

However, all I heard, was the subtle scraping from my butter knife, with a dollop of cream cheese raking across my toasted bagel.

Scccccrrrrrriiiikkkkcccctttt...

I gently curved the plastic knife into the cream cheese tub and smooshed it against the open face of my bagel again.

Scccccrrrrrriiiikkkkcccctttt...

I thought I had heard somebody ask me something from far away.

I looked up, and the large nose of a German woman was almost directly in my face.

I leaned back slowly.

"You don't mind, do you?" She asked in her thick accent. I saw both hands were gripping the back of a chair at my table that she'd partly already pulled towards her.

"I...I'm sorry. Not at all. Please." I replied as she thanked me and faced the chair around at an already full tea table adjacent mine.

I looked at my bagel and set it down slowly.

I was lost in my thoughts again. I was thinking about the trail and what was to come.

I was thinking about life, after the trail as well.

How could I ever go back to what I'd so purposefully ran away from? After everything, I'd gone through just to make it happen. After all of my experiences with life and to a lesser extent, the close calls I'd had with death. How could I go back to working twelve-hour shifts as a security guard again, feeling dull and dead inside?

I would grow bored, so quickly it didn't make sense to me anymore. Mortgage payments, car payments, insurance payments, a couch and a large flat screen. A life of going to work, coming home, eating, sleeping, going to work, coming home, eating, sleeping….

After the life I had lived, why would I EVER want to go back to that?

That kind of existence?

It was only the day before that Woodstock had sent me a text saying: *Where r u guys at?*

Woodstock had exclaimed over the phone that it was easy to fall back into his old lifestyle despite the fact that he missed the trail so much, every day.

I dropped my bagel onto the Styrofoam disposable plate and looked at it.

I wondered how Torry was enjoying his new life with Pam. With a job and with bills—while rebuilding his life.

I hadn't talked to him since he'd left my side back in Bentonville, Virginia.

Torry seemed to be so dead set on getting away from that lifestyle originally when we'd first set out on March 17th, that I couldn't imagine seeing him go back to it. But maybe that's what 'love' did?

Maybe his feelings for Pam, ultimately changed him?

Then again, maybe it was our bickering.

Woodstock and I had bickered quite a bit, and even once in a while though far more rarely, Wales and I did as well. And then at other times Woodstock and Wales bickered with each other.

But it didn't mean I hated them, nor did I expect as much that they hated me either.

While it wasn't hate I'd felt towards Torry, there was still a bit of contempt. There was an underlying anger towards him for some reason I couldn't explain. At first, I'd thought that it was his nonchalant demeanor.

Then again, maybe it was his leaving so abruptly after everything we'd done to make this trip a reality?

Finally, I had come to the obvious, observation. I was angry because I had felt dependent upon his strength to go on.

He had been my hiking partner.

And it had scared me, thinking of following him.

To think of that empty apartment back in North Carolina.

To dread and relive those lonely nights again, and to fear the self-destructive lifestyle I once had lived, all reawakening.

How long, before I would snap again? How long before I would say: "Forget this. I can't take another night of drinking alone."

Would that ultimately become the day I left again? Would it be the very moment that I decided to go on to my next adventure?

I'd learned that thru-hiking, was mostly about living for the moments. It had become a place for people to stop worrying about the future, and to forget about the past and live, just for the present. On that piece of trail, to escape civilization and responsibility and live only for yourself.

And many people chose to never go back from it either.

I became aware of that, after hiking beside people out here that would go on to die the very next day, such as Biscuit had in Damascus.

I had been in my own moments, where I was a breath away from death...and not a day after I found a tearful solace within the warmth of a shining sun beaming down upon me. All while I sat in a ditch with snowmelt rushing beneath my feet and with an ice cream cone in hand.

There was simplistic entertainment in watching a dragonfly dance through the air...or to sleep in the thick grass beneath an open blanket of stars atop a mountain bald.

I could never see going back to my former life after the trail.

Not after all of this.

Because in the end, it would only be a matter of time before I realized the money I was always saving for, was ultimately for my next adventure.

Not a comfortable future with a retirement plan. Instead, it was a chaotic, and unpredictable outcome. And that had become my ultimate desire.

The variables and multiple endings seemed limitless.

However careless, it may have appeared to others.

It was several days later, and I stood looking at a "No Trespassing" sign, obstructing my way forward.

"Well, you never find unusual places sticking only to the trail!" I tried to say positively out loud.

I had distanced myself more than 30 miles south over the course of a few days after Wales, and I had both been dropped off by the local trail angel, back onto the Appalachian Trail. However, as was becoming more typical, I had lost Wales along the way as I chose to orienteer and carve additional mileage out wherever I found this could be done easily.

"Let's see..." I said, looking down at my smartphone. I had taken a left on something called *Chateau Road*. Now I was at a dead end with old discarded tires and pieces of car parts littering a forests cul-de-sac. Rut-marks had torn up the earth, and worn clothes lay scattered around on the ground as if massive nudist parties had transpired there in the past.

If I ever needed to become rich off of recycling beer cans or bottles, this would have been the ideal location as I walked through literally thousands of them. My feet were kicking and skittering the huge amounts of litter across the destroyed, ruined Earth.

According to my phone, I wasn't far from Killington, Vermont. In fact, by orienteering off of the trail altogether, I had found that my alternative path passed within .4 miles from the town while the old Appalachian Trail that had been abandoned years before, actually went right through it.

However, my venture would prove quite dangerous as well. This was because the old Appalachian Trail that had been abandoned had slowly been taken back over by Mother Nature. I crossed nameless creeks and streams and navigated through briars along deserted logging roads that had become barely visible after more than ten years of non-use.

Sections of the trail had completely vanished by time from mudslides or fallen trees, and there were instances where I would find myself walking along remnants of a path only to stop, turn and realize I had taken a wrong turn quite a way back.

Faded Appalachian Trail white blazes, some which appeared to had been purposefully burnt off—marked my path.

I stopped momentarily, and looked at the spotty digital compass bouncing from left to right and up to down on my smartphone and sighed with disdain.

"Piece of crap," I muttered.

Above me, I heard scurrying through the branches. I looked up towards a crow cawing angrily as if I'd just invaded its home.

"Shut up!" I shouted at the thing, while its head tilted from side to side.

I sat down, and removed my backpack. I had decided that when you became lost, that the only rational thing to do was eat something and collect your thoughts. Maybe that's what I was missing? I needed to sit somewhere and figure out my next plan of attack.

The crow flew away as I removed food from my pack that my parents had sent me back in Hanover, in a care package.

I'd had my suspicions when I opened the provolone cheese packet, and it smelled much like Limburger cheese.

"Ugh…" I muttered, pouring out the clear oily liquid from the packaging onto the ground.

I took a bite and reeled. It smelled and tasted rather strange. I knew you could get away for four to five days without refrigerating cheese, but this hadn't been refrigerated for at least two weeks.

However, I didn't have much else to eat other than a little genoa salami that had turned a tad brown with age.

Later that evening after consuming half the block in hunger, my stomach screamed in sharp pains. It wouldn't stop grumbling and groaning. It had rolled several times before I made myself puke.

As I stood back up, my head felt like it was going to explode with pressure. That's when I felt my OTHER end, getting ready to explode as well.

I quickly got as far away from my camp as possible (which was only 10 feet) when I yanked my pants and boxers down…and essentially, as graciously and non-graphic as I can put this; I peed from my butt.

When I thought all was well, a massive gas bubble ran through my lower intestines rather painfully. I felt as if my insides were about to rupture—only it wasn't gas. It was more "sick" that needed to come out.

When I had finished, I took the cheese from the packaging and angrily launched it as far away into the woods as possible.

My phone buzzed angrily, seeking my attention and awakening me from my rest. What at first I thought was serious, was only the notification tone that my battery was dying.

A dissatisfied expression passed across my face, and I jammed my thumbs into my eyes to press the sleep still residing within them, out.

I glanced out towards my backpack.

"I think we're gonna be guessing our way towards Killington, today," I said to Gregory.

The backpacks response, was one of silence, much like anyone with a rational mind would have expected. However, it was very close to what would've been my own reserved and lackluster response.

While stumbling through the forest, I realized my sudden distaste in the path I'd chosen. Google Maps had identified a thin white line I traipsed back and forth along—as the Appalachian Trail.

Let me explain it this way, however.

There was no trail here.

I was walking through the woods over an invisible path Google called the AT. However, that invisible line supposedly led into Killington. That was at least if Killington actually existed as a place more tangible than this trail was.

I had been considering hiking along Route 4; straight into Rutland.

I needed to charge both phones, and my reserve batteries as well.

But even more than that, the majority of the food I'd received from my parents had been spoiled upon arrival, and I didn't want to risk any more foodborne illnesses like I had the night before. I needed fresh supplies.

The sun broke free from cloud cover at around 8 A.M. and by 10, after a breakfast consisting of water and a smashed cereal bar, I was on my way.

The majority of my day was spent pushing through maple and oak tree saplings.

This forest had a lot to throw at me, but mostly briars that shredded away the flesh of my legs as I crawled over, between or passed right through the patches unable to take any other route except straight at times.

Fallen trees, and washed out forest roads made the trek a chore, only because for brief spurts of time I believed I had found an actual path—only to see it vanish from landslides taken place decades before my arrival.

After a mile, I glanced down at my GPS and watched as the arrow that was supposed to account for "me" start to drift away from the "trail."

"No..." I muttered, in defeat. Suddenly my position according to the screen had begun to drift as much as two miles towards the west as the digital compass spun in odd and manic circles. I glared up towards the skies expecting some alien ship or magnetic cloud cover to have been the culprit, but found only clear blue skies.

"You piece of shit! COME ON!" I shouted, pounding my fist angrily into the screen. As soon as I did, the phone shut off.

For a moment, I stood there in awe of what I'd just done.

Did I seriously, just break my phone? I thought to myself. I attempted to turn it back on, but it wouldn't restart.

I laughed at first. It was everything I could do, to keep from taking the phone and smashing it into pieces against a tree until it exploded.

It was true that I had gone off track as a personal decision, but when I glanced back the way I had come I could find no visible trail there either. And that blame went to Google and their misinformed digital maps.

I removed the battery from the phone and plugged it back into the seating. I was immediately excited because the screen came back on again.

"There we go. That's what I thought." I said confidently. However, my confidence was short lived.

The phone proceeded to boot up as far as the logo screen before shutting down again.

Oh, I had grand scenarios playing out in my mind. I'd imagined round house kicking the smartphone up into the air and then shooting it with a rocket launcher, before decidedly jumping off of a cliff to my death.

I'd also imagined setting up my cook kit, boiling a pan full of water and then throwing the phone inside to cook to death.

So many ideas had come to mind, none more tempting than just twisting the phone between both angry fists until it shattered in a shower of screen glass and plastic splintered pieces.

I can go straight. It's noon. In the northern hemisphere if you walk towards the sun at noon you are walking TRUE SOUTH.

I'd remembered Torry telling me that little piece of information back when we were prep hiking before we'd ever set out on the Appalachian Trail.

It seemed so long ago now.

I took a breath and gave a final glance behind me, and saw nothing resembling a path.

It was time to go.

I'd managed a few hours later to get my phone to turn back on. However, the screen had been shifting into oddly different hues on occasion. I supposed I must have done damage to the screen in my fit of rage.

And strangely enough, I was comforted by that. As if I'd just taught the inanimate object a lesson.

I began breaking sticks and branches along the litany of interweaving and overgrown forest roads I traveled that barely bore visible ruts 10 to 20 years or more in the past. So severely eroded, they were indistinguishable from the rest of the landscape more often than not.

I did this in case I needed to backtrack. My "bread crumbs" of a sort. Eventually, the path I'd been hiking started to climb a steep summit, encased within a fenced off area of tightly woven pines, so thick it appeared physically impenetrable.

I stepped back and surveyed the landscape.

Helpful Tip 1,498: Your eyes take in so much at once, it's sometimes impossible to decipher a traceable trail even when it's right in front of your face. When faced with trying to visibly see where the trail continued on, I removed my camera and took a picture which narrowed my field of vision. It was easy to come to a conclusion as to why this trail had been closed, after looking at the picture I'd just snapped.

I scraped away gross amounts of leaf cover in a ten-foot diameter. Beneath it, I had found significant soil deposits that made me think the trail had vanished due to past landslides.

But it didn't explain the age of the trees blocking off the trail as well.

Unless those too had shifted downhill during the landslide I thought to myself.

I wiped sweat from my eyes and took a swig of water.

I knew the best case scenario for an individual being lost was to typically follow streams or flowing water sources downhill to where they collected in ponds or lakes or passed by roads into civilization somewhere. Luckily, as I had stopped to rest, I found that I had stumbled across a collection of wet leaves where water trickled downhill for a way. As the cut in the mountain widened further down, I found additional stream water coming out from multiple places along that same valley. All of which added to the slow trickle and turned it into a stream. By the time I had descended some 300 feet, I was now walking alongside a creek.

I refilled my water bottles with the cold spring water coursing straight out of the earth and from somewhere beneath the mountain. I would never know how a person could ever be able to readjust to fluorinated and chlorinated lead-filled tap water from a sink, after sipping the liquid heaven of a natural, fresh mountain spring.

After bushwhacking for what took 2 hours to cover a little over a mile; I came to Stony Brook road which was little more than a footbridge and an ATV trail.

I saw white blazes marking the AT, and then a switch back sign on the tree directly in front of me. I hopped out of the woods and found that there was a vehicle gate stating that the trail was closed to outside

ATV'ers unless you were a member of VASA. On the trees, however, red spray paint had been applied to the white blazes in an X fashion. Maybe this was no longer used as part of the AT anymore?

I looked around the general area and found were no white blazes further up the ATV trail.

"Not this shit again..." I muttered as my eyes scanned the enclosing tree canopy above me.

"AM I ALLOWED TO HIKE THROUGH HERE?!" I shouted out loudly to anybody.

To nobody.

A few birds chirped in response, and a squirrel tore off out of sight.

Other than that, I was only met with silence.

"That's good enough for me! Thanks!" I shouted out with a salute to the world.

So I followed the shortcut I'd found by phone which eventually brought me about 3/10's of a mile ahead into a clearing.

As I hopped down out of the woods, I rounded a dirt hump along the side of the road where two ATV riders had parked and were eating lunch atop their vehicles.

They watched me curiously as they chewed away at their bologna sandwiches and I crashed straight out of the shrubbery, waving my hands wildly before tripping and falling to my knees on a jutting root.

"Jesus, you okay?" one of them asked with a laugh.

I stood up slowly and wiped sweat from my brow. If my intention had been to avoid people in the area, I'd pretty much blown that plan all to hell.

"Do you guys know if this road goes to Killington? My phone goes back and forth exclaiming I'm on the Appalachian Trail...and then not. So I don't know what to believe anymore." I said, dropping my backpack in frustration.

"Hmm. You've been on this road here a while haven't you?" He asked. I nodded, taking a swig of water.

"Unfortunately you've got like 6 to 8 miles left before you even reach Route 100. Then it's about and additional four miles down into Killington." His friend said.

That was a lot further than Google maps had proclaimed.

"How about we give you a ride down to the road?" The other guy asked with his helmet still on.

I looked at the minimal amount of space he had available. Sitting on that ATV would have been about as close to making love to another man than I would have felt comfortable with.

"I appreciate the offer, though; I'll have to pass. I enjoy walking." I lied, still contemplating a quick ride towards food and civilization. My goodness, I had become spoiled.

"You sure you'll be okay?" he confirmed.

I nodded. "I always make it some way or another..." I responded.

About a half mile down the gravel path after leaving them behind, I saw a split in the road that led more South East according to my map.

The road went by a house with a wooden sign above the door with the words "Dads Cabin" engraved on it. I knew then that this had to lead to a main road.

After almost two miles of downhill walking, I noticed the forest road led out behind an automotive repair shop.

Across the street was a city park adorned with apple trees of four to five different varieties. However, it was absolutely was devoid of people.

Swings swung unused and dry-rotted in the warm breeze with only the ghosts of children's laughter to push them.

The "town hall" was next door, with nobody at work in the offices. There sat one town vehicle in the lot. The library would look exactly the same. Empty.

The local recreational center was abandoned as well, and strange haystacks with Jack 'o Lantern scarecrows adorned the landscape with nobody to appreciate the time and effort that went into the setup.

I found a picnic shelter with outlets and quickly went to charging all of my electronics and backup batteries.

According to AWOL's guide, there was a bus that ran from Killington to Rutland every hour. But the pickup station was four miles away, and the sun was already setting.

I was getting a little hungry for a snack, and the many apple trees in this park existed only to be ironic. Gaia apples as big as what you'd find in a grocery store lay rotten beneath the tree that had once bore them.

If only I had reached them a month before, they'd have been in better shape.

All the same, I knelt down and searched through a few promising looking ones. I removed my multi-tool and cut a small edible chunk out of a half rotten apple after scaring away the yellow jackets that had been swarming around it.

"Mine," I whispered selfishly, as I bit into the fruit.

River Road led to Route 4 along a scenic highway that showed off the striking colors of fall. The smell of autumn was so thick in the air, it had become nostalgic.

I remembered back to days from my youth when I once dived into ditches filled with leaves in front of my parents' house after having spent the day raking them. They had fallen from two-century-year-old oaks dominating our front yard.

It brought a smile to my face, as I smiled up at the sun.

"Outta the road, asshole!" a teenager shouted suddenly, tossing a beer bottle at my feet as the beat up Silverado sped by, and his friends in the bed of the truck all laughed. Glass scattered into a million tiny broken shards—some of which had impaled my pants leg. Luckily, however, nothing had cut me or stuck into my flesh.

I ignored them until they were out of sight, wanting to give the group no satisfaction of any sort for having done what they did.

Cars oblivious to anything outside of their metallic and fiberglass bubbles with wheels; cruised uncomfortably close as if I was nothing more than a bug on the side of the road.

When a 1970's VW Bus pulled over 50 feet ahead of me, I stopped my forward progression for a moment, cautious with uncertainty.

A guy that looked identical to the comedian Zack Galifianakis stepped out from the driver's side door. He watched momentarily in silence, as I picked the last remaining shards of the beer bottle from the bottoms of my pants legs.

"Yo hiker trash! I'm headed to Rutland! Get the fuck in!" He shouted, walking around the front of the vehicle and jerking the passenger door open.

No more beer bottles, thrown at you.

Quick access to real food.

Maybe a place to stay if the guy turns out to be kind of cool.

These were all real thoughts systematically running through my mind. Views of the ignorant and the naïve, looking and hoping for the best in a world that didn't always produce that kind of scenario.

I was less than a mile from the Inn at Long Trail, which was right by the Appalachian Trail. I could take a day off or two and get a ride back there to the AT having lost almost no mileage in the process.

"Are you coming, or what?" he asked as I thought of all these things at once.

"Well, you only live once. Right?" I asked myself out loud.

Here went nothing.

"ARE YOU READY TO DIIIIEEEE?" The driver screeched at the top of his lungs. He proceeded to turn up the volume on his radio to full blast after gunning the gas to his VW Bus. While doing this, he had decided to let go of the steering wheel so that he could air guitar, as death metal blared out over the sound system.

"We're gonna make it, and nobody is going to stop us!" he shouted maniacally as I felt my eardrums about to explode.

Well, it was official, I was about to die.

The driver purposefully began to weave the bus maniacally in and out of traffic as he floored it as fast as the struggling engine could possibly go. I felt like I was in the martial arts action movie The Transporter, and Jason Statham's fat, mentally incompetent brother-in-law was behind the wheel.

He stole a glance and saw the frightened expression upon my face.

"What's wrong? You worried about cops?" He asked. I was grasping the top of the front window with one hand, and the other was flat upon the ceiling.

I smiled warily, slowly clutching my unbuckled seatbelt against my chest.

"W...well...I'm worried about...something..." I managed to stutter.

"BECAUSE THERE'S NOT A SINGLE PIG AROUND TO STOP US WITHIN A 30 MILE RADIUS! SEE THAT SHIT OVER THERE?" he blurted over the music.

He pointed out of his driver's side window at what looked to be ten local sheriff deputies and town police along with an FBI vehicle and two state cops. They were swarmed around a red Pontiac Thunderbird on the northbound lane of Route 4.

"Hey, piggies got a drug bust there?! Oink, oink mother f-"

"Jesus Christ, dude," I muttered into my hands.

He had garnered a few looks, and one cop had even flipped him off in return. It was at this point he began laughing and head banging to the music again.

I tried to snap my seat belt in, but it wouldn't click.

"Hey, I can't get this to work," I shouted. Too bad the driver was in his own little world and hadn't heard a word I said.

I tapped him on the shoulder.

"What?!" He shouted bothered, and impatient.

"I can't get this seatbelt to work," I yelled once more before I finally reached over and lowered the music.

"This isn't clicking," I said at a more reasonable voice level.

The driver responded unfavorably, emphasizing the "F" word in a guttural growl as he explained just how much he didn't care that my seatbelt wasn't working. He then proceeded to blast the music volume up to maximum again.

"RrrraaaaaaaAAAAAGGGGGHHHHH!"

The driver had now started pounding his fists violently against the steering wheel as I tried to pretend I wasn't scared for my life. I thought of the knife blade on my multi-tool in my backpack and wished I'd had it in my hand.

I was almost confident that at this rate, the guy was going to pass by Rutland altogether. Maybe he'd never had any intention of ever taking me there at all, to begin with, and instead, I was really on a one-way ticket to the hospital.

When he pulled up to a Citizens Bank and jammed on the brakes, I braced myself, falling forward a bit as my pack skated across the floor in the back of the bus and smashed into the back of my seat.

He over dramatically pulled his sunglasses off of his face. His eyes were wide, vibrant but bloodshot. There were droplets of spittle in his beard as well and beads of sweat around the corners of his red-rimmed eyes.

I didn't know what to expect next.

"Are you ready to do this?" He asked, in a rather dramatic voice.

I looked around and stole a glance out at the bank. I saw bystanders walking by, eyeing the vehicle that was blaring death metal and that had skidded to a tire-smoke engulfing halt.

"Ready to do *what*?!" I asked with scared confusion.

He seemed as if he was trying to impersonate Jim Carrey now by being overly animated with his facial expressions.

If only I'd been holding my backpack in my lap. I would've bolted out of the vehicle right there.

"Are you FUCKING READDDDDDDDYYY?!" He asked, harmonizing the last part of that sentence like a coked out opera singer.

"THE HELL ARE YOU TALKING ABOUT?" I shouted back at him, getting angrier.

He pulled out a comically small knife from his keychain that was about the size of a thumb.

"We're gonna rob this place buddy. That's what I'm talkin' about. You with me, son?" He asked, gritting his teeth together and peeling back his lips.

That was it.

I was getting the hell out of here.

"Sure thing, I just need to get something out of my pack," I said, shoving my broken seatbelt out of the way and crawling into the back of the VW Bus.

"Sike!" He shouted, jamming his foot onto the gas and taking off. I flew forward and landed on my chest as he floored it.

"Jesus Christ!" I shouted, falling atop my pack and then rolling across the floor in the back.

The Zack Galifianakis look-alike hung his tongue out of his mouth and shook his head back and forth at me like a lunatic.

"Hold on tight! We're just getting start.....ted.....awwww....shoot." He said, turning and looking back at the road ahead. I looked past him through the front windshield and saw the red light he was pulling up on from my sprawled position on the floor. He seemed disappointed that there were cars in front of him and he wasn't able to plow through like a maniac. I truly didn't know where the hell I was or what was going on anymore. I thought for sure that this guy was certifiably insane or drugged up out of his mind. And one moment more.

I quickly got to my knees and fumbled with the side door...unsure of how to open it.

It seemed as if the handle had been broken off from inside. There was a tiny metallic tab that looked as if the plastic around it had snapped off at some point and the latch wasn't engaging.

The driver turned to look at me as I quickly pretended to be digging into my pack.

"Yo dude, forget it. We aren't robbing the bank anymore. Get your ass back up here." He said, turning the music up full blast again and growling along with the singer shouting over the speakers.

He started acting as if his hands were claws and began raking at the air while making dinosaur noises.

I had seconds before that light turned green and maybe a minute after that before I became a casualty in this guy's driving.

I fumbled with the door again as nervous beads of sweat cropped across my brow.

You have seconds, hurry up! I said to myself.

The driver revved the engine and began beating on invisible drums in the air as he swung his head in circles.

Come on, come on, come on!

I twisted the metal tab and pulled on what looked to be a jerry-rigged clothes hanger attached somewhere to the mechanics inside the door. I wasn't sure what this was supposed to do.

I glanced up front again, to see the yellow traffic light engaging. In less than five seconds it was going to turn green, and I'd be stuck with this guy until he potentially managed to wreck and kill us both.

Three, two...one.

The lock disengaged and the latch finally opened. I jumped out as quickly as humanly possible just as the light turned green.

The driver then screamed out at me in anger "The FUCK are you doing? Get back in!"

"No." Was my response, as I slammed the rolling door to his VW Bus closed. It didn't shut, though, or lock back into place.

Maybe the latch was broken or something. I didn't know, and frankly, I had no interest in the working mechanics of that Kidnappers Vehicle anyways.

I walked along the side of the road as he had shifted over towards the passenger's side window.

"Dude I was just messing around with you! Get back in!"

I continued to ignore him, though. I walked a block as he drove along beside me, yelling "Come on man. I was just givin' you shit. Get back in! I always like to mess with hitchhikers."

There was no way in hell I would be getting anywhere near that guy or his VW Bus ever again.

After I had continued to pretend he didn't exist, he slammed on the brakes along the side of the road, shouting "Fuck it!"

He got out, and I turned, facing him in the rare case he'd decided to make a charge towards me. This time I had my hand on my multi-tool in my pocket and I had already unfurled the knife blade.

Instead of rushing me, however, the driver said nothing and closed the side door himself before hopping back in and driving off without another word.

I had no idea where I was, or which way I needed to go at first. My phone signal had been acting up again, and as a result, I couldn't get GPS coordinates on my current position at the time.

I was still coming down from an adrenaline high, and I needed a place to sit and collect my thoughts.

I crossed Merchants Row and found a curb to sit on in the Walmart Parking lot.

Maybe no more hitches for a while, huh? I thought to myself. I removed my backpack and looked at Gregory like an old friend.

"Didn't get too bashed up back there, did ya?" I asked my silent partner. After a few minutes, I decided to call my parents which was both comforting, but risky as well. Only because I knew how my mother was going to react.

"Did you call the police?" my father asked me after I'd gone over the details of the incident with him.

"No, because all I was thinking about was getting out of the vehicle and getting away from the guy. I didn't think to take his license plate number." I replied.

"Well, we're both glad, to hear you're okay. We haven't heard from you for some time. We were getting worried."

I looked towards the earth and sighed.

"You know your mother, and how she worries about you." my father went on to say.

"Dad, just tell her I'll be okay and that I love her."

"You're out there trying to kill yourself!" I heard my mother shout in the background. It was evident he had me on speaker phone.

"Anna, knock it off." My father replied.

"No John, that's my son! I won't *knock it off*!" she shouted back at him.

Suddenly she had taken the phone from my father's hand.

"Richard?" she asked in a weak and fearful voice, calling me by my middle name.

"Hello, Mom."

"Richard, I want you to come home right now. I can't take this anymore! You're torturing me. You're going to end up dead in a ditch somewhere, on the side of the road!"

"Mom, I'm not going to end up dead anywhere. Okay? It was just one wrong hitch and besides. I got out of it just fine." I tried to assure her.

"I don't like you trampling around in those woods all day like some psychotic!" she replied.

I couldn't help but laugh, as my mother began to burst into overdramatic tears. This had always been her fall back weapon. To set herself off into a sporadic set of crying when she ultimately didn't feel she was going to get her way. She had perfected the art of it.

"Mom, if I'm a psycho then I'm in my element with the thousands of other psychos out here too. Which means I'm safer than you know. I'm in the town of Rutland, Vermont right now and I'm going to hang out here overnight."

"I don't want you sleeping in some tunnel, under some bridge, or in a trash can…"

"Mom, I've never slept in a trash can." I offered, with a chuckle.

"…and I don't want you sleeping in some back alley like a homeless man."

"Ma, would you listen to me fo' a moment ova' heer'ya?" I asked, trying to break her hysterics with my poor impersonation of an Italian man from Newark, New Jersey where she had been born. She had always loved my crappy attempts at humor.

"Listen, ah'm's 'bout to get's me one'ah dem subways subs tah eat. 'Kay ma? Youse stop worrying yourself down dere…okay? Den ah'ma gets me one'ah dem fancy rooms, filled wit nuttin but beautiful Italian women. Molto bene!"

My mother started to sniffle as she handed the phone back to my father.

"Okay…" was all she muttered as she stepped away from the receiver.

"Dad, make sure mom knows that I'm not stopping until I walk this rock I got you guys from the summit of Katahdin, all the way back home," I said.

"She knows, she just misses you. We both do."

I didn't immediately respond.

My attention had been stolen by the words in my guidebook. My eyes widened over the entry in AWOL's 2012 guide for the Hiker's Hostel located at the Yellow Deli.

"Well Dad, I'm gonna let you guys go. I need to find myself a place to sleep before it gets dark and I think I found just the spot." I said with a smile crossing my face.

"Just be safe."

"I will. Talk to you guys later." I said. I had wanted to tell them both, that I loved them. Only once again, it just felt too odd and awkward to do so.

And I hated that about myself.

I walked into the hostel, and up leather hide covered wooden stairs towards the bed rooms on the second level of the old downtown building.

There was a men's bunk room immediately on the right-hand side of the hallway. On the left, a women's bunk room had been in the process of being built. Drywall panels, paint cans, and tarps lined the uncarpeted surface. The wall putty patches had been recently sanded, leaving fine white dust upon the floor beneath them. Down the hall, there was a common area and a washer and dryer that were coin operated.

I knocked on a door that read: *Worker beez only pleez*. I figured the staff of the hostel or the Yellow Deli had probably worked or lived there.

There was no answer from my knock, however, so I began to explore.

The men's bunk room had a large bathroom with two private showers installed. There were four bunk beds and a single bed alone in the corner that gave nine bodies a place to sleep overnight.

Coming back out, I went to the end of the hall where there was a common area that had a sink, community-use dishes, a microwave and various hiking books on the shelves or the coffee and end tables there.

The World We Came to Find

Out back behind the common area was a large, second-story wooden deck that led to what looked to be a breakfast room of sorts behind a locked screen door. The other side of the veranda led down a set of stairs towards an enormous public parking garage, and a bus transportation system for the city of Rutland.

In the hour I had spent exploring, I came to find that many of the buildings on the block had been owned by the Twelve Tribes; the same religious group who owned and maintained the Hiker Hostel, as well as the 24-hour Yellow Deli down on the ground floor.

They were the embodiment of kindness, whenever I spoke to any of their members. The women dressed in what appeared to be more American-casual, middle eastern garb and covered their hair in bandanas or with hijabs. The men wore ponytails that they kept in a ball tightly cinched behind their heads, and almost all bore beards.

The men also wore a kind of tethered, interwoven string called "tzitzit," sometimes tied around their foreheads to express the "do's and "don'ts" of the Torah. It was worn as a sign of pride by their members.

When I went back towards the employee entrance on the second floor and knocked again, this time, I had received an answer.

"I'm a little lost..." I began.

"I'd say at this point; you are not lost. You're breaking and entering." The old man replied.

"Wait, what? No, no! I thought this was a hostel," I began as the guy started to chuckle.

"I'm just kidding around with you. The names Tyler." He said, offering his hand. I shook it, now a little more at ease than I had been in the moments before.

"It's getting cold out there on the AT, and it's supposed to get pretty low out here tonight in the city too. Can't have you sleeping in the cold now, can we? Let me show you around," he offered.

"I've already walked around, actually," I clarified.

"I just need to know how much I owe you," I added, removing my wallet.

His eyes widened, and a small frown crossed his lips.

"Well then. We ask for a twenty dollar donation per night." He explained.

"That's great!" I replied enthusiastically. A cheaply priced place to sleep was always welcomed.

"I have to say however it isn't hiker season much anymore and you're a little late headed north. You know you only have four days left to reach Katahdin, right?" Tyler asked.

Was it truly, already October 11th? I had been walking for so long, it seemed impossible to believe.

"Actually, I'm hiking *south*. I flip-flopped on the Appalachian Trail at Pine Grove Furnace State Park in Pennsylvania back in June. I've already hiked Katahdin back in August." I replied.

"When did you start?" he asked.

"March 17th, *this year*. I've been hiking for around six and a half months." I said.

"Well it sounds like you've got it all figured out then, don't you?" Tyler asked with a warm smile.

"Not nearly, when it's already taken me this long just to walk 1,600 miles." I replied with a chuckle.

I made my way into the bunkroom and took the small single person bed in the far corner by the window. As I sat down and dropped my backpack to the floor, I closed my eyes and listened to the familiar hum of the city existing outside of my window. I felt the warm breeze coming from between the cracks and gaps between the frames, borne sometime around the 19th century.

I'd always had a love-hate relationship with urban areas. At times, I could say the same thing regarding life within a rural environment as well. Still, there always existed these express differences and extremes each different atmosphere offered, which more often than not; gave way to both their energetic appeal and yet an "isolated" feeling all their own.

Living in the country, it was almost as if the surroundings had been made purposefully for your exploration. Such as, to get a sense of the terrain around you. Offering insight into the sort of world you would most likely find yourself coming into contact with more regularly, upon your living there.

On a mildly temperate day and with no responsibilities, pressing appointments or obligations to be anywhere—this atmosphere could at times, lure you out of your home for an afternoon walk through fields, pastures and deep hollows where life was very rich and alive.

These moments could quite often inspire thoughts outside of the claustrophobic confines of steel, glass and cement civilizations existing elsewhere in the cities of the world. The environment could whisk you away at any time into far away reveries and leave you staring off into the distance, correlating some scene of nature you happened upon as sparking an analogy. Maybe even a memory of the past. Perhaps it brought about a comparable metaphor you had attributed to work, or society or childhood adventures appearing much in the similarity between two worlds. Ones that you could later write down in your memoirs.

By hypostatizing Past and Present, these worlds collided.

Quite regularly the smell of fresh wildflowers and honeysuckles often drew memories like these out for me, and even in daydreams I could find myself lost and wandering through my thoughts without desolation or despair–if only because of my surroundings.

Always content.

Before I had known it, time could have elapsed so quickly that I had found myself walking back home, carefully picking ripened blackberries that would stain my fingers and palms with their dark, sweet juices. And with only the deep purple hues of dusk and the silhouettes cast by dark strings of clouds in the skies above to accompany me, I would find myself at a lonesome sort of peace.

I cherished, these empty moments of time, always attributing the harmonic atmosphere of the natural world, with that of isolation. It was a semi-euphoric feeling of being both fulfilled and conversely anxious, as night began to envelope my soul within those forgotten lands.

And then there was the city; dynamic, intrepid and alive.

A whole new energy existed in this electric environment. Nothing could feel more convenient or accommodating than stepping out from your cozy apartment, taking the fire escape ladder down to the alleyway leading towards Main Street and suddenly finding yourself eyeing all of the modern conveniences you could ever possibly need. The hankering promise of a greasy cheeseburger, a film in the local theater on a rainy day, a quick snack at a street vendor's cart and conversation to bide your time. There was always a warm cup of coffee or hot chocolate to be found on a chilly Fall day and a comfortable, welcoming seat at a corner shop café in your favorite sweater or fleece jacket. A place where tall buildings stood looking down upon you. It was here that the world was more rapid and hurried by short leashes and time constraints installed and embedded into everyday life out of efficiency. Conversations flowed quickly and only in passing, as groups of people walked by unperturbed or bothered by your existence. And why not? To quote Pinky Floyd, you were "just another brick in the wall"; the world watching you, as you watched the world. Living only as just a bystander with no background or meaning to anybody, or anything.

And oddly, one could sometimes find that they were fine with that.

With your favorite book in one hand and perhaps a spiced pumpkin latte in your other; you found your eyes were awash within the pages of your favorite tome—one which had been printed in bleeding black fonts, and laid gingerly upon warm butter-cream colored pages. It was here, that you were utterly numb to the atmospheric "hum" of the metropolis surrounding you.

I found I had more control of myself within this environment. I was less worried by the prospect that my hypothetical rural homes water pipes would suddenly burst by some extraordinary overnight permafrost freeze, or that power failure from a storm would leave me without electricity for days on end. I felt the world was more manageable in the city, because all I needed to find concern with was myself. My own physical wellbeing. Not the house, nor the woods and the acres of my property.

Not even the isolation in the expanse of the land surrounding me.

And while I could always exclaim that I was less "alone" in this populated urban environment; sometimes as that "brick in the wall" I found I had become exactly that. In the biggest cities in the world I was nothing important to anybody, anywhere. Ironically surrounded by millions of people, and just as alone as you'd find yourself to be in the woods.

One could stand to claim that indecisiveness came about in one way or another when thrust from one environmental extreme into the opposite. My hike had been the perfect example of that. There would always be a yearning, for those solemn hours alone at times when the subway rumbled the very structure of your dwelling, in passing or the sounds of sirens awakened you from desperately needed sleep long before the years had made you grown accustomed to their sounds and wailings.

Fall was here all the same. That much could easily be deduced by the colors of the decorative trees planted along the aged, splintered and crumbling sidewalks and cobblestone streets. And it pulled me from my thoughts in the city of Rutland, Vermont as I looked down from my window.

It had become oddly sudden to me, when the seasonal changes had hit though. In all my time whilst walking through New Hampshire and along the White Mountain Range, I felt the green leaves of maples and oaks were turning yellow and red with each step I had taken south. It had felt like that, walking from New Hampshire into Vermont as well. It had reminded me of country cottages, ones where neon moss grew on their dew soaked roofs in early fog-heavy mornings. Giant gazebos or open walled shelters where red and white plaid colored table covers danced lightly in the breeze. The kind that you would find draped across picnic tables on a sunny day. Picnic tables where Apple Pies had been set to cool. Apple pies with decorative graham cracker lattice designs resting across the tops. On lands where healthy green grass, black and white spotted dairy cows and your occasional apple tree lay nestled in the valleys of each rolling hill that the people living there called "mountains"; as far as the eye could see. At times, all it took to appreciate such beauty and the coziness it brought on, was remarking solely through the expression upon my peaceful face. The serenity brought about by a setting sun, shattered into a billion shapes and sizes, much like bright orange pieces of crystallized confetti; radiating like sparks and flames through the breaks in the trees towards the forests floors.

Splinters of luminescence that ultimately stole you from the binds and confines of responsibility and the lack of freedom you were unaware, you never truly had on a daily basis back in civilization.

Rutland, Vermont had become this place to me and my broken, blistered, wandering feet.

Massachusetts, Connecticut, and New York would also become these places to me as I hiked ever south, back to my family, to my parents, and to my home.

Chris was former Marine Recon, and a disabled veteran, who had been visiting the people of the Yellow Deli to gain closure amongst individuals he felt generally cared for him there.

Chris had completed four tours in Iraq and had served his country for 11 years.

While on tour in Afghanistan, his convoy had been ambushed. Of the three vehicles attacked, he and only one more marine would survive the altercation.

The first Humvee had hit an IED while the last two had been shot with RPG's launched from both sides. Chris had been on the turret at the time in the first vehicle, and had been thrown 30 feet. Having become riddled with shrapnel in the process from the explosion, he explained to me that he had landed on his side and broken three ribs from the fall.

While lying there, he was additionally shot three times. Once in the abdomen, once in the hip and once in the shoulder.

After a year of physical therapy, he had been able to walk again. However this was no easy task, and he explained the medicine he took daily didn't fully take away the pain. Chris could no longer lie on his right side, because of the pain in his shattered hip from the 7.62mm AK-47 round that had torn through him. Leaving only splinters of bone behind.

The other surviving marine in the attack was now deaf, blind and had lost three of his limbs.

Chris had been lucky, however his extensive facial and leg scars told a painful story. He lifted his shirt and showed me the bullet wound, now healed that had destroyed his hip as well as the one in his shoulder. His face was a massacre of scars as well, and his permanent limp left a note of sympathy for the man that had fought for his country and come back, battered, broken and bruised both physically and emotionally as well.

Chris hadn't been blessed with a comfortable life. He'd been married twice while serving, and both wives had left him while he had been overseas.

When he returned home to California, his 9-year-old daughter had passed away after suffering from leukemia.

It shamed me to think of all the times I'd thought I was having a "rough day" because of a little rain on the Appalachian Trail while I hiked. My having whined and cried about breaking up with a girlfriend who hadn't wanted to wait for my return home. And then you heard a story like Chris' and think to yourself that you hadn't experienced anything close to a "rough day" at all.

Nothing I had gone through could compare to that kind of pain. I felt my problems and experiences become so minuscule in a matter of seconds, and an overwhelming sense of respect for the man that had gone to war and came back crippled for my freedom. So that I could walk the Appalachian Trail, from Georgia to Maine.

"You don't have to believe anything about their religion. Just their sheer kindness alone is enough to make you forget about that world out there." Chris said to me, waving his hand dismissively at the window.

"It may make you feel awkward at first. They like to dance before they eat and share scriptures and stand in a circle, with everybody contributing to the sermon. You don't have to go if you don't want to. And nobody pressures you to believe in anything. But I think you should feel out the experience." Chris explained to me.

Truthfully, I was intrigued to see how this "hippie cult" as so many other hikers had called it, actually worked.

The history of The Twelve Tribes dated back to the early 70's where it had originally been created under the name "Light Brigade" by Gene Spriggs. Sermons and studies took place within a "communal setting" in his and his wife's home. Consisting mostly of teenagers, the Light Brigade took in mostly runaways or children seeking friendship and hope in a world they felt disassociated with.

The belief was that we were in the "end times," in a faith that had been based mostly on the Book of James. However, the Twelve Tribes refused to align their selves with any denomination, instead seeking out the creation of a new Israel consisting of Twelve Tribes in twelve geographic regions.

From there, it was my understanding that the details of their religion actually went a lot deeper. Sometimes involving rumors where different races were told to stick with "their own kind." However these claims had not readily been validated.

From the crew I saw running the Yellow Deli and working about the hostel—most of which were former thru-hikers, I got the impression most of these worshippers didn't actually understand the extent of the religion they had aligned their selves with. Instead, it seemed they were adopting the religion out of convenience and with a more casual approach. To work within a peaceful environment, within an atmosphere surrounded by like-minded people and hikers. Relating stories and sharing adventures from times long passed.

Chris had invited me to walk with him after the 12 Tribes community supper. He explained that after eating, he liked to maintain a little physical therapy from sitting down.

"After about 20 to 30 minutes of sitting, I gotta get up and walk to keep the pain from building up in my hip." he explained to me.

Our dinner had consisted of homemade biscuits, honey wheat bread loafs, and chicken noodle soup with massive chunks of chicken breast cut up and thrown in along with carrots and rice and other locally grown vegetables and herbs. All of the ingredients had been procured by one of the 12 Tribes members on one of their farms outside of the city.

"What'd you think?" Chris asked me.

I shrugged.

"It wasn't as scary as you'd described it to be. The food was great though!" I said excitedly. I imagined those warm baked biscuits being dunked into the chicken broth again and started to feel my mouth water all over again.

As we walked, I kicked a soda can across a crumbling sidewalk along our path of travel.

We took a right on Wales Street.

Chris laughed, though it was now a few minutes after the fact that I had responded to him.

"I wasn't trying to scare you away or anything. Some people just get put off by the kindness, the dancing and the sermons all at once."

"It didn't put me off. Everybody was very nice. And I am always very welcoming to friendly people." I replied.

In truth, this place psychologically did everything a cult truly did do...if you were to perceive it in such a way with honesty.

For starters, the $20 dollars was only a *suggested* donation. The rules were bent quite frequently. In fact I had even been told that it was all right if I didn't have the money and that I could still eat dinner with them if I'd wanted to for free.

Moreover, most of the preaching had been based on how important it was to be "needy" and to "help those in need."

How? By making this a law of their religion. As a rule, they accepted any and everybody. No race was excluded. However the intermingling of races, as I had read was still forbidden. How each specific sect of the 12 Tribes adhered to this, I was not certain. And I'd seen no enforcement of that rule during my time there in Rutland.

Ex-convicts, homeless individuals from the streets, former drug addicts and nomadic hikers with no clear destination seemed to make up the majority of the community. However, they now appeared differently, as if changed from their former experience. Their expressions were flighty, and almost "barely there." At times I felt I was being talked "through" more so than I had actually been engaged in any kind of conversation. It felt to me, that AT Hikers who'd given up their thru-hike or had completed it and weren't ready to go back home—made perfect potential "sheep" within their religious designs.

Always trying to find something about their selves or what it was they wanted from life by being out there.

I'd noticed that there were a lot of emotionally lost people out on the trail and I was no exception. As anybody was accepted and nobody was rejected from the group, you could view that warily with concern, or beautifully and fall with purpose, into that trap/nest. However, you perceived it.

Could you find rationale in taking somebody into your religious community who'd possibly been sent to jail for prior murder, robbery or assault convictions?

Many Christians could say: "Sure, forgive and forget" while keeping an untrusting and judgmental eye upon that person, thus completely contradicting their selves and their own beliefs.

In this, you could find fault, but only to the over opinionated.

Here, in the Twelve Tribes that judgmental blanket didn't seem to exist.

I was too trail-weary to be bothered by such trivialities regardless. I wasn't outwardly religious as much as I should have been, and despite their kindness, I wasn't too blinded or mentally clouded in grief to succumb to a belief based on my own painful life experiences thus far.

Wants and desires that never came true with questions like: *Why do bad things happen to good people?*

It was my belief that so many people ran to religion to cope with that inner angst. And for them, it worked

But while I am a dreamer, I also have common sense to realize WHY we searched for something greater than ourselves. We did this in my opinion to make sense of what didn't always, make sense.

If I could put off the worry of: "When I die there's nothing else. It's like going to sleep and never waking up. No dreams. No anything. Just darkness."

We as humans just cannot fathom that thought.

That dark space between when we fell asleep at night and when we awake the next day with no dreams.

If that was what death was like and if that time in-between isn't filled with answers...than that "gap" of missing time becomes frightening and terrifying. We can't conceive the thought, of no form of consciousness taking place. Because loss of consciousness is not a regularity in our everyday lives.

But by saying: "I believe in this *all-powerful-being*...and if I do *this* and *that* and if I'm paying in tithes and fellowship money that equates to at least 10% of everything I make, I'll go to heaven. I'll never *actually* die. If I say ten Hail Mary's, and fifteen Lords Prayers...everything cruel and rotten I've ever done is absolved."

We qualm that fear and guilt, and as a result, we live in an ignorant bliss of sorts for the rest of our lives.

But that's not a bad thing. Because I too wanted to die happy and ignorant of the turbulent and cruel world that surrounds us. To live out my days on earth happy, with a woman I loved and in the company of my friends and family.

And when my time came...I'd rather die, ready to go. Used up, broken...and of no further use to anything or anybody.

This community catered to the homeless and instilled "neediness" within their beliefs to gather those lost, broken souls out there looking for a friend. Looking for a home.

Looking to be loved.

And while that could be quite the beautiful dream, I'm sure reality wasn't always so forgiving. I'm sure mistakes and problems erupted from this venture.

But that was another issue, for another time.

The hostel had invited six local construction workers that hadn't been able to book a hotel anywhere else within the city for the night.

The workers had spent the day prepping work on the sidewalks throughout downtown Rutland. Out of the kindness of their hearts, and after the staff of the Yellow Deli served them a late night dinner only hours before—they also offered them a place to sleep for the evening as well. Despite the hostel's rules exclaiming the doors closed at 10:30 P.M., the workers, had had the rules bent for them just a bit. They had been drinking at a nearby bar, and even snuck beers inside the bunk room area despite being told alcohol was not allowed on the Twelve Tribes property.

It was midnight when they'd stumbled in.

"This place fucking sucks." One city worker said while another snickered.

"It's like a prison in here." He added as the giggling from the others continued.

"Shhhh. You're gonna wake these other people up." Another guy in a white wife beater whispered.

"Otha peepah? You mean *dose homeless* over dere?" He said pointing towards Chris and me. The comment had been followed by a round of hushed laughter.

I stared angrily over at the men from my side of the room. I had contemplated the thought of going over there, and smashing the guys face in with a brick, much to the horrified expressions of his fellow coworkers.

But bitter reality told me 6 vs. 1 wasn't going to put the odds in my favor.

"I could take a dump on my living room floor that would smell better than this place." The man in the wife-beater whispered with an annoyed sigh. They all erupted into laughter again.

It was painful to see a community that had opened their selves up out of kindness to complete strangers, only to be let down by the unappreciative actions of grown men acting like children.

It was sad to watch.

I thought about the Yellow Deli downstairs being open all night and knew that I'd never be able to sleep with these "children" masquerading as grown men; giggling over their insults.

I stood up and got dressed as they stopped talking and watched me.

"Hey, we weren't keeping you up...were we?" One guy asked as I walked by.

"Yeah, you were. Talking shit about a group of people kind enough to have the courtesy to take you slobs in for the night. I'd have left you pieces of trash out on the street to die, myself." I said opening the door to the men's bunk room.

"Hey, calm down man. We're only kidding around…"

"Go fuck yourself," I replied, slamming the door as I walked out.

I knew they were talking shit about me after I'd left. I could hear them laughing on the other side of the door. I wished Chris hadn't been sleeping through the whole fiasco across from me. Part of me wanted to believe he hadn't heard a word…only because I'd have hoped he'd have had my back.

An old, grizzled Marine who'd been shot three times and blown through the air by an IED and survived—sounded like the kind of backup I'd want in a fist fight.

I opened the door to the Yellow Deli downstairs and was greeted with the tired faces of the night shift service workers.

"Hello, John. How are you?" I was asked by an older gentleman tending the counter. He had already met me at dinner earlier that evening.

"Not able to sleep upstairs?" I was asked apologetically by one of the women staff members, peeling potatoes at one of the booths. I laughed, rubbing my eyes slowly as I sat down.

"Yeah. Not so much." I replied more into my hands than to them.

They offered me drink and food.

I took a muffin and a giant chocolate chip cookie.

I tried to talk about the current events of the world with them. Unfortunately (or fortunately. However you perceived it) they never watched television.

They didn't appear to know too much about what was going on. Ironic, living in a big city and being sheltered from knowing anything about the world outside with which they lived.

But that was by choice.

Irish folk music played over their stereo system.

It was odd to see a young, 12-year-old girl not enamored with Justin Bieber or mainstream pop culture music. Instead, she said excitedly while cutting up radishes at an empty table with what I assumed to be her older sister: "Oh! I love this part with the flute! Doolity doolitty doo..."

I chuckled softly.

"Why aren't you sleeping?" I asked her with a tired smile resting upon my face. It was 1:46 A.M., and I was surprised that time was going by in huge chunks as I nodded in and out of sleepiness.

"It's my night to work, silly." She said as if that should have explained everything to me all at once.

I wanted to ask if she went to school, or if she was homeschooled. I'd also wanted to ask her if she really was expected to work for the community at such an early age amongst a host of other questions. But I didn't want to pry either.

So I listened to soft Irish folk music and faded in and out of the burnt orange light that was absorbed into the old black oak wooden walls and soft leather hide-covered bench seats and tables.

Expansive airbrushed artwork murals painted the walls accompanied by hippy era fonts and quotes...whether indirectly Christian or spiritual and religious in nature on a subliminal level.

My bloodshot eyes ran over them dreamily as I listened to the sisters speak their bible quotes quietly to one another as if respecting my sleepy presence.

I nodded off after an hour for a few minutes.

When my head dipped, and I awoke suddenly, I was momentarily unsure of where I was.

"Would you like some tea?" The older gentleman asked me as I looked up at him slowly. He had appeared from thin air.

"I...uh..." I looked down and saw I had already finished both my muffin and cookie.

Only crumbs sat in the clear cellophane wrap before me.

"I think I'm good." I smiled up at him as he nodded and took my trash away for me.

"Have a goodnight," I called out to everybody. It was evident I now needed sleep.

When I'd gotten back to my bunkroom next door, the construction workers had all shut up and were sleeping off their intoxications and judgments of the only place willing to take them in for the night.

I laid down, physically exhausted, and initially restless.

I rolled onto my side and watched outside the downtown window, as passersby's from the nearby bars left and stumbled towards their cars or homes.

Loneliness can have rather strange effects on you.

At one point you're desperate for attention, making an idiot out of yourself by just trying to engage somebody in conversation, much like the way I had acted back in Hanover. The next moment you find you're sitting on city benches. Sometimes in front of grocery stores, people watching and hoping somebody approaches you if only to say "hi."

Anyone to give you an opening in regards to the weather and a chance to talk about everything, and nothing.

However with duct tape patches on your coat, holes with down feathers sticking out and the tattered leggings of shredded pants and a shirt two sizes too large hanging off of your sickly looking, unbathed body...nobody wants to take the risk. And who could blame them? What would I have wanted from them? Money? Food? A place to stay? And at that moment, the possibility of becoming a potential *bother* or *liability*, was ultimately what kept people away.

My hair was erratic and unkempt while my beard was scraggly and matted down on the one side I always slept on. I no longer even recognized my own reflection anymore in the mirror.

I'd wanted to go back to the trail, away from judgmental eyes. However, I was in no real hurry either. The weather had been calling for three days of torrential downpours, and I could no longer find the willpower to force myself into an environment I knew I was going to hate the second that first raindrop touched my shoulders.

I tried to watch a movie at the local theater there in Rutland out of boredom. Or truthfully, maybe it was to sleep?

I wanted to run away from the anxiety and depression trying to slink into my mind. This constant uphill battle where for no reason at all on random occasions—I felt alone.

True, I could sleep back in the bunkroom for free, but I didn't want to leave myself open for conversation from anybody whatsoever that may or may not decide to rent a bed for the evening. And truthfully, I didn't want to hand over another twenty dollars if I might potentially choose to hit the AT again instead.

"Anybody purchase tickets for *Don Jon* yet?" I asked the woman at the Flagship Cinema's counter. If it was crowded, sleeping there wouldn't be a very suitable environment.

The ticket cashier looked up at me, apparently bored with life and looking for somebody to take her away from the place.

"You're the first. That'll be $6.50." She said taking my card. I hadn't even agreed to watch the movie yet, but I supposed she'd decided to make up my mind for me.

"Is it any good?" I asked, trying to engage her in conversation.

"I dunno…"

She smacked on her gum, ripped off the receipt and gave it to me.

"I'm not from here originally…" I began, realizing I suddenly sounded creepy and desperate for conversation.

"Excuse me," She replied, stepping down from her high chair and walking away from the conversation starter I had employed altogether. I watched as she picked up a box filled with flyers for the movie theater, advertising a discount for Halloween. She proceeded towards the inside of the facility making conversation with another staff member as I walked away from the booth.

Next time John, just keep your mouth shut I thought to myself, feeling slightly embarrassed for having been snuffed so rudely.

As I walked into the empty theater, I saw dim lights waning from years of use, and many of the bulbs had been burned out within the main lobby.

I'd meant to come in here to fall asleep somewhere dark, comfortable and warm while a stupid romance movie played me off into LaLa Land.

Instead, thirty minutes in, I'm staring wide-eyed at what appeared to be a softcore pornography flick about a guy who masturbated too much.

"Jesus Christ…" I muttered, feeling immediate guilt and shame for having even sat down.

I suddenly felt very disgusted in myself for having been there at all and even more so for having the entire theater to myself. I cringed as each woman on the screen screamed into sexual climax left and right. I felt the whole world could hear the movie and everybody knew that "I" was in there alone.

Worse was how I crept out of the theater like some kind of pervert, noticeably looking either way and failing miserably at trying to leave quietly. I hadn't been paying attention and bumped into a velvet crowd control stanchion. I managed to stumble, fall over and knock the whole thing down.

"Sir, are you okay?" one of the staff asked, coming out from behind the counter.

"Yeah, I gotta make a phone call or something..." I blathered incompetently, as I reset the stanchions and sped walked from the building, looking and feeling very much like a criminal.

Inside the restroom at a nearby Subway restaurant, I splashed water onto my face and looked up at my reflection and at the bags beneath my bloodshot eyes.

Soft elevator Muzak played across the restaurants speakers. It was a poorly recreated version of Eric Clapton's song: "My Fathers Eyes."

My hands were shaking again. Dirt was thick beneath the fingernails.

My hands were always dirty.

Dirt in the cracks, in the prints and underneath the nails.

The jittering had started to become more periodic over the last couple of months. I closed my fists and opened them again, and it stopped. I was sure it had something to do with my having quit smoking, and my withdraw was becoming more prevalent.

Vibrations, probably related to some sort of tinnitus had come about my right eardrum recently as well.

Maybe I had lacked vitamins and proper nutrients as well.

Beads of water dripped from my beard as I took a couple of deep breaths.

I felt distant. My mind was clouded, and I was having an anxiety attack for some odd reason. I felt my chest and my breathing becoming more and more restricted. I was systematically shutting down, and the slow process was only making me more and more fearful as each second drifted idly by.

"What the hell is wrong with me?" I asked, gripping the edges of the sink. I was going to black out any moment. I was sure of it.

However, the next thing I knew, I was no longer looking at my hands or reflection in the bathroom mirror.

Instead, I was standing at the counter in the dining room area looking over various meats and vegetable toppings for sandwiches.

I didn't even remember walking up to the counter nor could I recall which way I had taken to get there.

I had sort of just...suddenly appeared.

"What can I get you today?"

"Foot long meatball marinara."

"What kind of bread?"

"Nine-grain honey oat."

Everything moved so seamlessly.

Everything felt so programmed and robotic. Every line fell into place.

"What kind of cheese?"

"American."

"Would you like this toasted?"

"No thank you."

The employee placed the last triangle of American cheese onto the sub and slid the sandwich over towards the vegetables.

"What else would you like on it?"

I then began to tell her each item, one at a time so that she didn't have to remember it all at once.

"Spinach. Banana peppers. Green peppers. Tomatoes."

"Anything else?"

"No thank you."

She then proceeded to fold the sandwich, cut it in half, and then wrap it perfectly just before sliding it into a baggy.

"Chips and drink?" She asked, while already ringing up the sandwich.

"Yes, please."

"$9.89, please. Credit or debit?" She asks as I'm handing her my card.

"Credit," I say.

"Have a nice day." She replies, slipping the receipt I never seem to want into my bag of food and handing my card back to me.

I wish her the same, accompanied by a smile she never sees, as she vanishes behind the counter to restock the layout bar. Passing the time till her shift is over.

I sit alone by the glass window at the front of the restaurant, eating my sandwich painfully slow—if only to bide my time a little bit longer. No rush to head back to an empty bunkroom and lie in my bed by myself with nothing but the sudden onset of depression and anxiety to accompany me.

As I eat, I'm people watching.

I'm watching couples.

I'm watching teens so absorbed within their angst-filled worlds they can't see straight. I watch mothers dressed too young. Alternatively, I watch parents dressed too old as well.

Then I come to realize I'm just as judgmental as everybody else out there that stares at *me* in fear. Looking at me as if I'm a second away from attacking them because of my disparaged appearance.

How quickly we could become hypocrites at the drop of a hat. We as a society like to believe we hate being judged while judging those around us all of the time. Whether it's our friends, our families...or our significant others, and I was no different.

I set my sandwich down and looked up at the gray skies outside the windows above me.

I just wanted solace. I wanted the pain that had been inside me to go away. I wanted this adventure to be my cure. I wanted to find some sort of strength, as I fumbled for the rock I had taken from the summit of Katahdin for my parents back home.

A foolhardy venture, no? Some stupid chunk of earth that was meant to epitomize my love. A word, I was too scared to utter out of shame to my own father.

I didn't know anything except that the following day, I was taking the bus back to where I'd left off on the trail in Killington. I'd continue through that cold, bleak forest filled with browning, dying leaves with the onset of fall steadily creeping in. And I'd be doing it alone.

All I'd have to keep me going were the words of my journal followers hundreds, or even thousands of miles away. Hell, they could have been in the same town, and in those moments I'd have still felt so far away and separated from them they might as well have been on an entirely different continent.

In everything I'd come across or done in my time out on the Appalachian Trail I had ultimately come face to face with how weak I truly was from the onset of day one when I said goodbye to a girlfriend and to a comfortable lifestyle forever plagued by "what if's."

Seven months later after all the other hikers were done, and everybody was gone, I was still out there, drudging ever slowly along south.

And as I sat there by the window of that empty Subway restaurant, I found it so strange that I couldn't even remember the last time I had actually hugged my own father.

I wasn't even sure why it was a thought that hadn't ever come to my mind before.

Always that male bravado standing in the way that made me feel like shaking my father's hand was a better recommendation than holding him ever was.

And it wasn't that he never told me I couldn't do so. It wasn't that I was brought up that way. It was always just one of those things that never seemed to happen. At some point in my youth, I had childishly touted: "I'm too old for hugs, and I love you's."

But still, I knew that wasn't the sort of thing you would ever say if you worried that one day you no longer had the opportunity to do so.

When it had become too late to do that very thing.

And so I wanted that hug now. Right then and there.

I wanted to tell my mother and father, that their son was okay...and to hold my mom and plead with her to stop worrying. To let me give them something to be proud of in me.

All I had left, was to walk home and give my father a stone. Something I had pursued through the blood, sweat, and tears attributed to my own self-consciousness and fear.

I wanted to tell my father that I loved him in person, and to hear him—to actually see him say those same words back to me.

That was ALL I wanted in this moment.

I'd had a hole in my life. A black hole that I had tried again and again unsuccessfully to fill with meaningless relationships and alcohol.

Relationships with people I ultimately knew weren't right for me.

I drank alone and lived in self-loathing while going to a job where it was mandatory I threw on a fake smile and left my malcontent at home.

And when I could no longer bottle up my aggressions, or hide my depression and my loneliness...I left.

That's was it. It was that simple.

I left, *everything*.

I went out in search of a way of life, outside the world of "obedient sheeple" I had surrounded myself with.

And I could say from the bottom of my heart that as I took that first step into the chaotic unknown, I had looked back on a world I never actually felt a part of, and I'd chosen to leave it behind.

But it didn't mean I wouldn't miss the people there.

It only meant that I had yearned to see a universe outside of that box.

I had learned to appreciate the time we had in this world, just a little bit more. I had become less controlled, by possessions. I had also learned to live, rather inexpensively and to be comfortable with that kind of lifestyle of having less.

I'd found out that the friends you make out on the AT, were the closest kinds of people you would ever find like yourself. Individuals, in search of answers just like you. Kindness and sharing that were so much more the human spirit than you would have ever known.

Given to you in such a moment of weakness…you couldn't help but break down and cry.

―⸺―

"We just wanted to let you know that we enjoyed having you stay with us. It was truly a pleasure." The caretaker said, shaking my hand.

"It was a beautiful place to stay," I replied, with a smile.

I sighed, as the look upon his face appeared as if he was readily waiting for me to shout out randomly: *JUST KIDDING! I'M LIVING HERE NOW! I'M NEVER GOING TO THOSE DAMNED WOODS AGAIN!*

Truly, I was never ready to leave a real bed, real food, and unlimited electricity. But two days in Rutland had been enough and financially I couldn't afford much more. I was running on credit cards I had no idea of how I was planning to pay off upon returning home. I kept believing that I could forego the late fees with excuses once the calls started rolling in from the creditors. It was a whole new side of irresponsibility I had never faced before until I was now in the thick of it, by my own making.

To think how much I had changed since the very first day I had started to step away from civilization. How fearful I had been at the beginning of making any little mistakes in my life, financially. And then to see who and what I had become. Hoping for free handouts whenever offered or given when my pride didn't step in the way of such things.

I threw my pack back on over my shoulders…wincing just a little. I didn't think it was ever possible to get used to Gregory's weight.

"It's been a pleasure," I said, shaking the caretaker's hand.

As I walked down the stairs, and out onto the street I took a picture of the Yellow Deli. I took in the atmosphere which felt so golden and beautiful in a cold, gray, cement covered city. As if an aura was radiating off of the structure.

"Did you hear about the free hiker's breakfast?" The caretaker asked, following me out.

I quirked my eyebrow as I looked back at him.

I was certain he was just making that up.

Why? Because I was the only hiker there and I'd never been offered such in the days before.

"Uh...no I didn't." I chuckled. What I had expected to do was to grab something to eat like a muffin to-go from the Yellow Deli on my way to the transit station behind the building. To take a bus back to the Appalachian Trail in Killington where I'd left off on Route 4.

What I hadn't been expecting were for these people to give me a free breakfast instead.

They had already been so kind and inviting with the free dinners they had offered in the days before that it had become hard for me to leave. Even if it was never truly their intention, I got the impression they had wanted me to stay. They had expressed so much interest in hearing my adventures from while I had been out on the trail, sitting in groups around me during dinner, asking questions and staring in awe as if they'd never heard the stories a hiker brought to their table before.

"Is there really, a *free hiker's breakfast* today?" I asked, suspiciously.

"There sure is, come on in." He said directing me towards the Yellow Deli.

I stopped.

"Come on. I appreciate it...but I'm not a charity case." I said. He looked to be momentarily searching for an excuse.

"Seriously. I don't mind paying." I added, already reaching for my wallet.

"John..." Yoshua began, by putting his hand upon my shoulder.

"One thing you're going to have to learn one day if you ever expect to finish your journey—is to accept people's acts of kindness. There is no reason to be too proud. You are our friend, and we want to see you reach your goal. And if we can help you do that in some way, then let us. You've been through a lot out there. The least we could do is give you a little breakfast. Now would you let us feed you? Please?" He asked.

I sighed in reflection, but after he had said those words, I didn't want to insult him by turning down his offer.

Being out there opened you up so wide inside. At times, it made you vulnerable. It could show you who you were through pain and suffering and everything else thrown at you in this gauntlet they called a "trail."

These moments of reprieve, truly were "magic." Because it was something so unexpected, you had no other word for it. And if you never abused it, you never got used to it.

Every successful hitch into town was a surprise.

Every mail drop from friends and family back home wasn't always expected.

Every monetary donation or even a piece of more than half an apple pie in some spontaneous occasion along some country road from a stranger, was a Christmas gift.

I could never get used to it, and ultimately I think that was what made these moments so incredible.

For breakfast, the Yellow Deli staff had made me an egg and cheese sandwich on a scratch-made buttered croissant, along with orange and apple slices.

After I had finished eating, Leb who'd been working behind the counter took my dishes and gave me a handmade cranberry, honey and blueberry muffin along with a homemade energy bar. Underneath the items was what I thought was the bill, but instead, was the following message:

"Dear John,
Have a safe and pleasant journey.
We are thankful to have met you. Come back again.
Your friends at the Yellow Deli."

I smiled as tears touched the edges of my eyes.
I wiped them away and left after wishing them a heartfelt goodbye.

"Big load. You doing the Long Trail?" An older gentleman with his wife asked as I stared out the window of the shuttle at passing scenery.

"Well, I'm doing *part* of the Long Trail," I replied. I didn't feel much like talking. Walking through towns as a ragged looking hiker, you get one of three things.

1. Everybody judges you as hobo trash and ignores you.
2. Everybody judges you as hobo trash and does everything they can to avoid your general area of existence.
3. Or, each time people see you heft your washing machine sized backpack on...they want to know why you're carrying such a load.

THEN the stories come. The same ones you've told over a thousand times before.

After a while, it had lost its flair.

I had reached the Inn at Long Trail, and I took Sherburne Pass to the Appalachian Trail.

Once there amongst gray skies, and rain clouds I felt spiritually weary, yet energetic physically enough to go on.

At Deer Leap Trail, a carved wooden sign touted a view .3 miles to the East, but it didn't hold much of my interest. After reaching the summit of Killington Peak, I had a view of everything.

I ate some cheddar and peanut butter crackers under a threatening sky and hated the ugly days that fouled my mood most times. I thought back to the White Mountains, and the occasional storm clouds I had seen brewing in the valleys beneath me. I had walked along ridgelines which had felt more like bridges in the clouds. It had felt like two separate worlds in that distinction. Above the chaos, and below it. Because I knew that above those rainy cloud covered skies, were bright blues and a radiant sun. There was comfort in that thought, of knowing it wasn't completely gone and never would be. All you had to do to see it, was rise above.

Eighteen miles fell beneath my feet that day in my anticipation and rush to complete Vermont. And then something amazing happened. Almost as if slipping back into the hiking culture, I would go on to push out an additional 36.5 miles in the following days.

At night the world was alive with wildlife and their calls into the darkness. Their answers were met with a distant train, which sounded its horn at road crossings intersecting its path somewhere in towns far away. The wailing called out to me and made me dream about long distance train hopping across the United States.

It had struck me more and more like an appealing way to continue my journey once I'd completed it. To instead of saying: "Time to go home…" I'd proudly shout: "The funs just getting started!"

Just dreams.

But sometimes dreams led somewhere. And if not directly, then they could indirectly impact your decisions and change the outset of your journey into something so wholeheartedly different—it no longer disguised itself as the original reason you brought this whole thing to fruition.

Hiking through the Green Mountain National Forest had taken me to Route 9 over the course of four days. Standing beside the empty road, I looked down at my phone and found that according to the digital map, I was five miles east of Bennington, Vermont. I looked with hungry eyes at the screen, almost drooling. I had been skimming over the restaurants that were said to have been available there in town. My gaze, however, stuck on a McDonald's establishment. I felt as if this place existed as the best option for a hiker.

Not only was the dollar menu food cheap, but you got unlimited drink refills and free Wi-Fi as well. To top it off, most times table side outlets were available to recharge your electronics while you ate and surfed the internet on your smartphone.

It seemed to be the most practical stop when in town and when on a budget. I stood on the side of the Route 9 crossing with the intention of heading into town for a couple of days.

I had managed to make contact with Wales finally, who had explained by text messages that he had gone quite some time along the Appalachian Trail without a recharge on his phone. As a result, he hadn't seen the messages I had been sending him and had concentrated solely on hiking. So much so, that he wasn't too far north of me.

"Well, Gregory, ready to go into town?" I asked my backpack, as I stuck my thumb up at an approaching car.

The driver sped by without so much as a glance, as I dropped my hand with a disparaged expression.

"Yeah, I know. It'll be hard to get a hitch out here and then back out here again to the AT when we're done. But I'm optimistic, dude. And you should be too. Besides, look how far we've made it already." I said to my nonresponsive, inanimate backpack.

An hour later, I had decided to walk along Route 9 with my thumb cocked before it became too late.

Ten minutes and two cars later, I was riding in the bed of a red Ford Ranger west, down the highway and towards Bennington. That was just a testament to the unpredictability a hiker potentially faced on a day-to-day basis.

I ducked down into the bed as far as possible, while cold, wet wind blew through my greasy, scraggly hair. As I had asked, my hitch had dropped me off in town. He had then offered me three bucks in cash to buy a hamburger. I began to politely refuse the money, however, because I wasn't a beggar. I didn't want to give the impression to this kind gentleman that I had staged this whole thing just to ask for financial aid from a guy already doing me a favor.

But then I thought about what Yoshua had said to me in Rutland and about how I needed to be more accepting of people's gifts and offerings.

I felt reserved until the driver told me: "If I don't give this money to you, I'm gonna be tempted to use it to buy a pack of cigarettes. And I don't need to be smoking no more."

He had said this with a rather world-weary expression and yellowed eyes. Thick lines of age were carved into his exhausted face. I felt sorry for him.

I took the money, if for no other reason than that maybe I was partly saving his life in some way. I thanked him and shook his hand.

"How far South you goin'?" He asked.

For the oddest reason, I almost told him Key West, Florida.

"North Carolina," I replied.

"Why *there*?"

"That's *home*," I said with a smile, as I tapped his door and waved goodbye.

None of the restaurants within the area had working Wi-Fi, and no outlets had been available either except at a Burger King.

After five hours of charging my items within the establishment and far too many free refills of soda, I decided that with the fading afternoon light quickly dissipating; that I had better head out and scout my place of rest for the evening.

Outside, I saw three people huddled beneath the bridge that led into the Kmart plaza I had been dining in.

I had taken the three dollars my hitch in the Ford Ranger had given me and bought three, one dollar burgers before heading out just in case I'd gotten hungry later that evening as I lay in my hammock.

I looked at the clothes and nutrient deficient bodies, of the three people standing underneath that bridge. They were young, but their faces had been ravaged by drugs.

Their eyes were hollow and their faces scarred by acne and scabs. A man in a Dale Jr NASCAR cap watched me with his hands in his pockets. Dirty clothes and missing teeth accompanied his smile.

It had started to drizzle, and I took shelter beneath the bridge along with them until it had passed.

"Hey, what's going on?" I asked as they sat with their backs propped against the cement bridge support pillar.

"Hi there." The woman said smiling, before hiding her mouth as if ashamed of her missing front upper row of teeth.

The other two guys acknowledged me without even glancing up.

They hadn't looked threatening. They appeared so sickly that if they had attacked me, I could've easily tripped them and possibly broken every bone in their bodies just by accident.

They appeared possibly homeless, and I was hoping they knew of some decent local places to set up and stealth camp without being arrested for trespassing.

"You care if we smoke?" A heavier guy on far end asked in a black and red lettered Red Sox jacket. He was packing something small, brown and crystal like into the end of a glass tube.

"Nah," I replied, leaning on the wall and looking up at the sky.

I heard a lighter flick and then the sound of someone inhaling through the tube.

I turned and saw the three of them were passing the glass piece with the charred end back and forth between each other, taking hits.

A burnt plastic/chemical smell came into the air.

"Hey, you hit man?" The guy in the NASCAR hat asked, holding the smoke in his lungs from the meth, or crack or whatever it was he was smoking. I wasn't familiar with either, so I was just guessing. Either way, I thought I had already answered the question just a moment before.

"Uh...no thank you," I replied.

I should probably get the hell outta here before a cop comes by, wondering what the hell four people are doing huddled beneath a bridge I thought to myself.

Before I left, I thought about those burgers in my pack. I was full and didn't need to be eating until I puked. Plus, I thought it would be nice to pay the kindness I'd been receiving as of late, forward.

"Hey guys, I got these for later...but I don't want them," I said, taking the burgers from the side pocket on my pack out for them.

I held my breath so that I wasn't inhaling any of the crap they were filling their lungs with as I handed the burgers over.

They thanked me, with confused and slightly untrusting expressions on their faces as they each took one.

Before leaving, I stopped and considered asking the three of them for a decent place to set up my hammock tent that evening. In all honesty, when I thought about it, though—I realized that I probably didn't want to sleep in the same places they may have been sleeping their selves since they were junkies.

I immediately decided upon setting up in the woods behind the Kmart directly in front of me. It had quick access to food, and a restroom and shelter from a storm should I need it. Trails weaved in and out of this town along highways and between old abandoned buildings and businesses within the area.

But for having chosen a place in the woods to sleep behind the local Kmart, it was also a very busy area. People walking the nearby trails at night, for example, came dangerously close to my campsite many times. Homeless people were drinking in the woods, surrounding me. And this wasn't just a couple of individuals. There had to have been nearly twenty to thirty others within the wood lines.

Teenagers having make-out sessions on rotting mattresses beside the river...and smoking weed beneath bridges or in the scant slivers of forest that riddled this town—seemed unbothered and unafraid by the likeliness of being within the same vicinity of potentially serious drug addicts.

It was funny how being homeless, and being a hiker—you could always so easily find the underbelly of a city or town within hours. Something others living in the town might have been blind to their selves.

It was late, but I couldn't sleep with all of the noise going on around me. Every shuffle through the leaves in those woods were either stupid squirrels or actual people walking here or there.

I was awake until the early hours of morning.

The following day, I had decided upon setting up across the Walloomsac River, otherwise known in town as the *South Stream* in Bennington.

"Ow, ow....owww!" I grumbled aloud, as my crocs slapped across the smooth bedrocks. Occasionally a rock would fall between the soles of my bare feet and the rubber shoes I was wearing. The intense pain would shoot up through the heel of my foot as more than two hundred and fifty pounds of weight would push down on to this one, tiny stone.

I hopped and cursed down the embankment until I had reached the withered flow of what might have once been a proud and prominent river, but now no longer.

I stood in a football field sized area of exposed, dried bedrock on either side of what amounted to be a ten-foot wide creek.

"Well, Gregory, any plans on how we're gonna cross this?" I asked my backpack. Gregory's response seemed more reserved than I would have initially wanted. But it gave insight all the same.

"We'll go around. It's too cold to be wading through that water." I planned out loud as I sat down, removed my boots from my backpack and got ready for a hike and exploration.

I took Hunt Street through your typical, New England neighborhood. When I reached an intersection, I looked at Google maps over my phone and saw an old railroad that ran across the street behind the Apollo Fuels gas station.

I decided on taking the tracks south towards the other side of the river.

The attendant watched me with an odd expression as I reached the edge of the property and found an old, overgrown section of railroad lying abandoned, and in ruin there.

The rusted road ties and tracks had been overgrown by weeds and bushes. Apparently no longer in use.

Overgrown shrubbery towered far above my head and created a tunnel of dried out vegetation or dead sunflowers along with other fluffy, seed spitting plant life species that usually spread their offspring by the winds that carried them far away.

I walked what appeared to be a well-established trail made by locals for a half mile down to where it came out behind a Tastee Freeze ice cream shop that had been closed down for the season. You could tell the establishment had seen happier days during the summer months when it had been surrounded and swarmed with kids and parents in shorts, tank tops, and sandals or flip flops searching for cold treats on a blistering hot day.

I eyed the "Closed for the Season" sign resting inside yellowed glass separators which read August 31st as its last day of operation.

I walked across North Street headed back towards the bridge and over the other side of the river. Once there, I climbed over a guard rail and traversed loose boulders down the side of the highway as cars sped by above me.

"Careful. Careful..." I said to myself out loud.

Suddenly, somebody called out to me.

"Hey! You a hiker?"

It was a woman's voice. I turned slowly and squinted my eyes, seeing only the silhouette of the individual and no obvious features to describe her otherwise. She was sitting beneath the bridge as nothing more than a shadow and had just snuffed out a cigarette. Now a puff of grayish-blue smoke emitted out into the air above her and curled beneath the bridge's support beams.

Great, another crackhead probably I thought to myself.

"Yeah, I am. Why?" I asked.

"Because I'm bored and wanted someone to talk to." She replied.

I bit down on the toothpick I had been chewing and thought about moving along and setting up my tent for the evening. I glanced down the bank of bedrock and the lick of land just beside it. If she had, in fact, turned out to be a fellow hiker, the possibility existed that we might have been able to find a safe area together to sleep for the night. Maybe she might even have known this area a thousand times better than I had. And if she was trustworthy, perhaps we could look out for each other's things as well as each other.

It was a tall order, and I knew I was being hopelessly optimistic. But I gave it a shot regardless.

As I approached her, she was already lighting up another cigarette.

Beside her, propped against the support wall of the bridge; I saw a red, rather ragged-looking external framed backpack that appeared so incredibly old that I was surprised it hadn't come along with shag carpeting and disco theme music attached to it.

It was literally, like…*1970's* old. It appeared ripped in several places, and poorly sewn stitches ran randomly along it like Frankenstein flesh. It was a good sign that she had been out here for a while, whoever she was.

Still, some spots hadn't been sewn at all and pieces of clothing, and a part of her sleeping bag was popping out of the sides.

That's when I believe I had recognized her from days before along the Appalachian Trail.

"You were at Spruce shelter a few nights ago, weren't you?" I asked. She raised her eyebrows as she took a drag on her cigarette.

"I was." She replied with a suspicious tone.

"Southbounder? Northbounder?" I asked, sitting beside her beneath the bridge, after clearing a few small stones and some grit away from the boulder I had chosen to be my seat. I had dropped my pack out towards the little flecks of sun spotting through the stormy clouds overhead. Already my back had started sweating while I had been carrying the pack around, and I wanted the pad to dry out as much as possible, but the misty air was going to make that a bit hard.

The woman replied to my inquiry by shaking her head slowly.

"Why do people keep asking me that shit? I just wanted to hike. I'm not north bounding, or south…fucking whatever. I was just bored." She responded with an annoyed inflection.

"Well *excuse* me. It's just the first thing we usually ask of one another when we see other hikers on the AT. Because it means we could hook up and…"

"I'm sorry, did you say *hook up*? *Really* dude?"

I sighed and lowered my facial expression into a tired sort of tolerance.

"Not *hook up*, hook up. I meant hike together."

"Hmph…" she replied, fishing around for her lighter in her pants pocket. She found it and relit her cigarette while offering me one.

And while the temptation was there, I decided to maintain my willpower and shook my head no.

I chewed more aggressively at my toothpick, however.

"What about you?" She asked, not even bothering to glance up.

She hadn't looked me in the eyes, once during our exchange.

"Flip-flopper," I said.

"All this trail jargon." She laughed, with a bit of irritability showing behind it.

"Okay, fine. I'll take the bait, dude. What…is….a…flip…Flopper?" She asked robotically.

I smiled while deep inside I felt like replying: *Nothing remarkable, really. Why don't I get the hell out of here and leave you alone, to your bitchy attitude?*

Instead, I answered her.

"I hiked from Georgia to Pennsylvania. Flipped at the halfway point to come up North to Maine because me and a few buddies I'd been walking with at the time thought that the park at the northernmost end of the trail would close long before we got there. Now I'm hiking back South to complete my trip. Then I'm heading back home, either by walking, or hitching or whatever." I said.

I broke out some trail mix from the cargo pocket of my pants and began crunching on it. I offered her some, but she declined.

"Where's home?" She asked.

"North Carolina," I replied.

She nodded and finally looked at me. Once she had, I realized for the first time how incredibly cute she was…in that tomboyish sort of way.

She removed her toboggan with dangling yarn pigtails on it, exposing a short pixie style haircut. Her hair was natural, and a dark and fiery burnt orange. She had freckles across the bridge of her nose that ended beneath either of her light-brown eyes.

"Well, I go by Daisy." She said, offering her hand. I shook it and noticed two things. Her hand was both cold and sticky as well.

I wiped my hand on my pants.

She noticed the gesture, immediately apologizing.

"Sorry, I've been eating jolly ranchers. Some of them got wet in the downpour yesterday."

"You just got here last night?" I asked.

She shook her head while taking a hit from her cigarette.

"I got here today."

"Oh, okay. I got here yesterday. Have you possibly met a tall hiker with curly blonde hair along the trail? Has a gray and red backpack and a blonde baby beard? He goes by the name Wales."

Daisy shook her head no, and I frowned.

As I looked at the rain clouds coming in, I thought about my tent again and stood.

"Know any good places to stealth camp in this town?" I asked.

"Not really. I thought I may just get a room. I wanna take a shower. It's been about five days." She said.

I thought that it would have been nice to split the cost of a room because I could use a shower myself and some decent sleep with the miles I had been pouring out to get to Bennington over the last few days.

So I asked.

However, when she scrunched her face into that: *Uh...I don't think... so* kind of way; I'd immediately felt stupid for even asking.

"I mean I dunno. I'm not sharing a bed with a stranger or anything."

"Don't worry about it. I should just save my money anyways."

She had made me feel awkward for even asking, so I put my backpack on in a rush to get out of there.

"Are you butt hurt because I'm not sharing a bed with you after having known you for like, 5 minutes?" She asked bluntly like I was suddenly the biggest baby in the world

"Nah. I understand completely. Better to be safe like that. But if you aren't busy later, did you maybe wanna grab something to eat at Burger King with me? Maybe around six?" I asked.

Daisy shrugged nonchalantly.

"Maybe. If I'm not there by 6:30, I probably changed my mind."

"Cool. Sounds good. Well, take care Daisy." I said walking from beneath the bridge and picking up my backpack. I began heading towards the woods and down the boulder bank when she suddenly called out.

"You too, bearded-guy-that-never-gave-me-his-name." She said in a sarcastic tone.

I turned.

"Oh yeah, sorry about that! It's Morris the Cat." I said with a smile and a humble bow.

"You'll have to explain that name. But later." She said, waving me away dismissively.

This area had been old farm land. It was not only noticeable by way of satellite imagery that still showed hayfields in the vicinity; but also the old human-made stream beds dug by hand (dried up as well) that had once diverted water from the main river to crumbling old mills along the shores. The streams had once flowed through some old barbed wire sections now cut or fallen after so many decades of age. There were dried up water collection ponds, possibly for cattle at one time.

Having read up on the history of the river, I found that supposedly around 1819 many water-powered mills had diverted the water for their businesses at the time. As a result, the Walloomsac looked like little more than a river-sized collection of bed rocks.

Over development and having sapped the resources led to the destruction of streams or creeks that once fed it.

The patch of trees I had taken residence in acted as a barrier between two vast pastures, a Child Abuse Services Center, the Vermont Veterans Home Cemetery and Mt Anthony Union High school.

Old shanty's put together with crumbling particle boards and wooden pallets lay in crumbling disarray or rotting within the overgrown vegetation. Hunks of vinyl siding and old torn tarp tents and trash bags stuffed with abandoned clothes laid strewn about in the flatter sections of the forest or propped against tree trunks as makeshift shelters.

I was so glad that I wasn't limited to these places—owning a hammock tent with the option to truly set up wherever I found two trees within reasonable range of one another.

It was 6:16 P.M. and I sat in the dining area of the Burger King alone, looking outside at the fading light. Occasionally I'd divert my attention at the wall art which consisted of advertisements for their varied products.

As 6:34 came along, I came to the assumption that Daisy wouldn't be joining me for dinner after all.

I washed my hands in the bathroom and looked at my ragged reflection in the mirror.

The hearing in my right ear kept coming and going periodically as the tinnitus started aggravating me more and more each day. Finally, it began to ring before fading away completely.

I held my wet, dripping hands before me and watched them shaking again, before closing my fists and holding them tightly.

I walked back out into the dining room and looked over at Gregory.

Gregory didn't look back at me.

Gregory didn't talk to me.

Gregory, the object that held all of my possessions and which I treated as a friend and hiking partner, lay propped in the seat across from me.

I didn't eat alone as I watched the headlights of passing cars outside. I ate with an imaginary friend.

I ate with Gregory.

I had received a text message from Wales, the following morning.

"hey where are you? Im in manchester center but im getting off the trail soon to meet my parents" the text message read.

Manchester Center wasn't that far away from where I was.

I called Wales over the phone, immediately after I had received the text.

"Manchester? What are ya tryin' to do? Finish NEXT YEAR?" I asked with an excited laugh.

"I've only been doing ten mile days. I think I've had the flu and have been incredibly weak lately. My joints hurt. Since I last talked to you, I've only managed one 18 mile day." he explained to me.

"Well, what are you going to do? Are you gonna take some time off and recover?" I asked as the tone of the conversation turned a bit more serious.

"I'm going to go and visit with my parents. I'm flying down to hang out with them further south for a while before coming back to finish. I'll probably be back in two weeks."

I thought that over for a second. I was going to be too far ahead by that time for him to ever catch up.

"Wales, I'll probably never see you again because I'm hoofing it man. I see the finish line, and I'm doing everything I can to get there dude." I explained sadly into the phone.

"I know. Maybe we could meet up and hang out a day together or something." he offered.

I told him he should start hitching south at that very moment before I never got to see him again for the rest of the trip.

Once Wales had finally arrived in town, we met up at a Dunkin Donuts.

"I was wondering if you'd ever catch up. You know you're the one usually blazing down the trails. I would have thought you'd have passed me a long time ago." I said in awe.

"Can't shake this sickness. I don't bloody understand it." He said, letting a little bit of British accent overtake his tone.

"So you're going to be quitting the AT?" I asked him.

"Not quitting. I just need some time off to visit my parents and relax a little. Eat real vegan food and come back out 100% to finish." He replied as I nodded in understanding.

Wales and I hung out for the rest of the day, in what I had suspected would be our last moments together. We caught up on how the many days had gone by since we had last seen each other and talked about the various adventures we'd had. I told him that he had missed out by passing Rutland, Vermont. Not only that, but he had missed out on meeting quite a few special people at the Yellow Deli.

As the hours started to roll by, eventually he brought up the obvious. We needed to set up camp for the evening. However, I had already packed everything up as it had been my intention to leave that very day for the AT again, before receiving his text message.

"Well, there's a place by the river. We can look back there I suppose." I told him. We proceeded to walk the stealth camping areas along the river. However, there was no real spot for Wales to set up for the evening safely with his ground tent without potentially punching holes with the vast amount of shrubbery surrounding us.

"There's really not a good spot for me to set up without damaging my tent." he muttered, looking around at the forest floor.

"Look at this," I said, showing him a picture on my phone.

"No way." he said immediately.

"Oh man, how awesome would a room be right now? Admit it!"

Wales shook his head, laughing as I mocked his classic line whenever Woodstock and I had tried to goad him into splitting a hotel room in the past.

"*I'm goin' to the trail, dude.* Let me guess, that's what you were gonna say, am I right?" I asked with a chuckle.

"I would split a room with you, but I already got one in Pittsfield for tomorrow on my way to the airport," Wales replied regretfully.

"Well, good thing I have this piece of plastic with imaginary money on it," I said, pulling out my credit card.

"What? No." He replied, pushing my hand down.

"HEY! YOU LISTEN TO ME YOUNG MAN! This is the last time I'll ever see you for the rest of my life." I began, playfully gripping him by the shirt.

"Or just this trip…" He interjected.

"THE REST OF OUR LIVES! I might die out there. You never know!" I shouted at him, overdramatically thrusting my hands up into the air.

"I can't justify it." he started in again before I cut him off.

"How about if it's less than eighty bucks, I get the room for us." I offered. He gave an uncertain look. I tilted my head to the side.

"Fine, no more than eighty bucks, though."

The price of the room had been $107 even after taxes.

"I thought you said that if it was over eighty, you weren't going to get the room?" He asked as we made our way towards our rented double bedded lair.

"Eighty *here*, one hundred and seven dollars *there*. What's twenty-seven bucks amongst friends?" I asked. Wales made his trademark move, by covering mouth and laughing bashfully just before hopping excitedly onto his rented bed.

After dropping our packs in the room, we walked a little over a mile to the Madison Micro Brewery for some beer and dinner, which Wales was kind enough to pick up the tab for.

When we had returned to our room, we played on our phones, each in our own world as we surfed the internet and watched YouTube videos or looked around on our Facebook pages.

We no longer talked to each other and existed in a comfortable silence—both well aware that the following day, Wales would be gone.

And while that was still many hours away, already I was missing him.

"Well buddy, it was fun," I said to Wales, as he nodded in agreeance.

"What are you going to do now?" he asked.

"Well, I'm gonna head eight miles or so east out of town, and get back onto the trail again where the AT crosses Route 9. How about you?"

"I'm just gonna hike out of town. It'll probably be easier to score a hitch further down into Pittsfield. I'll stay there overnight and then take a bus to Hartford, Connecticut. After that, I'll take a plane further south to meet my folks."

Our paths ran down the same roads for a while as we maneuvered through town blocks there in Bennington. However, this would be the last time we hiked together.

"Man, it's been an adventure, huh?" he asked me.

"The White Mountains, Mahoosuc Notch, Katahdin…" I said.

"Woodstock, and Steph." He added.

"The Warrior Hikers, your momentary girlfriend Sheila from the Golden Corral Restaurant. My nearly getting killed by a rabid German shepherd near Carters Notch in New Hampshire." I said as we both laughed.

"The huts, Manhattan, your aqua blazing down the Shenandoah." He added.

"Can't forget Woodstock nearly fist fighting that Motel owner in Millinocket and getting the police called on us."

"It's been a heck of a journey so far. I don't want it to end." He finished.

I honestly didn't want him to go, because I didn't want to be alone again.

"You could always skip ahead to Pittsfield with me if you wanted to stay the night in a hotel room." He offered with a laugh, almost as if he was reading my mind.

I looked up at the cloudy skies, feeling the urge. It was an urge that was always going to be there, but one I could no longer afford to indulge in. At the end of the day, I needed to finish this journey, and I wanted to experience as much as I could before I did and it all ended. I still had more than 500 miles to hike. I was too close to start giving up now.

"I can't do that," I said as we came to an intersection. Further east there was nowhere else for him to go. This was where we would split ways.

Wales of course understood.

"Well, text me when you get back onto the trail, brother," I said, shaking his hand a final time.

"I will." He returned.

As we started to walk away, I turned to him.

"Back at Lance Creek, in the very beginning of our hike,"

He stopped walking and looked to me.

"Lindsey and Jenna stayed with you in that tent. All me, CookIN, Woodstock, and Torry heard were giggles coming from inside, all night long. Like you guys were tickling each other. What were you guys doing in there?" I asked, cocking my eyebrow.

Wales smirked, confidently.

"Wouldn't *you* like to know?" he replied.

I laughed, and turned back east, to finish my hike.

To finish my mission for my parents.

And to head home.

From where Wales and I had stayed back in town, it was an 8.2-mile hike out of Bennington to the AT via Route 9.

I had decided to instead take Burgess Road headed east towards the national forest to where it transitioned into Stage Coach Road. That in turn, went all the way through to a highway on the opposite side of the forest supposedly.

Well, Google Maps was completely wrong, as was to be expected—AGAIN.

First of all, Stage Coach Road was nothing more than ATV trails and didn't exist as a paved state road at all. It intertwined back and forth through mud pits and bogs.

Eventually, in anger, I stupidly decided to go off trail to where Google Maps told me the AT existed. This involved me crashing through the forest clumsily and tripping and falling over boulders and rocks submerged beneath a sea of undisturbed fallen leaves. I continued for a few miles through thick brush and shrubs, taking minute established animal paths until I reached Lake Hancock mostly by luck.

What I'd thought were the markings for the Appalachian Trail, however, were actually white blazes that had been either burned, shot with bullets, or just poorly carved off of trees altogether.

Eventually, there were no longer any ATV ruts or forest roads to follow either, and once again I was plunking through the Vermont wilderness with nothing to guide me except the sun.

I came to notice a few things in a forest with overgrown trees and bushes and shrubs.

Old stumps.

These stumps likely hadn't seen life in over a hundred years. Some had been fully covered and enveloped in moss while others were crumbling so badly that their defiance against the weather, and time had quickly died quite a few decades before.

Still, some of the stumps were so well-preserved in their rotted state that you could still see the saw grooves and teeth marks of a perfect cut.

A human-made cut.

I no longer felt so helpless or lost anymore.

People had been here. Of course, while they maybe were no longer living there, still the fear that I was lost in some Amazonian Rainforest seemed to recede a little. Maybe this had once been a cleared field or an old farm road that was no longer visible because forest growth and time.

I was following tree stumps which when looking at Google maps—put me right atop what used to be the Appalachian Trail.

There were no hard places to step on the earth, and every third or fourth foot placement had me up to my mid-calves in mud. As I tried to go around these hidden bogs, the heavy leaf fall resting upon the forest floor made seeing any obvious features practically impossible. Eventually, one long step over a fallen log, had me sink almost immediately up to my crotch.

"Ugh, God!" I shouted out loud with disgust. I fell forward however before I could finish my sentence, into what I figured to be a hidden peat bog that had been covered entirely by fallen leaves.

The weight of my backpack caused my head to slip beneath the black, murky, stagnant water. When I withdrew from beneath the foul liquid, I was spitting and smearing rotting vegetation from my face.

"CHRIST!" I shouted out loud, as I retreated and scrambled up the log from the way I had come. I stood on the other side, sinking into foul mud up to my calves again as I looked for the way to go.

I had to go back the way I had come. It was impossible to traverse any further through this boggy forest. As I started heading back, I saw the remnants of a road which quickly ended in a wall of old bulldozed soil.

When I looked down at the razed ground, I noticed a small traceable path going over it. On the other side was a grassy field and beyond that, a boulder covered wet road.

The most ironic part about finding myself lost in this forest and unsure of where else to go came in the form of finally coming across somebody. And not just *anybody* in the same boat with me.

"And then I was like 'Oh God, I'm gonna die!' but truth was I knew what I was doing. I've kinda become a pro at getting lost out here."

Daisy continued staring ahead, walking on unbothered by my presence.

"I mean it's crazy, right? So you're here one minute stumbling around in the woods and then just out of nowhere find yourself magically popping back out into the right direction." I said.

"Mmm Hmmm." She replied, with no real urgency to engage me in conversation.

"So the real question is, what are YOU doing out HERE?" I asked, finally giving her room to respond.

"I already answered that question back in Bennington. I'm just hiking the Appalachian trail for a while." She replied, almost as if she was in a hurry.

"But this isn't the Appalachian Trail. This is some crazy old scribblings on a digital map. You're in the middle of nowhere, with me."

"Yeah, awkwardly convenient, isn't it? I happen to take the wrong way and bump into you again. Kinda like you were stalking me or something." She said, giving me a suspicious glance.

"Pffft. Lady, please, don't flatter yourself. You're not THAT pretty." I replied.

She stopped with her mouth ajar.

"Excuse me?"

"What?" I defended.

Daisy proceeded to pick up a small rock from the ground and then beamed me in the leg with it.

"Ow! What the hell was that for?" I shouted.

"That's for being a dick." She said, walking again.

I carefully followed behind.

We stopped at an intersection where piles of trash had been left, almost as if someone had created their own makeshift landfill within the middle of the forest. The road ahead of us was clogged for a good two hundred feet with old tires and broken window screens, or washing machine parts precariously creating a narrow passage only for those who were on foot. The other road, however, had a *No Trespassing* sign which at that point in my adventure held all the reverence of a candy wrapper on the ground.

Daisy turned to look at me with a frustrated expression, immediately holding her cell phone up.

"I hate Google Maps."

I smiled, removing my backpack and dropping it to the ground.

"Hang out here for a second Gregory, I'll be right back," I said to my backpack.

My backpack responded by falling over.

"Who are you talking to?" Daisy asked me suddenly.

"My backpack. Why?"

Daisy scoffed with an unbelievable expression.

"Because that's completely normal, I guess." She said sarcastically.

I walked into the woods to use the restroom and found myself looking at a tree that had been blown apart with bullets of every caliber. I ran my fingertips along the birdshot-peppered bark and shook my head slowly with disdain. Looking at my feet, I found myself standing in a world of beer cans left to rot over the course of hundreds or potentially thousands of years. Bullet casings and old decaying pizza boxes keeping them company.

I wondered how a person could so easily give no care to trashing the woods. How someone could remove the cardboard boxing from a case a beer and toss it so callously on the ground without any regard.

The forest in front of me had pools or puddles sporadically spread about, like large glowing ember pits reflecting the fiery afternoon skies above.

Swampy lands that held any number of waist deep mud pits looking to swallow or partially digest any part of me that it could.

I saw the carcass of a raccoon that had drowned in one of the pools and not far from it within another pit—a squirrel floating face down, lifeless. Flies landed on its back like a boat; trying to burrow into the decaying flesh and leave a senseless death for their potential larvae.

The pit didn't care. It just absorbed. It existed as a black hole, sucking these plants, insects, and animals into its dark, wet, watery depths and rendered whatever it had trapped into nothingness.

It left a chill within me, as I turned and made my way back towards Daisy after finishing my business.

As I slipped my backpack on, she had already started taking off without so much as a goodbye. I wasn't immediately insulted, but it told me a lot about her personality. In some ways, I think she was looking to be left alone, and here I came along wanting to get to know her and strike up a conversation. More dependent on her company than I maybe wanted to admit.

As conversations died off, I pulled ahead of her. Like the surrounding forest, the ATV trail with which we trespassed was rife with massive and wide puddles of water that looked like small ponds.

I had my earphones in, listening to music as we carefully navigated along the side of one such "pond."

I never heard the guy coming up behind us with his dirt bike, but Daisy had. When he came, it was a surprise we both hadn't been expecting.

I shouted a garbled, indiscernible grunt in surprise as a tidal wave of muddy water collapsed onto my entire left side, and the blur of a man in a water proof suit upon a mud covered white motor bike, flew by us both.

"What the fuck!" Daisy screamed out loud in rage, as I just stared at my dripping clothes and then the guy doing a U-turn and coming back towards us.

I slowly removed my earbuds.

"Well, *that* was unexpected." I said as I climbed up out of the roadway and into the woods completely.

Daisy was nowhere near as calm as I had been, though, in my response.

"The asshole saw us walking. We weren't hiding in the fucking woods! He probably thought it was funny." She said, seething with anger.

When we were halfway through the pond, the guy reached us and gunned the gas, flying through the water again. This time we were prepared and climbed back up the bank a little bit and into the wood line.

"He's *trying* to get us wet!" She shouted incredulously. The dirt bike rider then did another U-turn and came back, lifting his facial mask. He was smiling, as mud dripped from his face shield and he propped himself up in the middle of the pond water.

"Sorry, I didn't see you guys." He lied, with a smirk on his face.

"Come on dude? You're full of shit. You know that, right?" I asked. Daisy was blunter in her response, though.

"Seriously, you see two hikers here, and you *speed up* thinking it was funny."

"Who was I trying to make laugh? I'm the only one here. Besides. You're both trespassing anyways." He replied with that same grin on his face.

"Maybe you just get off on being an asshole, and you don't need anybody around to impress," Daisy replied.

"Nah. That's not me. If you wanna dry off though, you can hop on." He said, patting his bike seat.

"No, I don't want to ride on your loser-sissy bike. Get the fuck out of here." She said, kicking a load of water at him which sprayed up into his face. He shook the dirty water away a quick head snap and the smirk was no longer there.

"Don't fucking kick water at me, bitch." He said kicking it back at her.

"Hey, don't call her a bitch." I began as if I had suddenly decided to protect her and her dignity.

"Go to hell! You're a little pussy...on a shitty bike that mommy and daddy probably bought for you." Daisy said, kicking more water angrily at the dirt bike rider.

"Come on, let's just go." I said to her.

We started walking away when he suddenly revved his bike and spun his rear wheel tire at us, churning up water and spraying us altogether. He took off then, just as Daisy had started picking up rocks and chucking them at him as he sped off.

We were soaked now more than we'd ever had been before.

I sighed and threw my pack off on the other side of the puddle-pond.

Despite the rainy looking skies, brief patches of the sun were breaking through. Not nearly enough to dry our things, though.

"URGGHHH, GOD! What an asshole!" Daisy shouted angrily after him.

He vanished beyond a corner of hanging vines eighty feet ahead of us.

I sat down on the bank, telling her to calm down. Her yelling wasn't going to make the situation any better, nor would it re-dry our clothes and backpacks.

She sighed in defiant surrender, all the same.

I laughed a little in reflection, as I thought of a way to make her smile at the stupidity of the whole situation. She only shook her head angrily and threw her pack off as well. She fished out a cigarette...and began smoking as she sat beside me, offering me one.

I politely declined.

"Do you think we're pregnant?" I asked. She gave me a confused expression before looking forward and taking another drag from her cigarette.

She didn't answer at first, and instead, she hung her head down towards the earth finally coming down out of her adrenaline infused rage. After a minute or two in silence, she looked over at me.

"Pregnant?" She asked for clarification like I was the biggest moron in the world for asking it.

"Cause we just got, SCREWED," replied.

I offered her a smile, at my lame attempt of a joke.

It had worked. She laughed, dropping the cigarette from her mouth in the process.

The coal went out once it hit the cold, wet mud.

"Ah shit." She said, dropping the laugh as an angry look returned to her face and she picked it up to see if it was salvageable.

"Looks like you just got SCREWED again. You pregnant yet?" I asked, lightly elbowing her as she started chuckling once more.

"Shut up, idiot." She said replied, with a smile.

She flicked a hunk of mud that had been hanging from her shirt at me as I swatted it away, laughing.

Daisy and I had set up our camp, nearly two miles from what our maps had called, "County Road."

Monikers seemed to change quite a bit and sometimes one could come to find that a thru-way called "Woods Road" had wrongly been named, just to please the map creators. People who had no knowledge of what the roads actual name was.

What Daisy and I did know, however, was that we weren't far from the Massachusetts border. When I brought this up to her, she had seemed rather disinterested as she ate her ramen noodles.

"You gotta admit, it's kinda cool, though isn't it? You're about to walk into another state!" I said, trying to get her as excited as I was about it. She smiled, and finally caved into a forced kind of conversation.

"You're a bit of a pest, aren't you? I mean you *really* have to have constant interaction with somebody, or else you go crazy." She said, forking noodles into her mouth.

"Well no. Not really." I muttered, slightly insulted by the remark.

She saw right through my response though and rolled her eyes.

"Well okay, so I like to talk to people. So what? You shoulda saw me months ago. I was a lot less social in the beginning…" I had started before she cut me off suddenly.

"Why don't you bring *that guy* from a few months ago back?" she immediately interjected.

I shut my mouth at that moment and looked down at my food, anxious not to bother her any further with a dialogue of any kind. I stirred my bowl of instant mashed potatoes before setting it on the log beside me and staring at the fire for a while.

Daisy glanced up at me in silent confirmation to assure she hadn't hurt my feelings. The atmosphere was tense and awkward, but its creation hadn't been my intention either. I was merely trying to respect her request.

"Where are you from, Morris?" she asked finally.

"North Carolina. You?" I asked with a sheepish smile. She twirled some noodles onto her fork and looked up at me.

"Oregon. Can you guess where?"

"Easy. Portland." I said confidently.

She smiled, before setting her bowl down into the leaves beside her.

"I don't want you to take this the wrong way, but I'm not looking for a hiking partner out here. By preference, I'd rather hike alone." she said, picking up a small stick and probing the fire with it.

"If you want, I can make sure to sleep late tomorrow if you'd like an early start." I offered in response. She only chuckled and shook her head from side to side.

"Why are you trying so hard to please me?" she asked sincerely.

"I'm trying to be amicable. I don't want anything from you." I said in earnest.

"*Can I hike with you, Morris? Please? Please let me hike with you.* Isn't that what you want me to say?" she mocked, using a comedic, whiny voice.

"No," I replied, looking down at the ground with a befuddled expression.

"Why not? Don't you want to form a *friendship* and a *bond*? Maybe we'll start liking each other, and you'll get to lose that loneliness you so clearly have been holding on to for so long. Maybe you'll even get a piece of *ass* in the process? And then what? We'll run off and live happily ever after?"

Was I so transparent? It was incredible to realize that I had become so lonely, that the very thoughts Daisy spoke aloud became everything I immediately thought of when even minutely infatuated with someone.

I wasn't looking for 'the right one' in my life as much as I was looking for *anything* and *anyone* to hold on to. So desperate for affection, that I chased whatever might have even been slightly interested in caring and loving me. I was broken inside, and the realization of that was in a way uplifting. However, it was still my pride that she had challenged, and so I deflected by lying.

"Lady, you're full of assumptions. You seem to think I'm some lost, sick little puppy..." I began.

"But aren't you? You told me yourself you were hiking with a group of people that have all left. Some guy named 'Wales' that you thought I might have run across. A man named Torry that didn't feel like hearing your whining anymore. But now you're out here on your own, and I've even seen you talking to your fucking backpack for Christ sake."

"I'm just passing the time...when I do that...it's...for fun..." I tried to defend.

"I know what you're looking for John, and it bothers you that maybe I'm just a little more perceptive than you initially thought I was. But I see right through you. And I don't fault you...I mean. You're human. You're a social creature, and you're dependent on others," she went on.

Her eyes were fiery coals in the night as she stared and soaked in the warmth of the flames. She was oddly all-knowing at that moment, and it had started to creep me out.

"But see, I'm a very independent person John, and I'm not looking for anything other than alone time to get to know myself out here. I'm not trying to be who you want or need me to be, nor am I changing myself for anyone else."

"Don't believe I've ever asked that of you. I think you're getting way ahead of yourself." I tried to rationalize.

"I'm just laying out the boundary lines now so that they're clear from the get-go. You do understand me, don't you?" she asked with a grave intonation in her tone.

I nodded my head.

"Perfectly."

My eyes felt parched, and arid as I awoke the following morning and tried to rub the sleep out of them. I looked from my hammock and found Daisy's tent was gone.

She had left without saying a word and had packed so quietly; it was almost as if she had never even been there to begin with. I looked down at the spot where she had set up on a large patch of pine straw. I stepped out of my hammock and knelt down, touching the needles. I still felt warmth in the bedding and knew instantly that she hadn't been gone very long.

Daisy had been right about my loneliness. However, talking to myself was more than just a tool combat that. It also did a good job of calming me down when I got irritable.

"Come on Gregory, stop bitching! I know you don't wanna do it, but let's just walk!" I shouted at my backpack, as I tightened the straps on my shoulders.

Gregory bounced along, silent and possibly contemplative over my outburst.

I'd been following a dried up stream which eventually met up at another path called Risky Ranch Road. It was here; I'd come to a small bridge passing.

According to the satellite imagery, I wasn't sure as to whether it took me through people's property or not. However, it definitely went south into North Adams, Massachusetts. That was really all I needed it to do.

Fresh footprints in the road, meant that someone had been through there that very day. The puddles were slightly cloudy and only recently settling. I wondered then if Daisy had followed the same route, earlier that morning.

As I came down the ridge into town, grassy ditches transformed into broken cement sidewalks. Old buildings and architecture replaced the forest...and surrounded me as the trees disappeared.

I took Eagle Street down to Route 2, before making a sharp turn westward. It was 4:30 P.M. and the brief bit of bright blue skies looked to have turned to dark rainy ones.

As I walked along, I passed one of the sloppiest graveyards I had ever seen in my life.

Hillside Cemetery as it was called, was extremely overcrowded with plots. I had never seen so many fallen over or crooked tombstones before. Some were even propped up against other people's graves!

I immediately wondered how the cemetery keepers could ever keep track of where the bodies were buried.

But that wasn't all that I noticed while hiking through Massachusetts.

Besides the fact, that everybody looked like a tough guy, there were lots of smokers here too. People pushing strollers while smoking. People riding bikes while smoking. There were even two guys, jogging with lit cigarettes dangling out of their mouths.

And why was everyone so angry?

Merely walking down the street, I was running up on random conversations from women on their porches, clucking over the phone: *Tha bitch betta not come lookin' fah me. I'll drop her ass. You tink ah'm fuckin' playin'?*

Further down some punk kids on bicycles were throwing rocks at each other in the streets. Stray stones were occasionally bouncing off of people's cars, and nobody seemed concerned.

Finally, I came across a guy yelling at a woman on the adjacent sidewalk. I wondered how many times I was going to hear the "F- this" and "F- that" throughout the day. It had become almost every other word in these people's dialect.

"Eyyyyy! I'm walkin' ova' here and ya' fucking dog, fucking almost bit me."

The guy looked like he fit the exact physical description of your typical Italian Mafioso or Tony Sopranos henchman.

Meanwhile, the woman he had been shouting at was wrestling with the pit bull he'd spoken of, who was barking maniacally at the gentleman.

"That's why da sign says beware of tha dahg. You beware of da fucking dahg!" The lady replied, finally getting the mutt inside her house. She had high black hair in what almost looked like a beehive hairstyle. She was wearing leopard-print Spandex pants with a button up blue shirt she had tied in a bow at her stomach.

"You don't give a dog that bites people, a 400-foot leash, dummy." The guy shouted back at her.

"Ahhh get the fuck outta hereyah. You gotta job? You do any-ting but botha peepa, ya homo?" She shouted, waving her hands dismissively.

"I'm tellin' you's...next time that dog comes at me, I'll have control come down and put his ass tah sleep." He said walking off.

"Get tha fuck outta here! I'll have *you* put to sleep, ya fat fuck." The lady spat bitterly back at the threat.

Seconds later she had already transitioned into yelling at her kids inside her home.

After three miles of steady elevation climbing, I had finally entered Mount Greylock State Reservation.

I hiked the Auto road for 3/10th's of a mile up into the park, where I broke off into the woods for 200 feet to camp overnight for the evening once I saw nobody looking.

It was 10 A.M. as I pushed uphill the following morning towards the War Memorial.

Hungry for a real breakfast apart from the two cereal bars I had choked down earlier that day; I went into the lodge at the summit. AWOLs guidebook had stated bunkrooms were available for $35 a night there. However, when I checked the hiker registry and log book to find that nobody I knew from the Appalachian Trail had signed in, I was immediately aware this might have been a place to avoid staying.

In fact, nobody I had known that had hiked the AT that entire year, had signed it.

Upon investigating, I learned that it just so happened to be the lodges last day of operation for the season until next June. Luckily the kitchen was still open.

I went crazy once I had learned that. My mouth immediately began watering, thinking of all the greasy, fried things I could stuff down my gullet.

I sat at a table in the far corner of the dining area, mostly because I knew that I smelled pretty bad. My waitress looked bothered, and flopped her arms after looking over at me as if she was throwing a tantrum. She pouted, protruding her bottom lip in the process to one of her coworkers before trudging slowly over towards me as if dragging her feet through mud.

"How much would a burger, and some chili cost?" I asked at random, before even opening the menu.

"That would be $17.56." she said flatly.

My mouth dropped.

"Uh, how much for just the chili by itself?" I asked, looking at the few dollars I had remaining within my wallet.

"Chili will be $6 dollars not including tax, or tip. Extra crackers are $.50 cents each."

"Of course they are," I muttered miserably.

She gave a cutesy smile, as if that was at all comforting to a frugal, and hungry guy like myself.

"I'll take the chili," I said glumly, handing her the menu back.

She started to turn away.

"Oh, and uh. If you wanted to sneak me one extra pack of crackers on the down low. I mean I wouldn't say…anything…or…"

But the waitress didn't bother giving a reply, as if I'd just made some sort of smart-assed remark or insult towards her. I looked around at everyone eating their large meals there in the dining area.

Gorgeous green salads, with feta cheese crumbles and honey-coated pecans with apples. A man and woman were sharing a piece of strawberry cake, with pink frosting and moaning over each sumptuous bite.

The guy at the table in front of me crammed a fist full of tater tots into his mouth, and his wife took a sip of golden brown iced tea, with a large lemon slice clipped to the edge of the glass and fresh mint leaves drowning within the cup.

I began to sweat with anticipation, and my stomach groaned in contempt; restless and unwilling to wait any longer.

That was when I heard the cook in the back shout "order up."

My chili had actually come out quicker than I thought it would. That is to say, after he had probably just finished microwaving it.

There was a moment as it was carried out on a tray within a 6oz cup, that I thought it was a joke. I mean it had to be a prank, of some sort.

Someone was about to blast through the side of a fake wall and jerk me out of my seat—screaming into my face: YOU ACTUALLY THOUGHT WE WERE GONNA SERVE YOU THAT TINY LITTLE CUP OF CHILI, DIDN'T YOU, IDIOT? SMILE, YOU'RE ON CANDID CAMERA!

And I would nod my head stupidly with a dopey grin on my face as I realized what a complete moron I had been to think that the tiny cup of chili sitting on the tray, was actually *my* order.

Because surely the staff hadn't expected me to pay *six bucks* for a Sunday school sized, Daisy Cup of chili.

The cook had gone as far as setting my "meal" on the cashier registers counter, before completely abandoning it. My waitress looked over at me, and called out suddenly: "You can come up and get this whenever you're ready."

Oh, I can...huh I thought to myself, just a little bit pretentiously.

I could imagine the waitress just as smugly tossing the chili onto the ground at my feet and saying: "You can come get it whenever you're ready."

Well, she had at least saved me a couple of bucks, from tipping her at least.

I drank my 6oz lukewarm, microwaved chili in about 30 seconds and stuffed the two saltine crackers down my throat behind it.

Forget this dump I thought angrily to myself. I had seen what their nine dollar burger looked like on my way out.

You got a huge plate, with a teaspoon of coleslaw and a teaspoon of potato salad. The burger patty you might be wondering about? Well it consisted of your typical, pre-molded Bubba Burger frozen patty. You got six in a box for around five dollars in the frozen food section of your local grocery store.

However here, they charged nine dollars, for ONE.

"Never again, Gregory," I said on my way out, after paying.

"I'm sorry?" the cashier called out to me.

"I wasn't talking to you. I was talking to my backpack!"

The Massachusetts town of Cheshire had a church that according to AWOL's 2012 guidebook offered a place for hikers to lay their heads overnight. The church was called St Mary's Church of Assumption. A Roman Catholic Church; it offered no promise of laundry or a shower, but at least it would be a warm place to rest my bones.

It had begun to dramatically drop in temperature over the past few nights. The next few days, however, were calling for below freezing temperatures as well, and it was at that moment I realized once again that I was not equipped for this sort of weather.

When I had set out in March, I'd done no actual research and had no concept of the higher elevations being colder than that of lower level areas. As simple a thought as it might have been, it was the one that had completely slipped my mind. I'd thought: "Oh it's March and soon it'll be summer and Torry, and I will be long done with the trail before winter ever hits again!"

How naïve I had been.

I pushed down the mountain that day, walking along brightly sunlit ridges. Traipsing beneath golden leaves that shone brilliantly through—as rays of amber light illuminated them like gold.

The trail wove back and forth like yarn rolled out through old farmlands and fields where Mount Greylock looked down upon a hiker like a nurturing parent. In the afternoon sunlight, it was beautiful.

The fields were ablaze in the vibrant reds and dark oranges of fall foliage and dying shrubbery.

As I walked into Cheshire, I momentarily became a bit lost. My GPS had decided to play guessing games with me again, and now I was walking in confused, and angry circles trying to find my way south.

Once I had reached the Cheshire Elementary School, I'd mistaken it for the church. I'd hoped that the few cars I'd seen in the parking lot meant there were still teachers or administration staff inside with which to give me direction. I began buzzing doorbells equipped with cameras on them and knocking on windows to empty classrooms.

"Well, shit, where the hell am I supposed to go now?" I asked out loud.

After a while, I began to believe the school was in some way attached to the church I was looking to sleep at. It had to be, like some sort of Catholic prison camp for bad kids. When I finally found the church right next door to the school, I sighed at my own stupidity and circled the structure twice trying to find the right spot with which to make human contact of some sort.

I then decided to try the doorbell.

A short and very nervous looking priest answered the door. His expression was one of awe, as he looked up at me with his frail body shaking lightly. Had I awakened him? Was I truly that intimidating in appearance?

I took off the patadora my father had sent me back in Hot Springs and caught my "wild crazy man hair" in the reflection of his glass screen door.

Truthfully, I no longer recognized myself most times, upon stumbling across a mirror.

The priest kept eyeing my huge backpack with confusion as if the very idea of a hiker stopping by was completely alien and had never happened before.

"Hi, I was hoping I could get a room for the night. If they weren't all taken." I asked, smiling. I wrung my head cover nervously between my hands like a shy young child.

The priest gave me an odd, untrusting look and shook his head slowly as if in disbelief.

"I'm sorry, a *room*? What?" He replied, clueless. It was as if I was speaking an entirely different language to the man.

"You see...I'm a thru-hiker, and I have a guide that listed this church as having a place for hikers to sleep," I said, retrieving the guidebook from the side pocket of my backpack and waving it back and forth before him.

"Well yes, but that's during hiking season." He said while laughing nervously, almost as if he believed I was going to become enraged and attack him. He immediately stopped laughing once he saw the grave expression on my face.

"I...I mean. That's come and gone now." He said in befuddled contemplation.

I sighed and made it very clear and purposeful that I did this right in front of him. I left nothing to accident or chance and showed the real feeling within me at that moment. One of disappointment, as I now had nowhere to go that evening. It was going to be another long night of hiking into the darkness until I'd found a place to sleep.

"Is there somewhere to set up camp nearby that you know of? A section of woods or anything? It's nothing but pastures around here and I kind of pushed really hard to get to this church in time today. The guide never mentioned anything about a 'cut-off' date." I said, shoving the guide back into my pocket.

"Well, there are lots of woods around." He said directing me towards a patch of trees on the side of the building with the wave of his hand. They were overgrown with shrubs, and blackberry bushes. But I might just have had to make it work if he was offering no other solution.

"Over where those briars are, huh? Do you knew anywhere else I could hang a hammock without getting hurt?" I asked, just a little impatiently. It wasn't my intention to put fear into the man, but I was now consciously challenging him.

Over the course of the prior months, I found I had changed quite a bit. Formerly reserved, if I was ever going to get anywhere I was going to have to fight for what I wanted. There was no sense of entitlement attached to my resolve. Only the desire to prove to this man that I wasn't as bad or scary as he might have misjudged me to be by my looks.

"Well, could you go back the way you came? I'm assuming you came down Mount Greylock. There are woods along there, no?" He asked, stepping out the door.

"I'd just as soon push on hiking through the night than to go backward. Never mind. I'm sorry to have bothered you." I said with a saddened tone. I shook my head with obvious frustration and began to walk away. It was a bold move because I had a 50/50 chance of this sudden statement and gesture working. The priest was either going to be cold and uncaring, or he would take notice of the pitch in my voice and give me a chance.

"I'm sorry, so you're a hiker? What was your name?" He asked suddenly.

"John Morris....my trail name is Morris the Cat," I said, turning to look him in the eyes. His expression was distant and dreamy. Clouded over with thought, and a slight fear.

"Follow me. I'll find you a place to set up." He said suddenly, holding his arm out towards the East side of the building.

He walked around towards the back door of the church, with me heavy-hoofing it from behind. He then opened the passage to go inside the building.

"Oh no, I can just sleep out here. I'm not trying to make any waves or disturb anything." I said, stopping at the door. This was to show courtesy. To make him aware that I couldn't take his kind offer without showing just a tad bit of humility.

I knew this action made him feel more at ease. More connected, as if I was more human and humble than he had potentially, previously believed me to be.

"No, it's fine. You can use the Sunday school room for tonight." He replied, with a nervous smile.

"I'm really sorry for the miscommunication. If I had known there was a cutoff date, I would've never bothered you." I said.

"Oh no. I was just surprised. I'm not used to seeing hikers this late in the year. You just caught me a little off guard is all." He replied apologetically.

I knew now that I needed to be an ambassador to future hikers. I had to put this guy at ease anyway that I could. Grease the wheels a little and make a good impression. Particularly for those hiking this same time of year with nowhere else to go.

In the kitchen, three older women were cooking deserts and cleaning up dishes from what appeared to have been a picnic the congregation had earlier in the day.

"This way." He said leading me to a simple room with absolutely NOTHING on the walls except a rules list that exclaimed: *No hats. No food or drink. No gum or candy. No electronics of any kind. Bathroom breaks are taken only before or after class.*

There was a wooden cross and an old lamp from medieval times, on a bleak desk in the corner. In the middle of the room were two long rectangular particle board tables with metal folding chairs surrounding them.

There were some Appalachian Trail related items as well, such as poster boards from 2007, 2008 and 2012 with the pictures of several hikers glued to them. There were sets of newspaper clippings tacked to a bulletin board regarding past hikers achievements, speed runs, or even deaths.

"Funny you came today. We start using this room tomorrow for classes. In the afternoon of course. I was planning on cleaning these posters and things out tomorrow. Feel free to look them over and see if you recognize anybody."

"I'll be out early in the morning," I said, turning to face him. He looked at me with a sincere expression of peace.

"I won't leave a mess or anything," I said, trying to assure him. More than anything else, I just didn't want him to be afraid of me, and I was now starting to feel bad for my manipulative actions, having attempted to *guilt* him into giving me a place to stay for the evening.

"Well, we have mass tomorrow morning. People usually begin showing up at around 7 to 7:30 in the morning. But you don't have to be out of here *that early*...or anything. I'm not rushing you out."

I nodded my head and smiled, as he left me to set up.

He walked back towards the kitchen and began conversing with the women in there.

It didn't take long for my scent to fill the room, as I began to open my backpack and withdraw hiker essentials. I looked into my aluminum pot and reared back with disgust, slamming the top shut.

"I should probably clean that,"

The smell of parmesan cheese wafted up from my feet, after removing my boots and the absolute stink that my backpacks shoulder straps gave off was incredibly nauseating. I felt sick, from just smelling myself.

After I was done setting up, I walked out into the main hall to get some air and clean myself. As I approached the kitchen, the priest glanced out at me.

"You don't have to stand out there, come on in." one of the women exclaimed when she saw me standing off to the side.

"Sorry to bother you guys. I was just curious as to where the restroom was." I asked.

"Ohhh! Father David told me we had hikers. Honey, these are for all of you." the other woman said, suddenly handing me an entire tray of chocolate cupcakes. Beneath those, were Apple Maple Syrup bars as well.

Father David looked on, helpless.

"Well, I'm actually the only other hiker I've seen today." I corrected them. I looked at the Priest who began to have a worried look on his face.

"I should be the only one here tonight." I tried to reassure him. He nodded looking a little more at ease.

"You must be freezing. It feels like December outside!" the woman who had handed me the trays of goodies exclaimed. Suddenly, she handed me a whole pot of coffee with creamers, sugar packets and stir sticks as well.

I stood there in awe, balancing all of these things in my arms before Father David helped me with them.

We set them down on the table in the room I would be sleeping in that night.

I walked back into the main hall, thanking them appreciatively.

"But I probably will be the only hiker here tonight. I don't regularly see anybody else anymore." I reflected, thinking of how empty the trail had become.

"Well, whatever you can't eat tonight. Take with you tomorrow." one of the women offered.

I could have picked her up and kissed her on the mouth, right then and there.

In the room I had been lent for the evening, I scarfed down two cupcakes and two apple maple syrup bars along with two cups of coffee and was just beginning to start pouring my third when the priest leaned on the door jamb leading into the room.

"Looks like you came at the right time." He exclaimed as he saw my hunger, and ravenous behavior and smiled. I laughed and replied with a stuffed mouth: "I guessff sshoff!"

I covered my mouth and apologized for my being rude.

As I gulped down the creamy coffee and took a breath—I pulled out a $20 dollar bill from my wallet. I knew it was a lot of money, especially for somebody as monetarily destitute as I was. But Father David had taken me in when he didn't have to. He had then fed me as well.

"Thank you," I said, handing him the bill.

"Oh no. You don't have to do that." He insisted.

"Please. You've been very kind to me." I said.

"You *really* don't have to do this." He went on.

"But I want to," I said smiling.

He nodded, acknowledging finally in that moment for certain that I might not have been as scary as he'd initially assumed upon our first meeting.

You could see it in his eyes.

"You will be blessed, on your journey home." He replied, almost with prophetic vision.

"The blessings have already started, father!" I said, picking up my third chocolate cupcake and knocking it against an imaginary glass.

"Cheers!" I stated with a broad smile.

A bright yellow light cut through the darkness, and only my pacing shadow broke the beam to my sanctuary for the evening. I woke at 1 A.M., restless and unable to sleep within the Sunday school room.

When I had finally gathered my things to leave, I'd also left a note for the priest; thanking him wholeheartedly for allowing me to sleep warm, within the church that evening. I had also explained that the urge to move along had become too intense to fight. So I had decided to follow my feelings.

I missed home too much after so many months on the trail, and I wrote that down—in the message as if the priest had become my counselor.

My feet crunched over wet grass that had iced over during the night, and before long I had found a greenway trail that ran along the Cheshire Reservoir on my map.

It had once been a railroad that had been converted into a paved path for joggers and bicyclists, now named the "Ashuwillticook Rail Trail." Even better, it would take me twelve miles south.

The word Ashuwillticook (ash-oo-will-ti-cook) is a Native American name for the southern branch of the Hoosic River. The name stood for "the pleasant river in between the hills."

I saw the mountains around me.

They were radiant, clothed in their fall colored garbs.

The skies above the lake were a mix of both purple and pink, with strings of wispy clouds stretched out like cotton strands. Waning gray morning light would slowly start to erase the traces of dawn and the mist that carpeted the surface of the water; flowing without purpose or direction along the tops of my boots.

I made my way, to where the trail ended at the Berkshire Mall. I bypassed that area and traversed Route 8 until it reached the outskirts of Dalton and entered into Pittsfield.

Along the way, I'd had two different drivers stop and ask if I had needed a ride somewhere, anywhere. The first driver insisted after hearing that I was hiking back home to North Carolina, that I at least take some money.

"Please, let me help you." She pled to me, searching her purse and pulling out a wad of bills.

"Thirty-five dollars is all I have on me. Take it with you." She said, thrusting her hand as far as she could out of the passenger's side window.

"Listen. I'm not that good at taking charity." I shouted apologetically over the semi-trucks and big cars or trucks driving by.

She had her emergency flashers on and kept looking back cautiously at the traffic behind her as fresh blasts of cold air struck and shook her vehicle with every passing.

"I lost a son about your age to drunk driving about a year ago. He was always asking for $10 dollars here and $20 dollars there. I just got used to giving him a few bucks now and then." She exclaimed, with fresh tears sparkling along the edges of her light green eyes.

I wasn't sure how she had guessed my age, as I hadn't given it to her. I suddenly wondered how much I looked like her son. Had she been thinking about him before seeing me along the side of the road?

"Please take this." She tried again.

Guilt had me feeling too stubborn to give in. I had too much pride, though Yoshua had told me back in Rutland to give in and allow people to help me when they offered.

"How about just $5 dollars? I can get myself a breakfast biscuit from McDonald's or somewhere..." I was saying before she suddenly yelled out, catching me off guard.

"Oh! I have some right here! I bought two too many because I never know what people at the office want." She exclaimed, giving me two sausage and egg biscuits with the $5 dollar bill pinned between both sandwiches.

"I would hug you for this. But I smell bad. I haven't showered in over a week, or washed my clothes." I said smiling from ear to ear.

"Please be safe out there. And look out for drivers." She said almost out of reflection. I waved, walking backward and took a hearty bite from one of the biscuits, smiling.

Fresh steam from the hot sandwich clashed with the cold air and hid my face if only momentarily from the tears of appreciation that came to my eyes.

The priest from Cheshire had been right. Blessings were coming, one after another and they were impossible to ignore.

—⁂—

Sleep hadn't been achieved very easily along the side of a highway. I had ended the day before on the 19th mile and chose Kennedy Park and a spot far enough in the tree line along Route 7 to remain undetected from other people.

However, trucks or motorcycles barreling by in the middle of the night made so much racket that I was beginning to dread my decision in making a bed there at all.

My phone was dying, and my backup external battery charger was starting to fade away as well. Pretty soon, I'd have no way to search for places to set up camp or towns, or even parks I could sit at to make myself food out of the dwindling supplies in my backpack. I needed to reach Great Barrington, so I got back onto Main Street south and cut a left onto Walker Street. From there I walked the Veterans Memorial Highway until branching off southwest towards the town of Lee.

I asked a few locals of the area if they knew of places to camp. Instead of answers, I got strange looks or indifferent shrugs as responses.

In the process, it turned out that I had also accidentally asked the wrong person. While walking through downtown, I came across a group of people standing around a bus stop just inside the parking lot to a gas station.

Seven people, all waiting to board, and here I was, stumbling up to each individual with their heads faced down into the screens of their phones. I asked each person I came up to if they knew of any good places in the area to stealth camp without being hassled by law enforcement or run off of private property.

The last guy I had asked was a bit brazen, and irritated in his response.

"How da fuck would I know where you can sleep? Do I look like I go traipsing through tha mutha fuckin' woods?" He replied angrily at me. He had been listening to music via his iPhone when he had shouted at me.

"All I did was ask a question," I replied with a dull expression. I was in no mood for an attitude, and I believed the bags under my eyes had said that loud and clear.

I couldn't grasp how asking such a simple question could've garnered such an angry response.

"Man, go bother someone else. Wit' yo homeless lookin' ass..." He said as he started rapping some lyrics to a song he was listening to out loud.

The people around me all looked up, no longer hypnotized by their phones. And funy enough, nobody said anything either as their eyes dropped back down to their screens.

I bit my lip and turned away.

"All ya mutha fucka's talkin' shit...ain't doin' shit. All you fake ass niggas slinging crack, ain't doin' dick..." the man had started rapping out loud as I walked off.

I knew he was singing loudly and obnoxiously to get at me. To laugh in my face, without offering the expression with which to do so.

"Hey, can I ask you something?" I said, turning slowly. A few of the other people standing at the shuttle stop looked back and forth between us both.

"What'd I do to you? All I did was ask a question." I asked the man with confusion.

The guy began laughing and shaking his head while singing his crude lyrics louder, after turning his back towards me.

I walked away with grand visions of his response. Imaginary images of the man swinging on me as I evaded his punch, and my counter-attack being that of a jab to his throat, that would have left him on his hands and knees, choking for air.

I was always a tough guy inside my own head, though.

Never in the real world.

My boots scraped across the sidewalk as I walked along with my hands in my pockets. My destination was Great Barrington, and the name alone stole the anger and frustration that had been in my mind minutes before, away.

I imagined a castle sitting atop a hill. Surrounded by massive walls and a city tucked at its feet. Rolling green hills and farm-scapes as far as the eye could see. Windmills idly turning in the light cool breeze.

"Great Barrington," I said out loud, letting my imagination take me away.

I crossed the road and found myself at a laundromat in the center of the town of Lee. I looked longingly at the detergents inside and relished in the smells of clean clothes.

I realized at that moment that I was staring in at others more fortunate than I. They were all doing something as mundane as waiting for their large piles of blankets, comforters, or wardrobes to be completed washing or drying. All so that they could fold them, place them in laundry baskets, and take them home.

I stood on the outside of glass windows, splintered and cracked with age. Lined with dead bugs of every variety that would make any entomologist go wild with excitement.

I stepped inside and glanced up at a news program talking about the Governmental Shut-Down that had taken place. The signal was weak, and the image was pixelated and going in and out.

"Ah, turn that shit off! Stupid politicians. They should all go to Hell!" an old man said, sporting a Vietnam Veteran baseball cap. He looked up at me, and I nodded with approval.

I sat down on the far side of the laundromat and unplugged a washer no one was using so that I could begin charging my phone.

It was almost dark, and I'd need to hurry and find a place to sleep.

A strip of the Appalachian Trail in New York, headed south across a boardwalk through a bog.

CHAPTER 9

A Winter Daisy

She had stayed in Lennox, camping in the woods just outside of the Immaculate Heart Seminary at Schermerhorn Park. There, she watched students and staff from a distance, walking in straight, orderly lines through the trees.

She wondered to herself if in some alternate universe, she could ever have found herself in that same line without the urge to by character; purposefully lag behind or step out of sequential order.

When her stomach suddenly growled with hunger, she instantaneously removed herself from reflection, to attain to more important matters.

After warming herself a packet of oatmeal that cold, frigid morning, and giving herself a wet wipe bath; she was packed and standing along Route 7 in mid-thigh-high shorts, sporting knee-high rainbow colored socks and hiking boots. On her torso, she wore a thick red and black flannel button up shirt two sizes too large for her frame. Beneath that, a dark green tank top.

Her backpack looked like something straight out of the 1970's, with a worn aluminum weathered frame, dully glinting in the morning sunshine. But she was convinced the rips, stains and stitched up scars gave the thing character.

Her short, bright red, pixie haircut was certainly what caught most people's attention that day as she stood along the side of that road. Upon closer inspection, the bridge of freckles that ran like glitter beneath both light brown eyes stole the show, when one came face to face with her.

She had spent twenty minutes with her thumb cocked up, as she walked backward down Route 7, towards Great Barrington.

Eyes darted this way and that, as people ignored her on their way to school, work, or while running their errands for the day.

However, when the white Ford F-150 had passed by, it had waited in the entryway to a strip mall just 20 feet up from her.

The man inside the truck appeared to be in his mid-fifties. She'd thought he had looked harmless enough upon first impressions.

Talking to him, he had smiled and wasn't overly curious as to why she was out and about on her own, or if she had anyone nearby looking for her. These types of questions had always thrown up red flags in the past when hitchhiking. Because if the potential hitch knew no one was looking for you, then there was the possibility you might not be *missed*.

"Where ya headed?" the man had asked her, leaning against the inside of the door to his driver's side window.

She had replied that she was looking to hitch to Great Barrington, and his features immediately faltered almost as if he had partly hoped she had been seeking to make it somewhere else, further down south.

She'd suspected nothing bad about the exchange all the same, as she placed her pack into the backseat cab and then took the passenger side front seat beside him.

"I have a daughter about your age. She's beautiful, but you. Well, you're just *incredible*. Lauren would hate me so much if she'd heard me say that." He had said out loud, just before chuckling lightheartedly about the statement.

The comment, while it had made her uncomfortable, hadn't completely struck her as a red flag yet. It was the sudden automatic locking of the truck's doors as they pulled out onto Route 7 and picked up speed that had brought a flinching fear into her heart suddenly.

The hitchhiker had replied that it was kind of him to say the comment though all the same, and she felt immediately, that it might have been the wrong response. That was because the driver quickly seemed to have become emboldened by the response, as he adjusted himself in his seat.

Silence ensued for a minute until he had decidedly draped his arm around her shoulder.

Keep calm, Daisy. Just keep calm she had tried to tell herself, as the man's face began to become a little redder in color. Almost as if he was blushing. She could remember seeing the capillary bunches on either sides of his nostrils as he looked over at her; and the deep pockets and pores that appeared in grotesque detail upon his bulbous, swollen nose.

"My wife works in Great Barrington..." he rattled on, but the hitchhiker had no interest in hearing the words he was speaking. Only because now, he had started massaging her neck without request, with a rough, calloused mitt.

She smiled nervously and tried to shrug his hand away, while shying even closer towards the door. The man had kept his grip, tight.

"I...I'm okay. My neck feels fine. But thank you." she explained with a nervous smile pulling up either sides of her pale lips into a false expression.

"Oh come now. I'm just trying to get you to relax a little." He had responded, driving just a bit recklessly with one hand while occasionally swerving.

"You should probably watch the road." She said, shrugging her shoulders again.

"I'm watching the *fucking* road." He replied, sharply and with such a sudden bite in tone it frightened her.

Now you need to panic, Daisy she told herself.

She kept quiet for a moment until the driver had noticed her reluctance to engage in any more conversation.

"I've been driving for years, honey. Don't worry about me. Just stop being so uptight. I'm not gonna hurt you." He tried to reassure her in a calmer voice. His grip tightened a little on the back of her neck.

His fingers started to dip beneath the back of her flannel shirt, and the tank top she'd had on underneath that.

"Please don't…" she had asked, with the last bit of patience exuding itself in her nervous response.

"Oh alright. I just thought your shoulders might've been tired from hauling that backpack around all day." He said as he removed his hand, only to relocate it atop her upper thigh.

"Well where would you like for me to massage you?" he had asked this time, as he applied light pressure with his fingers to her bare skin.

"I don't need a massage." She replied, grabbing his wrist and attempting to pull his hand away.

Only he held on.

"Come on, sweetie. Don't be such a bitch. I'm just trying to make you comfortable."

She looked down at his lap and noticed the man had an erection at that point.

"Pull over now!" She had replied, sternly. She tugged at his hand, but it had become glued to her upper thigh and was slowly finding its way deeper between her legs.

"PULL OVER THE FUCKING TRUCK!" she had then screamed, as she began beating on his arm with closed fists.

"Calm down!" he shouted, removing his hand immediately.

"I'm calling the poli`ce if you don't pull the fucking truck over!" she screamed at him, as her face turned hot and bright and her heart felt as if it was beating through her chest.

"Stupid slut." He growled, accelerating on the gas. The engine groaned like a monster, as he swerved a bit off of the road, but corrected his path back onto Route 7.

She had removed her phone and had started dialing 911 when the man had immediately slammed on the brakes, and the car behind him blared on his horn, narrowly missing plowing into the back of the truck.

"Get out, you fucking whore! I hope someone *does* pick you up and give you just what you deserve, you bitch." He'd said as she reached into the backseat and pulled her pack forward. As she was opening the door and trying to get out, he had shoved her—causing her to stumble forward into the ditch, face first with her backpack landing beside her.

The man peeled off and left her in a cloud of dust, as she screamed out obscenities after him.

As she got up from the ditch, checking the fresh cuts on her knees and legs; the man that had been in the car behind them had gotten out of his vehicle and asked if the woman was okay.

"That asshole was trying to touch me. I needed a ride to Great Barrington. I was hitching." She had replied.

"Want me to call the police? I think I can remember most of his license plate number if you want." The man had answered.

She had shaken her head from side to side, as she grabbed her things and climbed into his vehicle.

"I just need to make it to Great Barrington. That's all." She replied.

I had walked into Great Barrington that very morning, to find Daisy sitting outside of the post office—sipping soda from a large McDonald's cup and rooting through a package on her lap.

"Well, well, if it isn't the Cat." She had said, giving me a passing glance as she brushed aside the Styrofoam packing peanuts from the box.

She withdrew some Skull Candy earbuds.

"Nice. Let me see those." I said, sitting down on the bench beside her. She handed me the package and then offered me some of her soda, but I politely declined.

I felt like I was getting a cold of some sort and I wasn't looking to share it with anybody. I had blown my nose earlier in the day, and it had come out a thick, dark green color.

"Got a knife on you?" I asked after handing her the package back. She shook her head 'no' so I broke out my Leatherman multi-tool from my backpack and gave it to her.

"Geez. Take care of your blade much?" She asked sarcastically, unfurling the knife and pointing out the spots of rust on it.

I supposed it was true and that I could've done a better job. I never used it that much anyways during my 2013 hike, as much as I initially thought I would have.

"I won it online...from one of those scammy auction websites. Surprised it works at all." I said, rolling it back and forth between my hands after she'd cut open the plastic packaging to her new earphones, and had handed it back to me.

"Must not have been a scam then, huh?" She replied, shaking her cup again and slurping loudly at the last few drops of drink.

"I dunno," I replied more towards the ground.

Across the street, an old woman was jerking the leash to her Maltese who wouldn't stop sniffing the sides of a light post.

"So why are you stalking me again, Cat?" Daisy asked, working open the packaging from the cut she had made with my multi-tool. She grinned happily at the new earphones dangling in her hands.

"Jesus Christ, here we go again. I think the truth is, you WANT somebody to stalk you." I replied, rolling my eyes.

"If that were the case, I'd have let the old dude in the truck feel me up earlier this morning," she said, draping the earbuds around her neck and posing with her hands on either side of her face.

"Whatta ya think? Am I boo-tee-full?" she asked with a comedic voice.

"Sure. Oops, shouldn't say that, though. Wouldn't want to sound like a *stalker*." I stated with a sarcastic tone.

She smiled and began examining the earbuds again as if she'd barely heard me.

I wasn't sure what she had been talking about in regards to the "old dude in the truck" she had mentioned. She had stated it as if she had been fishing for me to ask about it. Finally, after a few minutes, I took the bait not nearly taking the comment too seriously in the process.

"Old dude in a car feeling you up, huh?" I asked with a forced chuckle. Moments later, I would immediately regret having chuckled at all, regardless of its sincerity.

"Yeah. It was just an unfortunate hitch." She replied.

"You're not kidding around..." I confirmed.

"Nope." She replied, putting the empty Skull candy packaging into the box it had come in.

"Oh God. I'm sorry. I thought you were just..." I replied, generally disgusted in myself before she cut me off.

"It happens." She shrugged.

I laughed in disbelief and awe. Was it normal to be THAT nonchalant about almost being sexually assaulted?

"So you're either trying to project yourself as a real badass, or you don't care you were molested by an old man. Help me understand this." I asked.

"I wasn't *molested* really. He just kept getting a little too touchy-feely."

Daisy then proceeded to tell me the events of what had happened to her, in great detail as anger and rage slowly started to build up within me. On some level, I'd felt as if I was supposed to have protected her and instead had failed, only now gaining knowledge of what had happened just hours before.

"Did you call the cops after you got away?" I asked. I felt that I was more pissed off about her story than she seemed to be.

She shrugged.

"Nah. I got away, so it's not a big deal. Besides the guy was gone and I didn't think to get his license plate number anyways because I didn't want to wait around for cops. I'm mostly mad about *these*," she said, gesturing at the fresh cuts on her knees and legs from where he had shoved her out of the truck and into the ditch.

I shook my head in disgust.

"What a piece of shit. So he was talking about his daughter while trying to feel you up in his car?" I asked with a disgusted expression.

"Yep." She replied, standing up and tossing her cup and empty packaging into a nearby trashcan.

"Well, I'm sorry that happened to you. I'm glad you're okay, though." I said with genuine concern.

She nodded, distant and detached.

"Anyways..." She said, without a further care in the world about the incident.

"You know, you don't have to pretend to be a tough guy to me all of the time. That would have definitely frazzled MY nerves if I'd have been in your shoes. I don't care if that makes me sound like a wuss either." I explained.

"Yeah well, it's not like I was raped and there's nothing we can do about it now. Besides, you've told me about your bad hitch in Vermont. It isn't gonna stop you from hitching it again, is it?" She asked.

"You could choose never to hitch again unless you had somebody with you. That could be an option if you wanted to be smart about it." I offered, more out of deflection to her question.

"Oh yeah? You trying to get me to give you permission to tag along like a lost puppy dog?" She asked with a smirk.

"I don't get you..." I muttered.

"You can drop the *male bravado heroics*, John. I can take care of myself and don't need another man to 'protect me'." She said, gesturing quotation marks in the air with the roll of her eyes.

I shook my head angrily.

"I'm sorry, I'm confused. In the handful of times we've met, have I tried *attacking* or *killing* you, or *throwing* myself on top of you? Because I can just ignore you the next time I see you if you want." I said in all seriousness.

She was laughing and putting her backpack on.

"Cat, you're too sensitive. I'm just fucking around with you. Calm down."

She started to walk away, and I didn't bother asking where she was going...nor did I follow her.

Childishly I began to think that she had some deep seated mental issues and wondered if she might've made the whole "Hitch from Hell" story up altogether.

However, as she walked away, I immediately felt guilt and fear for her despite her exclaiming she didn't need me to be concerned, or to protect her.

"Daisy wait,"

She turned and looked back at me, with a satisfied, sly grin upon her face.

"Yeah?"

She was resting her hand on her hip.

I sighed, and bit my bottom lip; withdrawing my pride to be stubborn and just walk away uncaring.

"Just...be safe," I replied.

It was evident to me at that moment that she was the type of woman you could never hold on to. Flighty, flaky, independent and impatient. But there was a draw about her that always had the dependent chasing after her, either for conversation, friendship or more as she brushed them away like bothersome flies.

It was frustrating, only because it was accepting the fact she didn't need you.

"Don't go crazy, and start thinking of your backpack as a real person. Okay?" she asked, with a chuckle.

"What? You mean Gregory? That dudes my best friend and hiking partner!" I replied playfully.

I glanced back at my backpack resting on the sidewalk and propped up against the bench.

Gregory tipped over suddenly and fell from a brief wind gust. The onset of that breeze couldn't have been more perfectly timed as if it was in some way; the only way the backpack could respond.

Daisy immediately burst into laughter, as did I.

"You're crazy John." She said, walking away as I smiled after her.

I went inside the Post Office and asked the clerk behind the counter if the package I had been expecting had arrived. He disappeared into the back and then returned empty handed.

"So, you may be looking for about a five-day wait from the last location you had the box forwarded from. It appears like you had this shipped from Hanover, New Hampshire?" he confirmed.

I sighed with my face in my hands.

"Yes," I replied glumly.

Five days? I wasn't looking to LIVE in Great Barrington. I wanted to get out of there that very day.

"Also you're looking at a cost as well, seeing as how they were transferred here. Based upon the weight, I'd estimate probably around sixteen to maybe twenty-six dollars." He said with an apathetic smile.

Well, it was official. I hated the US postal service.

However, I needed the resupply of food and my thyroid medication stashed inside the incoming package, so it was looking as if I was going to have to stick around town until its arrival.

I started to turn away, when another customer who had been shipping a present to her daughter, overheard my dilemma.

"It's not all that bad. At least you live here." She said to me, as I hefted my backpack to my shoulders.

"Actually, I don't. I live in North Carolina." I replied to her as I started walking away.

"I think he's hiking the Appalachian Trail..." the postal employee explained to the woman on my way out the door.

Outside, I was sitting on the steps and was tying my boot laces when the woman came out and saw me.

"My brother hiked that Appalachian Trail too. Sometime around 21 years ago." She explained proudly.

"Oh yeah? What'd he think of it?" I asked her.

"Well that was back in the day when the trail went mostly along roads for significant periods of time or hadn't properly been marked. Took him a long time to complete it. I think he was gone for a year, if I remember correctly. But he had also hitchhiked out to California too after he was done with the hiking part." The woman explained.

"It's been a great journey so far. If you'll excuse me though, I need to find somewhere to sleep before dark and I'm trying to avoid spending the money for a motel room." I said, as I started to stand.

The woman would go on to explain to me that she and her husband were headed back to Rochester, New York after having already spent two days in and around The Berkshires. They had booked their room at the Days Inn down the road for three days but had decided to leave after two because they had already missed the Harvest Show at the Berkshire Botanical Gardens.

"You should take our room for today since we're heading out. As long as I can trust you won't destroy it or steal anything since it was purchased under our name," she explained to me.

"Ma'am, I would have no way to hike down the AT with a flat screen television strapped to my back on top of the 60bs already there," I said with a smile.

Now normally, I would've declined this kind offer. But since the woman had already paid for the room and nobody would be using it that night, why let a free room go to waste?

I explored the downtown area later that evening, realizing immediately from window shopping, just how expensive everything was, and simultaneously how monetarily destitute I had become.

After a mountainous dinner of nachos for two, I felt like I could use something warm to drink, to help relieve the pressure within my sinuses from my worsening infection. As I approached the door to a place called Fuel Coffee, I saw Daisy going inside.

I promptly turned around and decided *against* coffee.

"Hey! Where ya goin' dude!" she called out to me.

I pivoted on my heel reluctantly and turned to face her again. She walked over towards me.

"What're you up to, Cat?" She asked, fishing out a cigarette from her pocket.

"I dunno. Bumming around town for a while. Maybe thinking of going further South tonight." I lied. Truthfully, I didn't even know why I had done it.

I think I was mostly just put off by the aggressive tough-girl attitude for some reason. Maybe I was even intimidated by it?

"You want to go get some coffee with me?" She asked.

I thought about the time I had invited her to Burger King back in Bennington, Vermont.

"I dunno. Meet me there around say...6:30. I may or may not show so don't expect anything. If I'm not there by then, I probably changed my mind." I said almost perfectly reciting the same reply she had given me back then.

She smirked, putting her cigarette out by crushing it with her boot on the sidewalk.

"Fair enough." She said, walking off.

I awoke, struggling to open my eyes. They had crusted over during the night almost as if I had been crying in my sleep. However, the burning sensation down the back of my throat and the throbbing headache that had accompanied the conjunctivitis, told me that I was getting a sinus infection or cold of some sort.

I stumbled blindly into the bathroom, stubbing my toe once against the bed along the way. Feeling around for towels and then the sink, I ran hot water onto the fabric and spent the next ten minutes wiping my eyes clear from the gunk.

As I looked at my reflection for a moment, I found myself taken back by the redness of my eyes. The ringing in my right ear started to intensify and my hands shook as I gripped the edge of the sink. I closed my fists and opened them again until the shaking had stopped.

Though I felt absolutely miserable, I was too intent on moving along south as quickly as possible and was determined not to let my illness hold me back from doing so.

That day, I would go on to slackpack 18.71 miles into Salisbury, Connecticut just so that I could say I had crossed the state line and been somewhat productive while awaiting for my packages to arrive.

A couple of days later after receiving my resupply, I was walking through Salisbury again on a rather cloudy, and windy day that would meld into an overall melancholy atmosphere.

Random drops of rain would fall for five minutes at a time, and then taper off into a light misting. Roads, heated from the sun grew blankets of fogs, and the world became just a little bit eerie and abandoned around me.

A lone plastic grocery bag flew across the street, becoming tangled at the base of a street lamp. Leaves lay plastered to the sidewalk as if a severe storm had just come through the day before.

As I traipsed through the downtown collection of closed or empty mom and pop shops, I saw a guy purchasing a piano in a store called "Prime Finds."

The store appeared to have had older knick-knack and antique type items, and furniture for sale inside. Indeed, nothing that I would need for my hike. However, I was certain that some of the items would have looked great back in the apartment I had abandoned so many months before back in North Carolina.

I walked up and down Main Street, looking for a rogue Wi-Fi signal that had momentarily appeared upon my phone. I'd been trying to use the recently discovered signal to find my way to a nearby drug store for medicine, to combat the inhuman sinus headache I'd been combating throughout the day. My forehead felt a lot like a balloon, on the verge of popping.

My eyes watered in the sharp cuts of wind, slashing at my face as I continued down the road.

The town was vacant and uninhabited that day, however I was certain that somebody would show up eventually, and at that time I would probably come to learn that I had stumbled miles and miles in the wrong direction. Way too late in the evening probably to do anything about it, at that.

Maybe I would sleep underneath a bridge that night? Maybe I would catch a squirrel or a rabbit for dinner, or simply eat out of my own backpack? Who knew?

Such was the unpredictable future set out before myself, and my knowing that anything could happen at any time.

Now as I stood in the middle of this strange town, all to my lonesome—I had already learned, that miracles could take place at any moment during the many months I had already been out along the AT.

And I would never find that to be truer, than at that very moment.

I had music playing away in my ears as I walked south to hopefully stumble across the Appalachian Trail again, wherever that might have been.

However, when a rather attractive woman in her early 40's pulled her Toyota Camry over in front of me, I found my forward progression was blocked. She was saying something inaudible and I couldn't understand her, over the music in my ears.

I slowly removed my earphones and looked down at her. With general concern in her eyes, I was put off by a look of nervousness and reproach in her expression.

Have I done something wrong? Why does she appear to be so scared of me? I thought to myself.

"Do you need anything? Are you hiking the trail? Can I give you a ride?" She asked all at once.

Well wasn't this a surprise?

Immediately, I thought back to the priest at Cheshire who had prayed for blessings to follow me home.

Then I thought of Yoshua, back in Rutland, Vermont who had told me to embrace the service of strangers, whenever it had been offered.

I smiled appreciatively.

The woman had a kindness in her brown eyes that struck me immediately. I tried to instantly tear my heart from my sleeve, and tuck it away in my pocket for another days use—but it had already been shot by Cupid's arrow.

It left me willing to fall into her arms, then and there almost instantly. And in doing so, something told me that she would comfort me, hold on to me and whisper while running her fingers through my hair that everything would be just fine.

But as I searched for the words to reply, those same dark brown orbs held a distant sorrow of some sort. And the wear of emotional pain haunted the lines of her pale face.

Abandon all reason I thought to myself suddenly.

Wherever it is she wants to take you, go.

I could look at her and almost immediately "feel" her personality.

I had believed that in life, you occasionally came across, or met people that you could just 'understand' with nothing more than a glance.

And it wasn't a "sexual" or a "love" thing necessarily. It became transcendent of those.

I looked at my closest friend Paul Horner, from back at home and felt it.

I felt it with Keven Kirsch while talking to him by the river back in Damascus...and I felt it with Woodstock, Wales and Steph as well.

Whether the feeling was reciprocated or not, I believed that I just understood these people through and through. I could read their faces, their mannerisms and almost tell myself a story about their life.

It was a *friendship trait*.

And I had immediately saw it there, in that stranger driving the Toyota Camry and currently blocking my path of travel.

"I appreciate the offer. But I'm just looking for a place to eat around here and maybe a safe patch of woods to sleep. I'm also in need of a pharmacy in the area if you could set me in the right direction. Is there anything like that nearby? Something *cheap*? Like around the Falls Village area?" I asked.

The woman scrunched her face apologetically.

"It's expensive *everywhere* around here. Falls Village will be much worse. I could take you to the McDonalds in Canaan if you wanted to go." She offered.

Upon second thought, I declined after thanking her all the same. Not because I was too proud to take the offer, but because I was looking to make mileage. When I explained this to her, she nodded her head in understanding.

"Well let me at least give you something for luck. I give these to all the hikers I come across." She explained. She stepped out of her car and opened her trunk.

"Do you need any supplies? I keep supplies for you guys on the trail. I've got trail mix and some denatured alcohol..." She went on.

"No thank you." I assured her.

"Well, I make jewelry...and I have my own store where I sell it. Do you know Dungeons & Dragons?" She asked, rooting around in the box in her trunk.

I shook my head as she glanced up at me.

"These are the die they use in the game. You can take this with you. Here, pick one out." She said, offering me a bag with multi-numbered dice in it. They had been drilled through, to be strung as charms on a necklace or bracelet.

I chose a black one with varying numbers.

"Thanks." I said, with a smile, while rolling it around in my hand.

"Well, are you sure you don't need anything? I feel awful that I couldn't do something more for you." She said in a sad tone, as she closed the trunk to her Camry.

I paused momentarily, as I held that die in my hand. There were lots of things I needed. I needed the sinus infection I had been suffering from, to go away.

I needed the wind to stop blowing and the cold gray skies to vanish above.

I wasn't suited for the weather and its biting wind; clothed in thin, ragged synthetic shirts and a half emptied down jacket that offered no warmth.

And I didn't have the money for better alternatives.

Most of all, as I looked past the woman and stared down that long empty road ahead; all I saw was the same routine.

Dead leaves whirled in tiny little breezes and skittered across empty sidewalks.

The bared trees hung over the road with their craggy, skeletal branches reaching down to snag something or somebody passing by.

Brown grass pushed up against medieval-looking stone churches with crenellation battlements at the parapets of the towers. They reminded me of "teeth".

I didn't want to go down that road that day.

I wasn't sure I EVER wanted to go down that path.

But I had to, and there was nothing this kind woman could have offered to better prepare me for it.

The woman in the Toyota Camry had called herself Sara. Before leaving me, she had directed me to a nearby grocery store named LeBonnes, where I had ordered myself a huge submarine sandwich. With it, I got a $.99 cent Arizona iced tea, a bag of Sun Chips and some sinus medication.

Afterwards, I walked a country road along vast green fields and pastures to my right, and farmland with bales of rolled and packaged hay sporadically spread about to my left. The sun was setting in the distance, and the cloud cover above began to spit down upon me very spontaneously.

The first two drops of rain I felt were only warning signs.

I took off my backpack and went through the tired ritual of pulling everything out in search for my poncho, when suddenly a car pulled over about 30 feet ahead of me with their emergency flashers on.

Sara, the woman I had met earlier in downtown Salisbury; got out of the driver's side of the car and ran around from the road to meet me.

"This is crazy! I was just telling my mother all about *you*. Where are you going?" She asked, with an unbelieving expression. I smiled immediately.

"Well, I believe I found a shortcut by Havermill Road, that'll take me to the Appalachian Trail five miles down." I explained.

"That road goes near my place! Would you like a ride? Or *anything*? Please let me help you. It's raining, and it's so cold out here." She said going over to the passenger's side of her car. She opened the door, and her mother poked her head out.

"Mom, this was the hiker I was telling you about!" Sara exclaimed excitedly, gesturing towards me. I suddenly felt like a celebrity, for no reason at all.

"Hello! Sara was telling me about your adventures." The mother exclaimed happily from her seat.

"She was?" I asked in surprise.

"Now that I've run into you a second time, you need to just come back with me. Get yourself a shower, launder your clothes, get warm and fed." Sara pled, while I shook my head in disbelief.

Was this really happening? Was it becoming common that people just randomly opened their homes to complete strangers on the road? What had been so special and comforting about me that this woman was suddenly willing to let me stay with her?"

"I...uh. But I gotta get walking..." I began in protest, immediately feeling guilty for having to dash her good intentions.

"Oh, that would be so wonderful! I'll get out the inflatable bed. We can have a couple of drinks as well!" Her mother chimed in suddenly.

"Listen..." Sara said, as she came over to me. She took both of my hands and led me towards her car.

"This wasn't just a coincidence, that I came upon you again. It's clearly a sign." She said, walking backward with me in tow to her car.

"A sign, huh?" I asked, following.

Abandon, all reason I thought to myself with a chuckle, as I climbed into her backseat.

Alcohol can have quite an effect on lowering your defenses. I felt so incredibly welcomed in Sara and her mother Natalie's home, that I wondered why I had even thought to protest in the first place. With the vodka flowing from bottle to cup so frequently—I had become a wealth of information.

They both had quite a bit to share with me as well, about their pasts.

Sara's mother, Natalie, was a professional artist who had painted for a living. She had sold her paintings to friends and neighbors as well as to the Bronx Zoo and different businesses or corporations over the years.

Natalie had painted over 2,000 pictures altogether in her lifetime, and she had a few stored in her home that they let me look through.

Sara, on the other hand, worked for Prime Finds, the store I had seen earlier in downtown with a man purchasing a piano inside. It was a non-profit organization that took in donations for a tax credit and then re-sold those donated items. The money benefited Prime Time House which was a place that offered choice, hope, and opportunities to people living with mental illness throughout Lichfield, County.

As the night went on, and conversations flowed into the early hours of morning—one night suddenly turned into two, that I would be staying. They had convinced me, and I didn't speak one word of protest as my head swam with intoxication.

I glanced over at Sara, who was staring at me while she puffed upon a cigarette.

Warmth spread throughout my insides so intensely; I thought that I had caught on fire. She smiled, and I felt *real*. I felt like I was a part of something. I felt like a friend and that I was somebody of worth. I believed that I could give her every last secret in my life, knowing she'd go to the grave with all of them.

When she offered for me to sit beside her, I clumsily stood and made my way to the couch. I almost fell on top of her, as laughter erupted from either of us at my stumbling feet.

At her side, her perfume was lavender and lilac body lotion, and the fragrance sunk deep into my nostrils. It eased and soothed the burning pain, and pressure just long enough for me to raise my lowered, shy gaze towards her eyes.

The attraction had been instantaneous once again.

I had lost touch with reality, having boozed up so much during the evening—something I hadn't done in a long time.

Her mother, Natalie was asking me something from far away, as I drifted into the warmth of Sara's body, beside mine.

Suddenly, I was being guided into the other room with vision too blurred to decipher anything. Sara brought me to the inflatable bed that she and her mother had both set up for me, as the sinus pressure inside my skull had become so intense, it was accompanied by nausea at that point. The world spun within the darkness of that room, and all I could think about were the things that Sara had told me about her life.

As my stomach rolled with the intolerance to the alcohol I had consumed—she approached in the middle of the night and knelt beside me.

Beside my bed.

Her hand spread warmth across my cheek.

She had come to hold me.

To comfort me and to selflessly soothe my emotional and mental strain. And it was there, that I writhed painfully within her arms, sick and fevered with a hurt like nothing I had ever felt before, intensified by the alcohol sitting on my stomach.

But she stayed by my side.

She held me, in that blurred and broken darkness.

Bathed in lavender and lilac.

Her fingertips, running through my hair like the dreams I'd thought of the instant I'd met her.

And as I leaned into her embrace, she assured me that everything would be just fine.

I awoke in Sara's bed, with her tucked comfortably within the crook of my arm.

It was morning, and outside, birds were chirping loud enough to have stirred me from my intoxicated slumber.

While my headache was gone, my sinuses had drained heavily throughout the night, leaving behind a sore throat for me to agonize through for the rest of the day.

I carefully snuck out from the bedroom and went to find a bathroom to use. When I had returned, Sara looked up at me sleepily, with a smile.

"How are you feeling?" she asked. She sat up, and the blankets that had been covering her, fell.

They exposed the tight spaghetti strapped shirt that had hugged her pale, thin frame.

She was clothed in nothing other than panties.

"I'm sorry..." I said, immediately covering my eyes.

She quickly pulled the blanket back up and clutched it to her chest.

"It's okay. Come over here, and lay back down." She offered.

I walked back in, quietly closing the door behind me and laid beside her. She returned to the crook of my arm.

"I'm sorry about last night. My only intent had been to hold you and let you know that you didn't have to feel alone." she said with her head against my chest.

I was quiet momentarily.

I watched a cobweb attached to her ceiling, waving back and forth as I thought over what she had said.

"We didn't....well. You *know*...did we?" I asked. She quickly responded "NO! No, we didn't do anything like that. We just....well... you kissed me." She replied.

Oh boy. I couldn't even remember *that* having occurred. Had I forced an intoxicated kiss on her?

No, idiot. If you'd done that, she wouldn't be laying against your chest right now I immediately, mentally assured myself.

Why did I always have to make everything awkward? Had *she* found it uncomfortable to be in the situation we were now in?

My mind was racing.

"Did....you...uh. Well, I don't know...*kiss back*?" I stuttered, feeling my face turn a dark red.

She laughed a little.

"Yes, I did." She replied looking up at me.

The ice wall between us had melted; as I returned a smile. It was just as nervous as hers was.

"I don't know...we drank sooooo much." She added, rubbing her hands across her tired eyes.

"Do you think, we enjoyed it?" I asked in a serious tone. Her brown eyes fell into mine, and a soft smile crossed her lips. I wondered how so quickly, my feelings of regret could fade away with only this quick gaze.

"Maybe we should try again?" She asked with a mischievous smile.

I leaned down, and slowly touched my mouth to hers.

As we laid in her bed, talking about our pasts—I exclaimed that I hadn't gone out in a while.

"What do you mean?" she asked, twirling her hair while looking up into my eyes.

"You should let me take you out on a date." I said, with a playful smile.

"Oh yeah?" She replied, with a meaningful expression.

"I'm too old for…" she began.

"You're perfect Sara. There's nothing wrong with you." I countered immediately before she could talk herself out of it. Her eyes looked worried only for a moment and I thought she meant to argue that point.

But then she smiled, giving in to my request.

"Okay."

So after a movie, I took her to eat at a Mexican restaurant because it had been ages since I'd had anything remotely as good as Chori Pollo to eat.

Afterward, she told me that she knew where the Appalachian Trail was and wanted to take me by it so I knew where I would be starting again in the days to come.

She drove to where the AT went along the Amesville Bridge. Had I decided to take the road, (which was my original plan) this is a part of the trail I might not have ever seen.

Sara explained that she had always driven over the bridge before the city had closed it off to vehicle traffic a year prior, just so that she could see the water passing by beneath her.

Jersey barriers now blocked the way, and somebody had spray painted in stencil "YOU SHALL NOT PASS!" upon them.

We parked, and walked across the bridge together, holding hands like teenagers.

Sara had never really walked on the Appalachian Trail before, though she explained to me that she had always wanted to try it. The farthest she had ever managed to make it was 20 feet.

"I'm scared of ticks." She stated in defense.

I gave her dull expression.

"What?" she protested.

I grinned, taking her hand and guiding her down towards the waterfall.

"I don't know if we can make that." She exclaimed, looking at the state of a side trail leading down.

"If you fall, I'll catch you." I promised, looking up at her.

She looked about with wonderment in her eyes. These places were right in her backyard, and she had never seen them before that day. Never ventured out into the wilderness that was so close to home.

The sunset came riding in like a flaming horse, leaving fiery tracks and burning clouds behind like the ones that had bore it.

As Sara stood watching the waterfall, shivering slightly, I wrapped my arms around her from behind.

"Do you want to go?" I asked her.

"Not yet." She replied, turning her head and touching her lips to mine.

I had explained that I had wanted to cook a special dinner for Sara, and her mother Natalie as payback for the week they had let me stay in their home—while I continued to slackpack the Appalachian Trail, south.

Sara had helped me accomplish my hike by picking me up at the end of the day after her work ended. She'd find me at whatever pre-planned road crossing I had made it to. The following morning on her way into work, she would then drop me where I had left off the day before, so that I could continue to make mileage and be productive while staying with her and her mother.

"I'm pretty sure; I'm like the best cook ever." I lied, while she smiled and replied kindly "I can believe it."

Sara placated me, while I bragged about my nonexistent cooking skills, and helped me to indulge in my own narcissism.

She drove me to the grocery store so that I could shop for the ingredients to a special meatloaf I made. I had planned to serve my great Feta cheese, spinach, olive and cherry tomato stuffed meatloaf for dinner.

While we shopped, it was fun to see how loosened up, young-at-heart and giddy Sara had become since my arrival. She had traded a sad and lonely demeanor for a rather vibrant and exuberant sense of personality instead. I wasn't so egotistical as to believe the change had ultimately come from interaction with me. This was who she was all on her own. She was kind, loyal and devoted and she was intelligent—on top of being physically stunning and attractive; all things she had been long before I had ever stepped into her life.

If I had shown her anything, I hoped that it was she was still, and always would be all of those things and she didn't need me or anyone else to prove that to her as long as she believed it herself.

Her sense of humor had returned, and we spent most of our time together, laughing and playfully flirting with each other.

While walking through the store, in search of olives, she consistently and incessantly grabbed my butt as I'd yelp out loud in surprise, and run away.

Tears of laughter spilled from her eyes from the expression on my face after she had practically VIOLATED ME in the grocery store in front of everybody.

As we walked out with supplies in tow, she exclaimed: "I'm sorry. I had to walk away. The expression on your face was priceless. I couldn't stop laughing." She said as a fresh round of laughs erupted from her.

I liked her.

I liked her a lot.

I laid awake as Lisa continued to sleep. It was our last night together and I felt the pit of regret and sadness sitting within my stomach, just as it had so many times before in my past.

I'd felt this way when Torry had left my side on the river in anger back in Virginia and again when Steph had left to finish the trail with her fellow Warrior Hikers. I felt it when Wales and I lost Woodstock, and I felt it a final time when I said goodbye to Wales as well in Bennington, Vermont.

But it went deeper than that.

I'd felt this same way, the very day I'd started out back in Greensboro, North Carolina as I stepped onto that train headed South to begin, what would ultimately be the best adventure I'd ever had in my life.

Life on the trail was and always would be riddled with "goodbyes." I had come to understand it, but it never made it easy to accept it all the same.

I gently pushed the hair lying across Sara's cheek, away from her face. I then gently kissed her forehead.

Sara adjusted minutely to my touch before drifting off into sleep again.

I had been a little bit cross with her earlier that day.

When I realized why I had, I explained it to her.

"I was supposed to have only stayed here *one day*, and that turned into seven. Now, I don't want to leave." I told her.

"But that doesn't explain why your tone of voice is elevated, John." She replied.

I had looked down at the bed at that moment. I didn't have to think of an answer.

"I think I'm irritated with the trail. I'm tired of always saying 'goodbye' to the people I meet and come to care about." I replied.

"What do you know? I'm happy for the first time in a while. Now I get to leave again." I went on.

"Isn't that great?" I asked. The sadness and sarcasm was prevalent in my tone.

"John..." Sara began.

"Sara, I'm sorry." I said.

We had held each other then, and her face felt hot against my shoulder.

"I just want to finish this trail. That's all I care about anymore." I added.

"Look at how far you've come. Everyone is gone, and you're still out here. And you forget the most important thing about your journey. The reason you came out here to begin with." She said, as she reached over to the nightstand and picked up the rock I had taken from the summit of Katahdin.

She held it out to me now.

"You're doing all of this, to make your parents proud. Bringing this stone back to them to show what you've accomplished out here." She said, giving it to me. I held the rock within the palm of my hand.

"You have nothing to be ashamed of, and you're nowhere near as weak as you always proclaim yourself to be."

Hours later, I was now looking at her, wondering what she was dreaming about.

I had 360 miles left before I reached Pine Grove Furnace, State Park. The halfway point, where I had walked to months before.

I was so close to being done.

I wondered if Sara and I would keep in touch. I wondered if we'd always be friends, or if this week was just a moment in time that fate had crossed our paths, and helped us in mutually healing our emotional, mental and physical gaps. We had shared so much with each other. We had laughed, and we had felt like kids again.

I knew I wouldn't forget her, or her mother, Natalie.

I couldn't.

The first shelter I would pass in those early hours of the morning would be a decrepit old shed built in 1942. It had been called the Wiley Shelter and was a warped, crumbling and plain ugly structure. Trash and old ruined or abandoned tent equipment lie strewn about the grounds.

It was a disgusting display of littering.

"What makes people do this shit?" I asked out loud, as I shook my head from side to side and continued on.

A couple of miles later, I came to a green-blazed trail that led to a kiosk with schedules of the Appalachian Trail Railroad Stop nailed into a tree. It mapped out various times and days you could reach Grand Central Station in Manhattan.

It was such a strange thing to know that you could just hop out of the woods and go into one of the biggest cities in the world by way of a two hour train ride.

Passing the kiosk, I followed an orange blazed trail which led me into the outskirts of a suburban neighborhood.

I had come out to Sprague Road which I took to 55.

As I walked like a trespasser through this suburban, plastic, cookie cutter, soccer mom's paradise—I received nothing but looks of ill intent, and fear or disgust.

"Hello!" A little girl that had to have been no more than five years old said cheerily to me, while shyly waving and smiling.

I waved back with a smile of my own.

"Hello!" I said.

Her mother was on the phone about 5 feet away however and suddenly turned into Mama Bear.

"Hold on Deborah. Kylee come here RIGHT NOW!" She shouted at her daughter.

I was probably 30 feet or more away, clear on the other side of the road.

Yet the utter look of disgust this woman had given me was actually painful. I mean, I generally was not only hurt and insulted by the indirect assumption that I was some creep, but I actually got angry about it.

Her mother jerked the little girl's arm, causing her to fall on the ground and cry. I wanted to say something as I stopped and looked at the parent with bewilderment and confusion. However, I quickly figured I'd just as soon have had the cops called on me if I said anything at all.

Besides, who would they have listened to? An out of state homeless bum that smelled like parmesan cheese and boiled eggs? Or a woman who could've doubled as Snookie from Jersey Shore?

All I had done was wave.

I had decided to take the train tracks.

I barged past the highway of crazed New York drivers speeding by like lunatics and weaving back and forth or off of the shoulder of the road altogether, as they played on their smartphones while driving.

I had made my decision just in time it seemed. I say that because as I climbed onto the railroad, I noticed the terrain around me had started to turn into a massive morass.

Tall stalks of feathery swamp vegetation at least 4 to 6 feet taller than I, hugged the tracks on both sides. It then opened up exposing grassy fields half submerged by black boggy waters.

Birds of some sort, maybe pheasants frightened by my presence; took off loudly like the rotary blades of a helicopter pumping into the skies above.

As I traversed the wooden and steel tracks, I came across deer parts strewn across the railroad tracks for as far as 100 yards.

That's when I finally picked up on something about where I was. I was suddenly more aware of the predicament I had placed myself in, after seeing the deer carcass.

There was nowhere for me to GO in the event a train came.

This bed of gravel that the tracks sat on sloped down into the swamp on either side of me.

If a train *did* suddenly barrel along, I either had to hop into the water and soak or lose my things, drown, die of hypothermia potentially, or I could take my chances as an undiscovered Superman and get hit by the train head on; hoping to survive.

Taking the tracks might have not been such a good idea after all.

So I began to pick up pace, jogging with a 60lb backpack bouncing back and forth behind me.

I started looking, scouring the left and right for an emergency jump off point but found nothing accommodating. For all I knew, this muck could suck me in like glue and end up killing me just as fast as the train that hit me could.

Up ahead, I believed I saw the ground on my left beginning to solidify.

The land was taking shape, and so I began to run faster. My heart was pumping loudly, as I jogged towards that safe haven in the distance.

So close.

So very close.

That's when I heard the train horn.

"It'll be okay! IT WILL ALL BE OKAY!" I shouted out loud with nervous laughter mixed in, to encourage myself. It was a weak attempt at calming any fears I had.

My foot caught the edge of a railroad spike, and I stumbled momentarily but quickly recovered.

"Maybe they have good brakes?" I said to myself, huffing and puffing along.

I glanced back and still couldn't see the approach of a train. But the horn was unmistakable. Something you've heard a thousand times before in your life, and you never forget it nor the rumbling of the machine as it tore down the tracks at Rail Road crossings.

As I finally approached what I had thought to be stable ground, it appeared that I had misjudged it from a distance. It was a combination of water and mud with peat moss on top of it and far from the grassy embankment I had thought it to be.

Who knew HOW deep I'd sink into that crud, or if I'd ever be able to get back out once diving in.

Suddenly there was another train horn blast to remind me that I wasn't out of the situation just yet.

I thought about the deer that had been caught on the tracks, and its body parts that were scattered down the rail. Had that poor animal been a victim of the same predicament I was now in?

As I ran, my left foot popped painfully. I stopped running, completely out of breath.

Maybe there was ANOTHER railroad nearby, and I was freaking out over nothing? I swallowed large gulps of air and wiped sweat from my eyes.

That's when I heard the unmistakable rumbling in the distance. Still, I couldn't put a direction on the noise, so I touched my hand to the track and felt it vibrating.

"I have to run..." I said in awe. However, I was terrified and remained motionless and hunched down there, watching the sand upon the tracks quivering.

"I HAVE TO RUN!" I shouted, finally getting my head back into the real world

I immediately started jogging again.

There WAS no other track.

THIS WAS IT!

I heard another horn blast, and I looked behind me.

Still nothing.

That's when I saw the MTA passenger train flying around the corner in front of me.

I looked to my left as I ran towards the rapidly approaching train. I heard the horn blare again, knowing the conductor had to have seen me at this point.

"GO! GO!" I screamed at myself.

The MTA Conductor held firm to its horn, failing to stop its speed whatsoever.

I was now coming up on a thicker patch of vegetation existing within the peat bog surprisingly enough. Tall strands of grass that looked like a mutant species of wheat.

The train was closing distance with me, and I could now see the facial features of the conductor with fear on his face. He was waving his arms as if he couldn't believe the idiot, potentially attempting suicide on his work shift.

I couldn't risk it.

The land was too far away, and the train would have hit me long before I'd reached it.

I jumped off of the railroad towards the vegetation, falling short of reaching my mark by 8 feet or more and landed on the side of my foot with my full weight. I had landed upon the descending rocks, and my ankles response to this was to reply its protest, with a popping sound, followed by extreme heat and blinding pain.

A burning fire tore up my calve as I cried out and rolled down the rock hill with my backpack weighing me backward. I was instantly pulled into the 2-inch deep swamp water, luckily, however, I wasn't sinking atop the vegetation.

I laid there on my side, hoping I wasn't noticeable down in the weeds. I then crawled into the bushes further out of sight feeling scared, stupid, and exhilarated all at the same.

I was able to stumble to my feet as the train passed by, and dusting myself off as I climbed the tracks again and watched the train disappear from sight.

I was wet...but I wasn't soaked.

More importantly, I was alive.

The Appalachian Trail Metro-North Railroad Station in Dutchess County, New York was a train stop that went straight to Grand Central Terminal in Midtown Manhattan.

Its creation came about from a suggestion made by a fellow hiking enthusiast that also served on the Metro-North Railroad Commuter Council. Its construction cost a mere $10,000 dollars and connected city dwellers to the wilderness by way of a 2-hour train ride northwest.

Imagine the freedom of stepping out of your Manhattan apartment with everything on your back, taking a train right to the Appalachian Trail, and then just hiking either North or South for as long as you wanted to go. The idea seemed romantic to me, as I walked by its platform and thought it all over.

When I got back onto the trail, I found I was now walking a boardwalk that had two handcrafted chairs about a third of the way down it. One faced South with an AT insignia above it that said "Georgia." The northernmost seat was identical and had "Maine" inscribed upon the surface of the wood.

It was here I sat in the middle of the swamp and ate a meatloaf sandwich left over from the goodbye dinner with Sara from a couple of days before. Bright red dragonflies landed on my shoulders and wrist, and I watched them curiously as they watched me, canting their heads from side to side.

The trail came out through farmland and fields populated by gray skies and air so thin that it felt hard to breath.

Down in the valleys, light misting glazed the surrounding vegetation as I walked along beneath the canopies of trees, midway through the loss of their leafy coats.

It wasn't long that the isolation and the emptiness of my surroundings got to me, so I began walking down along Dover Road, towards Route 55.

Along the way, I passed by houses that appeared to have seen better days. Siding had been ripped off of some, and others seemed to have four or five different restoration companies working to combat anything from plumbing problems, black mold issues or septic tank removals according to the ads on the sides of their trucks.

I stopped to look at the map on my phone to see if I could find a different route, and when I did, I suddenly heard a woman calling out to me.

"Where the hell do you think you're going?"

I was bewildered and wondered momentarily if I had accidentally trespassed down someone's privately owned road.

I looked around for a moment before the woman shouted: "Yeah, that's right. I'm talking to you!"

I saw her now, in a flowery purple dress draped across her bulging frame.

"Home," I said back to her. She stood in flip-flops upon her porch within a group of teenagers. They had a 24 case of Yuengling beers.

My absolute, *favorite* kind of beer.

"Where's home at?" she asked.

"North Carolina."

She laughed and waved me over as did the rest of the teenagers all drinking beers their selves. I guess the mother didn't care that they were underage drinking because she was the one handing them out.

She tossed me one, and I caught it against my chest in surprise.

"No really. Where are you headed?" She asked as I gulped down the beer she'd just given me.

"North Carolina." I repeated, before turning my head away to belch quietly and respectfully.

She burst into laughter.

"Well do you want a ride, Forrest Gump?" She asked.

"A ride?"

Could it have been that easy? To simply hop into a car and make this all end just like that? The thought seemed inconceivable when brought up again and again. Like something that was impossible and out of reach.

And it was at that moment, that I realized I was the one that made it that way by continuing along. I was proud of that, so I politely declined but thanked her all the same.

"No thank you. Appreciate it, but I'm walking." I replied.

"Well Forrest, I hope you make it home safely. Take two for the road, you crazy stranger." She said as I smiled appreciatively and packed the two beers into my backpack and continued along down Route 55.

As the weather began to worsen, I took shelter from the rain underneath a bridge and stole the opportunity to finish off one more beer.

As I looked up at the skies, I knew I wasn't going to be able to make it to the Morgan Stewart Shelter before dark.

"Gregory, this is just our luck isn't it dude?" I asked my backpack.

Gregory met me with silence as I nodded and replied: "You got that right."

My backpacks silence told me just what I needed to hear, which was to carry on.

"Ohhhhh, the life of a wanderer. Walking down these roads...not caring where I go..." I sang out loud, as I propped my hands behind my head and watched the water flowing by in the creek at my feet.

When the rain finally shut off, I continued for another three miles down Old Route 55 to where the new route 55 connected on the other side of somebody's property. I began scouting for a way to make it to the road past the guy putting together pieces on a push mower, and I knew it was his property I would have to run across without being seen.

While he was busy, I quickly dashed through woods to the highway on the other side of his home and kept walking northwest to where the AT crossed the road.

It had begun to rain again, and as a result, I could no longer stand to hike in wet clothes, on a 59-degree day.

I set up on the southern side of Whaley Lake Stream and ate a dinner that consisted of another meatloaf sandwich and a Yuengling beer.

The next day, I knew I was headed for Carmel, New York.

I was looking to cut off some mileage by walking straight for Peekskill via roads and highways or simply crossing people's fields and pastures.

I heard a train in the distance, but the tracks I walked had been abandoned long before my arrival. Some sections had even been disconnected in the event a rogue conductor tried to press his or her luck out of defiance.

Rain clouds bid me a good morning with sad smiles and cold, fat teardrops as I clomped along the asphalt on that gray, dreary day.

Dead or crushed night crawlers and earthworms along the edge of the road, bounced their working halves back and forth while trying to figure out how to move their bodies after having been crushed by passing cars.

Beautiful rock boulder fields skirted either sides of 292, and the landscape rolled into distinct but gentle slopes that looked like ripples in a maroon colored blanket that had been tossed across the landscape. Wisps of fog drifted in and out of reality, leaving only the chill of their presence in their wake.

I ran a dirty hand down my tired face and felt sharp granule fields of dried sweat, collected within the hollows of my eyes.

Huffs of breath came from my mouth, leaving collections of water droplets in my beard, as I shook my greasy unwashed hair from my face.

Thirteen miles wasn't bad at all, for having reached my destination at 10:20 A.M.

I already had my Wi-Fi turned on, upon reaching McDonald's and stole a booth all to my own.

I began to remove my cooking gear, old tarps, and wet clothes as well as other filthy, grimy gear. I was setting up shop in the corner of the dining room area as if I owned the place.

And truthfully, it hadn't been the best idea. That was because quite a few people appeared genuinely afraid of me by my appearance alone.

Strange, though, that as I soaked in the warmth of the fast food restaurant, I felt emboldened by the looks of fear and detest I had received. I charged my electronics and batteries, helping myself to the restroom to give myself a quick sink-shower.

After 6 hours of camping out—the staff obviously started questioning my presence.

I had only spent two or three dollars, I had washed myself to the best of my ability in their restroom, charged all of my electronics on *their* power and used their Wi-Fi and free heat to comfort myself. Once again, in return, all they'd received was three bucks of my money in exchange.

I had become used to these situations and knew that you could stave off management's disapproval by purchasing some crappy menu item for a dollar and then milking the hell out of eating it.

However, it was safe to assume that my six hours had entirely been spent up. Especially when the floor washers and bathroom cleaning staff couldn't differentiate my smell from the smell of a toilet recently used.

The following day, my overstayed welcome hadn't been very much appreciated by the staff anymore, nor my purposeful neglect towards their immature comments given to me.

"Well look who it is! One of the dregs of society...back to leech off of McDonald's free internet and power." The smart-mouthed Italian kid behind the counter exclaimed.

"Don't you have school today Lil' guy?" I asked, setting my backpack to the floor and propping it against the table to a booth.

"Teachers work day." He lied.

"I understand. Makes perfect sense why you're flipping burgers. Gotta get ready for the rest of your life, right? Three sausage biscuits, and no mouth please." I said, leaning on the counter. I ran my hands across my sleep deprived face, pushing my thumbs into the sockets of my eyes.

It had dropped below freezing during the night. I had awakened to find that one of my water bottles had burst open at some point during the early morning.

Luckily it had rolled out of my backpack when it had decided to do that, thus averting me the trouble of a soaked backpack and the contents within.

"Hey Tina, look. It's the FATTEST homeless guy you will ever meet." The Jersey Shore reject continued on, in front of his coworkers. The girl he'd been trying to impress with that comment, just smiled and walked by.

"Come on, COME ON! Enough about your mother already, you wanna ring me up or what?" I asked, annoyed and raising my voice in irritation. His friends and coworkers joined, in a round of laughter at his expense, snagging the attention of the manager standing further back in the kitchen, by the fryer.

"Everything okay out here?" I heard him ask a few employees as he came up to the counter.

The other employees were looking away, and shrugging their shoulders pretending they had heard nothing from our exchange.

As the manager came around the corner, he looked straight at me.

"Everything okay, sir?" He asked me, while eyeing the kid behind the cash register. I knew I could get him in a lot of trouble for the hard time he'd been giving me.

The kid looked blankly at the monitor with no response for me or anyone else.

"I'm fine. How about you? Everything okay with you?" I asked, giving him just a bit of an irritated tone.

"Just makin' sure you were getting your order."

"Oh yeah, this kid is great. He's doing a great job pushing buttons." I said, with a smirk. The Italian kid smirked back at the comment, knowing he couldn't reply the way he'd wanted to.

I waited for the manager to leave before I said to him: "Hey, I was just kidding about your mom."

He looked up and smiled at me.

"I know, asshole. Otherwise, I'd have knocked your ass out for that comment." He exclaimed more to the screen with a grin on his face than at me.

I laughed.

I took Route 6 for fourteen miles southwest towards Peekskill, New York. No soda bottles filled with urine were thrown at me that day. No free food or money had been offered that day either.

I was satisfied with the tradeoff.

It would be 4 P.M. when I reached Peekskill Landing Park to find myself dipping beneath the 300-mile mark. I was excited beyond words, because while one could say: *Three Hundred Miles is still a long way to walk in the grand scheme of things*—it wasn't all that bad when compared to 2,188 miles.

I took alleyways, and gang-signed graffiti filled railroad tunnels and backways to a sketchy park on the edge of the water. It was definitely the kind of place I would have suggested to friends or family to visit if they ever felt like being mugged or killed while visiting New York.

It was called the Annsville Preserve Park.

In the distance, you could make out the Indian Point Nuclear Station as you walked along the desolate, trash covered shoreline of the Hudson River.

On my way there, I came across two gentlemen standing outside of the Jan Peek House Homeless Shelter, on Old Pemart Avenue.

They eyed me like I was there to steal something from them or as if I had come to harm them for some reason.

Untrusting, disturbed glares, reserved for those you wanted to leave you alone or otherwise, bugger off and die somewhere.

They mean-mugged me with sickly yellow eyes and pale unwelcoming complexions.

I asked the only one who acknowledged me in response, about how I could reach Bear Bridge on foot and cross the Hudson River.

"Yer gonna have'ta take dah *Goat Trail*. Ya heer'ya me?"

"Understood sir. I won't bother you again," I said, immediately dismissing the guy as a lunatic.

Well, so much for any help or guidance I thought to myself, as I started to walk away.

"Ya not hearin' me pal. Dah *Goat Trail* is what we call's Route 6. You'se from heer'ya?" he called out to me.

I stopped and turned to face him.

"Why of course I'm from here! I'm from Harlem. The next city over." I lied, trying to seem like a local so he wouldn't view me as some helplessly lost tourist he could potentially take advantage of.

"Da fuck you'se talkin' bout? Harlem's like an hour south from heer'ya by car. Next town ovah ya say? Dat shits 40 miles away, buster." He said as if I was the biggest idiot in the world.

Well, I was winging it to be sure, and truthfully enough my lie hadn't really been thought out too well. It was my goal to refrain from appearing hopeless and without direction and instead I'd looked like a complete moron.

"Yeah, yeah. Ah'course." I said, gesturing my hands in the air quite fervently, and trying to mimic a New Yorkers accent suddenly, for some reason.

Okay, what the hell was that I immediately thought to myself out of shame. Was that really going to be my sad attempt at trying to fit in with the locals? That was the best I had?

Before I had sounded like I'd been dug up out of a tobacco field, straight from South Carolina; now I'd adopted a northern accent out of apprehension.

"You'se got da semi's comin' round dose corners at 80, 90 miles an hour, bub." The man told me.

"And dey drunk as *shit*," his partner chimed in.

"Yeah, you'se know how dose New Yorkah's are." I added in, with a nervous laugh.

They both stared at me in uncomfortable silences as I cleared my throat and writhed my hands nervously.

Step one: Never attempt to make a joke that bad again, you idiot I thought to myself immediately.

"No, we don't know 'how New Yorkers are'. Why don't you'se tell us?"

"Well, this sure was fun! Better get going!" I said, chuckling not because I found it funny, but because I was probably about to be shanked. I gave a weak wave as I started to walk away.

So it was going to be a dangerous walk. I got that much from the brief conversation.

The Goat Trail was my next destination regardless, and there was no way I could complete it that night. I was too tired, and it was already getting dark.

"I made it ova Bear Bridge once by that route on foot, but dat was by dah grace of God!" The homeless man shouted out to me suddenly.

I stopped and turned.

"People don't die while trying to walk it, do they?" I asked, abandoning the former accent I had been stupidly using to try and fit in. The guy thought about it for a second and then shook his head.

"So then how's it dangerous?" I asked.

"People are smart enough, not to *try*." He ended, chortling heartily. He clapped his buddy on the shoulder, and they both went inside the homeless shelter while I walked on with my head lowered, and a nervous pit sitting within my gut.

The sun had vanished, and dusk was rolling in. However, I had found a footpath that branched into two different directions. One way went up to Route 6 and the other continued underneath the bridge crossing towards a sewage treatment plant.

I climbed the rocky embankment to the top and sat beneath the structure as a strong gust of wind tore through the Hudson River Valley. Dust sprinkled down, as cars passed overhead and I removed my sleeping bag from my backpack; covering myself with it. There was no conceivable way that I was going to walk that dangerous road at night, just to increase my chance of being run over.

So I sat in an upright position with my head propped against a support beam beneath the bridge instead, praying for a couple of hours of sleep.

With a restless night, that even blocking off sound with earbuds failed to help relieve; I had spent most of the evening reading "A Walk in the Woods" by Bill Bryson, with my head lamp.

At dark; a police car drove into the Annsville Park with its floodlights scanning the darkness on both sides. I shut off my light, not wanting to draw attention to myself. The cop car then did a circle in the center of the park once, before leaving.

Luckily he hadn't seen me hiding beneath the bridge above him.

When he reached the entrance to the park, he got out of his car with a cup of coffee steaming heavily in his hand. He proceeded to smoke a cigarette in between long sips while leaning back against his vehicle and looking over the mouth of the Annsville Creek where it met with the Hudson. When the cigarette was gone, he locked up the entrance gate and drove away. It was very routine, much like this was always the start of his night shift when on patrol.

As the MTA train ran along the Metro-North Railroad across the water in the distance, I wondered if the cop ever dreamt of taking it to places far away.

I watched its bright lights and the silhouettes of the people inside passing by. Destined to places like Cold Springs, Breakneck Ridge and Poughkeepsie further up north.

Come morning, I moved back down the embankment to the park and made my way to a bench. I laid out with my arms around my backpack and wrapped within a tarp and my sleeping bag.

I curled into a fetal position for warmth.

I slept unbothered on that bench until a quarter before noon.

When I awoke, I was freezing, and the only reason I had even awakened at all had been due to my own shaking.

I sat up, dreary and with bloodshot eyes. My hair was wild, and my nose was running so badly that I had rubbed the flesh around the nostrils raw.

I spent the better part of 30 minutes coughing up dark phlegm from my lungs that had settled into them, while I had 'slept.'

I looked around at my surroundings. Beer bottles or cans littered the ground and by my feet, I saw an open condom wrapper with two used Jimmy sleeves to accompany it. Beside those items, was an uncapped, used syringe and a bent spoon where somebody with a heroin addiction had shot up and carelessly left their crap behind.

Suddenly, I didn't want to sleep on that bench anymore, and I needed to move if for no other reason, then for warmth.

So I began my hike up Route 9.

Dodging cars is not fun.

Dodging semi-trucks and standing about a foot away from certain death as they fly by is even LESS fun.

"The hell are you doing, moron?" a woman shouted at me, while laying on her horn.

"Get off the fucking road, ya idiot!" someone else yelled out at me.

"You wanna gimme a ride then, asshole?!" I shouted back.

There was nowhere TO get off of the road. Was I supposed to balance my fat ass across the guard rails with a 60lb pack on and hope I didn't go teeter-tottering to my death down the side of the cliff?

Once I had reached Bear Mountain Bridge, it was an oasis if only because I was completely done and could get off of the "Goat Trail".

Here, I got back onto the Appalachian Trail and crossed a bridge that had a history.

The Bear Mountain Suspension Bridge had been built in 1924.

At one time, it was the longest suspension bridge in the world and was only surpassed by Philadelphia's Benjamin Franklin Bridge, 19 months after it had been completed.

At the southern end of the crossing, a tollhouse for vehicles stood, charging eastbound traffic $1.50 to pass. I took a left before reaching it, down an embankment and entered a zoo, surprisingly enough.

For someone that had given up reading his AWOL 2012 Appalachian Trail guidebook regularly, in lieu of finding his own way south—this was one hell of a surprise. But sure enough, there were white blazes there to prove the AT's existence. I couldn't remember reading anything about the place in the guidebook, but it appeared you did indeed go through The Trailside Zoo.

I crept through the park quietly, almost as if I was trespassing. It was late, and the park was already getting ready to close as I traipsed through it, thirty to forty-five minutes after the gates were getting locked.

While following the paved AT path, I looked down at one point into a cage to see the only bear I had seen during the entire seven months I had been hiking from Georgia to Maine.

The brown bear gave a disinterested look as I waved excitedly at it.

"Hey, buddy! Hey, how are you doing?" I shouted enthusiastically while waving my hands wildly.

The brown bear gave me a pathetic look and then stood and faced its ass towards me— letting out a fart just before laying back down.

"Nice..." I muttered, with instant disappointment.

I climbed Bear Mountain, where the scenery was on fire with ruby red leaves, and scorched skies.

Dark and maroon colored foliage blanketed the earth and faded into the distances atop huge granite slabs and outcroppings leading to expansive seas of blood. The views showed off the incredible beauty and isolation of my surroundings.

As the sun set, I was walking through the night guided by a large pale orb above, cocking its one crooked and cratered eye upon me. The dark skies were clear from cloud cover, and stars were vibrant and exposed. The distant smell of burning wood drifted into my nostrils, as my boots crunched across twigs, and fallen branches in the darkness.

The silvery eyes of deer watched me traverse through the black night, strangely demonic and otherworldly in their silhouetted appearance.

However unbothered by my presence as they were, their eyes left me feeling unsettled and alone.

I was walking a trail that had gotten so much use; people had begun to make paths of their own in any and every direction. Sometimes the clear line of sight would be straight, by the overabundance of use—only for you to notice after many minutes of hiking downhill; you were only following an old stream bed or water runoff from past storms.

AWOL's guide hadn't been very helpful either. All it had stated was "Shelter .6 East."

"Well, thanks for that vague description, asshole," I muttered out loud. My words disappearing into airy wisps before my eyes.

"Now all I need to do is figure out where you meant that .6 mile starting point to begin."

I was scattered in the shadows, stumbling and pushing through bushes and shrubs and young trees after losing my way. Instead, guiding myself by digital compass, and a digital Map to the spot it said West Mountain Shelter existed.

After the labyrinth I had traipsed through to get there, I saw the silhouette of the shelters two chimney stacks by way of an incredible sea of electric lights in the distance beyond it.

I dropped my pack in awe and stood on top of the world looking down. It was one of the most beautiful sights I had ever seen on the trail.

There in the distance, I could make out the NYC Skyline. I could swear I even saw the Freedom Tower and it's blinking Aircraft Warning Lights at the very peak.

Like a permanent sunset, the light pollution created a never ending pink hue above Manhattan even in the middle of the night. And as I thought it over, it was one that would never go away. Making it forever impossible to see the stars from within the city.

It was a spectral, patterned, and viral patch of civilization surrounded by obsidian night within the horizontal oval, with which it sat, and it encapsulated all of my attention for the evening.

After collecting a menial amount of wood to last me for a couple of hours, I found a metal push broom stashed in the corner of the shelter and swept a spot up on the busted, splintered floor. I then laid out a tarp and placed my sleeping bag atop it. When I went to sleep later that evening, I wrapped the tarp about myself like a blanket to further shield myself from the cold.

I watched the flames hungrily eat away at the branches I'd stacked within the fireplace, while finishing two granola bars, washed down with a Pepsi.

I read the digital map on my phone and found that I was only 29.3 miles away from the New Jersey border.

I had the urge and drive again, to go off trail the following day and find my own way south by running downhill through the trees and shrubbery and isolation of places the paths didn't usually take you. Part of that had to do with wanting to walk into Tomkins Cove towards the east as well. This hunger to explore was ravenous, and after a bit of coughing, I laid back and laughed between labored, wet and ragged breathing throughout the night.

I fell asleep watching the distant lights of millions of people, twinkle in the darkness from miles and miles away.

While laboriously struggling for breath by way of drowning, mucus-filled lungs; I looked out of my scenic "front porch view."

Morning fog drifted idly into town, off of Stony Point Bay and down towards the south of Tomkins Cove.

With no electric lights to illuminate or guide, I felt as if I was viewing an entirely different world that morning.

The fire from the night before was nothing more than smoldering coals, but those coals made good hand warmers. After collecting a few clean stones in the area and tossing them into the fire pit, 15 minutes later—I carefully removed the now baked rocks and wiped the ash off as much as possible before they cooled. This had to be done carefully so as not to burn myself.

I placed the stones into my emergency water bottle after cutting off the top of it, allowing them to quickly bring the temperature of the frozen water inside, up to snuff just enough to toss in a pack of instant coffee.

I hovered over the finished product, breathing the steam into my infected sinuses and raw lungs.

This caused me to cough a great deal. Sickly, terminal sounding hacks that produced thick, green gobs of mucus. And the medicine I had purchased to combat it all, was too weak to be effective.

As I stood, sharp spikes of pain ricocheted from the bottoms of my feet and up my thighs.

It was 6:48 A.M. when I started walking; my head absolutely swimming along in the process.

I couldn't think straight. Everything hurt too bad to think at all.

The coughing intensified, as I started to heat up internally with the movement from my hike. It felt as if I had inhaled a brick right into the left main bronchus tube in my lungs.

My ankles cried in their usual agony, pleading with me to decrease my daily mileage or to stop altogether, but I failed to listen.

I hadn't listened since March 17th so why would I begin trying to hear them out now?

I ignored the hotspots that had rubbed my feet raw the day before. My right pinky toe had been bleeding rather profusely for a digit whose only fault was that of losing a toenail. But the blister that had formed beneath it had popped and began to become infected as well.

My left foot was no better.

A flap of skin had come loose from the increase in mileage I had been putting in across the top of the pinky toe as well which caused tugging, pulling and tearing of the flesh slightly.

I stumbled, zombie-like and in a complete trance with no direction down the mountain.

The trail had started going in strange directions. Weird images appeared on the blazes, and I felt my eyes blurring over as I tried to make sense of them.

"Take a breath…" I said to myself. I looked around at the downpour of leaf cover falling around me.

I was no longer on the trail at all. In fact, I had reset my vision to find I was in fact in the middle of nowhere and there were no blazes at all.

I tugged slightly at the straps to my backpack, though and smiled.

"Gregory, can't you do anything right? Look at you leading me in the wrong direction." I said, before chuckling. The laughter turned into a short series of wet coughs and ended with me spitting out more mucus from my lungs.

Trails could curve in strange and sometimes arc like patterns up a pointless stack of boulders; failing to even reach these minute summits before vanishing completely off of a ridge line. Maddeningly at times the images or paths I would follow led to a perfect road or trail that would turn in an opposite direction at some point; yet offer no blazes to tell you it was doing so before dead ending into nothing but more forest.

Often I was left scratching my head in confusion asking:

What was wrong with me?
  It was hot. That was it.
  Dizzyingly hot, and I needed to remove clothing. Yes, that was indeed the problem.

Outside, frost covered the entire world but inside I was on fire, and my forehead had become the surface of the sun.

I dropped my pack, with an apology to Gregory of course for so rudely doing so…and then propped my back against a tree trunk, where I then slid down to the earth.

As I sat there, I began another unexpected coughing fit that left a thick greenish hunk of phlegm clinging to my uvula. I couldn't cough it out, no matter how hard I tried. It was like glue.

I had to literally reach into my own mouth, grasping at this thick, slippery gob; all while nausea swam over me.

As a result, my gag reflex kicked in, and I dry heaved for several seconds until bile, bits of granola and instant coffee came up.

Down the back of my throat where the sinus cavity met my esophagus, it felt as if I had snorted a line of sulfuric acid.

Every hard swallow burned like fire. I had to keep moving though, because sitting there was doing nothing for me.

I found a white blaze with a red dot in the center at an intersection where the blue blazes just up and vanished for no reason at all.

I took one emboldened step off of the trail, and my right foot slid out from under me. The leaf cover and frost had made everything slippery.

Who needed snow? I could've thrown a sled down right there and potentially slid all the way into town.

So as I slipped down along the hill feet first, small softball sized stones and rocks were worked up and tumbling down along with me. My boots searched desperately to find something to grip as did my hands as the speed of my descent increased.

My soles eventually found a boulder about the size of a seat cushion jutting out from the rest of the hill, but my downward slide had picked up so much momentum that I hadn't been ready for the sudden stop. Both feet landed atop the boulder HARD, as both knees buckled under my weight as well as the weight of my backpack.

I had landed in an awkward hunched-over position forward, which I accidentally over corrected. I teetered forward trying to balance back... but Gregory's weight wouldn't hear it. When I began falling forward face first down the side of the hill towards the ravine below it wasn't initially fear that struck me. No visions of the life I'd had, flashed before my eyes.

It was funny, because while I should've been worried about breaking my neck or my collar bone or maybe even a few ribs, instead all that passed through my mind was: *Well, here we go AGAIN.*

I slid chest first across loose dirt and leaves as if I had become a human bobsled. As I neared the bottom, I managed to roll sideways on my descent and finish in an upright position on my butt. I sat there stupidly, surprised I had escaped with nothing more than a few scrapes and cuts—as a world of loose dirt and debris came tumbling into the rear of my pants from behind.

I threw my backpack off and looked down at Gregory with anger.

"You know this is *your* fault, right?" I asked the inanimate object housing all of the things I needed to survive out here.

Gregory didn't appear to be very receptive to my accusations. In fact, out of either anger (or gravity); the pack turned its back towards me after falling over, expressing quite a bit of disdain towards me for my blame.

It wasn't the backpack's fault completely, but I had to blame *something* other than taking responsibility for my own careless actions.

Above me, the wind picked up and leaves swirled around in tiny tornadoes before me. More leaves broke free from the boney, skeletal branches above and joined the dancing fiery reds and bright yellows of the Fall foliage.

I breathed in the delicious scent of their vegetation, wishing I could smell them; longing for it actually maybe out of nostalgia.

The rest of the day, I stuck to staying top ground and walking high ridges which connected to others and continued in a generally straight line towards the outskirts of Tomkins Cove. I had to maneuver between stately eastern pines, big tooth aspens and silver birches amongst other abundant tree types.

Seventeen miles later would bring me to the outskirts of Southfield, New York.

The World We Came to Find

I took up residence for the evening, hanging my hammock low to the ground within the state forest running along the side of the road. I stretched out my tarp across the top of my rainfly and proceeded to toss handfuls of leaves across it. Wet leaves that stuck almost as well as if they had been bonded with glue adhesives.

This had enabled me to blend in quite easily, to my quiet surroundings on a road that didn't see much traffic for the evening.

My original plans had called for a 15-mile day into Warwick, NY.

However, it would quickly become 17 miles because I had planned to stop at the Subway restaurant next to Highway 210, on the outskirts of Warwick at Greenwood Lake and get something to eat.

I ate while hiking.

I could've gotten back onto the AT there since I was close enough to it to do so. But I'd of had to go straight through the woods to yet another unguided adventure, and honestly, I was just too ill to suffer through sleeping out there or pushing myself that hard, all while navigationally lost.

I needed to get to Warwick.

I needed vitamins.

I was tired of the nauseous feeling I constantly had over me, from the consistent digestion of rancid, infected post-nasal drippings going down the back of my throat in a constant stream.

I coughed painfully, feeling my lungs tearing away with each one. My head was still warm, and my complexion had turned a pale white. The bags under my eyes were dark, and the stomach muscles had grown sore from the hacking that had taken place throughout the night and then that day.

I bummed around until dark at the Veterans Memorial Park, laboriously wheezing into the frigid evening air.

I found a bench, which I had made a home and my bed until 10 P.M. when a cop pulled into the park and awoke me.

"Hey. Get up!"

The voice seemed so distant, as my sticky eyelids peeled apart and then closed once again.

"You can't sleep here, get up!" the voice shouted again, only closer to me this time. I suddenly felt someone shaking my shoulder roughly.

I sat up quickly with my arms raised, not initially knowing it was a cop and struck his arms away from me in sudden fear.

"Hey, calm down, or I'm gonna have to bring you in. Got it? What's your name? Where are you from?"

The questions were coming too fast for me. The blinding illumination from the officer's flashlight, was crippling as it lit my haggard face. My hands were shaking, and the ringing in my ear was sudden, and piercing as I opened and closed my fists to stop the jerking vibrations.

"J...John. John Morris." I said with a rotten voice and a raw throat. I began a coughing fit that only caused my abdominal muscles to cry and ache in nausea-inducing pain.

"Gotta get outta here John. You from this area?"

"North Carolina." I replied, slowly climbing out of the warmth of my sleeping bag. It had dropped down to the low 30's that night, and the scarce amount of heat I had momentarily found within my bedroll was now gone, having been instantly stripped from me within the darkness. I stood freezing, and shivering in place as the cop scanned over me with his flashlight. He was featureless and intimidating to me because of it. I'd left my boots on, and shook dirt and debris out from the bag as I started to roll it and put it back into my backpack.

"You have a place to stay tonight?"

"No." I replied, not nearly showing that I cared.

Because I didn't. I felt dead and too exhausted to care.

I would just walk.

"Which direction you headed from here?"

"West." I said, zipping up my dri-down jacket. Feathers escaped freely into the air, via the many holes and tears the coat had sustained over the past seven months.

The officer's expression was finally discernible as my eyes adjusted to the darkness. His eyes were sympathetic, even more so once he had heard my cough.

"There's a homeless shelter I think in Middletown, New York. I can't drive you all the way there, but I can get you a few miles down the road if you'd like." He offered with sincerity in his tone.

"I'll be all right," I answered, slipping my backpack over one shoulder and walking away without another word.

I trudged on through the night, into Westtown and reached a Presbyterian Church there after 13 miles. I figured they might have been a bit more forgiving of a sick, homeless hiker should they come across my body the following day.

I cowboy camped in the rear-side of the church by a corner. Warm vent air from inside, escaped the side of the building from a small structural crack in the foundation. The air was mixed with dust and mildew, but the menial amount of heat coming out from the cracks made it tolerable. There, I curled into a fetal position for sleep atop a deflating air pad.

Wrapped in my rainfly, my tarp and my sleeping bag—I fell asleep, wheezing with each sickly breath.

My fever had broken during the night, which was the good news and the headache had tapered off as well.

"Ten miles to Port Jervis…" I whispered aloud in a hoarse voice to my backpack, Gregory.

I slung my pack over my shoulders and looked at the red robin that had awoken me from above, just minutes before. Chirping and occasionally hopping from the branch to the earth to peck at potential food before taking off again. Sunlight broke through the trees and shined upon my upturned face as the robin flew off and then out of sight.

It was welcomed warmth, even if only given to me for a moment.

And then I was walking again.

I limped painfully down Highway 1, headed towards Route 6.

I was out of water, and my dry throat screamed out in agony with every dry gulp of air I took.

I needed something to drink, and fast, wondering to myself about the many survivalists shows I had seen on the Discovery Channel—how people ever got the gall to drink their own urine. When did you meet that breaking point, and what illnesses where you looking at after having done so?

After a couple of miles, I came across an old woman standing outside in her front yard and spraying down a child's highchair with her hose.

The elder sprayed table attachments laid across the grass and glanced up at me with the most god-awful look of contempt when she saw my eyes watching that precious liquid seeping into the earth.

I stopped staring and started to walk towards her. Only as I did this, she began to retreat slowly back towards her house as if she was indirectly saying I hadn't been welcomed.

"Hello. I was wondering if I could refill my water bottles with your hose…if it weren't too much trouble." I asked kindly, taking off my toboggan and writhing it in shyly in my hands.

The old woman looked at me with profound insult and hatred. As if I had lashed out at her, called her names or even threatened her with physical harm. If looks could kill, I would have exploded into bits of fat and hair, and hiking rags the moment she had seen me.

"I don't have any money." She replied distrustfully.

I was confused momentarily by her response, mostly because I hadn't asked for any money. I had only just asked if I could have a little water.

I had to think it over for a moment, as bewilderment encapsulated my expression in whole.

"I...I didn't want any money ma'am. I was just..." I had begun before she cut me off.

"Then what do you want?" She asked, crabby and grumpy as if my presence had just ruined her entire day.

It took only a moment to realize I might have actually not really *wanted* any of her water after all. Not after the attitude, she had been giving me.

However, my dry mouth and arid esophagus said differently, so I tried again, a little more patiently.

"Water. Just to fill this bottle." I said, taking an empty liter sized Brisk Iced Tea bottle from my side and showing it to her.

"Mmm. No. I don't allow strangers in my house. Have a nice day." She replied turning away.

I was a bit shocked because I was certain I had openly requested it from her hose. The one in her hand and the one pouring out water all over her grass...soaking into the earth as she greedily walked back towards the spigot and shut it off.

Just a mouthful.

I sighed and bit my lip in anger. I started to continue down the road with rage overtaking my heart when suddenly another woman called out.

"Betty, let that young man get some water for Christs sakes! He looks like he's about to keel over!"

I looked up.

"Oh mind your business, Mary." Betty waved dismissively at her neighbor. She had been watching the entire exchange from her window.

Betty hung up the hose on the side of her house, gave me a slightly sympathetic look as if second-guessing her actions and then went inside.

"Son, come on over here. I'll give you something to drink. It's amazing when people call their selves Christians around here, isn't it? Hey, Betty, did you forget the passage: 'Let not those that seek refuge be turned away'?" Mary shouted at her.

"You make that one up?" Betty asked her angrily from inside her house, before adding: "I was getting him water the whole time, I was just going to find a cup to put it in!" She lied.

"Come on over here young man. I've got some soda you can have." Mary invited.

While this back and forth between the women transpired, I got the impression that they didn't really like each other. However, that was none of my business, and I kept my mouth shut. I was merely there to go in the direction of drink, no matter which woman was offering.

When I knocked on the door to Mary's house, she appeared before me in a motorized wheelchair.

I opened the screen door, and she handed me an enormous mug.

"Here you go honey." She exclaimed. I greedily gulped down every drop of cola in the giant Steelers beer mug, which could've doubled as a pitcher. It was so cold it had been on the verge of being a slushy. I got an immediate ice headache that I didn't mind, only because my inflamed sinuses were momentarily numbed within the effect that followed.

"Thank you so much." I said, gasping for air as I handed her the giant mug back.

"Where are you from, sweetheart?"

"North Carolina." I said, using my sleeve to wipe the left over cola from my mustache.

"You're a long way from home. What's that backpack for?"

"Gregory here?" I asked with a smile.

She immediately appeared confused.

"I quit my job, sold everything I owned and decided to walk from Georgia to Maine. I flipped once I'd reached Pine Grove Furnace State Park in Pennsylvania, north to Katahdin."

"Katah...din?" she asked, still appearing confused.

"Northern most terminus of the Appalachian Trail."

"Oh, okay. How long is that trail? From Pennsylvania to Maine?"

"Georgia..." I clarified again.

"Well, that's quite an accomplishment! So you're almost done now?" she asked.

"A little under 300 miles to go, actually." I replied

"My lord! How long have you been out here?" she asked me.

"Almost eight months now," I responded, nodding my head in disbelief myself.

Betty came on over with a small glass of water and a single ice cube in it.

She handed it to me almost as if she'd been pressured to do it at gun point. I thanked her all the same.

I proceeded to pour all but the ice cube into my liter bottle. It barely gave me a mouthful.

I handed her the toddlers-sized glass back and thanked her again as Mary chimed in: "Next time don't be so rude."

"It's fine. I promise." I added.

"Oh shut up, Mary. Go back inside." Betty snapped back angrily.

She was walking away with the glass, towards her home.

"This poor young man was practically decaying away, right on your front lawn and you couldn't be bothered to give him a drink of water!" Mary shouted at her. Betty was already back inside her home though, and had slammed her front door in response.

"Well, I hope you didn't get a bad impression of New Yorkers because of that stubborn old wretch next door." Mary offered with a sympathetic tone.

I laughed.

"Not at all. I appreciate everything and anything anybody does for me. Thank you so much for the drink." I assured her.

I started to walk away when she called out to me.

"What about your parents? What do they think of you being out here all alone?"

I looked back at her.

"They're scared for my safety like good parents are. But they're proud of me too. Which is all I really wanted out of this adventure."

Crossing Bear Mountain Bridge and looking back north at "The Goat Trail" (otherwise known as Route 6). Precariously cut into the mountain, the tight curves and lack of walking space makes this an ideal section to avoid road-walking if at all possible. Down at the base of the mountain along the Hudson River you can see the MTA Rail tracks.

CHAPTER 10

Delaware Water Gap

I HAD ARRIVED AT THE Days Inn at 2:28 P.M. and found myself only 4.4 miles from the Appalachian Trail. Port Jervis was a border town on the Pennsylvanian, New Jersey, and New York state lines. From where I stood, I was only 230 miles away from Pine Grove Furnace State Park and my finishing point.

But none of that mattered to me at that moment, because I had officially declared that my day in Port Jervis, would be one of rest.

I was exhausted, and my sinus infection had turned into an upper respiratory infection as well which overall, had me reeling and feeling rotten.

As I lay in my bed, I coughed wet, terminal sounding hacks into tissues and listened over the phone, to the menial funds I had remaining in my bank account.

"Only gonna get more tough, here on out Gregory," I said, looking down at my backpack.

With a little over three hundred dollars left to make it home on, I started planning my trip for the weeks ahead more carefully. I wanted to celebrate one last night before I gave it my all and finished the last couple hundred miles I had left.

Part of my celebration included my deciding on seeing a movie, for old times' sake now that my crew was gone. Something that Woodstock, Wales and I would have done anyways after splitting the cost of a room together.

As I looked down at the map displayed on my phone screen, I found that the nearest movie theater was more than 18 miles away, in a place called Middletown, New York.

There was no way I was going to walk there, so I started looking up bus routes to take me instead. The following morning, I snagged a seat on a Coach USA headed northeast.

Once there, I walked to the theater from the bus stop and watched a matinee viewing of a film called "Enders Game" with Harrison Ford in it and left with the intention of grabbing a meal and getting back onto the AT that very day.

"Let's see. Something quick and easy, like a sandwich..." I mumbled out loud to myself as I brought up a nearby deli location over my phone.

After grabbing a roast beef sandwich to go, I purchased my return ticket for the bus back south to Port Jervis and then stepped outside to wait for its arrival.

Outside, I propped Gregory up beside me as I looked at the trails which lay ahead in the days to come over my phone and thought with dismay how truly long, 200 miles appeared to be on a map.

Just reflect on this, though. If you walk twenty miles a day, you could be finished in a week and a half. I thought to myself optimistically.

It was kind of fun to imagine my eight-month journey being completed in as little as ten days. However, it also seemed very impractical.

To make that timeline, I would have had to push myself a lot harder than I already had been doing up to that point—and my blistered, bleeding feet didn't want to hear anything about twenty mile days.

I looked over at my backpack and smiled all the same. I was so close to home; I could taste it. Excitement traveled through me as I imagined a big welcoming party upon my arrival from friends and family and everyone that had followed my journey on Facebook.

Everyone who had read my words about my time out there on my own.

I imagined Melody being at that party, oddly enough and before long, I knew I was most definitely dreaming.

Because Melody is gone, and so is everything and everybody else I knew back at home I thought miserably to myself.

I wouldn't be returning as the same guy. Instead, I would be transformed, and different in a lot of ways.

And deep down, I wondered if anyone would recognize *me* because of that.

"These mutha' fuckin' Cracka's are all ova da place, bruh!"

I looked up from my guidebook, hearing the hate words spewing from someone's mouth and looked for the voices of the individual speaking them aloud.

"Hey man, that nigga was 'bout to piss himself, yo! I ain't seen a mutha fucka so scared!" another voice said, as the group of three crossed a nearby parking lot on their way towards the bus stop.

"A flour-bag looking bitch. Dat's all he was, fam. Dat's all he was."

I kept my head down, pretending not to listen. However, as the subject was on race and I was the same color that the three black males were talking about; it was a little hard to keep from prying.

"Mutha fucka's don't understand. Man, we grew up on tha streets! N-Y-C, baby. You see dose niggas out on 18th ain't fuckin' sweatin'. Cuz those mutha fuckas don't give a shit. Dey get they asses deported, and they come back a day later through the same damn hole they crawled out of!" One of the men ranted. He appeared to be the ringleader of the group.

He was a considerably tall black male, with dreadlocks halfway down his back. They were professionally woven, with different colored beads in some of them, representing the Rastafarian culture even though the man sporting them carried no accent of the sort.

Wales was a 6'5 giant, and the tallest person I had ever known. The man before me, however, appeared to be an inch or two taller than even him, and just a little more built in comparison as well.

"Dreads" as I called him, wore unlaced open-tongue baby-blue Timberland boots on his feet and sported old military style camo pants three sizes too large. On his torso, he wore a white wife beater beneath a thick, Arctic North Face coat.

"You got these crackas' pulling strings on everythin' we do. EVERYTHING, MAN! We don't got a black president, we've got good ol' Uncle Tom in office who's gets puppet'ed 'round by dese fools all day. What does Black America do about it? We watch BET all day, or another Tyler Perry movie and don't give a SHIT!" He shouted, while his two buddies agreed, nodded, laughed or said things to embolden him like: "You know that's right."

Other African-Americans within the vicinity began to tire of the man's racist rhetoric after a while. Or that's what I would have liked to have believed, as they passed sympathetic looks my way. Others just rolled their eyes or shook their heads while putting their earbuds in and cranking up the music on their phones or iPods.

"Did you know *this* guy," Dread's said, pointing down at me.

"Will always make 10 to 15 thousand more a year than you will? These mutha fuckas' jest don't know. And you know *his* ass ain't gonna feel sorry for you." He said, using me unwillingly as an example in his flawed design.

"They don't hire niggas. Plain and simple. White trash looks after white trash. Ain't no jobs out here for niggas. And they wonder why we slinging dope and hustlin' in the streets all day? You expect me to live on sixty dollars a day flipping burgers? Man get out!" He said with a violent anger hidden deep within his words. It was almost frightening to be there at that moment because I felt as if he could have exploded at any second on me, raining down blows.

"Actually, that deli down the road there is hiring. There's even a sign in the window." I said suddenly in response. I didn't even know why I had opened my big mouth because instantly, there was a hushed silence that grew over the area. I wasn't oblivious to it and immediately regretted having said anything at all.

Dreads turned to look down at me, with disguised rage behind his dark brown eyes.

"I uh…I just came from there." I stuttered, holding up the roast beef sandwich I had to show him as proof—if it all even mattered at that point.

I quickly looked down towards my feet, to appear and keep from looking as if I was challenging him.

It wasn't hard for me to believe that America still had its issues with racism on all sides of the front. I wholeheartedly agreed that black people were still treated unfairly to this very day. There are thousands of official statistics to prove this point beyond a doubt. But I also didn't believe that you fixed that problem by repeating the same cycle of hate and racism that was brought down on you—to others.

That wasn't how I believed you solved the problem.

Furthermore, while I might have ultimately been assuming things, I felt Dreads in particular may have utilized racial divide as a reason to separate himself from dealing with outcomes and circumstances he had created himself. To have a reason to be angry. Or possibly even a reason not to look for a job and call himself a "victim" rather than trying to stay strong and rise above.

"Tha fuck did you say?" He asked, laughing incredulously.

I looked up at him calmly. I then pointed down the street towards the deli I'd come from.

"I said, there's a job hiring."

He looked at me momentarily, as I took a bite of my roast beef sandwich and stared right back. I offered no sympathy within my eyes.

I wondered how things would have played out differently if Torry had been with me, or Woodstock and Wales.

Anyone actually, while I sat there in a town I knew nothing about—alone.

"Man scratch this dumb ass cracka, dude." His friend in light blue basketball sweats said, waving his hands dismissively at me.

His third friend in a black oversized Steelers jacket laughed out loud, while Dreads simply gave me this convoluted look of wonderment, almost as if he hadn't been used to being talked back to.

"Man, yo' expect me to find a job with the color of MY skin? You REALLY expect some bleach-boy mutha fuckas gonna hire MY black ass?" he asked.

"Well I'm going to assume by 'bleach-boy', you mean a 'white guy'. So when you go out into the world already tossing around racial slurs like that coupled with a mindset that says: *THIS WORLD OWES ME SOMETHING*; then no, probably not." I replied.

"Who tha fuck is THIS homeless ass nigga?" Basketball Threads scoffed. Dreads didn't like my response at all. And though he still had a look of amused wonderment upon his face, his eyes spoke of a growing violence within. I imagined his quick reflexes and the sinuous muscles of his arms grabbing me by the throat and choking me out right there on the spot.

"WHAT COLOR IS MY SKIN, DUDE? Look at my arm. WHAT FUCKIN' COLOR IS MY SKIN?!" He shouted angrily, slapping his forearm and shoving it into my face. I winced and withdrew back against the wall. But I had nowhere to retreat to and instead—clenched up, waiting to be hit.

He was hovering over me, shouting in a rather intimidating manner.

"I'd say a creamy...coffee looking color." I replied. I took another cautious bite of my sandwich while he and his friends laughed.

He stood back with his hand over his mouth...jumping and laughing excitedly while shouting: "No this bitch didn't. Oh, mah gawd... no this guy didn't!"

The taste of the meat from the bite I'd taken of sandwich in my mouth, soured. Maybe because it had turned, or maybe because of the adrenaline and fear coursing through me at that moment. All the same, the flavor had changed, and as I looked down at my half eaten sandwich, I realized I couldn't eat any more of it.

It was disheartening, considering how much I had paid for it.

"How about you go FIND ME A JOB...white boy. It's so easy. Go out there and find me a job. Go on BOY!" He shouted getting up within my comfort zone.

I didn't immediately reply because I was opening my sandwich and looking at its contents in disgust. I suppose that what Dreads did next was solely out of anger and the appearance I gave off by dismissing him.

He smacked my sandwich out of my hand to the ground, where it flew apart into broken chunks.

"GET UP, *BITCH*! I SAID GO FIND ME A JOB!" He shouted angrily down at me. This time he'd grabbed me by the front of my shirt and was shouting. I flinched and closed my eyes, pulling my head back against the wall in fear.

"Whatchoo gonna do? Huh? Do something nigga. Do something, you trick ass wonder bread lookin' bitch." He said as he let go, and his friends erupted into a flood of laughter.

In truth, I didn't miss the sandwich anyhow.

I stood up slowly, and his friends came in close, ready to pounce on me at a moment's notice if something physical erupted between their leader and me.

Dreads was a lot taller than I.

I began to measure the three of them up as I stood there, afraid. The male in the black oversized Steelers coat was short and fat and didn't appear to be much of a threat. Basket Ball Sweats was about my height and skinny, lanky even, and he looked about 19 or 20 years old. Dreads curled his head, pressing against me with his chest as if he dared me to move.

"That was my sandwich..." I said, sadly.

"Fuck yo' sandwich!" Dreads shouted as I flinched again.

"I mean, it tasted bad...don't get me wrong. But what pisses me off is, what if I was going to finish it? What if that had been all I had to eat?" I asked, almost trying to rationalize with him.

"What you gonna do? Huh? You gonna gimme me a kiss, *faggot*?" He asked, coming in face to face with me. I knew now that Dreads wasn't looking to resolve or talk out his anger. He was seeking to get it out of him physically, and I was the perfect person to take his rage out on.

Alone, looking homeless and with no friends to support me or back me up I was already at a disadvantage.

My complexion was the sole "definition" he needed to justify hurting me. I was every racist white male that had done anything to him or friends and family in the past. I had denied any loan he had wanted and any purchase because of credit. I was every white officer that had pulled him over to check his I.D. for warrants.

I existed to him as everything he believed to be wrong with his life, his home, his country.

"Please let me get by," I said, as I made to push past him.

"Let me prove I can get you a job. If I'm wrong, you win this argument. Okay? Do we have a deal?" I offered.

"You ain't gonna get me no job, nigga. You'se all talk..."

I looked him dead in his eyes with nothing but seriousness laden in them.

"Let me try..."

He laughed and stood back; waving his arm and granting me permission to leave.

"Pussy-ass, bitch. Nigga says: 'They're hiring across the street'," he mocked, imitating a nerds voice that was supposed to have been *me*. The three of them erupted into laughter at his comment.

"Forget your Fanny pack?" He called out to me, kicking my backpack around on the ground.

I had everything of real value on me anyways. Most importantly my money and both my phones. I wasn't bothered by them kicking around my pack. However, I stopped and turned all the same.

I remembered my camera was still in the side pocket along with all the pictures and video I'd taken of my eight months out there on the Appalachian Trail.

But the most important thing of all was the rock I'd taken from the summit of Katahdin for my mother and father. The sole reason, and mission in still being out there. Some misguided sense of "pride" I sought out, to feel included and prove my worth to the rest of the world.

If you go back and try to take that rock that they don't know holds any real meaning to you, they will take it away and toss it over a bridge somewhere I thought to myself quickly.

Don't be stupid. Don't let them know how much that stone means to you.

I took a deep breath and turned, walking back towards the deli I had bought the roast beef sandwich from fifteen minutes before.

The black woman behind the counter looked up at me as the bell above the door rang with my entry. A smile crossed her face.

"You're back rather quickly." She said with a laugh.

"Yeah, I was just curious about something," I said, nervously writhing my hands together.

"But I guess you kinda already answered it," I explained with a timid laugh.

She gave me a confused look.

"What do you mean?" She asked.

"You guys are hiring, right? Could I get an application?" I asked hurriedly.

"Yeah, sure." She said, reaching and bringing up the form from beneath the counter.

"Could I fill out an application here if I was, say…*black*?" I asked.

She gave an odd expression of confusion, unsure of my angle. It was too bad she hadn't been aware of the situation that was brewing at the bus stop outside.

"*I'm black*, aren't I?" she responded, with suspicion in her tone.

"The guy over there out the window, the tall one with the dreads on his head said that he couldn't get a job because white people won't hire him. I was trying to prove him wrong."

"Oh, okay. Seriously, forget that dude. He's stupid. And if you're bringing an application to him, then no. Cause he has an attitude problem. Always comes in here wit' his dumb ass friends, trying to flirt with me and demanding extra meat and cheese on sandwiches and doesn't expect to pay extra for it." She said, withdrawing the application and slipping it back beneath the counter.

I sighed, knowing that wasn't the answer I'd been looking for at all.

"He and those guys are always showing boatin'. They always end up screaming at the manager back and forth. He usually tells them to get out." She went on.

I looked back outside at the three of them. It wasn't the point I had been trying to make at all. Had I'd known he'd already created a bad reputation for himself in town, I wouldn't have bothered at all. It had solely been my intention to grab an application and bring it back to the three of them. To show 'Dreads' his whole: "I'm a Victim, and the World Hates Me" act was just that.

An act and a poor excuse to dodge responsibility and consequence.

I walked back out of that deli empty handed with my head hanging.

"Yo nigga, you get me that job?" He asked; as his friends were chortling like hyenas beside him.

I ignored him, as I made for my backpack that they had stuffed into the garbage can during my absence.

"HEY BOY! YOU GONNA ANSWER ME?" He asked, shoving my shoulder aside.

"Don't touch me."

I reached for my backpack again, and he smacked my hand away.

"What'choo gonna do? Huh?" He asked. Shoving me hard enough to cause me to stumble.

I turned to him as my face flushed red with anger. Defiant, yet still too much of a coward to do anything about it, other than facially express my detest.

"You jest a big 'ol pussy, aren't ya?" He began in a low whisper. His two friends were crowding nearby now.

I felt humiliated.

Meanwhile, everybody else; the other bus riders, went on with their lives, pretending they weren't watching what was going on. Acting as if they hadn't heard any of the exchanges taking place.

I reached out again, and this time he smacked my face hard. I looked down in shame, with the fresh sting still tingling upon my skin.

"Do something, man. You just gonna let me smack you around? A grown ass man like you? J'est gonna take it?" he asked, smacking the back of my head hard while his friends laughed at my cowardice.

I reached for my backpack again, only to be shoved away by Basketball Sweats this time.

I looked to the others around me at that bus stop, for help again. The other riders who stared like zombies down at their phones. Acting like they were unaware of what was taking place.

But they were aware.

Only they wanted no part in my problems.

Nobody stepped up for me.

Nobody backed me, because nobody cared.

What are you going to do John Torry's voice suddenly called out to me in my mind.

What are you going to do when I'm no longer here to fight your battles for you? He had shouted at me back on the Appalachian Trail, long before he had finally left my side for good.

My teeth clenched and quivered with fear, along with my closed fists. I took a deep breath, and let my thoughts flood out.

"You want to know why you can't get a job? It's not because of 'evil white people.' It's because you grew up thinking the world owed you something."

"YOU DAMN RIGHT THEY OWED ME SOMETHING! FOUR HUNDRED YEARS OF SLAVERY MUTHA FUCKA! THAT'S WHAT THEY OWED ME!" He shouted back into my face.

"You were never a slave. Your parents weren't slaves, and neither were your grandparents. You want to be babied and catered to for the rest of your life because of what your ANCESTORS went through, and that's fine. Don't grow up and don't be a man. Because it's clear you're too lazy to TRY or WORK for the American dream." I said, feeling the anger within me burning like a wildfire.

My response caused the other people at the bus stop to look up at me from their phone screens.

"Aw, WAHHHHH. So you went to apply for a job and got turned down. Guess what asshole? So do thousands of other black people every day and white people and Latino people. But you seem to think you're 'King Shit' and your problem is not only race specific, but because ALL WHITE PEOPLE SINGULARLY HATE YOU. But it doesn't take long, just hearing you run your big fat mouth to see the only reason you can't get a job is because of your own racist outlook on life. How do you think we change the world? Fix racism? By repeating the same cycle over and over again? Retaliation? Or by *understanding* WHY the cycle never ends?" I asked.

"Bitch, what do you know? Your white-privileged ass never had to *fight* for a job." He replied as if he had been there, to see my entire life unfold before his eyes.

If only he had known the truth.

I was a high school dropout who's best paying job had been as nothing more than a security guard. Whatever had been at my fingertips because of the color of my skin, remained oblivious to me as it had my whole life that I had scratched, clawed and scrounged to get by monetarily.

My lack of education and the chances that I had squandered didn't have a skin color. Nor did it have a *race*, when I applied and failed for jobs, I had no college degree for.

I had metaphorically walked out of that same door he had, jobless with my head held in shame. Only I didn't have a "race card" to play and blame for it because being white, should have been all I needed to have succeeded in life.

"You know what? You're right. You win. I'm done arguing with a dummy. You apparently feel you know a lot more than I ever will." I said reaching for my backpack. As far as I was concerned at that moment, Dreads could live in his messed up reality making excuses for why he did what he did and how he lived the way he had.

Because unfortunately in this country—selling drugs got you more money, a lot quicker and far more easily than working some minimum wage paying job all day at McDonald's, or at a deli making sandwiches. And because blaming someone *else* was always an easier pill to swallow than taking responsibility for your actions or lack thereof in life.

"Who you calling a dummy?" He said shoving me again.

I was done playing scared all of the time and worrying about the consequences.

Being shit on.

Told not to express myself or who I was and to not have an opinion.

I didn't WANT to be there anymore.

I didn't WANT to be in Port Jervis.

I didn't want to be in New York or New Jersey...and I no longer wanted to be on the trail.

And if that made me a coward, or a chicken shit then so be it.

I would be the first to laugh at the feathers growing on my back.

But what I wasn't going to do, was to stand there at 30 years of age, be insulted because of the color of my skin, have my things thrown in the trash and then be physically assaulted without defending myself.

Without standing up for myself now that I no longer had Torry to fight my battles for me. Or Woodstock's car to drive away from the situation.

In that backpack, was my whole entire life.

Everything I owned.

In the waist belt was the rock I'd gotten for my father all of the way back at Katahdin.

My thyroid medication was in there as well as my clothes, my food and the things I needed to survive.

Suddenly, this man wasn't just taking away material objects.

He was taking away my life, and I'd gone too far, to give that up now.

"Here man. I was jest playin'. Take it." He said, standing back.

I reached for my things again, and he shoved me back against the wall, saying in a sports announcers tone: "Get'cho ass back!"

His friends barreled over with laughter, apparently finding their leader to be the funniest man they'd ever known in their lives.

"You's a stupid ass...nig-" was all he managed to get out.

An incredible rush of adrenaline filled me, sparked and grew into an explosion—and I swung on him as hard as I could, without thinking.

Without feeling anything other than pure rage.

My fist, or maybe I should say more so the SIDE of my balled up fist connected with his cheek.

I wasn't a boxer.

I knew I couldn't fight, either. I hadn't been in a physical altercation since high school, and even back then I was frequently getting my ass kicked.

I simply threw a wild punch at that moment. A haymaker; which hit hard enough to cause Dreads to stumble back for a second, but to ultimately do nothing more than anger and insult him.

His basketball sweats-clad friend was on me in seconds. He had thrown his weight into me, catching me off guard and shoving me up against the building.

There, the back of my head snapped back and bounced off of the brick wall. He was throwing fast punches into my midsection, almost as if his life depended on it. Each blow tearing with more ferocity into me than the one before it. I tried to tighten my abdominal muscles to better take the hits but coughed out in pain as air seemingly escaped my lungs from the attack.

There was no way I was going to match the guy hit for hit...so I grabbed his sweater at the shoulders and shoved forward with my foot jutting behind his.

He sprawled backward onto his ass, while the third guy in the black Steelers jacket was trying to hold back his friend Dreads.

"Yo, you don't want your parole officer to find out 'bout this shit! Yo chill, dawg! Chill!" He shouted. He had wrapped both arms around Dreads waist and was dead weighting him in place.

"Imma fucking kill yo' bitch ass!" Dreads screamed out at me in rage. There was enough fury within him exuding out at that moment, that if I had let it cause me to second guess my decision at the time—things would've turned out a lot worse for me.

"Yo' chill dude!" Steelers' jacket shouted at him.

"I'm calling the police if you don't all stop it right now!" An older black woman cried, but she was only a millisecond of distraction. Others at the bus stop were now shouting out in protest at what was taking place as well.

Stop it!

Calm down people!

Guys, just separate!

Where had they been before? Suddenly becoming good Samaritans now that everything had boiled over.

We heard their words but paid no heed to them.

"Hear that? You'll be going *back* to JAIL you racist piece of shit!" I shouted angrily at Dreads, holding my stomach in pain while hunched over, still gasping for air.

Dreads had about a second before he broke free from his buddies grasp and I knew I couldn't take him toe to toe. I was already hurting, and Basketball Sweats was getting up to his feet now.

Dreads grabbed both of his friend's wrists, which were locked around his waist and started to wear the strength within his grip.

"Don't man...just...chill..." the man in the Steelers jacket pled to Dreads, struggling against his strength.

I didn't know what to do.

Dreads broke free from his buddies grasp, coming for me, so I charged him.

I shoulder rammed my full weight into his stomach and buried myself into his gut as hard as humanly possible. His feet left the cement momentarily as he was suspended in the air, while we both trampled the guy in the Steelers sports jacket that had been trying to hold him back, beneath our feet.

I grabbed on to Basketball Sweats shirt in the downfall, as the three of us, tumbled out into the street.

As we went down, a car driving by jammed on the brakes and screeched to a halt about ten feet from where the fight was taking place, bearing down on the horn in the process.

Dreads had a tight hold around my head after I had charged into him and we had all hit the asphalt. He had managed to use my own attack against me, by smashing the left side of my face into the road. He repeatedly slammed my head down, face first into the blacktop as I fought to keep my head from striking so hard.

I felt him beating rapidly on the back of my skull and upper back with one fist while he held me locked down with my head beneath his right arm.

I was able to pull myself free in the struggle, by prying his grip off from around my neck and feeling various places in my spine pop from struggling to do so. I raised my left fist in an attempt to rain down punches upon him as he drew up his knees and held up his hands; ready to deflect any attack I sent his way.

Only instead, and before I could land a single punch, Basketball Sweats had gotten up and grabbed my raised arm, pulling me backward. He had also wrapped his other arm around my throat from behind.

Cutting off my air supply.

I struggled violently, feeling my eyes bulging and capillaries bursting within the whites of my eyes, as he squeezed with all of his might and I felt my world wavering.

My vision began to blur, and I felt the heat of my blood radiating like lava, and beating with a struggling pulse inside my exploding skull.

"Gonna kill yo' mutha fuckin' ass." He whispered between clenched teeth as his grip tightened. I kicked wildly and without direction into the air, and felt the warmth of fresh tears stream down my cheeks from the corners of my eyes as I fought against the strain. I was struggling so hard to breathe, as the world darkened over.

I jerked sporadically in the last few seconds of consciousness remaining, as the sparks in my eyes showed me warnings that I was about to lose it all.

"Go to sleep, bitch. Go...to...sleep...bitch..."

The words were so distant and inaudible from the roar of blood trapped within my head. Only exhausted squelches escaped my strangled throat, as I thrashed weakly. Unable to fight back, and wholeheartedly believing this was the moment I was going to die.

I pulled, the only move I knew to do. The only thing I *knew* could hurt the man, choking me to death.

I was scared for my life and fighting with everything left in me, and I was far too weak to hit anything or anybody with any kind of force.

But I knew that I could *grab*.

I reached back behind me, gripping Basketball Sweats by the testicles and squeezed with all of my might.

He screamed out in pain and jumped back, causing me to lose my grip on them. However, he had also weakened his grip from around my throat in the process, and this gave me the opportunity to fight back.

He cried out as I pounded my balled up fist again and again against his crotch, trying to block his testicles with his hands. Had I been able to grab ahold of them just once more, I'd of probably tried ripping them off too.

Tears from strain ran down my blood red face, as I continued to kick at Dreads directly in front of me, trying to fight off two attackers at once.

Basketball Sweats took his arm from around my neck to protect his crotch and deflect my blind, awkward attack; raking his fingernails across my neck in the process.

I fell backward with Dreads in front of me, kicking back at me while sprawled out on his back. He'd hit my shins, my knees and once just below my gut.

I went to get up and start for him again, but Basketball Sweats had already recovered and had begun throwing punches at my head from behind.

I felt his knuckles bouncing off of my skull, glancing as he missed direct hits in his discomposed rage.

The most painful had been the one that connected beneath my right eye and then the one that had caught my bad ear, causing a "pop" and the slightly muffled sound of ringing within it. I struggled to my feet, trying to cover my head, but blinding myself in the process.

I made for Basketball Sweats legs and grabbed one. I managed to pick him up off balance and push with just enough force to cause him to fall backward, where he struck his spine against the corner of a cement planters curb. He cried out in pain, as he rolled over to his side in a fetal position and reached out for his back.

Suddenly, I felt the arms of someone new behind me.

I attempted to break free, kicking and stamping wildly and believing that somebody else had been trying to attack me as well.

Only it was the black elderly woman's husband. The woman that had threatened to call the police. Two more arms surrounded me then as well, and they belonged to a heavy-metal-dressed fellow, with long brown hair he kept in a ponytail and a black leather jacket covered in chains or rivets and spikes.

"Hey, calm down. You ain't wanting to go to jail, son." The older black man said calmly to me.

"Yeah dude, it's over," Heavy-metal-looking-guy said.

Basketball Sweats made for me again, and managed to get a punch in that landed just below my neck within the struggle. But the Heavy Metal guy that had broken up the fight shoved him back with one dominant hand.

"Enough! It's over!" He shouted.

Dreads was still wrestling with his friend in the black sports jacket in the middle of the road.

"Let go of me homie. Let go of me." It was all he kept saying.

"I ain't lettin' you go back to jail, man. Damn, chill out, bruh. It's over. Homeless ass nigga got his ass kicked, man. It's all good." Steelers-sports-jacket-guy added.

I felt like laughing at that comment, maybe even challenging the statement since it was a three versus one fight.

But I didn't want to continue anymore either.

It amazed me how exhausted I was, from a fight that couldn't have lasted longer than a minute. I was absolutely drained.

I couldn't fight anymore even if I'd wanted to.

"Alright, I'm good," I assured both guys holding me back.

"You sure? Cuz I ain't lettin' you go till you are." Heavy Metal guy said to me with concern in his tone.

"I'm leaving." I assured him.

"No the fuck you ain't leavin' nowhere!" Dreads shouted at me in response.

I ignored him.

"I won't let him go for you." Heavy Metal guy assured me.

I had barely heard the promise, though. I didn't care about anything but getting away from there. I grabbed my backpack out of the trash and peeled a honey bun wrapper and some bodies gum off of the bottom of it.

People looked on at me with shocked expressions at what had all just transpired as I threw my backpack on and stumbled down the street, holding my bruised midsection.

"Hey, homie. Come back, bitch! Pussy-ass bitch-ass cracka! I see you out here mutha fucka. You dead, son. Yo, you got me homie? I SAID YOU GOT ME HOMIE?! You're dead!" He shouted after me.

I ducked into a nearby pub, where I nursed my wounds in the bathroom. I had a small rising bruise beneath my left eye, and all over my head, I felt the throbbing of punches that had landed or had glanced off of my skull.

My ear was sore to the touch, and I tongued a small tear on the inside of my cheek where a blow had connected and ripped the flesh against my teeth.

I spat blood into the bathroom sink and cupped my quivering hand beneath the faucet. I took warm water into my mouth and swished, spitting the metallic taste back out.

I walked back to the bus station, 30 minutes before my bus was scheduled to arrive.

Nobody that had been present during the scuffle was there anymore. Just a whole new group of people oblivious to what had just happened, 2 hours before.

Upon reaching Port Jervis, I decided that I shouldn't head back out into the impending winter weather after having been attacked so viciously. I used the fight as justification to get myself another room for the night and to sleep somewhere soft, and warm and away from the outside wintry elements and the potentially dangerous people out there.

The next two days were calling for Arctic weather blowing down from our northern neighbors. Temperatures in some eastern states would stay in the mid to low thirties during the days while dropping down to the teens at night.

It was in this weather that I headed back to the trail where I had left off; 4.4 miles south of Port Jervis.

After my scuffle in Middletown, I was a bit reluctant to finish the trail at all. Not out of fear so much, but more so just out of that "burnt out" feeling and exhaustion that plagued me. The knowledge of the cold, the shorter, darker days to come and walking on alone. At times I wanted to stop living in the "chaotic unknown" and actually know what my day or week was going to look like. The hard part was the balance in ever finding an equal amount of each, and never straying too far into the extremes on either side of the spectrum.

"I really appreciated you coming out to see me," I said to Sara as she drove me back towards the trail.

She had read the events that had transpired in the days before on my Facebook page and journal. She had seen the pictures I'd posted of the aftermath as well and had chosen to come and pay for a night at the Days Inn.

Only this time, she had opted to sleep beside me throughout the evening.

She smiled over at me from the drivers' seat.

"I had fun." She exclaimed.

She had driven two and a half hours from Connecticut, because she had cared for me so in just the week she had gotten to know me. And for a short while, we got to drift in and out of that "comfortable space" we had yearned for one more time after I'd left her home.

And then here I was again.

When she dropped me off, we said our goodbyes, and then she was gone once more.

As she drove away, I stood there on that frozen, snow covered and desolate hill New Jersey residents called a "mountain." The wind blew heartily, sending shivers down bared oak and birch trees whose leaves had already fallen long ago. Their skeletal fingers reached down for me, looking to snag pieces of me away as I walked beneath them.

Across the ground, wisps of fallen snowflakes traipsed about in small whirlwinds if only to find a warmer place to die, within that waning sun.

I listened to the "silence" around me and found no comfort in it. No solace whatsoever at that moment.

Only fear and loneliness.

I had reached Sunrise Overlook, which offered a view of a huge, glacier-scraped valley. The crenellations, mounds and parallel ridgelines (called till) that were created by glacial deposits as far back as millions of years and as recent as 21,000 years ago. When you imagined sheets of ice as high as 10,000 feet tall where you stood on that summit, it was simply overwhelming.

Weather-worn, eroded outcroppings of exposed bedrock atop summits offered the pathways and periglacial boulder fields that were devoid of plants or vegetation of any type.

Freeze-thaw weathering occurred when water that was trapped in micro cracks in the surface of the stones expanded and contracted due to temperature changes above and below the freezing point. As a result, the fields of boulders which were made up of glacial rock deposits made for a relatively taxing place for life to grow.

That's because they were considered to be in constant motion to that very day.

I broke out of the wood line and found I had reached Culver Fire Tower.

I threw off my backpack and made ready for an ascent with a decent view only to find that there was a 'No Trespassing' sign up.

Then as I looked over AWOL's guide, I wondered what the point was in even bothering to list the place as a view to begin with?

Beneath the sign was a phone number, you could call if you wanted to access the tower.

As I looked around, I found it might be hard pressing to expect a Ranger to drive all the way out here in the middle of nowhere, just to let me stand inside a fire tower for a few minutes and then walk back down.

However, I was just too curious not to try the phone number.

"I'm sorry. The number you have just dialed appears to be disconnected. Please hang up and try your call again." The recorded voice said to me over the phone.

"Hmph," I pouted.

Apparently, the phone number was a sham.

With daylight burning, I took off after a PowerBar and half a liter of water for lunch.

The trail wound lazily back down into the valley where I crossed over Highway 206 through Culver's Gap.

As I began the next ascent, I noticed brown, black and white fur across the trail as well as splatters of fresh blood on the rocks and boulders I was climbing.

I began to wonder if something had killed a skunk, but the patches of hair weren't that dark. Maybe more a dark grayish hard brown, than black.

There were patterns synonymous with dragging, across the ground as well.

That was when I realized that somebody had shot a deer on park property and had then pulled the body downhill.

The further up I went, the more gruesome the scene. Blood was literally all over everything, in huge puddles that bugs had already started to collect in.

I began to wonder how much blood a deer could actually have in it, having never hunted one before myself.

When I turned the corner, I almost ran face first into a fellow hiker. He had black shaggy hair, and just enough above his upper lip to call it a mustache. His complexion was pale, but he looked as if he spent a lot of time in the woods by the weathered lines on his face.

He looked at me, offering nothing to say.

"What do you think about all of this blood?" I asked, laughing.

He only stared at me momentarily, as if attempting to read me. His black, beady rat-like eyes flashed, and then he spoke in a dry, hoarse tone.

"I don't know. What do *you* think about it?" He asked me back.

Just by the way he had answered, something felt "wrong" about him.

It was his voice.

"I was gonna guess *illegal poaching*," I said, a bit hesitantly.

"Is it illegal, to kill deer this time of year?" He asked, almost with a hint of cynicism in his voice.

"I...uh. I actually don't know. I don't hunt regularly." I replied.

I made to move around him, but he had blocked the entire path. When he saw me make my move, he made no gesture to step aside and instead, stood there and looked at me as if the thought hadn't yet registered.

"Can I get by?" I asked finally.

He was silent as he stepped to my left and watched me with widening eyes as if there was suddenly a spider crawling across my face, unbeknownst to me.

I shook my head with confusion as I passed by and continued down the trail as the sun dipped behind the horizon and all that greeted me were gray skies and dying light.

As I hiked along, I would glance back every once in a while and see the man walking 70 to 80 feet behind me through the trees.

Whenever I would speed up, so would he.

When I slowed, he would slow down as well. Never bothering to pass me.

Finally, having become bothered and annoyed by his tailing me, I sat for 15 minutes drinking water and eating a granola bar, while hoping he'd finally catch the hint and pass me. When I looked back in his direction, however, I saw he had found a log to sit on. He was eating an apple and looking over at me.

No offer of conversation was made, but I hadn't been asking for it either.

When I started walking again, he got up, tossing the core of his apple into the woods and followed.

Finally, I stopped. I turned and I stood there, staring directly at the man for exactly one minute.

I actually counted the entire minute in my head, and I didn't move, I didn't blink. I watched him with no facial expressions, no coughs, not anything. My intention was to give the guy the impression that I wasn't all there in the head myself, so that he might leave me alone.

The man, however, did nothing but stare back at me.

"Did you want to pass me?" I finally asked with an exasperated tone.

He didn't answer at first.

Finally, he began walking West, off of the trail altogether.

"No." was his reply.

The mountain ridge I walked, sat between Culver Lake and Kittatinny Lake. It was like a bridge of land that had separated both glacial lakes.

Looking down into Owassa, you had the perfect view of the valley below while pink horizons and strings of clouds hung above.

The summits and outcroppings were covered by fields of wild grown golden wheat.

I ran my hands across their tops, as I walked the narrow trail.

While admiring the view, I took a moment to walk into the woods off of the trail to use the restroom and watch cars miles and miles away drive in the distance. Already turning their headlights on in preparation for the coming night.

As I peed, I wasn't initially bothered when I had heard leaves rustling behind me. I figured that with all of the squirrels I had seen, that had probably been the source of the sound. But after I had finished urinating and had zipped up my pants, I turned to see the strange hiker from earlier just within view. He stood behind a tree 40, to 50 feet away, staring at me.

I was both surprised and angered in my response.

"What the *fuck* is your problem?" I shouted at him.

He didn't answer and instead walked back out towards the trail.
When I reached the AT again, he was gone.
But deep down, I knew he wasn't.
Sometimes, you can just feel a person's eyes on you without them ever being visible, and I honestly felt his eyes on me in that very moment.

It was dark when I'd reached Brink Shelter, and as I stumbled about without light to guide my way, my ankles screamed back at me in pain.

Boulders and stones were so expertly hidden by the fallen leaves that I counted myself lucky I hadn't fallen flat on my face several times throughout the day.

I had hiked 18 miles, and was absolutely beat as I threw my pack off. I searched unsuccessfully for a water source in the dark before turning my headlamp on. Even with the flashlight, though, it was too hard to decipher what was a trail leading to the spring and what was merely old deer paths that led further into the dark forest.

I could find no blazes to guide me on the trees.

There were two shelters here, one new and then one probably half a century old. The older of the two had been the one I had approached first.

It appeared as little more than a shed large enough to cater to maybe five or six people, and even then there would be no room for packs.

Only sleeping bodies.

The newer shelter had benches large enough to sleep on and stood adjacent to the old shelter. It also had windows as well.

Despite the fact that they both looked swept clean and habitable, I chose the newer one for the evening. I ate a cold dinner, shivering as I pulled my sleeping bag over my head and prayed for warmth.

As the night went on, I shook uncontrollably despite the fact I had all of my clothes on, and thermals as well. Adding to that, were two tarps and my fleece liner.

I tucked my head beneath everything and tried to use the heat of my breaths to warm the inside of my bag. The problem was the humidity in my breaths.

The heat from the inside of the bag, coupled with outside condensation building beneath me began to make the fleece liner wet.

I had managed a whole two hours of on-and-off rest throughout the night until the numbing cold, and the sharp pang of my bladder woke me.

Outside of the shelter, I suddenly heard the rustling of leaves.

I slowly unzipped my sleeping bag and liner and crept painfully to the western window. I looked out and saw a figure walking around in the dark. No flashlight, no pack.

Nothing.

Just the silhouette of somebody walking through the darkness as the moon brilliantly shone from above.

I began to wonder if it was the same weirdo from earlier in the day.

I looked over at my backpack, and muttered quietly to Gregory: *We gotta get outta here.*

It was 3 A.M., and I quickly began packing my things. There were no intentions of following the conventional route, via the Appalachian Trail. I'd have to pass the figure in the dark to do that.

I packed as silently as possible and prepared my knife in my pocket by unfurling the blade. I was ready to grab it if I needed to defend myself, for whatever reason.

Being so close to the end of my journey, I felt I had started to lose a small piece of my sanity.

As I took down my tarp, I peered through the darkness. I could hear the circling footsteps but saw nothing.

I headed out, taking an old abandoned forest road in the area, instead of the trail.

I was moving fast enough that I was no longer shivering. Power walking that occasionally turned into a light jog when the terrain permitted it.

Sometimes I would stop and turn back, looking over my shoulder into the darkness. I didn't have my headlamp on, mainly because I hadn't wanted to draw any attention to myself when I was leaving the shelter in an attempt not to be noticed.

The moon gave off more than enough light for me to see through the shadows anyhow. The downside was, it could also give off more than enough light to give away my position as well.

I broke from the trail and started rushing even faster down the mountain, crashing through the woods. I was certain in my own paranoia but playing it safe all the same.

Low hanging branches and shrubbery slapped painfully against my face, as I took the occasional fall, on a hidden boulder beneath the carpet of leaves covering the forests floor.

It was a maze that surrounded me, and only the digital compass on my phone guided me southeast, towards Delaware Water Gap.

Be calm, be calm. I tried to assure myself.

I held on to my knife tightly in my pocket and then withdrew it once I had heard the rustling of leaves nearby.

"If that's you, I promise you…"

Promise you what I immediately thought to myself.

Was I ready to cross that boundary and make that declaration of physical violence if it was, in fact, the man who had been following me earlier the day before? Was I even *ready* for an altercation?

Two deer emerged from behind a wild holly bush. They looked at me with blank expressions.

He's long gone, stop worrying about him. I thought to myself.

I took a few deep breaths and checked my GPS. I was 5 miles away from the shelter at that point and I felt a little safe and more comfortable in that thought.

Through my running, I had come across an abandoned forest road that ran alongside the Delaware River, where a series of buildings and old barns had been washed over by past floods.

Some of the sheds, or uninhabited houses had completely fallen over while others had massive logs that had crashed into them, shattering their foundations which helped with the collapsing of the structures.

It was at an intersection that I came to a broken, crumbled bridge that had been sealed off by metal grates to keep from allowing vehicular (and foot) traffic from passing. As if this entire ghost town had been quarantined from the rest of the world.

I threw off my backpack and approached slowly, slipping my fingers between the bars as I stared like a prisoner at the other side. There was no way to cross, as the banks were too high on either side of the bridge from many years of erosion.

I looked through the metal barricade into a window of the past.

Across the bridge, logs, great chords from broken trees and branches had been washed atop the pathway blocking any history of a real crossing ever having been there. The boards were rotted through or missing altogether.

While there had been a relatively identifiable forest road leading up to the bridge, on the adjacent side, there was nothing but overgrown fields of marshland to accompany it.

I grabbed my pack, climbing the slanted grate just enough to be able to lower my backpack onto the adjacent side of the barrier.

I looked down at the 15-foot drop and took a deep breath. There was no other way to get across that I could see. I believed I could make it, as long as I was careful and stuck to the support beams on either sides of the bridge.

I held on to the edge of the bolted, rusty barrier gate and swung a leg around the outside of the fence.

However, my finger got caught in one of the grate holes, and when I went to let go, it tugged me back towards the 15-foot drop below.

Utter shock ran from my heart to the heels in my feet, as I grasped desperately at something. *Anything*, with my right hand and managed to grip the blockades support beam as a last resort.

I pulled myself forward and shook my finger loose as I took my first step upon the planks. Sure enough, as soon as I had, my foot punched through a rotted board.

My leg fell through the hole to just above the ankle, before stopping.

I yelled out in pain, falling awkwardly to one knee. The only saving grace had been that I hadn't drawn blood in the process.

There were some light skin scrapes, but nothing more.

I threw my pack back on, and the structure groaned angrily, as I carefully crossed.

Old metal support beams laid gnarled and twisted atop the bridge as a testament to the strength of a flooded river and the trees that had crashed into it. It was unbelievable to see the remnants of such raw power that a wooden log could have against steel.

When I had made it to the other side, I tossed my pack over the rusted metal grate barricade there and watched it roll down into the waist-high grass on the other side. I then had to drop to all fours, and crawl on my stomach into the tiniest little ball to reach the stone support embankment five feet below the bridge. I clung to the sides and walked a jutting rock lip until I was able to pull myself up and over to the other side.

"Well Gregory, we did it," I said, picking my backpack up and dusting it off as I looked back at our accomplishment.

Gregory wasn't really much for words in times like this; choosing to keep a sort of "reserved calm."

I supposed that was excusable, being a backpack and all. As I turned around, I sighed with dismay however.

There was no definable "road" or "path" on the other side of the bridge.

Simply an old wild animal trail that eventually led to an overgrown brook side road.

It was once your typical country dirt road that had half washed away by time and then been overtaken by dry, dead vegetation and briars.

Whole chunks of the road had fallen into the river, making it impassible so I climbed the ridge and looked down into the distance to find Old Mine Road.

"It DOES exist!" I said out loud, excitedly.

I had read a lot about this road as it had a long history on it, as did the entire valley.

The road had been famed in lore to be one of the oldest in America. Old Mine Road had a length of 104 miles stretching from Delaware Water Gap to Kingston, New York and it was believed to have been first established by Dutch miners in the 17th century.

Many locals claimed it had been used to transport copper ore, from several mines that remained within the gap to that very day.

With such a minute amount of yield for the supposed amount of resources left in the area, those beliefs had thus been discounted by historians and geologists alike.

Before existing as a mining road, it was also theorized by local archaeologists to have existed as a Paleo-Indian trail dating back to 10,000 B.C.

As I walked through old settlements and abandoned houses, even more history began to unfold before my eyes.

Homes built long ago stood as decaying monuments to the past. These structures were left standing, to rot away into oblivion and extinction from over half a decade before.

The interwoven trails that barely existed anymore led in and out of the main modernized highways. You could follow these paths to crumbling barns, or boarded buildings destroyed by vandals and painted in graffiti.

It was surprising to me that the park hadn't torn them down long ago. There weren't even signs stating "No Trespassing" and warning of prosecution for doing so.

It looked as if nobody cared.

The history of the government's takeover of the area could be rather infuriating when learning about it.

And it all boiled down to "eminent domain."

In the 1950's with the Federal government finding interest in the area (mostly due to flooding damages coinciding with hurricanes) the land had been condemned, and people were kicked out of their homes for a hydroelectric dam which was to be built within the area. The Army Corp of Engineers exclaimed that the building of the dam would control flooding in the area as well.

This was of course at the cost of seizing private landowners' properties, some of which had been passed down through many generations.

For a dam, that was ultimately never built.

The original proposed project would have left a 37-mile wide lake, reaching depths of over a hundred feet in some areas.

The project began to falter due to budget issues at the time. It wasn't long that the residents who had been displaced when their lands had forcibly been condemned by the government, began fighting back by claiming their property had been unfairly requisitioned.

They joined the sides of environmental protestors claiming that the damage the government would be doing to local plant and animal life within the area by flooding it for the creation of a lake and the hydro-electric dam; would be insurmountable.

Eventually, the condemned lands were turned over to the National Forest Service for public use.

The houses never vanished though and the road that held so much history remained, no longer under threat of disappearing beneath a lake.

I explored some of the abandoned homes out of curiosity. Some of which had been torn apart by Mother Nature, and others by bored teenagers.

Some homes were empty, save for a few freezers rusting away in their basements while others looked as if the owners had said: "The hell with it, I don't need any of my things" and just walked away.

The homes were scavenged, clothes and beds were torn apart, and old televisions from the 60's had been smashed. Plates, glasses, and dinnerware were shattered into dangerous little shards across the ground or walls.

I knelt down and brushed aside the broken glass on a family picture taken sometime in the early 1920's, by the looks of the clothes they wore in the image. A mother and father, with two twin daughters on each parents lap. Nobody smiled.

The background told a tale of the lands they once worked and lived upon.

I placed the broken frame upon the peeling kitchen counter, hoping someday that someone, maybe even a family member of those in the frame would find that picture they'd thought had been lost decades before.

Back during a time, when this entire home would have once been beneath 100 feet of lake water.

It would be 4:40 P.M. when I reached I-80 and began my walk along the interstate; crossing the Delaware River into Pennsylvania.

New Jersey had been short, but I was also always taking different routes other than the twisty, curvy path of the AT.

A footbridge had been built along the side of the interstate, with white blazes to guide the hiker along the way.

Semi-Trucks and cars raced by more than 70 miles-per-hour, causing the bridge to rock up and down as I traversed. The wind, the carbon monoxide and the noise from their engines were unbearable.

I hated walking that bridge, and when I reached the other side, I was glad that I never had to go back across it again.

I found a street curb along a desolate sidewalk where I sat and pulled out AWOL's guide.

I looked up hostels in the area, and smiled wide with excitement when I found the "Church Of The Mountain Hostel." However, when I called the number, I got no answer. I knew it wasn't hiking season anymore, but I left a message regardless out of hope.

The Appalachian Trail curved up along streets on the outskirts of the town of Delaware Water Gap, clearly trying to stay as far from the center as physically possible.

I walked to the church, on what would be another of my longest hiking days thus far while on the trail at that point.

It would end as a 25.8-mile day.

At the church, I waited an additional thirty minutes after finding the hostel door to be locked. But truth be told, I was tired, hungry and cold.

My feet didn't want to hear anything else about hiking for the day, and so I decided to celebrate my long hike by getting a cheap room at Pocono Inn for thirty-six bucks, feeling I had deserved it.

After showering and collapsing on my bed, the Reverend from the "Church Of The Mountain Hostel" called me back.

He informed me that he would unlock the door and that the only reason it had been locked to begin with was that this time of year, it usually filled up with homeless people that never wanted to leave. Maybe I would end up being one of those individuals myself?

My friend and former coworker, Keven Kirsch, had been enjoying the vacation from one of his regularly scheduled suspensions from work.

Keven was the type of individual that had no problem talking back to supervision and didn't hold back thoughts or feelings for the people he didn't like being around. His lack of filter, usually caused fellow sensitive coworkers to report him to management, which repeatedly led to suspensions from work on a systematic basis.

Utilizing the "vacation time" he had now acquired, he had decided to drive up and visit me at Delaware Water Gap.

After heading out at 2 A.M., he drove throughout the night from North Carolina and arrived at around 10 A.M., hyper and wide-eyed—having been fueled with coffee and cigarettes the entire drive up.

"So what do you think?" I asked him after he'd pulled up to the hostel. I stepped out from the door with my hands in the air, doing a runway spin. I scratched my beard and bowed to show off my haggard appearance since he'd last seen me in Damascus, Virginia.

"You look like shit." He replied.

"Still the same old jerk. Why did I invite you up here again?" I asked.

"Probably because I'm the only one who would come." He responded with a laugh, as he shook my hand and brought me in for a hug.

"You're right. Thanks for coming, pal." I said, patting him on the back.

During breakfast, we talked our typical banter, hopping right back into conversations about work, despite the fact I no longer worked there. It seemed like the natural thing to do with an acquaintance from back home though the subject always left me with such a feeling of peace, at having quit.

After we'd eaten, I challenged him to hike a piece of the Appalachian Trail with me.

So we walked seven miles from Delaware Water Gap to the Kirkridge/191 road crossing via the Appalachian Trail.

"I couldn't see climbing this with a 60-pound pack on like you do all the time," Keven exclaimed, huffing along as sweat poured out of every pore on his body.

Meanwhile, I felt great clomping along, with nothing but a phone and my camera in my pockets. It was like my own personal vacation away from Gregory after the 25-mile hike I'd had the day before.

"This is only a 1,200-foot climb, *gramps*. You've already missed the 4 to 5,000 footers back up north." I replied while charging up ahead of him. He stopped for a breather, panting heavily against a tree trunk and shook his head from side to side.

"I think I need a cigarette." he muttered, before charging on.

We had planned on either hitching or getting a taxi ride back into the small town of Delaware Water Gap once we'd reached the 191 road crossing. Unfortunately, after contacting a local taxi service, we both stood around waiting for 45 minutes before decidedly resorting to other means.

"It's cold, and my shirt is soaked from sweating all day." Keven explained.

"Yeah, and I don't think that taxi is coming any time soon.

I had gotten used to this behavior from taxi companies.

Usually in Trail Towns where private drivers taxied part-time or for supplemental income, if you weren't running up a massive charge a lot of the time nobody was coming out for you.

When we called back, we were told: "Oh don't worry, somebody will be up there for you guys soon enough. Eventually."

"Forget it, let's just hitch," I said hanging up and sticking my thumb out.

Keven really got into this part of the hike, laughing every time a car passed us by. Having never hitched a ride before in his life, the concept was a bit new to him.

"What are we supposed to do?" he asked me as if I had all the answers.

"Watch and learn," I said confidently.

I lifted my pants leg and shook my butt back and forth to passing motorists that either honked or laughed; ultimately nobody bothering to stop.

Meanwhile, Kirsch was either humping the air or making rude and pervasive sexual gestures with his hips.

When that didn't work for us, we tried dancing with each other or jumping up and down and wildly waving our hands back and forth. We flashed sad faces, crazy eye faces, and overly excited faces as cars flew by.

"This is ridiculous! You and Torry made it sound so easy!" Keven said in disbelief.

"Well, that was also during hiking season. We don't have backpacks on, it's November, and you look like a maniac. Of course, no one wants to pick us up!"

"Oh, I look like the *maniac*? Says the 400lb gorilla with the serial killer beard standing right beside me?" Keven replied.

We both laughed, and then went right back to trying to get hitches.

I held my hand to my chest, trying to sing like an opera singer on the side of the road, while Keven hit high pitched notes in his poor rendition of Carrie Underwood's "Before He Cheats."

I began pleading with passing motorists on my knees and with my hands clasped into the skies above me, feigning crying. Meanwhile, Keven jerked his body manically as if he was breaking out into sporadic muscle spasms upon the ground, writhing back and forth.

A Jeep finally pulled over, and a blonde teenage girl got out of the passenger's seat and popped the chair forward as she climbed into the back.

Keven sat up from the ground and looked over at me with a confused expression and dirt on the side of his cheek.

"Uh...what do we do now?" he asked.

I was still in shock and awe that somebody had finally stopped for us.

"I uh...I guess we get in?" I said, rather unsure myself.

"Come on! You guys in or not?" a man's voice shouted from the driver's side seat.

"Thanks!" We yelled simultaneously, as we jumped up, dusted ourselves off and climbed in.

"We're headed for Bangor so we can take you that far," the driver exclaimed as we shut the passenger side door behind us.

"That's great! We're headed to Delaware Gap if you could drop us off along the way." I said.

"Wait, *Delaware Water Gap*? You're hitching in the wrong fucking direction, dude!" He said, laughing.

"You idiot!" Keven said, immediately smacking me in the back of the head.

"What? Sorry! I've got a crappy phone with an atrocious navigational system." I replied, shoving him back.

"Well, I guess we could take you there." The driver said a little reluctantly.

"We'd be more than happy to give you $10 bucks for your trouble," I offered.

I looked back at Keven.

"Right Keven?"

"Who's got ten dollars? You?"

"You do!" I said, grabbing for him as he laughed and smacked my hands away.

"Now just wait a moment." He said as his face dropped into a serious expression, and he fished out his wallet.

"Moochin' off me..." he muttered, as he slammed the ten dollar bill into my palm.

I handed the driver the bill when Keven's phone began ringing.

It was the taxi service we'd called for earlier that had left us high and dry.

"Hey, my driver has been all over the place looking for you guys. Where are you at?" I heard the voice say.

"Well, we ended up hitching a ride because you fuckers kept us waiting for over an hour on the side of the road," Keven replied to the dispatcher, before hanging up in their ear. He passed a goofy smile as I shook my head from side to side.

Keven Kirsch, once again proudly displaying absolutely no filter whatsoever.

I stood on the outskirts of Lehighton, where Keven had dropped me off on his way back south to North Carolina. I was 10 miles northwest of where the trail crossed PA 248/145 at the Lehigh Nature Center.

I spent an hour with my thumb cocked by the side of the road until I was able to snag a hitch to the Center via two different hitches. I then spent the rest of the day hiking back north towards Kirkridge and the 191 road crossing over the course of two 14-mile days, so that I didn't miss any mileage in between along the Appalachian Trail. As I stood at Fox Gap where Keven and I had hitchhiked just two days before, I marveled at how truly lucky I was to have snagged a ride within the first 20 minutes of hanging my thumb out into the cold air there.

"Where ya headed?" the man in the passenger's side front seat asked me after the car had pulled over.

"Trying to get back south to the Lehigh Nature Center. I'm hiking the Appalachian Trail." I replied.

"The dude loves nature, Jeff. Whatta ya say?" he asked his friend who was playing on his phone behind the wheel of the Honda Civic he was driving.

"Ask him if he's Republican or Democrat." the driver said, not even bothering to look up.

"Well?" the man in the passenger side seat asked, looking up at me.

"I'm whatever I'm supposed to be, to answer your question correctly and get a ride south..."

The guy behind the wheel suddenly made a "buzzer" sound and shouted: "Wrong answer!" as he started to pull away.

I chased after them momentarily.

"Democrat! I'm a Democrat!" I pled.

The driver slammed on the breaks and looked over at me while his friend laughed.

"You better not be full of shit. Get in the back." he said, as his buddy opened the rear door for me.

As they drove, they asked various questions about my hike including the very obvious one.

"Why are you hitching to Lehigh Nature Center if you're a *hiker*?" the driver asked, looking suspiciously up at me in his rearview mirror.

"I've just spent the last 2 days hiking north from there, to Fox Gap where you guys just picked me up. I was connecting a piece of the trail that I'd missed while hanging out with a friend visiting from home."

"Where's home?" the passenger asked, looking back at me.

I turned and looked out the window before replying "A long ways from here."

When they dropped me off, I ran a tired hand across my face. After the full hiking day I'd had, I was looking to just go to sleep at the first chance I could find. I watched the staff coming out of the Nature Center, and one woman in particular as she turned to lock the front doors to the building.

I glanced down at my phone and found it was already past 5 P.M., so I decided to make a run for Woodpecker Trail which I had seen reconnected with the Appalachian Trail; before anyone told me the area was closed off for the evening.

Luckily I hadn't been seen.

As I disappeared into the shadows, I found the place I'd call 'camp' in the darkness and solace of the forest. I managed to discover a pile of leaves and brushed them aside to make sure they hadn't been covering a dead animal carcass or a nest of fire ants. I then laid my hammock down on the bed of leaves without bothering to hang it and placed my sleeping bag inside. I knew that I was still protected by the bug net I had repaired, when I zipped myself up in the hammock tent. This meant that I wasn't too worried about any insects invading my sleeping place that evening.

Instead, I managed to obtain a rather restful slumber throughout the night, tucked warmly into my nest of leaves.

In 1911, the New Jersey Zinc Company created a smelting plant in the western part of the town of Palmerton, Pennsylvania. The following year, another station was constructed on the East side.

The effects of the pollution were disastrous over the next seven decades as the technology to control it was nonexistent at the beginning of its creation. Later, when cleaner and safer means of production were made available, profit came first, and standards were never implemented. The health effects at the time were not known, and claims were promptly dismissed.

The scarred landscape could still be seen to this very day, as vegetation had died out on the eaves and summits of the ridgelines.

Whatever it had once looked like, I'm not sure I'll ever know, because at that moment it looked almost exactly like the surface of Mars, or some barren, craggy wasteland.

The EPA had discovered over eight inches of toxic metals in the topsoil's within the area once cleanup had begun. People had been breathing in these fatal substances for years, fueled by the local industries

The World We Came to Find

with which they had been employed. Three hundred homes had to be decontaminated in the area and hundreds of thousands of diverse wildlife within the 3,000 square miles affected by the pollution, were killed off.

In 1980 the West Plant was shut down due to a market decrease in zinc and an increase in EPA regulations to control the pollution.

The East plant still runs to this day, but more cleanly and under closer scrutiny now.

Palmerton would become one of the nation's worse hazardous disaster zones, and ended up on the US Governments Superfund List. Thirty-three years later, vegetation and wildlife were still struggling to grow back in some places.

I walked through rock fields and down old forest roads, waiting for cancerous tumors to begin cropping up on my arms or legs sporadically.

While a bit of an exaggeration, upon reaching Metallica Spring, I second guessed my decision to get water.

Lead and arsenic contamination in the water existed to this very day, according to the EPA Website.

Why this was considered a viable drinking source according to AWOL's guide book was beyond me.

I wouldn't have risked even filtering the stuff myself, but left that decision up to others to make on their own.

It would be a few days later after connecting the portions of the AT further up north, that I would cross 248/145. The smell of sulfur was thick in the air, and the barren hillsides that led up the ridge felt depressing and gloomy on such a gray, rainy day to match.

But I wasn't going to let it bring my spirits down.

I sprinted up the ridgeline with renewed energy from the caffeine pills and four miserable cups of instant coffee sloshing around in my stomach.

Pennsylvania was known to some as "Rocksylvania." A funny name that would instantly make you chuckle once you got to sample the terrain for yourself. Stumbling across stones as big as softballs made it tricky, and even dangerous at times at steep grades.

A hiker had to get used to the constant danger of twisted ankles and prepare for it with a slower and more deliberate hiking pace.

More often than not, I found the Appalachian Trail almost purposefully went over great lengths of these sections where walking two or three feet into the wood line would have you stepping upon relatively flatter surfaces instead.

So very often, I would abandon the AT altogether and hike through the woods, over fallen trees, and through shrubbery instead. Because if there was one thing I'd learned about the Appalachian Trail, it was that you were sure to find your way to it again by always climbing towards the top of a mountain or a hill of any sort.

Halfway up the first major climb of the day, I found a woman bending over and examining a bright yellow stone on the ground in front of her.

"Looks good to me..." I said approvingly, having been speaking about the rock between her fingers.

The woman looked back at me with contempt in her eyes, despite the hoodie still hiding her face.

You could feel the sudden anger.

Something seemed recognizable about her though all the same. She had dropped the rock and was wiping mud and dirt off of her butt.

"Ya done looking at my ass, ya fuckin' pervert?" She asked me.

"I m..meant the...stone..." I tried to clarify.

"Sure ya did. While lookin' straight at my butt," she said with a cynical expression.

I suddenly realized who it was.

"Daisy?"

The girl slowly dropped her hoodie and smiled.

"Well, well...if it isn't the Cat. Look'it that beard! I hardly recognized you dude!" she said with a hint of surprise all of her own.

She reached over and punched me in a buddy-like fashion in the side of the arm.

"How've ya been?" She asked, fishing out a pack of cigarettes from her front coat pocket. She flicked me one which I caught but tossed back to her.

"Not gonna help my chest congestion," I replied.

She shrugged, putting the rejected cigarette between her lips and lighting it.

"Suit yourself."

"I can't believe you're still out here, and that you're still going! This is kinda exciting! Now we can have a slumber party and talk about all the hot guys on the trail..." I said jokingly, with a flip of my hand.

"Whoa, hold on buddy. I'm not going any further. You see a pack on my back?" She asked, taking a drag as she sat down on a boulder and grinned up at me.

I looked around momentarily.

"Actually no, I don't. What are you doing up here?" I asked.

She blew a thin stream of smoke out as she pointed downhill behind me; the way I had just come up.

A young guy that looked like a John Travolta wannabe from the movie Grease Lightning was walking up the hill. Or struggling, I should say.

"Ohhhh. Nice!" I said, nodding my head with snubbed approval.

"Are all badasses accessorized...with that same leather jacket?" I asked sarcastically.

"Ha. Ha." She returned, mocking my joke with a slow clap.

"He happens to be kind of cool," She responded just a bit defensively.

"Sometimes." She quickly clarified.

'John Travolta' was struggling up, in what appeared to be snakeskin cowboy boots. The loose gravel and sliding stones beneath his feet made this task impossible. There was nothing on the boots bottoms but a slick surface that had no traction. They were terrible for hiking in.

He continued to slip and fall comically.

"You know. I'm a pretty cool guy, myself. Plus I come equipped with a few accessories of my own." I said to Daisy, as I kissed each of my flexed biceps.

"Oh God. Shut up." Daisy laughed.

"Yeah, it's real funny isn't it?!" The John Travolta look-alike shouted up at her. He must have confused her laughter as being directed at him.

"If you're having a hard time, take off your fucking boots then you idiot. Don't get angry at me!" She shouted back at him.

"Yeah, and hike in my *socks*? You're a smart one." He yelled back.

"Clearly you were both made for each other," I whispered to her, patting her on the back.

I removed my backpack just as she passed me an annoyed kind of look.

"At least he doesn't talk to inanimate objects like *you* do." She said, kicking at my pack.

"Shh! You'll hurt Gregory's feelings saying things like that out loud." I replied, gently petting my backpack with a goofy smile.

"We didn't have to come up here you know. We could've seen everything just fine from *down there*." Daisy's guy friend called out to her.

"Yeah, but then you'd be missing out on the excellent view of mankind's destruction of nature. Don't you just love the lack of plant or animal life here? Can't you...just like...take a breath and ENJOY the smell of lead and arsenic filling your lungs?" I asked, in a kidding tone.

He didn't seem too enthusiastic or jovial about my comments. In fact, he hadn't even responded or looked up at me.

"I can't believe you're whining and you haven't even made it a quarter of the way up yet," Daisy spat rather diminutively at him.

While the young man looked as if he should have been in rather decent physical condition, he was swallowing so much air and sweating so profusely that he had started to make me feel tired, just looking at him.

"Would you like to sit?" I asked, offering my seat. Of course, his Alpha-male bravado only made him shake his head no as he leaned forward onto his knees, panting.

"I'm good." he replied to me before turning towards Daisy.

"But I'm not going way the fuck *up there*." He said, gesturing his pointer finger towards the top of the mountain.

"That's fine. Me and the Cat will go by ourselves." She responded in an irritable tone. She stood and looked down at me as if expecting me to chime in like some kind of shoulder parrot: *Yeah! You tell em' boss!*

Her guy friend was looking up at me suddenly like I was the world's worst enemy. How I hated being dragged into the middle of a lovers quarrel.

"Maybe you could just borrow MY boots, then give them back on your way down." I offered. My heart had been in the right place when I'd said it. I didn't mind taking a break there while they went up together to enjoy the view.

"What are you, dense?" He asked me irritably.

I widened my eyes and looked away immediately.

"Don't talk to my friend like that, asshole," Daisy burst in, defending me. Now suddenly I had become her friend? Up to that point, I thought she was always bothered by my presence. Or at least she did a good job portraying that sort attitude.

"Why not?! Were you fuckin' him too or somethin'?" The John Travolta look-alike shouted; his face getting red.

"Well, on that note. I'm gonna get the hell outta here..." I said standing and throwing my pack on.

"Yeah Mark, I was fucking him. Just like I was fucking your brother...and your best friends and everybody else you think I'm fucking." She replied sarcastically.

Oh boy.

I started hiking uphill while they argued back and forth. Finally, Mark waved both of his hands dismissively at her and began trudging... or well....slipping and falling back downhill.

When I reached the top of the summit, I looked back down on to the valley I had come up from.

Daisy arrived shortly after.

"Listen, about all that shit..." She began.

"Nah. Don't worry about it. I just hope that your boy-toy didn't drive off and leave you behind out here." I said with a smile, as she sat down on the ground across from me.

"He couldn't. Not when I've got his car keys," she said with a mischievous smirk while patting her front pocket.

"Smart. So what's your story? Why did you decide to get off of the trail? Where have you been after Great Barrington? Who's *that* guy? I mean I've got a ton of questions." I rambled.

"First and foremost, as I said, in the beginning, I was never on any 'Appalachian path.' I was just exploring towns and trails and going wherever I'd wanted to go."

"Well excuse me. My apologies to the lady who never hikes the Appalachian Trail, but who've I've come across on it *twice* now."

"And twice in towns out of the way, in case you forgot that. Kinda like you're stalking me," she added.

"Oh, here we go again," I said, rolling my eyes.

After I had ditched Daisy for coffee back in Great Barrington, Massachusetts; the next day she had lucked out on a hitch down into Torrington, Connecticut where she had met Mark outside a diner there. She had run out of money, and was hoping to get a temporary job and had asked to stay with him while she earned a few bucks to get back on the road.

A little bit of a "thing" had developed between them, though, complicating the situation. Despite the fact that she was quick to ensure me it wasn't "love."

"I just...I needed him for a while." She tried to explain in a nice way. Well, she had failed miserably and ran a shameful hand across her face immediately apologizing to me as if I was somehow going to absolve her from all sins.

After a while of saving a few bucks as she did part time waitressing, they decided on a random road trip down to Louisiana together. Along the way, she had wanted to see a few notable spots along the AT, despite the fact, her new guy friend wasn't exactly enthusiastic about it.

"Don't you have a family? Life or people waiting for you? Somebody missing you? I mean damn, I feel like with as many times as we've run into each other I should know just a LITTLE bit more about you. But all I've got is questions."

Daisy laughed.

"Why do you care, Cat? I'm just a wanderer. It's what I do. Wander from here to there and all over. Besides, when I reach Louisiana I'll probably ditch Mark, and head for California alone." She said unapologetically.

"And then what? End up dead on the side of a highway somewhere after another unfortunate hitch? Like the one you had before where you were almost sexually assaulted?" I asked in a serious tone.

She laughed again, not nearly taking me seriously before reaching over and taking my hand into both of hers.

"Still determined to protect me, a complete stranger; from the rest of the world, huh?" She asked.

I looked down, as she ran her thumbs back and forth across the palm of my hand.

"You're a good guy." She said.

"But you forget that I'm a big girl and that I can take care of myself." She added.

"I know....it's just..." I began.

But I stopped myself. Nothing I was going to say would change Daisy's mind and it certainly wasn't my place to try. I had latched on to her, finding someone that had heavily appeared so very independent, where I was too much the coward to go it all alone.

This was another goodbye.

And unfortunately, this was the life of "the road" or "the trail" or whatever it is you called or categorized my hike to be.

Living out here, everybody had their own paths, and at times you tended to forget that in lieu of your own selfish wants.

Admittedly, I enjoyed the banter between Daisy and I. It was fluid, and playful and almost always sarcastic, but flirtatious.

Daisy looked up at me, with a soft smile on her face.

She searched my eyes, for once staring into them. She waited for my response while a part of me felt she didn't really even need one.

"I was lost once, as an introvert," I said to her finally.

"But each act of kindness that came from complete strangers made me a little more social. More outgoing, and more included in the rest of the world I had felt so distanced from when I first started walking out here back in March. I opened up more and more as each person took a swing at my defensive walls with a sledgehammer. And simply talked to me." I said.

"I don't know, what life has in store for you down the road, Daisy. But I have learned that if you don't allow people to help you. If you push away those that care, you'll find exactly what it was you were looking for. To be alone." I went on.

I'd remembered what Yoshua had said to me back in Rutland, Vermont when I had stayed at the Yellow Deli.

It had made sense.

"And that's not a place anybody of a rational mind, actually wants to be." I finished.

"Cat, you're making it sound like I hate the world..." She insisted.

"No. I think you're just afraid of it. Like I was." I interjected.

She sighed, looking down momentarily.

"Why do you care? You don't even know me?" She asked, more at the earth than at me.

"Because despite the fact that you can't see it yourself..." I said.

"You're friendship, your conversation. *Your presence* is worth the effort." I went on, squeezing her hand.

She looked up into my eyes.

"You're worth caring about." I ended.

She stood, and I followed. Daisy then wrapped her arms around me.

"Cat, I'm gonna miss ya. And your corny-ass jokes." She said, against my shoulder as I hugged her back.

"Be safe out there," I said, letting her go.

I knew I'd probably never see her again from this point on. But there was always some little piece of hope that made me think once I headed out on those lonely roads across America again someday—I just might cross paths with the crass, blunt redhead who called herself Daisy.

"By the way, did you actually sleep with that guy's brother?" I asked her.

She looked back at me with a smirk, as she walked the trail down the mountain.

"Not yet, but I was thinkin' about it." She replied with a wink.

"Nice,"

She waved and then she was gone.

When she was out of sight, I turned and looked down the trail ahead of me.

Devoid of emotion, it was a blank, unpainted canvas. Waiting, to be painted with the tale of my story.

There weren't any sentimental feelings or longing for it.

It existed only as an obstacle from that day forward in my mission to complete my journey. The magic from the trail, the *real magic* came from the interactions with the people that walked it. The friends one made along the way.

I looked down at my backpack.

"Let's finish this, Gregory. We have family waiting for us back at home."

Bake Oven Knob had been vandalized with spray paint and graffiti upon arrival. I turned my attention away from the scarred rocks and looked out over farmland, from between the pine trees.

Throughout Pennsylvania, New Jersey and New York; I had seen a lot of graffiti painted over natural beauty. Even down south as far as Virginia. Only in the more desolate extremes and beginnings and endings of the AT, did Mother Nature seem to have prevailed.

The Pennsylvanian "Knifes Edge" tore out of the earth like old, snapped bones ripping through the earth's crust.

Precariously slanted like the blades of a knife, a hiker passed across the terrain at dangerous and slanted angles which overlooked the eastern valley carved out by time—thousands of years ago during the ice age.

I stumbled, slid and fell often enough that the bruises from days before became reactivated in shocking pain. I could barely walk, my feet hurt so badly.

I had lost two more toenails with my rapid increase in mileage over the weeks before, and the growing reemergence of a new pinky nail had caused infection as it grew at an oddly misshapen angle. This meant my steps had to be careful, and thought out to avoid any more pain or injury than I already had.

The AT eventually crossed Highway 309 where .2 miles west existed the Blue Mountain Bed & Breakfast.

And of course, it was closed.

This was rather unfortunate because I had planned on buying a cheap burger or something to eat after reading of its existence in my guidebook. My many days and my lacking budget on the AT had dried up what little food I had left in my pack.

I usually fought an empty stomach with lots of water to make me feel full over the course of the next few days, as I rationed out what few items I had left. And in my journal entries, I left this information out with the knowledge my mother would read it, and become even more scared and fearful for my safety than she already was.

Upon arriving at the Allentown Club Shelter a short time later, it was dark.

The wind was terrible, and the temperatures had dropped to 16 degrees in the area. I put up a tarp across the opening of the shelter, though it barely helped. My tattered pants clung to my scarred legs, briefly rising and falling with every wind gust as I shivered in the corner of the structure.

You weren't ready for this cold weather, John. You should have been done months ago.

It wasn't a depressing thought, as much as it had made me actually laugh. I resolved my laughter quickly, into a series of sickening, wet coughs that produced spots of blood in the phlegm I spit up.

I touched my head but felt no fever. However, the pain within my lungs had become restrictive and tiring, leading to labored breathing.

For dinner, I had Instant Mashed potatoes, in between coughs.

I can't eat anymore I thought disparagingly as I tossed my aluminum bowl to the dry rotted flooring of the shelter.

I stared, lost in a daze as a mouse came out after several minutes and inspected the contents of the bowl.

The mouse propped itself up upon its hind legs, and its tiny little phalanges lightly gripped the edge of the massive structure standing before it. It took a whiff of what was inside and shook its head almost as if in disgust, before sprinting away.

"Believe me. You're better off, little buddy." I said as the mouse disappeared back into the hole it had come from.

Throughout the night, my sinuses continued to drain down the back of my throat leaving me to awaken to a raw esophagus the following day.

My abdominal muscles ached as I sat up, from the constant coughing throughout the night.

Early morning, the temperature in my area stood at 12 degrees as I combated the cold with my tattered and torn quick dry synthetic pants, thermal shirt and pants, and a light down jacket that I'd started out with 8 months earlier. Now, amidst the many holes and rips the jacket had no more feathers within it.

I shivered over the embers of the fire I'd created the night before.

I had spent the night, watching the flames and hoping that they'd lull me to sleep like they had back at Sam's Gap in Erwin, Tennessee when Torry had created a fire to calm me, and take my mind off of the Norovirus I had been infected with at the time.

I stumbled out of Allentown shelter and down the road at day break, dragging my sluggish feet across the asphalt like a zombie.

The sun was barely over the horizon as I pushed 5.7 miles down the road into Hamburg, Pennsylvania.

I was coughing again, and didn't make it very far before I felt my legs collapsing and my fever starting to take hold.

"I can't go on, Gregory..." I muttered miserably. Every time I felt I might be getting over the sinus infection, turned upper respiratory infection—it seemed to come back ten times as strong.

It was dusk, and truly I was surprised at how little I'd actually accomplished in mileage that day. My camp for the evening was going to have to be in somebodies shed.

I'd stumbled across it while crossing through their pasture at dusk. It was far too dark to continue on, and so inside I found myself bundled up in a bed of hay, tucked into my sleeping bag unbeknownst to anyone.

That following morning, my vision was blurred and packed in the corners with mucus. The sinus headache I had been plagued with was so heavily onset, it made each step nauseous. I fought the urge to throw up, as I stumbled along.

My throat was thick, and when I tried to vocalize anything, I sounded like a 50-year-old, 3 pack a day, chain smoking truck driver.

I pushed on past frozen fields, and frost glazed yellow lines in the middle of the road that twinkled like millions of microscopic diamonds.

Upon reaching the center of town, I booked myself a room at the Microtel there. I had been given a last minute cancellation room priced at only twenty-eight dollars for the evening.

"You're in luck, pal." the woman said with a smile and a thick New York accent.

"Oh, don't 'cha lemme forget to tell ya, 'bout dah box I made for youse guys." She added.

I tilted my head with nauseous results, in confusion.

"Dah hiker boxes ya guys trade stuff in," she clarified.

"Oh. Yeah..." I replied with a grim demeanor.

She handed me the laundry detergent I had purchased from her for a dollar.

"Thank you," I said as I started to stumble away.

"Youse okay? You sound pretty rotten," she called out to me.

I was too tired to answer.

I proceeded to spend my time resting and taking many showers over the course of the day to break up the mucus in my lungs and sinuses. I washed my clothes and nursed my feet when I wasn't attending to my lungs by inhaling steaming, microwaved cups of water.

I had managed to cough up even more phlegm, dotted with spots of blood in it, before collapsing on the bed with my head swimming.

I had cranked up the heat full blast, but laid beneath the covers of my bed, still shivering.

Still feeling frozen despite the sweat beads resting upon my forehead.

My phone suddenly buzzed, showing that I had missed a call. Maybe I hadn't heard it during the 3 hours I'd spent breathing in steam from the shower.

I looked at the message.

It was from my father.

"You're gonna die out there!" my mother cried into the phone. I pulled my ear away from the receiver.

"I can hear your last, dying breaths, Richard!"

My mother always had a flare for the dramatics. I took her comments loosely.

I was definitely hurting to be sure, and I knew I needed medical attention immediately—but at no point did I feel as if I was about to *die* at any point.

I hadn't hit that threshold where I felt I knew: "This is the moment I get help, or I've reached the end of my road."

However, my father whom was a little calmer and collected expressed fear of his own. Especially once he'd heard, I'd been coughing so much, that there was now blood coming out of my lungs as well.

"Richard, all I'm saying is—be careful. Your mother is scared and..."

"She doesn't have to be, Dad. I'm all right." I said in a hoarse, whispered voice due to my inflamed vocal chords. I could hear my mother crying in the background.

"My only son is going to kill himself," She said, between bursts of tears.

I sighed.

"Maybe you should go to the doctor," my father said finally, breaking the silence.

"I don't have the money, Dad. I don't want to spend anything else. I have nearly $250 bucks to make it home, and I'm only 117 miles away from finishing. I think I should be okay."

"If you need some money..." he began to offer, only I cut him off.

"Dad, just let me do this on my own. I don't want any money, and I don't need any help. I came out here to prove to you..."

"You don't have anything to show to us." He interjected.

"We love you, Richard, whether you finished your hike or came home right now." He said, as his voice broke a little.

I felt tears burning on the edges of my eyes at that moment, much as I had heard they were burning in his.

I wanted to hold my parents in my arms, more than ever. Something I hadn't done in years. To tell them face to face that I loved them, instead of pushing them away like I had in the years before.

"Try to get to a hospital or doctor that will bill you down the road. In the future somewhere and some time. Okay?" he asked.

I acknowledged and agreed that I would try—just before hanging up.

As I connected my smartphone to the Microtel's Wi-Fi, I searched for the closest hospital nearby.

"Reading, PA. Thirty-three miles away..." I muttered out loud, as I wrote down directions on my note pad. I tapped the pen against the side of my cheek.

Thirty-three miles. Might as well be a hundred I thought pessimistically to myself.

I scribbled a few numbers to get estimates of taxi cabs to and from that hospital as I laid back in bed. Projections were given of eighty to one hundred and twenty dollar estimates.

That was far too much money for a one-way drive to the hospital. What was my grand plan now?

Cars flew by at incredible speeds the following morning, as I ducked and ran away amidst the splashes of water from puddles their tires threw up at me in their passing.

At times I shielded myself using the cardboard sign I had made myself. It wasn't very effective, though

My sign was simple and read: *In Need Of Medical Attention. Need Ride to Hospital in Reading*

I coughed painfully, as the rain and cold crept into my clothes. My breaths came out in shallow, sickly, labored clouds. I tried blowing heat into my frozen, wet hands on the side of Interstate 78, barely feeling the strength to hold my sign for any longer. The roar of the car or truck engines and their horns were distant. Blurred streaks of headlights and rear brakes or turning signals dominated my vision. Accompanied by the drowning sound of rainfall.

I'd spent two hours in that spot, and in the 36-degree weather managing to do nothing but lose my faith in the kindness of people.

My entire upper torso was numb, and my down jacket was a soggy clump of fabric clinging loosely to my frame.

"I hate you Pennsylvania!" I shouted angrily, giving up and slamming my sign onto the muddy ground. I received strange looks from nearby drivers at the stop light, and a few laughs from those not nearly taking me seriously. And why should they? Who was I? They didn't owe me a thing.

I leaned down and grabbed my cardboard sign. The words I had written upon it, had run and bled, and at that point looked like nothing more than black streaks and smears on a soggy chunk of cardboard.

"Well, this isn't helping me," I muttered miserably.

I began coughing again as I pulled my collar up tighter in the drizzle that was coming down, and walked back to the Microtel.

It was 7 A.M., and it felt as if somebody had poured wet cement into my chest. My breathing became so labored, I felt I actually had to remind myself to try harder to breathe, with each breath.

The World We Came to Find

I downed three ibuprofen to help reduce the inflammation in my lungs and removed my wet clothes and jacket. I knew that I would need to get warm and dry again before I was shoved back out into the cold at check-out time later that morning. The only problem was, I didn't have any change or cash to break for quarters to run the dryer.

I crept out of my room to the housekeeping closet down the hallway. Microtel had a few washers and dryers that only the staff had access to. However, somebody had left the door ajar, and the key to the room in the doors handle. I looked either way down the hallway and towards the ceilings from both directions for any video cameras. There was nothing and nobody to catch me in my act.

You're clear I thought to myself.

I entered the laundry room, tossing my wet clothes into the industrial dryer, and closed the door behind me as I left.

Finally, back in my room, I looked up nearby Urgent Cares or family doctor practices just down the road from the Microtel. This was my last act of desperation.

"This is Hamburg Family Practice, how can I help you?"

"Hopefully you really *can* give me a hand. I'm an Appalachian Trail thru-hiker. I've got absolutely no money or medical insurance, and I'm here in Hamburg. I would go to the hospital, but the closest one is 33 miles away in Reading, and I don't have the money for a taxi. I've had no luck standing in the rain hitching for the last two hours. I believe I've got pneumonia...and I've got no way to get around. I was hoping one of your doctors would possibly see me for free out of the kindness of their hearts. I wasn't sure if they offered pro bono visits, but I've barely got enough money to make it home." I pled. I was exhausted, sick and on day three of a swimming headache. Indeed, I was expecting the answer to be no long before she'd said it.

"Actually no they don't. And we don't take walk-ins either...which is why I don't know what to tell you since we couldn't help you even if you did have money." She replied sadly. I could tell she honestly felt bad for me. The sympathy in her voice felt good to hear, all the same.

After standing on the side of an interstate in the rain, with a sign stating I needed medical attention, in part, I was still upset and pissed off that nobody had given a damn to stop, let alone even inquire as to if they could help in some other way.

"Well, I don't know what I'm supposed to do? I'm so close to being done. I'm only 117 miles from completing my hike. Couldn't I just be billed or something? I mean all I need is antibiotics. I'm not a druggy. I'm not a scumbag...I'm a human being. If I didn't need a prescription, I'd buy them myself. I just need five minutes with a doctor, to give my symptoms to and have him write a prescription. That's all."

"Oh sweety. God bless you, let me see what I can do...honey." She said as she put me on hold.

When she got me back on the line ten minutes later, she asked: "I got good news for you. How's 9 A.M. this morning?"

I smiled, with tears of appreciation in my eyes.

"T...that sounds...incredible..." I stuttered, wiping my eyes. I erupted into a series of wet, ragged coughs that produced more blood in the sputum than usual.

"My God honey that really *does* sound bad. How far are you away from our clinic?" she asked.

"Two...and a half...miles," I whispered with a throat completely on fire.

"Seeing as I've got to walk there, how about 10 A.M. instead?" I asked.

"Actually, that would be perfect." She replied.

After the doctor's visit, I was walking back towards Wal-Mart with a prescription in my hand and an exhausted smile, but a smile all the same upon my face.

The antibiotics would cost me forty dollars, and it didn't seem like an expense I could avoid.

I ate a five dollar Chinese lunch, while my Z-Pack antibiotics were prepared.

"Two Hundred and four dollars," I muttered out loud, as I looked at my online bank account over the Wi-Fi connection on my phone.

"I'll survive," I said with a smile and a positive outlook.

That evening, I was telling my story to the woman behind the counter at the Microtel that had checked me in the day before. She had become absorbed with my story and exclaimed she wanted to know how she could help. She had approached me after seeing I had been sitting in the lobby all day, now that my room stay was over and I had checked out. I had explained to her that I was trying to stay warm as long as possible before I went back out into the cold rain to find a place to set up my hammock tent for the night.

"I don't have a place to sleep, and I can't afford another room," I stated with a shrug.

She nodded her head with a grave expression on her face. I was well aware that what I had just said was a tall order for any hotel worker or manager.

"I have kids…and I doubt my boyfriend would…be okay…if you were to stay at our house…" she began apologetically.

"Oh no! Don't worry. I'm not asking you for a place to stay." I clarified, though in truth I really had been trying to work that angle.

"And I can't really just pass out rooms here," she added.

"No worries, I'll figure something out," I replied with a smile, as I lifted my backpack on.

I started towards the automatic doors when she called out to me.

"It's snowing outside. Or well, it will be later tonight they're saying. For Christ's sake, look at it out there." she said, with hurt in her eyes.

"I've been in worst places. Don't worry." I tried to assure her.

"Where will you sleep? You're sick, and you've got pneumonia." She said with a mother's fear in her voice.

"Maybe I'll hike through the night to keep warm? If I don't stop, I won't get cold." I explained.

"No," she said, shaking her head from side to side. She furrowed her eyebrows, looking at a laminated map of the Microtel's rooms.

"Come here." She said.

"Don't look up at the camera behind me. Just smile and nod a lot. Okay?" she whispered.

I walked over just as she had said, keeping my mouth shut and nodding my head.

"The camera doesn't have audio, but I don't want them reading your lips either. Got it? Room 148 is under repairs for new carpeting. The toilet flooded onto the floor in the room. You could probably remove some of the shampooing equipment and tools off of the bed and stay the night in there. I don't want you going outside and getting any sicker than you already are." She said, secretly slipping me a card to the room.

"I...I don't want to get you in trouble..." I stuttered.

"You won't. And if someone complains, I'll pay for your room. Your life is in danger being sent out into that snow with pneumonia. I think any company would be okay with my saving your life." She said with a smile.

"I...want to...I could kiss you....right now..." I said, feeling my eyes well up with appreciation.

"My boyfriend probably wouldn't like that. So let's just say you'll owe me one. Okay? And make sure you're out of there before 8 A.M. when dayshift takes over, and I leave for the night." she winked at me, as I smiled and took myself to my free room for the evening.

I carded into the room and found it to be absolutely clean, with the heat already on. I had expected the area to smell like raw sewage and for large sections of carpeting to have been ripped up and piled into corners. I expected flooding stains on the floors or walls and sheets covering furniture or for the furniture to have been removed from the room altogether.

The woman behind the counter had either purposefully or accidentally given me an average, clean room.

I collapsed on my free bed, with the heat cranked on max whispering out prayers of blessings to befall that wonderful woman behind the counter that had saved me from the cold.

"You 'sposed to be hikin' da Appalachian Trail?" A Tilden police officer pulled over to ask me, as I walked down Hex Highway.

"Sometimes," I replied.

"Well if so, you're a bit lost. Trails back *that way* and West." He said to me.

Only I wasn't lost. I was exactly where I had wanted to be. I wasn't feeling too confident in being in that forest within the frigid weather, cut off from the rest of society, only because I didn't have the gear to hike in below freezing weather.

"Got anything to drink?" I asked him.

He laughed.

"You need a ride somewhere?" He asked, choosing to ignore my question.

"No thanks. I'm walking." I replied.

He offered me the last mouthful of a bottle of water he'd been drinking from, but I kindly turned down the offer.

Eventually, he wished me well as traffic started flowing more steadily behind him and he drove away.

I passed through a few townships such as Jalappa, Shartlesville, and Straussburg.

I ultimately ended my day behind the Dunkard Brethren Church School.

Despite the size of the forest patch I'd seen in the satellite image on Google Maps, all the leaves on the trees were gone, and the vegetation had all shriveled and died.

If anyone drove into the lot behind the Church school, they would see me potentially trespassing. But all I was doing was sleeping and trying to survive. I wasn't vandalizing anything or making fires...nor was I leaving trash, or hurting anything or anybody. I doubt I'd have been written a ticket or have been prosecuted for that. If anything, seeing someone in such a state usually incurred acts of kindness instead, from my experience out there thus far, so it gave me hope rather than fear.

There was a stream passing through the middle of the small lick of woods, where I could rehydrate. As I pumped water via my purifier, it still looked dirty.

My pump was screwing up, as the liquid inside had frozen a few days before and caused an internal crack within the mechanism. It wasn't working correctly anymore.

Just what I needed. A broken water filtration system.

Several days later, I re-emerged onto the Appalachian Trail and reached Stony Valley Rail-Trail at Rausch Gap. It was 11:30 A.M. when I arrived, and I was confused as to which way I was expected to go.

This is because white blazes painted tree trunks opposite the rail trail yet, other sets of white blazes took a left down across the bridge as well. I took pictures of the water here, which looked an unnaturally metallic light blue as it not only flowed out from a grate in the earth but a nearby stream as well.

Having originally been settled in 1824 due to fresh water springs and coal; Stoney Creek Valley was a thriving village at one time which in 1850 led to the creation of the Schuylkill & Susquehanna Railroad.

A two hundred room resort was built to entice tourists (which would later burn down) to the area by way of a railroad for people to drink from the "divine mineral springs" said to cure all kinds of ailments.

This seemed to be a reoccurring theme of the time because the town of Fuquay where I had grown up as a child was also famed for that very same reason...having hotels and inns built up and around Fuquay Springs because of the "miraculous mineral water" there.

As the town of Stoney Creek Valley ran through its resources, it eventually began to be retaken by nature as people just up and left, leaving it as a ghost town.

When the railroad stopped running through the area...tourists stopped coming.

Eventually, it simply faded away and was retaken by Mother Nature.

In 1945, the Pennsylvania State Game Commission would purchase the land, and to this very day, it was used for hunting.

I didn't see any hunters out there though and instead was met only with blasting winds, gray skies, and solace.

When the wind became too much to bare, I decided to refill my water bottles before heading out to hike and warm up again.

I threw my pack off and grabbed my malfunctioning water pump out of the side pocket.

I then began an awkward descent along an eroded bank.

"Careful..." I whispered out loud to myself, with reassurance.

I hadn't heeded my words that well, however, and I ended up slipping and falling down as the dirt crumbled out from beneath me.

As I fell, I spun around and tried to grasp anything, but there was nothing there to grab.

How pathetic I must've looked when I fell butt first into the stream.

I was in shock at how freezing the water actually was and how it hadn't just been a sheer block of ice at its current temperature. As I went to stand, I stumbled, panicking as I couldn't suck in ANY air. I tried to climb the bank only to fall backward again.

I felt my lungs seize up in immediate shock as I scrambled and clawed my way back onto the shoreline. Seventy-five percent of my body was soaked in icy water, met with a blast of wind.

I climbed up the shoreline, stripping my clothes as fast as humanly possible and grabbed my dry reserves out of my backpack.

I threw EVERYTHING on. My thermal pants and thermal shirt and then my second pair of dry synthetic shirt and pants. I had two dry pairs of socks left as well. I was glad I hadn't decked myself out in my full clothing to combat the cold that day, if only because of this now very real and freezing scenario that had taken place.

My clothes were bringing me no warmth though as the wind began to gust in massive waves, that swayed the trees and caused branches to collapse and fall in faraway sections of the woods unseen by my eyes.

I had no intention of slipping my cold, wet boots back on and instead put on my crocs. Along the rail trail, I stopped and crawled down into a dry ditch to get out of the wind.

"Jesus, I'm gonna freeze to death out here," I said to myself, working fast.

I punched a hole into the layer of ice that had grown across the murky swamp water the bridge was passing over. I pulled out my sleeping bag and wrapped myself in it. I then retrieved my aluminum bowl, and dipped it into the filthy water before beginning to boil the muddy liquid.

I revived my hands by cupping them around the flames, and I continued sipping the hot, dirty water until I felt my core was warm enough to continue on.

But none of this had helped my feet or legs, nor the skin around my stomach and lower back. With the wind picking up with ferocity and cutting through every layer of clothing—I began to jog. To heat up my core as much as humanly possible, even if it meant doing so by exertion.

The outer layer of my flesh was frozen, but I knew I was keeping my core alive.

I had wrenched and rung my wet clothes out and then tied them in various places to the outsides of my pack to try and get them as dry in the gusting wind as possible.

Both my down and fleece jackets were wet, however, and my Walmart thermals weren't nearly doing enough to keep me warm.

Within minutes of having tied my wet clothes to the sides of my pack, they had already lightly frozen in the freezing wind.

I lifted my shirt to check the skin around my stomach and found that it had turned a dark maroon color.

I was reliving the same scenario I had encountered back at Sassafras Gap Shelter, after climbing Cheoha Bald in North Carolina.

I was rather frightened and what made it worst, was that this very trails length was 21 miles long. I wasn't even sure at what mileage the Appalachian Trail had joined it.

I had reached the Dauphin town line indicated by a cement pillar at 12:45 P.M., however, there wasn't a single building in sight to suggest that I was anywhere near civilization of any sort.

Finally, I came across what I believed to be the trailhead because a forest gate had been placed in the roadway.

I walked around it to find an empty parking lot which only dampened my mood even more.

It was almost dark, and I had maybe an hour of light left.

When I finally began to reach civilization, I stumbled down the road and eventually stopped to pull out my phone.

I found I had finally gotten a signal.

I was shocked to realize that according to my GPS, I had walked 27 miles that day! If it told me anything, it was that the fear of freezing to death could really put some pep in your step.

I sat on the side of the road for a moment, while my feet begged to be put out of their misery. I could feel two huge blisters beneath both feet and removed my crocs, only to see there were blood stains on the fabric of my socks.

I was a mere eight miles away from The Doyle which was a hostel in the town of Duncannon. However, if it was like any other hostel it had a closing time, and on a Sunday evening that might've been early for all I knew.

I didn't want to cheat, and it was the hardest decision I had to make in a long time; because I was so proud of walking as much as I had.

But eight more miles on top of the 27 I had already pumped out, was too impossible an undertaking and I was risking another night out in the cold with none of the clothes to make it work in my already injured position.

With weather reports on my phone explaining that within my area it was going to drop to the mid-teens that night and result in a flurry of snow, I called a nearby taxi cab company which immediately turned me down.

"Sorry, but I can give you a number for the night crew." He said, bored and maybe even bothered by my call.

"Listen, I'll give you whatever you want to charge me," I said, which actually meant only the roughly $200 dollars I had left.

"Look, I'm really sorry about your predicament and all buddy, but I'm probably an hour's drive away from you in Harrisburg."

"It says on Google maps, you're only 3.4 miles away! PLEASE HELP ME!" I shouted angrily into the phone.

"Look, I can give you the number to a night crew...or you can go fuck yourself. You gonna take it down or not?" He replied.

I sighed, feeling hopeless.

"Yes," I muttered.

So he gave me a number for a "night crew" working out of Harrisburg. Whatever that was supposed to have meant to me.

Turned out, however, that the number he had given me was disconnected.

"I'm sorry, but the number you have dialed has been disconnected. Please try your call again." The recorded voice said into my ear.

As cars passed, I stuck out my thumb, with each speeding up every time they saw me.

After the sixth passing car, I began waving my arms at them wildly as if I had been in some great emergency or wreck.

I got two angry honks from two different vehicles.

After a while, I lost my anger and rage, and just "existed" within a plane of hopelessness.

I swallowed my pride, my shame, and fears of face to face rejection— and began approaching houses along the side of the road.

I knocked on doors, rung doorbells and got no answers.

At one point somebody looked out of their window because I saw the shade move. But they never came to the door.

Finally, at the next house, somebody did.

"May I please step inside for a moment sir, I'm freezing."

I felt so embarrassed and humbled for just an inkling of reprieve. If only to warm myself for five minutes from the gale force winds tossing me around, before moving on.

I felt this odd mix of anger and sadness for bothering these people. Asking for nothing more than to stand in a shed or garage...anywhere for a moment's chance at warmth. Something you may potentially take for granted, every day.

The man decked out in woodland camo looked past and around me as if I had people hiding in the shadows, waiting to spring out the moment he said yes to my inquiry.

"No. I'm sorry, but you're gonna have to move along." He stated in a dull, southern drawl.

He didn't ask why I had stopped at his door and he didn't look at my backpack. Only briefly did he look into my glazed over, and exhausted eyes.

I turned, walking away into the darkness.

I tried the house next door where an older woman answered with untrusting eyes.

"Ma'am, I fell in a river about 18 miles back in that state game land. I'm currently hiking the Appalachian Trail on and off on my way back to North Carolina. Right now I can barely feel anything. I was hoping you had a shed or a garage that I could stand in out of this wind for a few minutes just to warm up. This is my driver's license. You can hold on to it if you think I'm a bad guy. I'm just asking for a moment of warmth while I try to find a taxi." I said, handing her my license.

"Hold on. Let me talk to my husband." She said, disappearing inside her home with my I.D. in her hand. She closed and locked the deadbolt on her door behind her.

I felt I actually might have a shot, and smiled at fates kindness.

But when she had returned, she handed my driver's license back to me.

"I'm sorry, but my husband and I are about to go to bed. We can't help you." She said.

My heart dropped, and I felt off.

I didn't accept her apology.

I didn't thank her for her time or consideration, had it ever even been there.

I wanted nothing from her anymore, as I turned and walked away.

The last house I tried was answered by two children. The girl looked to be about six and her baby brother was maybe three or four years old.

"Hi! You can come in!" the older of the two exclaimed immediately, trying to open the door for me.

One could look at the naiveté in a child's response like that one, and momentarily find it to be absolutely beautiful. The sheer kindness and thought of an innocent mind, oblivious to the outside dangers of the world; so willing to let a complete stranger in out of the cold.

It was beautiful in that "perfect world" kind of way—but in a different light, it was absolutely terrifying.

"Oh no, no, no. That's okay. Could you get your parents for me, though, please?" I asked, pressing back against the swinging glass screen door so that the child wouldn't open it. I didn't want to alarm her parents. I was the stranger here.

So the little girl ran off while her little brother stared up at me with his thumb in his mouth; wordless.

I smiled, and he smiled back.

When the mother appeared, she led the boy away and threw me a glance, like I was the biggest piece of trash she had ever seen.

When her husband came to the door; as he opened it, she shouted from another room: "Tell him we don't have any money!"

He ignored her request in my presence.

"Yes?" He asked.

"My names John Morris," I said, handing him my driver's license.

He looked down at it as I went on.

"I'm hiking the Appalachian trail. I've been walking since March 17th. This is the coldest it's been out here since I've been on the trail. I need to call a taxi, but I don't know this area, or if there are any motels around...and if I stand still for more than a minute I'm freezing. All I'm asking is a garage to stand inside or a shed. I don't even have to come into the house." I begged.

"Well, there aren't any motels or taxis around here that I'm aware of. Where are you trying to get to?" he asked, looking over my license.

"Duncannon," I replied, shivering as another blast of wind passed right through me.

"Oh yeah, you're only about 10 miles or so away. But that's nothing for a hiker that's gone from Georgia to Maine." He laughed.

"Sir, I've hiked 26...maybe even 27 miles today already. I can't feel my fingers. I fell into a river earlier today at Rausch Gap, and I haven't recovered from the cold. It's too hard to recover in this wind." I pled.

He looked at me for a moment, before nodding his head.

"Tell him 'no,' Jason!" His wife shouted from the other room.

"Stop it." He replied to her, in an annoyed tone.

"I could unlock the shed for a couple minutes." He said, thinking out loud.

"Our wedding pictures are in there Jason!" She howled, at him.

I couldn't believe she'd said that. As if that would be the first thing I'd want to steal if I had actually been there to rob her.

The man was still contemplating when I felt my knees give out from under me.

I got light headed, and sick suddenly...and simply crumpled onto their stoop. I didn't lose consciousness, but I was so cold, and my feet and ankles were in so much pain, I couldn't stand any longer.

The guy looked down at me with a smirk on his face.

"No need for the dramatics, man." He said, as his wife shouted at him: "Just close the door!"

"She's gonna bitch all night if I let you in. Look, I can call an ambulance if you want."

He handed me my license back, as I slowly, painfully stood—clambering to my destroyed feet with no response for him.

Nothing to say, to such an unwelcoming household.

I felt dead inside as he called after me.

"Hey, I thought you said you were cold?" He asked.

Cold wasn't the term for what I was. Hypothermic seemed a better fit.

He could "open his shed for a couple minutes" he'd said.

How gracious, was this guy? To open his shed in 15-degree weather for a guy to stand in, who was suffering from hypothermia?

Could you get any more kind than that?

I had remembered that Trail Angel Mary had been suggested as a Facebook friend by Stephanie, back before she had completed and left the trail. Steph had given me that information in the event I needed to utilize her shuttle services.

I looked in AWOL's guide and found Trail Angel Mary's phone number.

I stood uncaring, halfway in the middle right lane of the road, as people swerved around me in the darkness or honked.

I never even bothered to look up at them. I was so mentally and physically exhausted I didn't give a rat's ass about being an inconvenience to them. Besides, if they had run me over at least, I could concentrate on a different kind of pain.

Maybe somebody would call a cop?

Maybe I'd even go to a warm jail cell for the night, with a free meal.

I just didn't care anymore.

And that eight miles that I'd be skipping to reach The Doyle?

Well, I didn't give a damn about that either.

I had reached Trail Angel Mary Parry over the phone, who told me that she knew the road I was on.

She had heard my story and had grabbed a large cup of hot cocoa along the way, to picking me up.

When she arrived, I all but fell into her van on the side of that dark road.

While she drove, she talked about the trail. We talked about life, but most importantly; she cranked the heat full-blast in the van as I soaked in the warmth and gratefully gulped down every last drop of that cup of cocoa.

"Your face looks so pale. You're lucky you were able to reach me because I was about to go to bed." She exclaimed.

My right ankle panged painfully as if my joints were held together by jagged, sharp bone shards. Simply readjusting my legs, sent tendril shocks of pain throughout my calves and thighs.

I asked that she take me by an ATM, where I withdrew a hundred bucks. After giving her a generous tip, I thanked her wholeheartedly while she tried to give me some of the money back.

"I had nowhere to go. No motels, or hotels around here. People weren't even opening their doors to me. I was standing in the middle of the road waving my hands and cars wouldn't even stop. You saved my life, Mary. You deserve a whole lot more than this."

It was only money.

I had no value or desire for it anymore, except that I needed these used pieces of paper printed with green ink, to survive out here just a little longer.

If I hadn't needed it to get back home, she could've had the rest of my cash for all I cared.

When she had dropped me off at The Doyle, she gave me directions to her place if I needed anything else from her.

I thanked her and waved goodbye...as I made my way inside, where I paid $53 dollars in cash for two nights.

I needed the rest.

The Doyle was quite the legendary place it had been built up to be by other hikers. Its longtime association with the trail and the hikers passing through Duncannon spoke for itself.

The Doyle had been built in 1905 atop what was formerly called the National Hotel. Originally named the "Johnson Hotel," it was owned privately by Adolphus Busch who had once owned several other properties in the area as well. When he died, his hotels and land were given over to his company, Anheuser-Busch (Budweiser). It was one of several hotels purchased (and currently left standing) which existed if only to sell and market their beers before prohibition hit.

After Prohibition came and went, the laws had changed, and the hotels were sold away.

It became the Doyle in 1945. As I was looking for history on it, I stumbled into the online archives of a local newspaper company. I found some of the articles written in it to be rather humorous. It's funny how politically correct we had become as a nation. A lot of the things written in the newspaper at the time seemed of have had no professionalism in them at all.

For example, when was the last time you read a "Wanted AD" in the newspaper seeking a "good little girl"?

Then there was this: "A certain judge has just affirmed the right of a man to swear in his own home. We do not precisely see where the judge got his law since, in most of the states of the Union, profanity is a punishable offense. And if it be against the law we do not see how it is allowable anywhere else."

And that was the end of the article! Nothing else to be said about it.

Then there was this bit of news on August 3rd, 1904 via Town and Country:

"Wm. Heiser, a worthless character, and Katie McCormick, a girl 14 years old of Atco, New Jersey were apprehended in Newport last week as runaways and taken to New Jersey. Heiser who was 20 years old, had enticed the girl away from home."

I found it hilarious that the journalist got away injecting personal views and beliefs of the man's character into the story.

I think we all agree that when you report a news story, the best way to do that is in a nonpartisanship manner; utilizing "journalistic objectivity."

I had spent most of the day in bed, with my feet propped up, which had caused a bout of cabin fever.

My ankle was in such a state of disrepair that my teeth automatically clenched, whenever I stood.

Even gathering the gall to pee had become a chore. I simply held it in for hours on end, until I could no longer take the ache of my bladder adding to the pain of everything else.

It was snowing outside rather heavily, with high gusts of wind that sent snowflakes furiously scattering about in the air on their forever downward spiral towards the earth. Blankets of snow gathered against doorways and lightly dusted the old floorboards beneath crumbling awnings, and abandoned buildings in the town of Duncannon.

Several structures had been condemned, and their windows and doors boarded up. Others had fallen victim to vandalism.

As I limped along the splintered, broken sidewalks...it felt rather foreboding. I always sensed I was being watched.

Window shades, yellowed by years of cigarette smoke and age would move minutely as if ghosts of the past watched me as I stumbled down those abandoned streets. Maybe even desperate to tell me their stories.

People looked out from the upstairs apartments of businesses boarded up, or structures condemned below.

And it was strange, in that I could almost always hear far away laughter or conversations.

Only nobody walked the streets.

I shuffled, limping along, my face frozen, wind burnt and weathered. Dried tight by the cold. My beard scraggly, like a hundred thousand octopus tentacles all thinking, moving and writhing in their own directions with every gust of wind. My face barren, and devoid of emotion and my toboggan drawn down tight to hide the rat's nest, that was my hair. My clothes, my body filthy. Dirt, in the cracks along the sides of my calloused hands. Blackened beneath the fingernails.

I was no longer the person I once was, back in North Carolina.

No matter how financially destitute, or disheveled that I now was within the rags clothing me, I was okay with having changed. If anything, I felt stronger and more experienced than I had been in my sheltered life back at home.

Upon my return to the hotel, I talked to the owners, Pat and Vicki. I bided my time by playing billiards, dabbling in passing conversations, watching television with them and mulling over the current events on the news programs.

Often Pat shook his head, going on about how much worse the world was turning while offering me items off of the menu intermittently if only to steer clear of any conversation leaning towards politics.

Meanwhile, Vicky spoke of the big dreams she had of playing the lottery and wishing that they could afford to fix up the place with the winnings. Every time, while eyeing another Powerball ticket she had purchased, or while rubbing scratch-offs.

She was by no means reserved to The Doyle's current state, proudly saying: "It's the best/worst hotel on the trail!"

It was truly a beautiful building, The Doyle; with that mysterious age-old charm about it. If the walls could talk or project the things they'd seen in the years of its existence, you could make movies out of the lives of the people that had passed through there.

But that wasn't to say it wasn't without its fair share of problems either.

The bathrooms ceiling tiles had all but caved in, exposing the wires, the pipes and rusted inner workings of the building.

Sections of sagging or water warped sheet rock had fallen away, exposing the decaying skeletal innards of wood beams and joints.

Pits or holes in the floors...or toilets that had been in disrepair for over a decade that stood unused, and forgotten in darker parts of the building.

The second floor had once been a ballroom but had been converted into the owner's living area.

Meanwhile, five town locals rented out and lived in rooms on the 3rd and 4th floors.

The Doyle had survived three floods. One of which the water had risen from the nearby Susquehanna River by as much as 39 feet!

There was so much story to the building, and if you sat at the bar, Vicky and Pat were more than happy to break out the "family portraits" of The Doyle and tell you ALL about the history.

I had stopped by Trail Angel Mary's place, to thank her again for the events of the night before. She had, in turn, invited me to Thanksgiving with her at the local Veteran Affairs Center. But while I would have loved to go—I was also undecided of taking her up on that offer, only because I needed to make miles and finish my hike, being that I was now so close to the end of my journey.

It would have to be a decision made in the morning, depending on the weather.

Sitting out front of The Doyle, I read over the map of what I had in the days ahead of me.

Suddenly, I saw a ghost from the past walking up in thermals with an impossibly small ultra-light backpack on.

The thru-hikers name was "Prada" and the last time I had seen him was with Woodstock and Wales at a grocery store back in Gorham,

New Hampshire. But even before that, I had seen him in the 100 mile wilderness at Pierce Pond, in Maine.

"Well look who it is," I said with a smile.

"I'm bad with names, but I'm sure I remember you." he replied.

"I was hiking with Woodstock and Wales way back north in August and September."

"That's right! You walking the AT anymore?" he asked me with genuine enthusiasm in his voice.

"Off and on, I guess you could say. Still out here, but I sometimes hike the roads and through towns instead of along the AT. How about you?" I asked.

"Well, I've still got over a thousand miles to go. I'm southbound hiking to Springer Mountain. I hope to be done sometime in late January or February." He replied.

He looked over my clothes and scrunched his face slightly.

"Aren't you cold?" he asked.

"Freezing, actually," I replied with a laugh. Prada was decked out in thick thermals and a down coat that looked so warm, I immediately envied him.

"I mean dude, you've got paper-thin, quick-dry synthetics on in below freezing weather. You crazy or something?" he commented.

"I didn't prepare properly. I was one of those idiots that expected to be busting out 18 and 20-mile hikes every single day—and I was supposed to have been done in four or five months."

"Yeah, those itineraries are always bullshit aren't they?" he said with a chuckle.

"We never factor in getting hurt…" I said.

"Or getting sick…" he chimed in.

"Or wanting a few days off," I added, smirking at how truly slow my journey had been.

We caught up and talked about how brutal the trail had been through Pennsylvania thus far. He explained to me that he was miserable because of the cold and the snow, but at the same time, he had expected it.

"But just not yet. You know? I've still got so far to go, and I don't want to be bogged down with snow on top of everything else for the next thousand miles."

"I've only got three days left till I reach Pine Grove Furnace, where I flipped back in July," I said, with just a little bit of pride. However, that had been five months before and when I thought about it—it didn't seem really that impressive to me after all.

My kindergarten teacher once asked me: "What do you want to be when you grow up?"

Children never regularly reply to these questions with answers that they wanted to be Sewage Treatment Specialists or Bank Loan Officers. I can't honestly say I've ever heard a child state that they wanted to manage IRA's either. You could say a big part of that is because as children, there aren't many Investment Banker Superhero cartoons out there for them to identify with.

We want to be Astronauts, because of the mystery, exploration and the adventure.

We want to be soldiers and heroes renowned for the service to our country and keeping friends and family safe on domestic or foreign soil.

We want to be police or firemen to protect and save lives or nurses, and doctors to take care of people.

When my Kindergarten teacher Mrs. Eason asked what I wanted to be when I grew up, I told her I wanted to be an "Ambulance Driver." An EMT, like my father, had been at an early point in his life.

It was true, that he was my role model growing up. But that wasn't the sole reason as to why I had prematurely chosen that potential career path.

Instead, when the teacher had exclaimed with genuine pride in her voice that my father had "helped people," my vision of him had become instantly solidified. My mother would go on and on about how many lives he had saved, grossly exaggerating the details almost all of the time while all I cared about was making him as proud of me the same way, someday, that this teacher was proud of his service.

It was instilled in me, at a young age.

As I grew up, and as I failed in school I felt ways apart for my entire life. Shoved into one special education class to the next, I couldn't understand the numbers and equations when it came to math. I had no interest in complicated scientific theories or the biology of frogs and animals.

Instead, my mind wandered, as I wrote stories in the back of the room that had nothing to do with the subject matter we were supposed to have been learning. I would pretend that I was miles and miles away, within my own world. Writing adventures of fellow school girls and crushes I had that had been saved from school bullies by me of course. Stories that would never find the light of the day and either eventually vanished or were thrown away by myself as I read the cliché and clunky storylines and cringed in disgust.

Eventually, lack of self-confidence in myself and my own abilities helped in my decision to drop out of high school.

I never married, never gave my parents the grandchildren they wanted and at 30, I sat around all day after work and grew depressed at what little I had actually become. How little impact I had made on the world or even in my own life. When the whispers of my disapproval grew too much to handle within my own mind, I turned to alcohol to numb my emotions.

I didn't enjoy my job because I never felt like I was doing anything substantial. I didn't enjoy my life with Melody because it felt like a ruse. And with each wrong decision I made, the hill I fell down felt taller and taller.

So here I was now.

I had made a change and reset my life.

And with each hardship I faced, I remembered my past and how I had given up thousands of times before. How truly hopeless giving up had made me feel.

It was a goal, to never become stagnant and float in place like I had done for my entire time on this planet thus far.

If I was ever going to change the outcome of my life, I couldn't sit back and wait for *somebody else* to take the wheel and weather out the storm for me.

I would have to find that courage to stand. To take hold of the wheel and take back over my life once and for all. To navigate the rocks and hurdles and waves seeking desperately to sink me under like the millions of other people did each day their selves.

For the first time in my life that I could remember, I was actually proud of myself and everything that I had accomplished thus far.

And as I laid in bed, unable to sleep—all I could do was anticipate the very ending of my hike. The one that I'd dreamt about almost every day, for more than eight months.

They were good thoughts that brought smiles to my face.

I thought of model bikini-clad women, waiting to greet me at the finish line with beer and endless steaks, ribs or marinated grilled chicken breasts.

In November, and twenty-six-degree weather? I thought counter-intuitively.

"Yes, in twenty-six-degree weather. Asshole." I replied to the cynical part of myself out loud.

It was Thanksgiving Day, and the weather had turned worse for wear. I went to Trail Angel Mary's house, seeking her out but found that she was already gone.

Outside of The Doyle, Prada was trying to get a signal on his phone and find a place to eat for the holiday.

"Bro, somethin' ain't right about not having anything to eat on this day." He explained to me.

"I know. I just went to see Trail Angel Mary, and take her up on her offer to eat at the VA Center, but she had already left. I don't know where we can eat and everything around here looks closed." I replied.

As we walked hopelessly around town from one restaurant to the next, our "feast" was turning out to be a bologna sandwich from the one open store in Duncannon; a gas station.

So I thought to myself for a bit and put a dash of shame aside.

"Well, what could it hurt?" I muttered out loud finally.

"What's that?" Prada asked, blowing into his rose colored hands for warmth as he looked away from the abandoned pizza shop in town.

"I'm gonna see if any local churches have any Thanksgiving Dinners going on today. Maybe if there is one close enough, we could walk there and get a free meal." I replied optimistically.

"Dude, that's an excellent idea!"

"I know, I know…" I replied egotistically.

"When it comes to food, I have the *best ideas*. Believe me." I added confidently.

I had Google searched "Free Thanksgiving Dinner Duncannon, PA."

The first listing to come up was a link to a local churches Facebook page.

So after clicking it, I found that the church was reminding people on their Facebook Pages own timeline to RSVP if they thought they'd be making it to the dinner.

In the comment section of the announcement, I posted a plea, and we proceeded to have the following exchange:

John Morris: *Hi, I am an AT Thru-hiker currently staying at the Doyle in Duncannon. Me and a fellow thru-hiker here have*

nowhere to go for Thanksgiving and we're curious if we could join you for dinner.
Lindsey: *Hi John, you are more than welcome to join us for our dinner at Noon. We have plenty of food out at the church.*
John Morris: *Thank you so much. Is there a cut off time? Because we don't have a car, so we will be walking there.*
Lindsey: *It should be going on until 1:30 P.M., but we can arrange a ride if you'd like.*
John Morris: *That would be incredible. Thank you so much. What time should we meet somebody out front of the hotel?*
Lindsey: *A guy named Tom will be down with the church van at 11:45.*
John Morris: *Thank you very much. God bless you all.*

Cornerstone Christian Church proceeded to pick us up exactly on time and fed us without end until we had turkey and stuffing and pumpkin pie coming out of our ears.

When we had ingested as much as we could physically fit within our stomachs, they then gave us each three "to-go" boxes each to make meals for the days ahead.

Prada and I laughed happily at how such an unusual turn of events could come across in such a moment of need.

Because as I said before; food, water and a warm place to sleep were your most precious commodities while out on the Appalachian Trail.

When we had returned, Vicky and Pat decidedly let us stay the night for free—because it was Thanksgiving. A testament to the kindness you regularly found on the AT.

I sat up slowly and glanced out the window, watching the snow falling down in fat clumps. It was morning, and I packed my things quietly;

preparing to head across the street for breakfast before heading out when Prada came from his room.

"Yo dude, you hungry brother?" He asked, seeing I was packed and ready to head back out to the trail. It was 6:34.

I had time for a sit-down meal.

"Yeah. I'm saving the Thanksgiving leftovers for the trail and going across the street for a warm, cheap breakfast before heading out. You wanna join me?" I asked, zipping up a couple open pockets on my pack.

"Bro, I've been eyeing that place for the last half an hour. Let's hit it up."

And so we were both off.

We left our keys to our rooms, in the locks on the doors like we'd been told by Vicky and Pat before leaving, and then headed out of the Famous Doyle with our packs in tow.

As we ate, we talked about how we had lucked out the day before.

"Still can't believe they just up and snagged two complete strangers dude," Prada said, forking some eggs into his mouth.

"You know, it's gonna make me sound like an asshole for noticing it. But churches are probably the best place to receive a free hand out anywhere you decide to walk in this country." I replied, stirring the sausage gravy onto my biscuit before taking a bite.

When the waitress came to drop off our check, I decidedly paid for both of our breakfasts.

"Dude, you don't have to pay for me," Prada said, taking out cash.

"Listen, I'm only offering if you promise me that you'll finish," I said.

"Oh yeah bro, I'm definitely finishing this hike. Nothing short of death is gonna stop me, dude." He reassured me.

We said our goodbyes, and I was hiking by eight. I left town via Bloomfield Road which took a left onto Dellville about a mile and a half down.

Old structures and ruins stood along the side where houses had once so clearly been mere feet from the path of vehicular travel.

It made it hard to find room to walk the 6-inch shoulder, as cars flew by at ungodly speeds on icy roads.

When I reached the large expanse of open frozen fields, I began long treks across harvested corn flats. The sounds of soft wisps and dried husks accompanied my walk as I randomly stumbled across the rows and raised mounds, so dream bound and wrapped up in the beauty of my location.

It was a few hours later, when I came across the Dellville Covered Bridge several miles down the road, that crossed Sherman Creek.

The bridge had been built in 1889 and was still standing; albeit no longer in use to vehicles.

I took a few pictures and carried on along that narrow slice of blacktop in the middle of nowhere while looking up at dark gray clouds that had attempted but ultimately failed all the same to block out the sun.

The fields were golden and rolling and despite being midday—the grass crunched and crumbled along the side of that road beneath my feet; still frozen.

When I reached Highway 34, I was on a ridgeline that looked down into the valley at several cities and townships randomly dropped about here and there.

In a nearby rain ditch beneath a dead bird, I found a ten dollar bill with a few frozen drops of blood on it.

I threw it into my pocket and began hiking again down the highway. A few feet from the ten dollar bill, I also came across a burnt spoon, a shattered lighter and used hypodermic needles.

Had I really just come across somebodies heroin kit, right there on the side of the highway?

I began making my way towards Middlesex and east Carlisle on foot by dragging my boots loudly across the pavement.

The land here was very eclectic, going from lush farmlands to crowded highways to subtle hills and valleys with soft dips or pits in the earth amongst a rural landscape.

I walked a mile along a horse pasture where one such creature followed me along, expecting to possibly be fed a treat. Had I anything to give, the horse would have gotten one as well.

My last stretch of hiking had me passing through one more two-mile section of fields.

I took a moment to catch my breath on the side of the road and heard the approach of a car engine from far away. I brushed aside the ice droplets that had accumulated around my mouth and nose, and watched from a distance, as a woman approached in a 2013 Jeep Cherokee—swerving all over the road.

As she drifted towards me, I dropped my pack and flew into the ditch. She swerved at me and over corrected herself wildly towards the other side of the road—jamming on the brakes and creating a huge cloud of smoke and tire marks as she slid to a stop.

She had been texting on her smartphone and driving at the same time and had narrowly missed clipping my dropped backpack by a foot or less.

"Oh my God, are you okay?!" She shouted frantically as she ran out from around her car parked at an angle in the middle of the road.

"Jesus Christ lady, what are you trying to do?! Kill me?" I shouted angrily at her as I picked myself up out of the ditch and started dusting snow and bits of shrubbery off of my clothes.

"I am so sorry, I didn't even see you there..." She replied, horrified.

"YEAH! BECAUSE YOU WERE TEXTING AND DRIVING LIKE A MORON!" I shouted at her.

"I should be calling the police on you right NOW!" I added.

The woman's face appeared so guilty, immediately felt bad for the threat I'd given her.

I thought of this as not only a learning lesson for *her*. But a bit of compensation for *me* as well. My thought process had changed, and I was adapting, and learning how to survive. I was learning different ways to get food or to get money when I wasn't finding it along the side of the road. I attributed a lot of that to spending hours and hours on end while hiking, thinking of possible scenarios taking place and their potential outcomes.

It was because of this, I instantly began to fake a limp when climbing out of the ditch.

"Oh no, did I hit you?" She asked fearfully, with tears in her eyes as she ran towards me.

She placed her hands on my shoulders, but I gently pushed her hands away. I needed to complete the act.

"Please don't touch me, lady...you've done enough damage already. I still had 13 miles to hike today..." I lied.

"Now that I've potentially broken my ankle while dodging your damned car, I can barely walk. Now I'm gonna have to use money I don't have to get a motel room. I should really be suing you for this." I muttered, throwing it all on extra thick.

"Can I take you to a hospital? I can take you wherever you need to go. Please. I am so, so sorry." She pled.

I ignored her, acting in pain as I attempted to rotate my "hurt ankle."

"Yup. I probably won't be walking normal ever again." I said, shaking my head from side to side. Maybe that was a little *too* much drama because the woman's expression began to fade from fear to suspicion.

"What if I fixed this whole situation by paying for your room for tonight?" She offered, brushing both of her eyes with the back of her hand.

I felt a smile growing inside, but I knew I could not take her up on an offer that grand. I would have felt way too guilty for doing so.

"Listen. If you really want to help me out, I could use ten dollars so I can sit somewhere for a while, eat a warm meal and let this ankle rest up some."

"Ten dollars? Sure, anything! Are you sure that's enough? I can give you more if you want." She said, searching through her purse.

If I was a complete scumbag, it could've been PAYDAY for me.

But I only wanted her to learn a lesson. I wasn't trying to get her in any trouble and I had no intention of calling the police. I wanted her to be more careful on the road, that was all.

If anything, she was getting off easy, and I didn't feel a bit apologetic about my request.

She went on to offer me a ride which I turned down. I was only 1.7 miles away from the Econo Lodge, and it was only 3 P.M.

I had hiked 15.5 miles already.

I left the limping act on as she drove out of sight and then began walking regularly again.

Not only had my motel practically paid for itself with the ten dollars I'd found earlier that day on the side of the road—but now I had dinner as well!

Ten bucks bought me three hot dogs, a big bag of chips and two, one-liter bottles of Brisk Iced Tea. For dessert, I added two packs of Reese's Peanut Butter cups. Ten bucks went a long way in towns, away from the Appalachian Trail.

I couldn't sleep.

Not so close to the finish line.

With only 11 miles left to go, it was early when I took off. That was because at 1 A.M. when I had awoken, all I found myself doing was staring with anticipation up at the ceiling.

I had started packing my things, hoping that if I could exert a little energy by moving quickly enough, I might just exhaust myself with the intent to fall back asleep.

Instead, all I found myself doing was staring at the alarm clock as I sat on the side of my bed.

I glanced down at my backpack, with reflection; counting the rips and tears on the fabric. Making a note of the hole that had been chewed through its front pocket back in the Smoky Mountains.

"This is it, Gregory. This is the day it finally all ends." I said.

Gregory didn't have much to say in response, but I'd like to think he was appreciative if for no other reason than because he hadn't fallen over.

So that was how I found myself hiking early.

Three in the morning, to be exact.

"Freezing. Yes, I'm freezing. Ohhhh, but I'm walking. I'm walking. I'm walking!" I stammered to myself out loud as each word quivered past my lips into the frigid, wintry air.

It would be about an hour and a half later when I reached the Sheetz gas station in Mt Holly Springs, Pennsylvania.

There was a line, even this early for food.

When it was my turn, I used the food ordering screen to throw together an oddly custom created barbecue sauced BLT on a pretzel roll with a hash brown on top of it.

A Strange concoction, sure, but fuel to your average hiker all the same.

As I paid for my things, I felt a lot of eyes on me.

A lot of locals staring me down and eyeing my pack as I weaved in and around people standing in the way or waiting for their orders to be completed.

"That'll be $6.72." the cashier said, as I tried to get the money out from my pocket. I was scrambling and searching and found that I had come up $1.16 shy as I counted my change and placed it on the counter.

There were hurried sighs behind me, and I felt my face flush with embarrassment. I quickly dropped my pack and started searching through the side pocket when I had heard a young teenage girl mutter: "This guy is gonna take all day."

I stopped searching and looked up at everyone all looking back at me. It was silent in the line, and I turned back to the counter with an apologetic expression.

"It appears I don't have the money," I said with a shameful tone. The cashier handed me the crumpled dollar bills and coins I had given him with an understanding nod.

Outside, I was walking across the parking lot when suddenly I heard someone call out to me.

"Yo homie. Where you goin'?"

I kept walking, not believing anybody had been talking to me.

"Hey, guy...hol' up a sec." I heard somebody call out again. Finally, I turned around to find a rather large black man with tattoos covering his body walking towards me.

I was admittedly taken aback and intimidated as the guy appeared to be the Incredible Hulks twin brother. Built like a body builder and a professional NFL player, he had tattooed tear drops beneath either eye.

He had names I couldn't read tattooed to his neck and philosophical quotes painted down either forearm as well.

He had designs, pictures, and stories inked into his broad jawline down to every inch of his veiny arms and hands.

"Where ya headed, brah?" He asked, towering over me like a giant. I could swear I almost felt the ground tremble with his steps.

"Pine Grove Furnace, just down the road," I replied with a gulp, wondering if I should've done that. Was it a good idea to tell him where I was going?

"You need a ride?" He asked. On his chest, a company badge of some sort with a barcode was dangling.

"Nah man. I appreciate it, though." I said as he began to reach into his back pocket.

He pulled out his wallet suddenly.

"How much you need?" He asked as I gave him a confused look.

He pulled out maybe three hundred, in twenty dollar bills.

"Whoa...dude. I'm good. I promise." I laughed, anxiously holding up both hands and stepping back. What the heck was going on?

"Where you headed for the holidays, yo? You got some place to go?" He asked.

Apparently, unbeknownst to me—I had passed up a homeless shelter back in Carlisle, and he was willing to drop me off there. He went on to say that the shelter in Harrisburg allowed you to stay for up to 10 days and he'd drop me off there if I had wanted to go.

Truthfully, that sounded rather promising, only because temporarily speaking I was in fact, homeless. Part of me wanted to take him up on that offer and hop into his vehicle.

But that was also *north*, and I was no longer going in that direction anymore.

When I thanked him and declined, he then folded up maybe $60 to $80 dollars in twenty dollar bills and held it out to me.

"Man, I can't take that. I really appreciate it, though..." I began, pushing his hand away as he cut me off.

"I ain't offerin' brah, I'm tellin' you to take it. Here." He said, insisting I receive the cash as he opened my palm and pushed the bills into the center.

"But why? I don't even know you?" I asked, handing him the money back.

"I had a chance to right a lot of peoples wrongs at a point in my life. And my dumbass didn't do it because I was greedy. Well, I'm doin' it now. Or tryin' to at least..." he hinted, holding the money out to me.

"Listen. You wanna help me?" I asked.

He nodded his head.

"Yeah, I do."

"Offer the next guy you see out there needing money, what you just offered me. I've been out here since March 17th, and I've come across more acts of kindness than you would ever believe from complete strangers."

"Let me stop you right there. Because you best believe the next guy I see stumbling around in the cold, half-dead as you look...no offense...

ah'ma help out ANYWAYS. I was homeless once but got a second chance at life, and I make a lot of money now. I'm offering to help you because I was on the street and a complete stranger talked to me. Got to know me. Realized I wasn't an alcoholic or a drug addict and handed me a thousand dollars in cash right there in the streets of Philly. Got me a job at a packaging plant where he was a manager and even hooked me up with a carpool to and from work. This guy didn't know my black ass from Adam...you hear me? And he decided to just up and help a brotha out, panhandlin' on the street. Because he knew I weren't no junkie. Now I saw you struggling to find money to pay that cashier in there for your breakfast. Took out your last few dollars and you was even countin' coins n'shit. Couldn't even afford to buy yourself something to eat." He went on.

"Yeah, but that doesn't mean..." I tried to say, but he cut me off again.

"Hey. This is play money." He said waving it back and forth in the air.

"Listen, I can't take this," I said, looking down.

I proceeded to lie and to tell him I was financially complacent just to further insist he give the money to someone else that needed it more than I.

Could I have used the money? Sure I could. Besides, when he had shaken my hand, $60 dollars started to look more and more like at least a $100 and some change. But there were more deserving people out there than I.

I was almost done with my journey, and within a week or two I would be back home with my family.

But I wouldn't be lying when I say I was touched.

"You're an awesome person, though, for this..." I assured him.

"Dude, you sure? People don't jest hand out money e'ry day nah..." He asked, flashing the cash again with a smirk on his face.

"Yeah, but I really appreciate it, though. Pay it forward to the next guy you see in need. And thank you." I said, offering my hand.

He shook it, pulling me in for a "bro hug." His hands felt like cinder blocks, as he patted my back.

"Homie, it ain't no thing. Lemme give you mah numba in case anybody tries to fuck wit you out here. Yo'r Grizzly Adams lookin' ass, stumblin' through the woods n'shit." He said, as I took down his phone number and laughed.

"I'm sorry if I find it hard to believe that if I was being attacked by a bear, you'd roll up in your whip and start poppin' 9's at it," I said.

"Ey' you neva know..." He laughed.

I walked through the Dellville Covered Bridge, in Pennsylvania while hiking down one of many country roads.

CHAPTER 11

The Way Home

I walked into Pine Grove Furnace State Park at 8 A.M., and followed a paved greenway past Laurel Lake.

The air was crisp and silent, as my boots scraped across the surface of the blacktop.

A rush of excitement filled me, as I passed Fuller Lake to my left and crossed a bridge to the field I had reached so many months before.

There it was.

Cold, and neglected. Sitting in the browned grass beneath the shade of an evergreen by the stream.

The dark brown splintered and weathered picnic table I had rested at 5 months prior, acting as a landmark to my victory. And for the months...years, decades to come—nobody would ever be more aware of its importance than me.

I came to a halt half expecting something grandiose to happen.

I awaited confetti to burst from the skies, and a collection of people to run up to me, telling me the obvious.

That I had completed my journey and that I had crossed the finish line.

Letting me know, that I could finally go home.

But…none of that happened.

The park was barren, and I was alone.

I stumbled, my ankles and the pads of my feet screaming out in agony as they had every day for the last year, begging for me to sit and to take a load off.

And instead of ignoring them as I always had, I limped painfully towards the picnic table, ready and willing to give them their well-deserved rest.

I shambled aimlessly, abound in silence with only the sounds of my stuttering steps crunching through the frozen grass to accompany me.

Loosening my straps, I allowed my pack to fall from my shoulders…as I began to jog.

My heart thumped as heavy as the ton of bricks I had just dropped to the ground behind me.

I ran, feeling broken but alive.

Weary, and exhausted but overwhelmed with emotion.

Empty, and burnt with all of my energy spent. Yet every muscle ache was a victory. Every bleeding blister and wound, a sign of perseverance.

And as I felt my knees give out, and as I fell to all fours; I was hit by a rush of emotions existing within the memories of the trail. People that I had met. Friends that I had made and the places and sights that I had seen.

Lessons I had learned and the trail angels and journal followers that had cheered me on.

When I reached the very spot my feet had touched, back at the beginning of summer, I sat; mouth open. Breathing heavily as I ran my hands across the surface of the picnic table in wonder.

"I did it…" I breathlessly said to nobody. To anybody.

To myself.

"I actually did it," I whispered into the cold air, still unbelieving. The words dissipated into small clouds before me.

"Sir, are you okay?" A woman in a red jacket suddenly asked, running over towards me with her husband.

They were decked out in matching jogging sweats.

"I'm...incredible..." I tried to verbalize, with a broken, quivering voice. I looked up at them both with weary eyes. Tears that I'd tried so hard to fight, ultimately ran down either cheek.

"Oh, honey." She said, resting her hands on either of my shoulders.

"What's wrong?" She asked, kneeling beside me.

"I can go home," I said, with all the sincerity of a man on his last leg of strength.

My complicated, vague reply had possibly conveyed insanity on my part. I knew she didn't understand.

"I can see my family again." I cried, my voice shattering into a million pieces.

I was homeless, sitting in my tattered clothes at a picnic table... in the middle of some random park before two complete strangers. My coat was a patchwork of duct tape and poorly sewn holes. The soles of my worn boots flapped and lolled like a dogs tongue when I walked.

I must've looked piteous, and hapless.

However, the look on the womans face at that moment almost said that some part of her understood.

"That's beautiful then, isn't it?" She asked, with tears reaching the edges of her own eyes. Sincerity in her voice, despite not knowing why exactly I was so swept with emotion.

I emphasized a final time, and as the words left my mouth, I could no longer hold back my tears.

"I can finally go home..." I cried; as this woman took me into her arms, and held me.

I looked at the stone in my hand that I had taken from the summit of Katahdin. I sat on a bench outside of the General Store; a place where AT-Thru Hikers could take on the Ice Cream Challenge during warmer months in the year. Now it appeared empty, and closed for the season.

I tossed the rock into the air and caught it, before securing it back into the waistband of my backpacks pocket.

"We still need to get home, Gregory," I said to my backpack.

"My finish line is back in my parent's arms in North Carolina. The only difference is, I don't have to walk there anymore." I explained out loud.

Gregory didn't respond. Then again he never normally did anyways. Instead, as I looked over the battle scars he'd gained over the course of 8 and a half months, I felt a sense of pride in this inanimate object that had helped me out so much along my journey.

After walking around the park, searching for a phone signal—I had managed to secure a ride into York, Pennsylvania by way of Trail Angel Mary.

And when she had arrived, she had even brought me a lunch of chips, a bologna sandwich wrap and an apple in a brown paper bag.

She'd dropped me off at another Econo Lodge in York, where I'd been able to secure a room for $39 bucks.

I'd spent some time plotting out my route for the days to come.

From my motel, I was about a mile and a half from a Greyhound Bus station which couldn't have been more than a thirty-minute walk, tops.

I had JUST enough luck to overdraft my account, and purchase a $108 dollar bus ticket destined for Danville, Virginia.

Unfortunately, it would be a 15-hour trip leaving at 6:00 P.M. and arriving at 10 A.M. the day after. Furthermore, the bus wouldn't be there to pick me up until the following evening which meant I'd have to hang around in York all day.

On a positive note, once I had arrived in Danville, Virginia I would only be 88 miles from my parents home, just barely over the North Carolina border.

"Housekeeping!" I heard loudly, which broke me out of sleep. Whoever had called it out had already begun opening my door.

I looked at the clock, and it was 10:40 A.M.

Half naked, I groggily stumbled to the entrance of my room; rubbing the sleep from my eyes.

I peeked my head out from around the door, and two Indian housekeepers stood there; a man and a woman.

"Check out time, sir." The man said, which brought a burst of anger from within me.

I looked down and saw I had even put the "Do Not Disturb" sign up.

"Checkout is Noon." I reminded him rather irately.

"Checkout is *now*, sir." He said, rolling his eyes which pissed me off even more.

"Checkout is now?! NOW, HUH? 10:40 A.M. IS SPECIFICALLY CHECKOUT TIME??" I argued, raising my voice with rage.

"Sir, you could to please, calm down." The woman pled, struggling with her sentence structure.

I walked away from the door and picked up the phone, calling the front desk.

"Hello?" the assistant manager answered.

"What time is checkout?" I barked into the phone.

"Yes sir, checkout time at the Econo Lodge is 11 A.M. Did you need anything else?" The voice replied robotically over the phone.

"Your door, you know...the ones WITH THE RULES ON IT? It says check out time is noon. Maybe you'd like to get that fixed." I slammed the phone down as the housekeepers both just barged their way on into the room.

I was in nothing but my boxers.

"Sir...we can come back." She began.

"No! By all means, come on in. I'm HALF NAKED ANYWAYS, but you don't seem to give a damn. Would you like to see the rest of me?" I asked hooking my thumbs beneath my boxers.

She didn't appear to be phased nor did she appear to have been listening to me much anyways.

"Sir, we apologize for knocking on your door early. That was all I wanted to say." She clarified.

I stood there silent while she looked at me.

"Okay, please sir?" she asked since I hadn't answered her.

"Can I get dressed now? Or were you going to watch me?" I inquired, impatiently.

"Yes, have a nice day sir." She said, finally leaving.

So I could be a dick sometimes.

It was true. Especially when I was forced to wake up due to the rush to shove me out the door without allowing me to stay the full allotted time. The truth was I hadn't needed to read "Rules" on the door to give me the answers I had sought. The motel clerk had actually told me Noon as well, and my alarm had been set for 11:30 because of that.

It took a few waking moments for me to realize I'd blown up way too much at the woman. This overall "irritability" I had, became more and more present around all of these people now that I was back in civilization. The trash blowing uncaringly in the streets and the rude, take to our environment once I'd stumbled back into the city was shocking. I had seen police officers, dropping fast food bags of trash out of their cars at stoplights. People tossing lit cigarettes into trashcans on their ways inside stores as the material inside them had started to burn.

Garbage covered everything here, and attitudes were rampant about the city. Including mine.

It was hard to breathe.

Everything felt cluttered, crowded together and claustrophobic.

It took only a few hours in the extremes of a city, to wake up and realize why I had gone away in the first place. Why I had left these cement and asphalt civilizations behind.

There was nothing beautiful about these cities.

I hadn't even gotten home, and I was already missing the trail.

I made my way to the Downtown district of York, walking busy train tracks or semi-dried city canals on my way to the Greyhound Bus Station.

The trickling water was brown; rotten with filth and algae and less than a quarter inch deep. For the most part, though, the canals didn't have any water running through them. Anything from old baby strollers to halves of couches laid crumbling away in these giant cement drains.

I found old pieces of cracked china glasses, and big wheel bikes—to pieces of an office desk with pencils still in one of its decimated drawers.

There was a woman's pink purse, with six dollars in it and nothing else to identify whom it had belonged to. And there was a man's credit card that was almost faded away from the weather, wear and time.

I followed the city canal through suburban neighborhoods or industrial areas to Coduras Creek, as old Weeping Willows hung over the edges of people's property, swaying their leaves in the breeze against my face.

Upon arrival at Coduras Creek, I'd found it to be nothing more than another man-made dumping area. Its existence, just an excuse for people to drop their tires, washing machines and old televisions into. Nothing more.

When I entered the bus station, it was mostly empty. Everybody was outside, awaiting the 2:30 to Baltimore. The structure was noticeably old. It had been converted from a train station at some point during the 20th century. The old "Capitol Trailways" signs were still up and hadn't been touched, though.

It appeared as if Greyhound had purchased the property, slapped a few posters and stickers up and said: "This is ours now."

I sat in one of the tacky 70's orange bucket seats for the next 3 hours, trying to avoid conversations regarding my backpack and succeeding for the most part.

Upon arrival, the bus was hushed, lights turned off, and one person sat to each row and section—closed off in their own individual worlds.

Some played on their phones and others played on their tablets.

There were several times I drifted in and out of consciousness if only for a minute or two of sleep, which did nothing to ease the exhaustion from more than eight months of hiking.

I arrived in Danville, Virginia at 10 A.M. and took off on foot, much to the protest of overzealous taxi cab drivers at the Greyhound Terminal.

They shouted and yelled out at me, or offered "discounts" of some kind as I walked along the side of the road, ignoring them or waving them away.

"Not interested!" I shouted.

"Come on buddy. It'll be the cheapest twenty bucks you've ever spent."

"You don't even know where I'm trying to go!" I said incredulously. The driver passed a sly smile.

"Eh, big brotha Danny will look out for you. 'Kay?"

"No!"

Danville looked like a struggling monolithic city that had been forgotten, with grand bridges over river crossings, statues and memorials faded or crumbling with time. However, they were all amidst abandoned or decaying warehouses and old factories no longer in use.

Cars drove by loudly; their tires sending up sprays of road mist as they passed. As I crossed the Dan River, I remembered going tubing down it with my family when I was a lot younger. However these days, it was quite disgusting and polluted looking down at it from atop the bridge. Positively filled with trash and hundreds if not thousands of swollen, bulging, half-filled soda bottles bobbing like little buoys along the shoreline.

It was a straight shot down Highway 86 and by the time I had walked into Yanceyville, I was soaked only because a rain poncho lasted so long before succumbing to the elements.

I ended my day behind the Piedmont Community College in a beautiful patch of woods there.

Before setting up, I refilled my bottles using a hose on the side of the building.

Unfortunately, it utilized one of those unique water-key handles that separated from the valve so that nobody could use it but maintenance employees. However, I had managed to get around that obstacle by breaking out my Leatherman and using the pliers on it.

When I set up my tent later that evening, the air temperatures were starting to lower, and the wind was picking back up.

I gathered a bunch of semi-dry leaves and laid them out underneath my hammock. When I tied my support strings, I set my tent low enough to the ground to become half submerged in the leaves I had gathered. I'd done this to keep the wind from passing beneath my hammock and freezing me throughout the night.

And because I was so close to the College, I threw armfuls of leaves across my rainfly as well for camouflage.

As I laid back in my hammock, I gave an update of where I was at currently online for people that had been following my journal entries.

Little did I know, how much of a mistake that had been.

At around 2:59 A.M. I heard voices and peoples feet crunching and stomping through the woods about 300 feet away from where I had set up camp.

"Morris the Cat! Come out kitty, kitty!" Somebody whispered in hushed calls.

I awoke, barely moving and seeing only my breath disintegrating into the air before me. The moon was rather bright that early morning.

"Where are you, kitty, kitty?"

I peeked out from beneath my rain fly.

There were three people, stumbling around through the forest I was camped in carrying cheap, dollar store handheld flashlights. Short cone-shaped yellow beams cut through the darkness. One of the guys flashlight wasn't even working correctly, and he kept bashing it against trees until it finally broke apart.

"SHIT!" He shouted as his friends joined, in hushed laughter.

"Guys, shut up!" one of them said.

"He's probably not even out here, dude." The third man chimed in.

"He probably wasn't even hiking this whole time."

"I think he was walking, but he probably made up everywhere he's been." Another person from the group said.

"Yeah."

"Yeah, you're probably right."

I laid as still as possible in my tent. They had started in my direction, and so I grabbed a rock the size of a ping pong ball laying in the forest beside my hammock. If they got too close to my tent, my plan was to throw the rock adjacent to their right or left to distract them as I possibly snuck away. It was just a thought and I had needed a possible escape plan.

"Dude, his journals are full of shit. He's not out here. He probably sits in his parent's basement and makes this crap up." One of the guys said as they walked closer towards my hammock.

"Which way did we come in here?"

Scattered laughing, followed by silence. They were getting closer to my tent. They were maybe a hundred feet away now.

"Dude, I thought YOU knew?"

With the way they were talking, they didn't appear to be any friends or real fans of mine. As a result, I had no intention of popping out and saying: "Oh, but I'm right here fella's!"

Honestly, I wasn't aware of the type of person who came looking for somebody they didn't even know in the woods, at 3 A.M. or how normal that was.

After they'd left, I got up and began packing my things.

It was time to go.

I wasn't much of a fan of walking in the dark.

Maybe you're just paranoid I thought to myself.

It wasn't hard to second guess myself at times. However, I felt that being alone had ultimately contributed to my increased anxiety. So it happened that every time I saw the headlights of an approaching car; I ended up diving into the wood line to keep from being seen.

Yep, you're officially paranoid I said to myself, as I watched an old woman who could barely see over the steering wheel of her Buick, drive by.

I hiked for seven miles, and it was 10 A.M. when I'd finally been able to snag a ride. I had been hitchhiking on and off, and for the most part been grossly unsuccessful.

When I had finally received a hitch, I had been dropped off at a gas station, where a sign across the highway had stated Hillsborough to be 29 miles away. That was good because Hillsborough was only a 40-minute drive to my parents' house.

I was getting closer every day.

As I thanked the man for the ride and walked into the gas station, I eyed a treasure trove of empty cardboard boxes stacked to the right of the open cashiers counter.

I knew if I had a funny sign, I might have better luck at scoring a hitch to take me further into North Carolina.

So I asked the Indian guy working behind the counter if he had a box and a Sharpie I could use to make a sign.

"Sign for what?" He asked, eyeing me distrustfully.

"I'm trying to hitch a ride to Hillsborough," I said.

"No. I don't have any boxes for that." He replied, with general disinterest.

"What are *those* being used for?" I asked, pointing to the heap of discarded cardboard boxes to the right of the counter.

"We're recycling those."

I scoffed, finding the response to be a bit incredulous.

I couldn't just have one piece to make a sign with? I thought to myself.

"What if I bought it from you?" I challenged, dragging my hands from my face with an amused, and unbelievable expression.

He laughed, and shook his head no.

"Five dollars." I offered.

"It's not for sale, sorry." He replied, looking at the time on his wrist.

"Sorry, did you have somewhere to be?" I asked with a hint of anger in my voice.

"I have better things I could be doing." He replied, clearly bothered by my presence.

"*Ten dollars.*" I returned. I just wanted to know the guys breaking point. I couldn't understand how asking for something so minuscule could become such an issue to the man. And while I had no intention of giving the guy ten dollars, I was perhaps misguided in my belief that I could get him to eventually give in.

"You're going to give me ten dollars for a cardboard box?" he asked, with an unbelieving pitch in his tone.

"Well, you're too stingy to give it to me for free..." I replied.

"Fine. Here." He said impatiently, walking over to the heap of empty cardboard boxes and picking one up.

He tossed it at me, and it skidded across the floor. Stopping at my feet.

"Okay. Ten dollars." He said holding out his hand.

I mocked patting my pants and reaching around in my pockets, or coat before I slowly withdrew my middle finger.

"Well, would you look at that? Guess I'm fresh out of tens. OH WELL!" I said shrugging comically and making a sad face.

"Get out! Get out of my store, you!"

I laughed, kicking his ten dollar box across the store and back into the cardboard heap.

"Leave now, or I'll call the police!"

"OHHH GODDDDD! NOT THE POLICE! PLEASE GOD, NOT THE POLICE!" I shouted, slapping my hands against either cheek over dramatically, before shoving open the door to his shitty corner store and nearly breaking it off of the hinges in the process.

I walked down Highway 86 for the next half a mile where I came across an Ace Hardware store. The business had boxes stacked up outside next to their trash bin. They didn't seem a bit bothered when an employee caught me ripping off a chunk for my sign either.

It read: "Hillsborough: Hiker Headed Home." I continued my trek down the highway, occasionally flashing my sign at passing motorists until a Sheriff's Deputy saw me and pulled into a driveway I was passing.

"Oh boy..." I sighed, shaking my head from side to side.

"Hey there!" The officer said politely, stepping out of his car.

I prepared myself, but put on my best smile all the same.

"Hello, Officer."

"I figure I might as well ask...before I get a call anyways..." He said, eluding to something I might have already needed to know about, or that was expected I know.

Had this stop been about the Indian guy back at the gas station? If so, all I'd done was flip him off and then left. I hadn't broken any laws or made any threats, so I wasn't sure why I was suddenly so nervous.

"Can I ask what this is about?" I replied, dropping my pack to my feet and propping it up against my legs.

"Well...now. I don't mind being the one asking the questions. Where were ya headed today?" He inquired. I thought the sign I'd made had made it pretty clear where I was headed.

"Well, let's see. I slept behind the Piedmont Community College in the woods last night, and today after a few hitches I can probably get quite a bit closer back to my hometown," I replied.

"Now what town would that be?" he probed.

"Little place, about thirty minutes outside of Raleigh."

"I see." He looked me over and then knelt down beside my backpack, thumbing one of the many rips along the side that I had poorly sewn up.

"How long you been out here?" he asked.

"Little over eight months now," I replied, with just a hint of exhaustion in my tone. He caught it and gave me a sympathetic look.

"Well if you show me your I.D. I'd be happy to give you a ride down to the Orange County line and cut off a significant amount of hours of walking for you." He offered.

"You want to see if I have any warrants. That's what this is *really* about, right?" I clarified for him.

I wasn't an idiot. And while he was in fact potentially trying to do me a favor he had to at least make sure he wasn't helping out a convict either.

He smiled and canted his head slightly.

"I'm sure a fella like yourself ain't got nothin' to worry about now do ya?" he asked.

I shook my head from side to side.

"I'm legit. I don't mind showing you my driver's license in exchange for a ride." I said, retrieving my wallet for him.

I handed him my I.D. and sat on my pack as he asked me about my adventure and waited for a reply from his dispatcher about my background. He was probably breaking policy by picking up a hitchhiker anyways...so I was actually very grateful for the lift.

"You don't have any weapons or drugs, or anything in that pack... and blah-blah-blah, do you? I gotta ask these things." He inquired apologetically.

"Got a rusty, Leatherman multi-tool. That's about it, other than body odor as far as carrying any weapons go." I said with a smile.

He lightly chuckled, handing me my I.D. back and then proceeded to open his rear door for me.

"You can put your pack here and get in on the other side." He said, opening both rear doors for me.

The back seat was cramped, and my knees painfully drove into the bulletproof wall separating each other from the front and rear cab.

There was NO leg room, which I suppose helped with keeping arrested persons from kicking.

Sure as he had promised, he dropped me off at the Orange County line.

"Well I'd like to take you further, but I'm on duty." He said, opening both rear doors for me.

"No really, thank you very much," I said, shaking his hand.

"Ah, it was nothing. From here you're about 11 miles outside of Hillsborough. Much better than 29. Just stay to the left up ahead at the fork." he said with a smile.

"Once again, I can't thank you enough. Even though I know the real reason you stopped was that you just didn't want to deal with me in your area." I said, smirking.

"Well, I just know how the locals are...and somebody would've been calling us about you. Probably complaining about some guy hitching on the side of the road. I thought it best to just get you outta my hair at least and maybe help you out at the same time in the process. Take care now." He said, waving me on as he hopped into his cruiser.

I waved back and pushed on down the road.

It was only a few more miles before I came across a converted Elementary School, now turned Child Services office. Behind it was an abandoned park, where I sat down to eat at a picnic shelter. With the woods that had encompassed it; practicality had me believing it was the perfect area to set up and sleep for the night. Each mile I walked, brought me closer into downtown Hillsborough. The further I went into the city though, the fewer options of stealth camping I would have readily available.

Reports were calling for sleet and rain the next two days, and frankly, I didn't want to deal with it anymore.

"I don't really have to, either." I reminded myself out loud.

The wind picked up suddenly, and I pulled my coat closer against my body, trembling slightly.

When my phone buzzed, I looked at the notification to find I had a missed voicemail message. It was from my mother.

The message she had left, was simple.

Please, come home.

I wasn't sure why I was still here anymore. My hike, however anti-climactic as it had ended was over back at Pine Grove Furnace State Park. I had been offered rides by former coworkers and friends in the area that had followed my journal entries.

However, there was still some part of me that didn't want to let go of wandering and walking. The winter wind was cold, and the rain, sleet, and snow were never wanted partners when it came to hiking.

Being alone wasn't preferable to having a hiking buddy by my side either.

But still, I clung to this lifestyle, no matter how badly I simultaneously wanted it to end.

It was the familiarity of jumping back into a scheduled life and living like I had before. Now the very thought of it all terrified me.

When I looked over at Gregory, the backpack unintentionally helped me come to the biggest decision of my journey.

To return home.

Sure, I could have said it was the breeze that tilted the pack over. But I liked to think it was Gregory giving me a sign.

Telling me to finally rest my bones.

At least for a little while.

"Just so you know, you're not allowed to camp here." A local maintenance employee exclaimed a bit cautiously. He looked down at me warily as if I was bound to jump up at any moment towards him and start screaming crazy rants about the end of the world coming through bible scriptures.

I had no intention of sleeping in that park anyways. But something spoke of a kindness that existed in the man's eyes.

"This can go one of two ways," I began too tired to argue and too cold to care.

"You can give me a ride into town and earn ten bucks for a seven-mile drive when you get off of work today," I said, taking out a ten dollar bill and handing it to him.

"Or I can just sneak off into the woods and camp here anyways when you leave," I replied.

"And please don't give me the whole 'You'll call the cops on me' spiel. You know there won't be a search party going through every inch of those woods looking for little ol' me." I added.

The man looked at the money and then to me. He seemed hesitant, almost as if he was about to hand the money back. So I played a different angle.

"Please, I really have nowhere else to go," I said, with earnest exhaustion in my voice.

He nodded, biting his bottom lip.

"I get off at 3:30." He said, pocketing the ten.

I had been dropped off at a McDonalds and was now only 48 miles from home.

My friend, and former coworker, Devin Payne lived in the area and when he had learned that I was only 15 minutes away—he drove to meet and greet me with his two children.

"You look…wow." He said, glancing up and down over my haggard appearance.

"It's okay, you don't have to be kind," I assured him.

"I mean, you look great, buddy." He said, slapping me on the shoulder. Somehow I believed he was full of it. I smelled horrible, I was dirty and my beard had anything from twigs to pieces of leaves in them.

I smiled at his kindness, however.

Even more so when he ordered me an eggnog milkshake and we caught up on old times.

From McDonald's, Keven picked me up and gave me a ride to his home in Cary for the next two days. It was there, I rested and recuperated from the cold. I was only 22 miles from home now.

The weather had called for more rain and sleet on the way, and the roads had already started to ice up.

When it was finally time, I asked Keven to drive me to my home. I had a mission to complete, and I was holding it right there in my hand when I said so.

We didn't have much time to make it home before my father went to sleep. He had been notorious for never staying up past 8 or 9 P.M., and as of that moment, it was already 8:17.

The roads were slick, as Keven floored the Jeep to meet the time limit. In the process, he was skidding and fishtailing as he weaved in and out of traffic.

"GET OUT OF THE WAY!" He shouted at other drivers, as I held on for dear life with eyes wide open.

"I uh…I don't think this story ends the same way if I arrive home, DEAD." I exclaimed, gulping the lump in my throat.

He laughed, as the cigarette in his mouth bobbed up and down.

We parked Keven's Jeep at an abandoned parking lot down the road from my house.

This was it.

"You ready?" He asked.

I took a breath.

"Ready as I'll ever be," I replied.

My eyes burned, and I became transparent at that moment, as I slowly opened the Jeeps door; standing in the cold drizzling rain.

"This is it, John. The moment you've been waiting for." Keven stated excitedly for me.

"I'm nervous for some reason," I replied as I pulled my pack from the back of his vehicle.

Orange streetlights created mysterious atmospheres like illuminated protected zones in the dark; as I turned down my street.

The place I had grown up as a child.

The route I walked was splintered; cracked and shattered in some areas by time.

Old, wise and yet foreboding; this road had been my playground when I was younger, less experienced and knowledgeable in the workings of the world to know how dangerous some of my endeavors had been.

This asphalt had seen me and my sisters rise and grow up through the years from nothing more than a handful of bean sprouts.

It had seen our family the first time we'd driven to our new home here back in the 80's.

It had greeted my older sister after she gave birth to her first child, and then her second years later. It had seen my younger sister's son, as well and then had seen us off every time we'd driven away to live our separate lives.

Now, a year later it still welcomed me back home.

Unrecognizable as I thought I was, I still felt this "living consciousness" in that pavement. The familiarity and welcoming warmth it gave me.

I looked down at the ground, feeling embarrassed as a couple of drops ran from my eyes. Looking over at Keven, I apologized as he looked on.

My last hike home.

"I'm sorry..." I said.

I tried to appear cheerful while I limped painfully down my road. Blistered, raw feet touched down on an unforgiving hard surface. My boots barely held together and crumbling apart. The soles slapped against the surface.

My torn jacket held together by duct tape and super glue while my tattered pants that had clothed me for more than 2,000 miles, dragged behind me in weathered, worn strips of cloth around my ankles. The threads only holding together by sheer luck.

My journey had taken me so long, and all I could do was hike with almost 9 months of excruciating exhaustion to keep me company most times.

I didn't remember the life lessons of the trail, and I didn't think about the moments I had almost died out there. There was no regret or care over anything I'd lost to make this dream come true.

All I wanted to do was see my parents.

All I wanted to do was stop walking.

Nothing mattered to me but an old road that had become a tunnel.

And my mother and father were the light at the end.

As I reached the edge of my yard, I stopped.

I couldn't see anything as I wiped the tears that had ran down my bearded cheeks. I climbed the front porch steps and knocked on the door. I didn't initially get an answer except for the bellowing barks of my parent's surprised dogs, inside.

Then the door opened, and my father answered with my mother behind him.

"I'm home."

My mother's answer was typical of most loving parents. Or maybe not. My mother was prone to screaming, and as a result, she let out her love for me in the form of nearly tearing her vocal chords as well as deafening everybody else's eardrums within the vicinity.

As I walked in, my parents stepped back with an unbelievable look of awe.

Oddly enough, I felt like a stranger amongst them both.

I pulled at the shoulder straps on my pack as Gregory fell lifelessly from my shoulders, for the last time.

The World We Came to Find

"Richard!" My mother shouted again with tears in her eyes. She was crying, as she threw her arms around me. "Richard, why did you leave? Why did you go away?" she asked with a defeated tone.

I smiled, with tears spilling from my own eyes.

"I had to make myself better, Mom. I had to clear my head, and get things right in there." I tried to explain.

I looked to my father then, who had a smile on his face.

"Dad...I hope I made you proud." I said.

It was all I had left to ask for.

I handed him the rock I'd brought back home from the summit of Katahdin. A symbol of everything I'd given up in pursuit of it, and the appreciation towards life that I had in turn gained.

In the days to follow, I rested. I watched television, and I took up residence in my parents' old attic that my father and grandfather had converted into two bedrooms for my sisters when we were all younger. I sat on the window seat and looked out at the sturdy oak tree that had stood proudly beside our house growing up.

The rain came down, and the pitter patter of the drizzle atop the leaves made it peaceful.

But I was uneasy.

It was too quiet, back at home.

There's something to say, about living outside for almost 9 months.

Being back inside, could quickly make a person feel claustrophobic. And while outside it was pouring down with rain, I'd have rather been out there, back on the Appalachian Trail than in that room.

I sighed quietly to myself, watching water streams drip down the glass of the window.

I helped my father with menial tasks around the house and yard to help earn my keep. It would be a while before I got a new job, and was able to get back on my feet again, so it was only fair I helped out in the meantime.

One day, my father and I had just finished raking the leaves in the backyard and were sitting down by the fire pit. The sun was setting, and bright wisps of clouds disintegrated into the horizon.

I looked over at him after he had thanked me for the help. I was silent momentarily with my response before speaking up.

"Dad, I wanted to apologize for something," I began.

He looked a little confused, as he tossed a small broken limb into the firewood stack next to the pit.

"For what?" he asked.

"I didn't mean to give the impression that you weren't proud of me while out there on the Appalachian Trail. Or that the only way you ever *would be*, was by my going out there and hiking, to begin with. It wasn't what I was trying to convey at all, actually." I said, looking down at the ground.

"I know that. You don't have to apologize." He replied, nervously shuffling his feet.

"It's just—I've always failed at everything I've ever tried at, and it was my own lack of self-worth that had me thinking you had nothing to be proud of in me. You know, despite your never having said that to me."

He nodded, as I continued.

"It was all in my own head, and it took a lot of thinking while hiking that trail to realize a lot about myself. Most importantly that a lot of the demons I had, were created all in my own mind." I explained.

My father took a deep breath, and let it out slowly. He appeared mildly uncomfortable, because talking about feelings and emotions was never his strong suit when it came to me.

When I had started to notice the expression of uneasiness upon his face, I had the sudden urge out of embarrassment to make an excuse, get up and then leave if only to avoid it.

I had just started to stand when he finally answered me.

"I worked my whole life to provide for you, your mother and your sisters. I didn't make the most money in the world and I certainly didn't do any of it for a badge of honor. I did it because I had a responsibility to look after you all. Because I loved each of you," he said, as I slowly sat back down.

I looked up at him finally.

He was searching for the words to say, but the hardened part of him made it an almost impossible task to overcome.

"It was hard. You and your sisters are all different and have your own unique personalities and trying to get to know you guys individually could sometimes be difficult. Sometimes *impossible* to do, when you're working 12 hours a day, 7 days a week." He went on.

His eyes suddenly became glassy.

I noticed that my father looked anxious and that tears sat on the edges of his eyes.

"But part of being a father, on top of taking care of his family is also getting to know his children and being as much a part of their life as he can be. To show them the way, and hope that they aren't just successful, but are more successful than you ever dreamed of being yourself. And I think I know enough about all of you," he said, as a tear fell down his cheek.

"To have never once in my life, thought of any of you as *failures*."

I sat, motionless and silent. Seeing tears in my father's eyes was a rare occurrence I had only witnessed a handful of times in my life. He wiped his cheeks with the backs of his hands.

"Richard, you *never had to leave* to make us proud of you." He said softly.

"Your mother and I love you and your sisters, and have been proud of you all since the days you were born."

I swallowed the lump in my throat, as my eyes welled up, and a couple of drops fell down my own cheeks at that moment.

I stood and hugged my father for the first time in years.

She had drawn the rules up over the phone, before our face-to-face meeting. She had been acutely aware that I wrote an online journal and had posted my status updates on Facebook speaking of my journey along the Appalachian Train in 2013.

She was also cognizant of the parts that had been written about *her* as well, and had never truly accepted or appreciated it; instead choosing to ignore its existence altogether.

In her opinion, I had given out far too many details about our personal lives and she had become embarrassed by the things I had willingly shared with the rest of the world.

So before our meeting in person, she had requested that if I was going to write up our last interaction together, that I change her name and the details of the meeting just a bit to throw people off. She didn't want friends or family to know that we had both met a final time.

She had no interest in being a part of my story. However in truth, she had played too big a role to not be remembered or portrayed at all.

"How about you pick a name for yourself then, Melody? And when I write the last part of my journal, I'll change it up just for you." I offered, irritably.

"Call me *Samantha* when you write up your blog. And make me sound like an ex-girlfriend from four or five years ago." She demanded.

"What about a *secret agent*? Should I write that you work for the CIA too?" I asked sarcastically.

"John, just do me this one favor, before we go our separate ways and never see each other again." She asked, hurriedly.

"People are going to want to know about my story, Melody. They're gonna want to know how it all ended." I defended.

"If you even ever write a book, which I honestly don't see happening anyways—as long as you don't use my real name I won't care *what* you write that we did or talked about here. But for now, this is all just too fresh and soon, and I don't want mutual friends of ours asking questions tonight or tomorrow about our meeting up. Asking if we're getting back together, and…" she trailed on before I finally cut in.

"Okay, okay. You've got it. I'll call you Samantha, and I'll say you're an ex-girlfriend from years ago. Deal? How about we meet at our old coffee shop." I explained over the phone.

"That'll be fine."

Melody was on her way out of town, moving back to Connecticut to be with her family and friends and to start a new job and life there. Before making the long trip up, she wanted to see me a final time and congratulate me under the terms already discussed. I was agreeable, if only because I wanted to see her once more before she disappeared forever.

She was her usual, beautiful self upon arrival.

But time had changed us both so very much. The age of *past mistakes* was set so deeply into her expressions, I felt like nothing more than a stranger she had made every attempt to distance herself emotionally and mentally from.

"Before we start, I want you to know that I'm happy for you John," Melody said, as she looked me over.

My face was still burnt and peeling from the recent months I had spent in the cold. My lips cracked and scabbed over from where they had split. My gait awkward, as I limped towards her with glass splinters crunching between the joints on my feet and knees. The pains of readjustment, and letting "rest" sink into bones and muscles that had gotten so used to the day-to-day walking they once suffered.

"Thank you," I replied hoarsely, as I pulled her seat out for her.

My voice hadn't yet recovered from the month and a half of untreated Walking Pneumonia I had been subjected to through Connecticut to Hamburg, Pennsylvania. But I knew it too, would someday get better as well.

Melody stood momentarily, looking me over as if I'd been gone for years, before touching my wily beard with her fingertips.

"You seem so..."

"Old? Raggedy, maybe?" I asked in an attempt to start things off with a dash of humor.

"Different." She said, with a gentle smile.

"How'd you know I was back home?" I asked as I helped push in her chair after she sat down.

"Timothy told me you were back." She replied, as I limped over to the other side of the table and sat down. Tim was a mutual friend of ours and one of the very few still shared between us that had decided not to take sides in our separation.

"Really? I haven't talked to him since..."

"He says I was too hard on you." She cut in suddenly.

There was a hint of both contempt, and regret in the way she had said that.

"I disagree," I countered, much to her surprise. Truthfully, I hadn't met with her to hash out old grievances and arguments. Nor did I arrive in person to pass the blame back and forth, on what had come to pass between us in the early months of my journey.

I had merely wanted to see a familiar face, even if it was no longer in the same context as what had once existed between us.

"I never *actually* stopped reading, you know." She said, looking down at the table.

"I mean, I know I told you I did and that I didn't care. But honestly, I couldn't just give up and stop my feelings for you. I may be robotic, and 'surgical' like you said, but I'm not heartless."

I smiled, and she caught the expression as she looked up into my eyes with regret.

"Melody, if you came here to apologize for something, please don't. You didn't do anything wrong. Our paths, just went in completely different directions and it was nobody's fault. Years down the road, we might not have even known what was going to transpire between us—if I hadn't left to hike some trail." I said, trying to show her I wasn't as critical of her as she might have thought I would be.

"Clearly, while suffering from an early mid-life crisis mind you," I added, with a chuckle.

She smiled painfully.

"I gave you an ultimatum…"

"And I made my choice. Just like you made yours. I understood a long time ago why you gave me that ultimatum. You were just as scared for me, as I was being out there." I explained.

"You were so stubborn, and set in your way," she began with a hint of impatience in her tone.

"I'm sorry." She said softly.

She set the coffee she had ordered down and cupped her hands around the base for warmth. It was chilly, that December day outside of our favorite former coffee hangout. I touched her hands, as she looked up at me with wet eye lashes twinkling in the setting sun.

"I will never, be sorry for the time I had with you. The good and the bad moments. I got to know a great person while being with you," I said, holding her hands lightly.

"And you helped heft a lot of my emotional and mental weight as well as my feelings of worthlessness as long as you could. You'll never know how many days early on, the thought of getting back to you—carried me each day. And maybe even saved my life, when I was suffering from hypothermia. Getting back to you, was all I thought about." I explained.

"John, I don't hold on to moments or relationships from the past though like you do: You described me, as surgical. And with good reason. Because *I am*." She said, tilting her head slightly.

"Yeah, but you're also stronger because of that. And I understand how things need to be done, from here on out." I insisted.

This was our dance. Promoting each other's strengths upon our meeting. Imbuing confidence in one another to make up for the fact that we both knew, there was no longer any love shared between us. Just a mutual respect for what once was.

Melody nodded her head, taking a drink from her cup of coffee.

"I just don't want you to believe it was all *you*. It could have taken us years down that road, to see the distance growing between us both. Maybe this was for the best?" she offered.

"It was," I assured her, with a sad smile. It was always hard to admit mistakes, but it was an easier pill to swallow when you both acknowledged it was ultimately for the best.

"How are you readjusting? To life, after the all that time out there? Is it hard?" she asked, changing the subject quickly. She was very tactful with it.

"The high fades quicker than I thought it would. I sleep on the floor, or outside sometimes in my hammock still. It's just so very claustrophobic, surrounded by four walls."

"So you're saying, you miss being back out *there*? In those woods?"

"Every day," I replied, looking up at the skies above.

"Strange, isn't it?" I asked.

I had lived my dream. In a sense, I could even say that at 30, I could now die happy. Because I had done what so many others had wanted to do, but for whatever their reason was—family, financial status, age or even fear; couldn't.

One is quick to think I should have been happy now. Quite possibly, even believe: *This guy did what he had always wanted to do. He brought pride back home to his parents, he had a grand adventure, and he made it back alive. So what's he have to complain about now?*

Many of those nights that I had been home since completing my trek, I spent on my parent's front porch—looking up at the skies. I often thought of faraway places and the people I had met along the Appalachian Trail that I would probably never see again. I thought of the sights I had seen, and places I had always wanted to go in the future. But while my journey of self-discovery and pride was over, the dream hadn't entirely ended or died either.

In fact, I didn't believe the dream ever *really* ended at all. Instead, I found it transformed. It had become something different.

Now it was hiking the Continental Divide Trail, and the Pacific Crest. It was rafting down the entire Mississippi River or hitchhiking across America. It was hiking through Patagonia down in South America, or backpacking across Europe.

It was anything other than another 9 to 5 job for the rest of my life. Sitting calm, safe and collected amongst my gaudy unused house furniture, and surrounded by expensive televisions and computers. So absorbed by materialistic things, and zombified by movies and TV shows, politics, and media that I gave up living in trade of watching celebrities live THEIR lives instead.

I wasn't anybody special. With seven billion of us in this world, mine was the story of one ordinary guy that got fed up with his life and went out in search of something; *anything* that he could find to make sense or justify his existence on this planet.

"Where are you right now?" Melody asked suddenly.

I ran my hands across my face, curling my fingers into my wild and unkempt hair.

"A thousand miles away from here," I said into both palms.

I felt her cold fingers clasp around my wrists, and slowly pull my hands down from my face. I looked down at them, as she interlaced her fingers into mine.

"I'm going away again," I said, withdrawing my hands suddenly.

"What are you talking about?" she answered with a surprised tone.

"It was good to be home, but I'm not here to stay. This..." I said, holding my arms open on either side of me to account for my home.

"*This* isn't where I want to end. It's a beautiful place to live but I've been home a week, and I already want to go." I exclaimed.

Partly, I was hoping for reason.

Deep down, a piece of me was hoping Melody had some answer of rationale. I wanted help, to understand my feelings. My thoughts, and my own heart. I wanted to make sense of a world that I no longer found sense in.

But mostly, I wanted her to give me the reason why I shouldn't go.

In that moment I needed her to have the answers when she was the last person on this planet that would.

But it was at that exact moment, I realized the flaw in my own design.

Here I was, reverting back to my old self. The part that clung to *other people*. The "dependent John" that needed *others* to be strong himself.

And that was no longer who or what I wanted to be. If I was ever going to continue to make my dreams a reality, in a sense, I would have to grow up and take charge of my own life.

"It makes sense now," I said, with a breath of excitement.

"Don't take this the wrong way John, but you've got me confused. You go back and forth about what it is you want in life, and you've got no definable answers for ANYBODY. I don't think people will enjoy a book where you bounce back and forth, over and over again—never understanding what it is you want in the end. Never making up your mind." She said, shaking her head in disbelief.

"But don't you see, Melody? I have." I said, finally coming to a sort of clarity.

"I can't *lie* to everybody. I can't tell everybody that I KNOW what I want to do with myself now. Because I believe I am still changing, still evolving."

"But you're home now. There's nothing else out there…" she began.

"So what would you have me do? Tell everybody going out there in search of something like I was, that once you complete the Appalachian Trail…THAT'S IT? PROBLEMS SOLVED? Life goes back to normal, and you live happily ever after?" I asked, passionately feeling my heart begin to flutter once again and come back to life.

"One of the principal things I wanted to achieve by telling this story the way I did—was to strip away the 'Sunshine & Rainbows' that everybody made every moment out there to be. It's NOT sunshine, with clear days and warm nights all the time. Sometimes it's an overcrowded shelter on a freezing, rainy night with two sick people on either side of you, coughing in your face. Sometimes it's going hungry a day or three because you misjudged your food load out. Sometimes it's falling in a freezing river, or being confronted by a feral dog in the middle of nowhere. One time it was getting my ass kicked in Middletown, New York." I explained.

"What are you saying?" she asked, confused.

"I'm saying, that a lot of times, it's falling down mountains, with blisters beneath your impossibly painful feet, and day after day torture and exhaustion as you live off the empty carbs of Ramen Noodles and Instant Mashed potatoes over and over again," I exclaimed.

I was coming to a realization all at once, and it was exciting. I was no longer holding back my thoughts, and I needed nobody else to help me grasp life and take hold of the reigns. Because hadn't I done it? Hadn't I made it back home?

"Well with the way *you* explain things, why would anybody ever want to go out there and hike the damned thing at all?" she asked, laughing at first until her expressions turned serious, and a hurtful expression crossed her face.

"What was this all for, John? What was your great epiphany that was worth giving up everything for, including *our relationship*?" she asked as if I'd just openly insulted her.

In her tone, there was pain. She needed reasons greater than what I had given her to justify my escape. She needed to understand what I had found to be so important about resetting my life, when it had affected our relationship so.

"There are these moments…" I said, softly.

"Moments, of such inferential beauty. They come hand in hand with the trials, and obstacles you face out there. Crowning achievements when you're on the verge of quitting or giving it all up. And then a trail angel comes along and provides you with a warm bed for the night. A meal to eat and a place to shower and launder your clothes. You push and push all day to summit some mountain in the middle of nowhere on bad feet, and weakened knees—and when you reach the top it's almost impossible to restrain yourself from tearing up at the sheer magnificence and awe of a view unlike any other you've ever seen." I explained.

"Being unhappy when you've got no reason to be, is a state of mind Melody. I get that now. *It's not a prison*. And anybody dedicated enough can break free of the shackles we bind ourselves with and head out for adventure. Or *escape*, like I did."

I wanted to be able to state that I had lived my dream before I died.

I wanted to be able to impress a woman, who had nothing to be excited of in me.

And I wanted to give myself SOMETHING, to have pride in—even if I was always looking for a way to tear it down.

"I…I think I should go now," I said, standing suddenly.

Melody looked up at me with a surprised and bewildered expression.

"What are you talking about? What's going to happen to you? What are you going to do now, and where are you going to go?" she asked, clearly unsatisfied with my explanation. But that was okay because it was no longer my job to make her understand.

I beamed her the brightest smile humanly possible, as I shook my head from side to side.

"You know, I don't really know yet," I said, with a chuckle. I rested my hands on my hips and for once, held my head up proudly.

Finding that 'chaotic unknown' and the unpredictability it saturated your life with was part of the adventure. I knew that now. Others that had hiked the trail knew it as well.

But it was something, she might potentially never learn.

"I don't know, where I'm gonna go, or what I'm going to do next," I said, looking down at her.

"But that's also what makes up half the adventure, right there," I replied with a wink as I turned and walked away.

The End

John Morris AKA Morris the Cat; went on to publish the three-part story of his adventure that began on March 2013 and ended December 1st of the same year. After going back to school, he obtained his TEFL/TESOL (**Teaching English as a Foreign Language/Teaching English to Speakers of Other Languages**) certification.

He met his beautiful wife Xinwei Wang in June 2015, and married her on March 23rd, 2016. Their future plans included traveling and teaching English around the world.
Time permitting, maybe he'd sneak in a few more long-distant hikes along the way of life and write a book or two about them as well.

Hey everyone! Morris the Cat here.
If you enjoyed my book, please let me know!
You can post ratings and reviews on Goodreads and on Amazon.
Be sure to visit my website www.theworldweleftbehind.com and sign up for my newsletter to receive firsthand knowledge of future releases, see exclusive sneak peeks at all future titles and enter to win free books or even a Kindle.
Follow my Facebook and Amazon Author page.
I respond to ALL reviews, good or bad, with the upmost respect for your opinion.
Thank you for your support,
John R. Morris a.k.a. Morris the Cat

www.ingramcontent.com/pod-product-compliance
Lightning Source LLC
Chambersburg PA
CBHW070712160426
43192CB00009B/1159